CW00516274

OXFORD ENGLISH MEMOIRS AND TRAVELS

General Editor: James Kinsley

MICHAEL KELLY

Reminiscences

MICHAEL KELLY

Reminiscences

Edited with an Introduction by

Roger Fiske

LONDON

OXFORD UNIVERSITY PRESS

NEW YORK TORONTO

1975

Oxford University Press, Ely House, London W1

GLASGOW NEW YORK TORONTO MELBOURNE WELLINGTON
CAPE TOWN IBADAN NAIROBI DAR ES SALAAM LUSAKA ADDIS ABABA
DELHI BOMBAY CALCUTTA MADRAS KARACHI LAHORE DACCA
KUALA LUMPUR SINGAPORE HONG KONG TOKYO

ISBN 0 19 255417 4

Printed in Great Britain
by W & J Mackay Limited, Chatham

Contents

Illustrations

ACKNOWLEDGEMENTS

We are grateful to the following for their kind permission to reproduce the illustrations in this book: Brighton Corporation: facing p. 302; British Museum (Prints and Drawings): 63; Iveagh Bequest, Kenwood: 78; Mander and Mitchenson Theatre Collection: 62 (bottom), 79, 174; National Portrait Gallery: 190 (top and bottom), 286 (top); Radio Times Hulton Picture Library: 286 (bottom); Victoria and Albert Museum: (Harry Beard Theatre Collection) 62 (top) (Enthoven Theatre Collection) 191, 287.

The editor has kindly provided the illustration opposite p. 175.

Introduction

On 1 May 1786 the curtain rose in Vienna on the first performance anywhere of that unsurpassed masterpiece, Mozart's *Marriage of Figaro*, and, astonishingly, two of the cast were British. Susanna, the heroine, was sung by Nancy Storace, and Michael Kelly doubled on the only tenor roles, Don Basilio and Don Curzio. These two singers enjoyed Mozart's close friendship for more than three years, and when Kelly came to work on his *Reminiscences* he was able to give the only first-hand account of Mozart in English; it is one of the most intimate first-hand accounts in any language. Kelly could also count other important composers among his friends, for instance Haydn and Gluck, and his remarkable gift for vivid description and anecdote brings to life a very wide range of people not only in Vienna but in Italy and Sicily where he had trained as a tenor.

Kelly's later career in London embraced both the Italian operas at the King's Theatre in the Haymarket and the mixed repertoire of plays and operas at Drury Lane. No British theatre today attempts such a repertoire, and no British singer today could hope to acquire the detailed knowledge of plays and players that Kelly shows. There is much here about the Kembles, Mrs Siddons, and Edmund Kean, and the book is a major source of information about Sheridan; few other writers of the time give as convincing a picture of this selfish, infuriating, charming, talented man in all his complexity.

Together Kelly and Nancy Storace raised Drury Lane's vocal standards to a height they had never attained before, and so made possible the Mozartian operas that Stephen Storace, Nancy's brother, wrote for this theatre in the 1790s. Kelly's singing made history, in that he was the first playhouse tenor who did *not* sing his high notes falsetto. In his *Life of Kemble* James Boaden described Kelly's high A in 'Spirit of my sainted Sire' from Storace's *The Haunted Tower* (1789): 'His compass was extraordinary. In vigorous passages he never cheated the ear with feeble wailings of falsetto, but sprung upon the ascending fifth with a sustained energy that electrified the audience.'

Kelly's *Reminiscences* were published in the year he died, 1826. When Cyrus Redding met him on Brighton front that summer, he was in an invalid chair and riddled with what he called gout; probably it was arthritis. 'A dissipated man,' wrote Redding many years later,[1] and added with Victorian smugness, 'Few of his contemporaries in past times were free of the charge.' 'Not a man of mind', Kelly was 'a good after dinner man', though he laced his stories with words 'which polite manners have banished from good society of late years. He looked flaccid from past indulgencies,' but on a full stomach he rallied and 'began to talk in his wild way, upsteaming with loyalty.' The loyalty had been strengthened by invitations to Brighton Pavilion from George IV, who enjoyed the stories and the wild way of talking as much as anyone.

Theatrical reminiscences were suddenly in the air. The tireless Boaden wrote lives not only of John Philip Kemble (1825) but also of Mrs Siddons (1827) and Mrs Jordan (1831), all of them padded out with a great deal of stage history. The dramatists John O'Keeffe (1826) and Frederick Reynolds (1827) and the oboe player William Parke (1830) wrote similarly padded but readable lives of themselves. It will be noted that Kelly's reminiscences were among the first to appear, and with good reason, for his musical and theatrical experiences both abroad and at home made him of very special interest. But he had been plagued with rheumatism throughout his retirement in Brighton, and his publisher, Henry Colburn, must have realized that a man so obviously in decline would never produce a book without help, especially as he had had no experience in putting words together. Accordingly Colburn decided to have Kelly's memories ghosted by Theodore Hook (1788–1841), a professional writer with a good knowledge of music and enough debts to make the task acceptable. Kelly was paid £400 and given fifty copies.[2]

Theodore got his knowledge of music from his father, James Hook, who had composed more than two thousand songs for Vauxhall Gardens; they included 'The Lass of Richmond Hill'. Parke tells us James Hook much preferred talking to listening. Theodore combined an inherited loquacity with an eccentricity that was all his own, and rivalled Horace Cole in his love of ingenious practical jokes played in a blaze of publicity.[3] His fame as a wit also depended on his ability at parties to improvise verses about anyone and anything, and his popularity was by no means decreased by his having been accused as a young man of embezzlement. He had spent from 1813 to 1818 as Government Treasurer in distant Mauritius, a position for which he was far from suited, and when a new

[1] *Fifty Years Recollections* (1858) ii. 308–12.

[2] *Drury Lane Journal* (Society for Theatre Research, 1974) 107.

[3] See A. J. A. Symons, *English Wits* (1940).

Governor was appointed it was found that a large sum of money was missing. Hook's responsibility was certain, though he may have been negligent rather than criminal. He undertook to repay the money, but an increasing love of gaming and alcohol prevented his ever doing so. He found it a struggle to earn any sort of living, in spite of his having founded in 1820 the very popular periodical, *John Bull*. He also wrote novels that sold well. Some thought them second only to Scott's, and the largely autobiographical *Gilbert Gurney* might still find a public today.

In 1849 the Rev. R. H. Dalton Barham published *The Life and Remains of Theodore Edward Hook*, and in the 'New Edition, Revised and Corrected' that appeared four years later there is a reference (p. 203) to Kelly's *Reminiscences*, 'which we are told Mr Hook, "from motives of pure kindness, rewrote, that is to say, composed from rough illiterate materials"; the style and dialogue are pointed up, and an occasional reflection, betraying *ex pede Herculem*, is introduced, but the staple of the two volumes is the genuine experience of the veteran himself.' The words in quotes seem to have been taken from notes made by Barham's father, a close friend of Hook and the author of *The Ingoldsby Legends*.

The 'rough illiterate materials' can hardly have included a detailed diary. So easy-going a man as Kelly was not likely to have kept one, and it is significant that in those pages that describe his years abroad there is an almost total absence of dates. Hook would not have been able to uncover such dates, whereas he could quite easily supply them for Kelly's time in London. No doubt Kelly started scribbling in a haphazard way as soon as he retired to Brighton, and then lacked the skill and energy to put into shape what he had written. The liveliness of the dialogue in his *Reminiscences* must owe something to Hook's abilities, but there can be no doubt that he got much of the material from Kelly in the form of conversation, and as a talker Kelly was liveliness itself.

The secret of Hook's share in the writing was well-kept, but Cyrus Redding knew of it from the first. When he told Kelly on Brighton front that he had just read his *Reminiscences*, Kelly replied, 'But you could not have read what that rascal Hook omitted.' Pressed for an example, Kelly told the story of Taylor, the Opera House manager, being pursued by bailiffs. Kelly had bored a hole in the wall large enough for Taylor to creep through into the next-door house; he suggested that Hook had left this out because he thought he might one day need the same method of escape himself.

In his benevolent review of Boaden's *Life of Kemble* and Kelly's

Reminiscences,[1] Sir Walter Scott described Kelly, not unreasonably, as 'this singular compound of genius and carelessness'. There can be no denying that the book is not always reliable as to facts. 'Being born an Irishman,' Scott added, 'he has some of the reckless humour of his country, with a large share of its good-nature', and it would be surprising if some of Kelly's anecdotes had not gathered a few accretions with the passing of time. Inevitably he is sometimes misleading about himself. Can he really have been thought a brilliant character actor in Vienna in 1786? In London a year or two later he was thought a very poor one, though it is only fair to add that he and Nancy Storace did teach the Drury Lane company to respond in the Viennese way to the action ensembles that Stephen Storace composed, instead of standing stiffly in line facing the audience as they did during ensembles at Covent Garden.

No one should assume from the imposing list of Kelly's 'operas' on pp. 346–8 that he had any ability as a composer. At no time in his life could he write down more than a tune; he always left harmony and orchestration to others. As Tom Moore put it in a letter to his mother (who had known all the Kelly family in Dublin), 'Poor Mick is rather an *im*poser than a composer. He cannot mark the time in writing three bars of music; his understrappers, however, do all that for him, and he has the knack of pleasing the many.' According to Parke[2] he was 'but little acquainted with harmony, and I had his own word for this; for in the year 1803, he candidly told me in the garden of Watson, the proprietor of the theatre at Cheltenham, that he merely wrote the melodies, and that the old Italian, Mazzanti, did the rest.' Kelly saw no reason to include this information in his *Reminiscences*, but he did at least write in kindly fashion of the old Italian.

Nothing would have been heard of Kelly as a composer had not the very talented Stephen Storace died young in 1796. At first Drury Lane tried to fill the gap by engaging Samuel Arnold and Thomas Attwood, but when these composers failed to give satisfaction they fell into the way of accepting music allegedly by Kelly for the sake of having a famous and popular name on their playbills. In our own times musical comedies are usually composed in Kelly's way, but the method can hardly hope to succeed in the field of opera.

Kelly's *Reminiscences* include two pages of music, 'the Melody composed by Michael Kelly, and arranged by Mozart, with Variations at Vienna in

[1] *Quarterly Review*, June 1826.

[2] *Musical Memoirs* (1830), ii. 127.

the year 1787' (pp. 114–15). There is no doubt that, for friendship's sake, Mozart arranged a tune that Kelly hummed to him, but this cannot be his arrangement. Colburn made the plates in July 1825, and there should have been plenty of time for Kelly to notice the wrong time signature, the misprint in the piano part in bar 4, and the absence of 'Fine' at the end of the main section (bar 15). Though the middle section in the minor is rather inept, the main tune is agreeable, as Kelly's tunes sometimes were. Mozart's arrangement survives, and consists not of variations but of a vocal trio for soprano, tenor, and bass (K.532); he began to write an accompaniment for wind instruments but never finished it. The music is a semitone higher than in the version Kelly gives, and it differs for the better in small details.

To his credit Kelly made no attempt to conceal or distort his then famous liaison with Mrs Crouch. So far as is known, she was the only woman he ever loved, and he would have married her if she had out-lived her legal husband. Mrs Crouch was born Anna Maria Phillips. Her father, who was half-French, gave public readings of poetry to which very few people came; he does not appear to have had any other employment. Miss Phillips became an articled singing pupil of Thomas Linley, who got her into the Drury Lane company in 1780 when she was seventeen. In both 1783 and 1784 she spent the summer break singing and acting in Ireland. On the first trip she nearly married John Philip Kemble who was acting there with her (see pp. 255–6), and on the second she got as far as the altar with a young Roman Catholic; however, her father's henchmen overtook them just in time to prevent the wedding. This information is given in a somewhat ill-written book by M. J. Young called *The Memoirs of Mrs Crouch*; it was published soon after her death. On 9 January 1785 Miss Phillips married in Twickenham a naval lieutenant called Rollings Edward Crouch. She was quickly pregnant, but as a result of her falling the baby was born prematurely and died in two days.

She first met Kelly in March 1787. As M. J. Young puts it, 'From his long residence abroad, Mr Kelly arrived in England almost a stranger to the language, in which he obtained an excellent instructress in Mrs Crouch, and she was equally benefited by his scientific knowledge of Italian music. Mr Crouch proposed his residing with them', which in the event was not very wise of him. When Kelly made his Drury Lane début as Lionel, Mrs Crouch was Clarissa. 'He taught her new graces for her songs, and she taught him to give proper expression to the dialogue.' This *ménage à trois* lasted until 1791; by this time Kelly and Mrs Crouch had made at least one summer tour without Mr Crouch, and he will not much be blamed for leaving her.

When Mrs Crouch died, the *Gentleman's Magazine* for October 1805 said that 'she sought for happiness with the most dazzling and illustrious of lovers', and it would seem that Kelly connived at her brief period in 1792 or 1793 as the Prince of Wales's mistress. This might suggest that his loyalty was stronger than his love, but it cannot have been an easy situation for him—or indeed for Mrs Crouch. Thereafter he was unfailingly affectionate and patient, even when she drifted into alcoholism. In her prime her abilities had been remarkable. Romney's portrait at Kenwood testifies to her beauty, and Storace's scores to her vocal agility, for she could sing difficult operatic arias as effectively as she could act Shakespeare heroines. Her voice was a high colloratura, and Storace took her up to high Ds and Es in all his full-length Drury Lane operas. As an actress she was placid rather than animated, excelling in such parts as Perdita, and as a matter of course playing Olivia to Mrs Jordan's Viola. She chose Celia for her stage farewell in 1801. By this time her singing voice had deserted her, though she was only thirty-eight.

Kelly lived on, consoled by friends among the aristocracy of whom perhaps he was a little too proud, but it should be remembered that singers had only just risen high enough in the social scale to have such friends; in Kelly's day they were a subject of justifiable pride. Leigh Hunt describes him in old age as having 'a quick, snappish, but not ill-natured voice, and a flushed, handsome, and good-humoured face, with the hair about his ears. The look was a little rakish or so, but very agreeable.'[1] The same might be said of his *Reminiscences*. They are also remarkable for their lack of malice, even towards Sheridan, who constantly owed Kelly money and who hardly ever repaid what he had borrowed.

Kelly's honesty is suspect only when he is writing about France in the early 1790s. At this time revolution was more than a possibility in Britain, and many people went to Paris primarily to see what life in a republic was like. Kelly was there in 1790 and 1791 and though he brought back librettos and a little music for use at Drury Lane his main reason for going must have been his latent or overt republican sympathies. On the other hand Stephen and Nancy Storace preferred to stay in England, their royalist leanings confirmed by their close friendship with Joseph II, Marie Antoinette's brother. By the late 1790s such leanings had become general, owing mainly to the Napoleonic Wars; and by the time Kelly

[1] *The Autobiography of Leigh Hunt,* ed. J. E. Morpurgo (1949), p. 123.

was working on his *Reminiscences* those who had been in Paris thirty years before were at pains to conceal their real reason for going, and expressed a moral indignation of which they had scarcely been conscious at the time. Kelly's evenings with the King at Brighton Pavilion must have tilted a number of his sentences.

Kelly assumes a knowledge of London's theatres that modern readers are unlikely to possess. Until his last years there were four theatres in London's West End. One of these, the King's Theatre in the Haymarket, presented exclusively operas in Italian together with ballets on (usually) three nights a week from December or January until the following June. The other three theatres offered a varied repertoire of plays and operatic pieces in English. Each evening there was a mainpiece lasting more than two hours and an afterpiece (often a pantomime) lasting about an hour. The proportion of operas to plays was surprisingly high, and even though they nearly all had spoken dialogue the music was their main attraction. (An opera without speech was Arne's full-length, all-sung *Artaxerxes*.) Colman's Little Theatre in the Haymarket was allowed to open only in the summer months when the two winter playhouses were closed—usually from mid-May to mid-September. This arrangement allowed Colman to draw on actors, singers, and orchestral players who would otherwise have been temporarily out of work, but he could not draw on the most eminent, who tended increasingly to spend the summer months at the theatres in Edinburgh, Dublin, and other provincial centres. Because Kelly worked for most of his career at Drury Lane, he scarcely mentions what was going on at Covent Garden, where the repertoire was neither more nor less operatic than at Drury Lane. Gossip about Covent Garden's operas, in particular those by William Shield, can be found in the *Recollections* of John O'Keeffe and in the *Musical Memoirs* of W. T. Parke.

In Kelly's day there was no producer or director in the modern sense. At the playhouse rehearsals were run by the prompter, though an actor-manager such as John Philip Kemble would take charge if he himself had a part. The prompter was empowered to fine any actor or orchestral player who was late for rehearsal.[1] In a playhouse opera, the composer, sitting in the orchestral pit at the harpsichord or piano, would take over from the prompter during musical items, and he would do such conducting as there was at performances. When the composer was not present the leader of the violins often took over the direction; Drury Lane's leader

[1] See p. 197.

at this time was Thomas Shaw. Italian opera rehearsals and performances were similarly directed by the composer when present, and for new operas he usually was. Otherwise the theatre's official harpsichordist sat at the instrument, and no doubt prompted when the singers forgot what came next. The King's Theatre also had what was called a stage manager to see that rehearsals went smoothly; Kelly held this position for nearly thirty years.

Note on the Text

Kelly's *Reminiscences* were first published by Henry Colburn early in 1826. A second edition, completely reset, appeared in the same year, presumably because demand had exceeded expectation, and in this, Volume I runs to four more pages and Volume II to thirty-eight more pages than before. I have not found any additions. A large number of foreign names and words, most of them Italian, which were wrongly spelt in the first edition, are correctly spelt in the second, and inevitably most of these improvements occur in those pages which describe Kelly's years in Italy; but even in the second edition foreign names are wrongly spelt from time to time. Punctuation was also improved in the second edition.

I have preferred the text of the second edition, as Kelly himself would have done. Names that are still spelt wrongly are spelt correctly in my Index, and on the few occasions when the difference is confusing a cross-reference has been supplied. Thus the composers Kelly calls Galupi and Rigini are listed in the Index as Galuppi and Righini without comment; but few readers would suspect Kelly's Cecchi of being Schetky, so there is a cross-reference. As the Contents pages are unlikely to have been devised by Kelly himself, I have taken the liberty of correcting a few errors and standardizing the punctuation. The numbering of the sections is editorial.

Both editions ended with an Appendix of some thirty pages giving a history of the King's Theatre since the year it was opened, 1705. Early on, whole sentences have been lifted word for word from other books, for instance from *An Apology for the Life of Mr. Colley Cibber*. Kelly cannot have written such an Appendix, much of which has nothing at all to do with his life and memories. The latter half is in a kind of shorthand that does nothing to make the facts palatable; for instance:

> 1786. Opened 23rd January; Gallini manager. The following season opened 23rd December.—1787. Opened 8th December, under the same manager, for season of 1787–8.—Opened 9th January; Gallini manager, and Mr Taylor proprietor. The theatre burnt 17th June, between ten and eleven in the evening . . .

The Appendix is not included in the present edition.

The last plate in this edition, a portrait of Kelly in old age, was the first edition's frontispiece. (In the second the chair-back has been cut away.) There were no other illustrations in 1826 apart from the song by Kelly that Mozart arranged (see pp. 114–15).

Select Bibliography

The Reminiscences of Michael Kelly were reproduced in 1968 in facsimile from the second edition by the Da Capo Press of New York, and reprinted from the first edition in 1972 by the Folio Society; the editor, Herbert van Thal, cut about a third of the text, added Biographical Notes, and called the result *Solo Recital.*

BIOGRAPHIES. *The Life of Michael Kelly* by S. M. Ellis (1930); *The Irish Boy, a Romantic Biography* by Naomi Jacob (1955). The latter has imaginary dialogue and reads like a novel.

KELLY'S CONTEMPORARIES. A useful though slightly inaccurate two-part article about Kelly in the *General Magazine* (May–June 1788) includes an engraving of him as a young man. *The Memoirs of Mrs Crouch, including a Retrospect of the Stage during the Years when she performed* by M. J. Young, 2 vols. (1806), is sometimes of interest though the writing is poor and the information often irrelevant. References to Kelly in the writings of Sir Walter Scott, W. T. Parke, Thomas Moore, Leigh Hunt, and Cyrus Redding are identified in the Introduction.

THEATRICAL AND MUSICAL INFORMATION. *The London Stage,* (11 vols., Southern Illinois Press, 1960–8), gives the author, composer, cast, and date of every theatrical performance in London's West End from 1660 to 1800; the last two volumes cover Kelly's career. Almost equally detailed information about the King's Theatre in the early nineteenth century can be found in *The Italian Opera and Contemporary Ballet in London, 1789–1820, a Record of Performances and Players* compiled by William C. Smith (The Society for Theatre Research, 1955); and less detailed information about the playhouses in John Genest's *Some Account of the English Stage* (Bath 1832, 10 vols.), and in Allardyce Nicoll's *Early Nineteenth Century Drama* (revised edn 1955). Dates in my Index come mainly from *The Dictionary of National Biography* and *Grove's Dictionary of Music and Musicians* (5th edition, 1954), which, however, have both Stephen and Nancy Storace born one year too late and in rare instances make other mistakes. I have also consulted Baker's *Biographia Dramatica* (1812 edition) and, with less profit, *The Thespian Dictionary* (1805). Kelly's many errors when writing about his Dublin performances were first pointed out in *Opera in Dublin 1705–1797* (Dublin 1973) by T. J. Walsh, to whom I am indebted. My thanks also to Colin Hardie and Genevieve Hawkins who identified quotations for me.

Chronology

KT: King's Theatre in the Haymarket (home of Italian opera)

DL: Drury Lane LT: Little Theatre in the Haymarket

		Age
1762?	Kelly born in Dublin on 25 December but no baptismal entry has been found	
1777	He makes his début in Piccinni's *La buona figliuola,* and also sings Lionel in Dibdin's *Lionel and Clarissa*. (Kelly incorrectly implies that these performances were in 1779.)	14
1779	He leaves Dublin on 1 May to study singing in Naples with Fenaroli, and arrives 30 May. Immediately after Christmas he has a fortnight sight-seeing in Rome	16
1780	He leaves Naples (in the summer?) for Palermo with Aprile who gives him a home and teaches him singing	17
1781	Kelly leaves Sicily in May (?) for Leghorn, where he meets Stephen and Nancy Storace, who are 19 and 16 respectively. Kelly is in Pisa for the Giuoco del Ponte (28 June). He is engaged for the winter in Florence; 'Ortabella' the soprano	18
1782	On Storace's recommendation Linley invites Kelly to DL, but his father is able to veto this, Kelly being under age. In September Kelly leaves Florence for Bologna and Venice where he is engaged for the winter, but the engagement falls through and he is briefly destitute. He is invited to sing in Graz 'for the autumn and carnival' (held in October); Benini the soprano; they open in Anfossi's *La vera Costanza* and perform (in Italian) Grétry's *Zémire et Azor*	19
1783	Kelly in Venice without steady employment. He is engaged to sing during the Fair at Brescia (held in June); 'Ortabella' the soprano; Kelly leaves hurriedly for fear of assassination. After a concert in Verona and a six-week season in Treviso he is back in Venice and being patronized by Signora de Petris, in whose house he lives	20
1784	Kelly sings in Anfossi oratorio in Lent. Early in the summer (but Kelly implies this was in 1783) he is engaged for the Italian operas in Vienna, where he again becomes friendly with Nancy Storace, the prima donna there. He sings and probably makes his Vienna début in Paisiello's *Il re Teodoro* 23 August (see p. 122, *n.* 1)	21
1784–6	During his three years in Vienna Kelly meets Haydn and Gluck, and becomes friendly with Mozart. He sings in Paisiello's *La Frascatana* and *Le gare generose* (1786, = *Gli schiavi per amore*), in Gluck's *Alceste* and *Iphigenia in Tauride,* in Storace's *Gli sposi*	

	malcontenti (1 June 1785) and *Gli equivoci* (27 December 1786), in Salieri's *La grotta di Trofonio* (12 October 1785), in Martini's *Una cosa rara* (17 October 1786), and in Mozart's *Figaro* (1 May 1786), &c	21–4
1787	Early in February Kelly leaves Vienna with the Storaces who have engagements at the KT. After some theatre-going in Paris they reach London, 18 March. Kelly's DL debut (20 April) is as Lionel; Mrs Crouch Clarissa. In June he goes to Dublin, his mother having just died, to see his father and to sing there with Mrs Crouch. In the autumn Mr Crouch invites Kelly to live with them. For the next twenty years Kelly sings at DL, where Sheridan is the manager	24
1788	In the summer break Kelly and Mrs Crouch tour the north of England; according to M. J. Young Mr Crouch goes with them	25
1789	Kelly and Mrs Crouch spend the summer singing in Dublin, Cork, Limerick, etc. In September, the KT having been burnt down, Nancy Storace joins the DL company. Stephen's *The Haunted Tower* establishes him as the leading English opera composer, and he takes over the direction of DL's music from Linley	26
1790	Kelly, Mr and Mrs Crouch, and Jack Johnstone spend August in Paris	27
1791	Kelly goes to Paris in June. He returns just in time to take Mrs Crouch to the Oxford Festival early in July, but she is taken ill in Henley and does not sing there. After more provincial concerts they set up house together, Mr Crouch having made off. While DL is pulled down and rebuilt, the company moves into the new KT, which has so far been unable to get a licence for Italian opera. Mozart dies in Vienna	28
1792	Kelly probably spends another summer in Paris, apparently without Mrs Crouch; it may be now that she is briefly the Prince of Wales's mistress	29
1793	From January the KT is at last licensed for Italian operas. Sheridan has Storace and Kelly put in charge of them to facilitate alternation with the DL company which, on Italian opera nights, moves over the road to the LT. The arrangement proves unworkable; it is agreed that from September KT shall present only Italian operas, and that Colman shall, exceptionally, keep the LT open in the winter. He engages the less eminent performers while the more eminent tour; Kelly and Mrs Crouch spend much of the winter in Dublin	30
1794	New DL opens 12 March, at first only for oratorios. Kelly, while still singing there, continues for the rest of his life to	

stage manage at the KT without pay, apart from an annual benefit night. He and Mrs Crouch spend the summer singing in Edinburgh 31

1796 Storace dies suddenly in March. In April Kelly sings at the KT with Banti in Gluck's *Alceste*. In the summer Nancy Storace leaves DL, and in the following year she starts a five-year tour abroad with Braham. Kelly and Mrs Crouch are now spending less of their summers singing in the provinces and more in visiting their friends 33

1797 Kelly's first opera, *A Friend in Need,* produced 9 February. As in them all, his tunes are harmonized and orchestrated by Mazzanti. In the autumn he and Mrs Crouch move from Suffolk Street near the bottom of the Haymarket to 9 New Lisle Street north of Leicester Square 34

1798 *Blue Beard* produced; it is Kelly's most ambitious and successful opera, and it stays in the repertoire for a quarter of a century. By now Kelly is DL's music director. He begins to publish his own music from Lisle Street 35

1800 *Pizarro,* Sheridan's much acclaimed but now forgotten adaptation of Kotzebue, produced, with music by Kelly and Dussek 37

1801 Mrs Crouch leaves the stage; her singing voice has gone, and she is becoming an alcoholic (mainly on port) 38

1802 Kelly opens his Music Saloon at 9 Pall Mall, where he is soon publishing operatic music by Winter, Portogallo, Cimarosa, etc., and selling wine to the clientele of the near-by Haymarket theatres. The Peace of Amiens makes possible a trip to Paris 39

1803 In the summer he sings with Mrs Billington in Edinburgh and Liverpool 40

1805 Mrs Crouch dies in Brighton 2 October, much mourned by Kelly 42

1807 Kelly is invited to run Italian opera season in Dublin starring Catalani; he sings too 44

1808 Nancy Storace (30 May) and Kelly (17 June) both choose for their farewell performance at DL Storace's much-loved *No Song No Supper*. In August Kelly runs another Italian opera season in Dublin with Catalani 45

1809 DL burnt down 24 February; the company takes over the Lyceum. Kelly still writes 'operas' for them; most are only plays with a few songs 46

1811 Organizing another Italian opera season in Dublin, Kelly sings there on 5 September for the last time on any stage. On the same day he is declared bankrupt in London—the result of his having given too little attention to his music shop. The business is taken over by Falkner and Christmas, and Kelly moves to 13 Great Russell Street 48

1812	New DL is opened 10 October	49
1813	Kelly sets off for Dublin to fight a legal battle about the pirating of his publications, but overtaken by gout he never gets there	50
1814	His sixth and last trip to Paris, with Jack Bannister and others. He returns again riddled with gout	51
1816	Sheridan dies 7 July. Kelly increasingly arthritic and decreasingly active	53
1817	Nancy Storace dies 24 August	54
1820	Kelly composes his last opera, *The Lady and the Devil*. By now his work at KT is virtually over. He spends more and more time at Brighton, where he works on his *Reminiscences* and is treated as a friend by George IV	57
1826	Kelly's *Reminiscences* published. They are so successful that a second edition is called for, but he is still an undischarged bankrupt. On 9 October he dies in Margate, and is buried in St Paul's, Covent Garden. 'His body was brought to London by the steam packet in a packing case.' (*Drury Lane Journal*)	63

REMINISCENCES

OF

MICHAEL KELLY,

OF THE

KING'S THEATRE,

AND

THEATRE ROYAL DRURY LANE,

INCLUDING

A PERIOD OF NEARLY HALF A CENTURY;

WITH

ORIGINAL ANECDOTES

OF

MANY DISTINGUISHED PERSONS,

POLITICAL, LITERARY, AND MUSICAL.

TO THE KING.

SIRE,

I MOST respectfully, and dutifully, lay at the feet of my Sovereign the Memoirs of a Life which has derived its happiest, as well as proudest passages, from His Royal condescension and patronage.

Your MAJESTY rules over millions of affectionate Subjects, all bound to bless your illustrious name for benefits, either conferred or secured; but, out of that multitude, not one heart can beat with a more fervent sense of obligation, than that of the very humble Individual who has been graciously permitted, thus publicly to subscribe himself,

Your MAJESTY'S

Ever grateful, and dutiful

Subject and Servant,

MICHAEL KELLY.

Contents

I

The following Memoirs of an active life have been thrown together, somewhat in the manner of a journal; incidents are recorded as they occurred,—scenes are retraced which have long since passed,—and characters recalled to literary life which have long quitted this sublunary stage. I aim at nothing but setting down facts as I remember them; and thus deprecating the severity of criticism by a candid avowal of my object, proceed, without further preface or apology, to my narrative.

I was born in Dublin.—My father, Thomas Kelly, at the period of my birth, was Master of the Ceremonies at the Castle, and a wine merchant of considerable reputation in Mary Street. He was known for his elegant and graceful deportment, and no lady would be presented at the Irish Court, who had not previously had the advantage of his tuition. My mother's name was M'Cabe; she was of a very respectable family in the county of Westmeath. At a very early age, she was placed for education in a Roman Catholic convent on Arran Quay. My father (who was of the same religious persuasion,) having a young relation placed also at this convent; when visiting *her,* had many opportunities of seeing Miss M'Cabe, and the results of those meetings were,—a mutual attachment, an elopement, and a marriage. Her father, who was extravagantly fond of her, soon pardoned the runaways, and, as a proof of the sincerity of his forgiveness, added to it £.5,000, which was considered no mean fortune in those days!

My father and mother were both excessively fond of music, and considered to sing with taste: all their children (fourteen in number) evinced musical capabilities, and I, the eldest of the family, was, at three years old, daily placed with the wine on the table, to howl Hawthorn's song in Love in a Village, 'There was a Jolly Miller', for the entertainment of my father's company; for company, unfortunately for his family, he had every day; and no man in the city, so justly renowned for hospitality, gave better dinners or better wine.

At the age of seven I began to learn music. My first master's name was Morland;—he was the very prototype of his namesake the painter; a wonderful genius. But dissipation was his idol, and he who might have selected the very best society, preferred that of the lowest orders. He was continually in a state of whiskey-punch intoxication.—He would sleep all day in a cellar, and I have often heard him say, somewhat *nationally,* that his *morning* began at eleven o'clock at *night!*

His first visit was generally to our house, for he was partial to my father, or rather to his currant whiskey, and so anxious was my father that I should receive instruction from him, that I have been kept up till one o'clock in the morning on the mere chance of getting a lesson. My improvement under him was rapid, and before I had attained my ninth year, I could execute with precision and neatness Schobert's Sonatas, which were then all the fashion. I also possessed a soprano voice, on which my father was determined to bestow every possible cultivation. My first singing masters were Signor Passerini, a native of Bologna, and Signor Peretti, who was a *vero musico*. He was the original Artaxerxes when the opera of that name was first performed at Covent Garden; he taught me the beautiful air, 'In infancy our hopes and fears', which was composed for him, and it made an impression on my mind never to be forgotten.—He had a fine contre altro voice, and possessed the true portamento so little known in the present day. He also taught me the song of Arbaces, 'Amid a thousand racking woes', which I executed with the greatest facility: but the songs which delighted me most were, 'Oh too lovely, too unkind', and 'Oh, why is death for ever late?' I never sang those without tears. Another great favourite of mine was that in Lionel and Clarissa, composed by Galupi.[1]—By the way, all the Lionels of the present day think proper to omit that fine song; perhaps they are right, and for the reason once given to me by an Irish post-boy, whom I was scolding for not driving faster; he turned round, and exclaimed, 'By Jasus, master, it is not an easy thing to work hard.'

I was sent, with my brother Patrick, to the best academy in Dublin, kept by Doctor Burke, a clergyman of the Church of England. He was a worthy man, and considered an excellent scholar. His daughter was one of the first piano-forte players of the day. The late Mr. Francis Goold, and Mr. Thomas Goold his brother, the Irish barrister, were on the same form with me. At a beautiful villa, which their accomplished father had near Dublin, I frequently spent the vacations with them. Mr. Goold was an excellent judge of music, of which he was very fond, and all the men of genius then in Ireland used to meet at his house on Sundays. Kane O'Hara, the ingenious author of Midas, had a puppet-show for the amusement of his friends; it was worked by a young man of the name of Nick Marsh, who sang for Midas and Pan. He was a fellow of infinite humour; his parody on 'Shepherds, I have lost my love',[1] was equal to any thing written by the well-known Captain Morris; and with many others of equal merit, will be long remembered for the rich vein of humour which characterises it. The love of company, joined to a weak constitution, condemned this truly original genius to an early grave, regretted by all who knew him. In the performance of this fantoccini I sang the part of Daphne, and was instructed by the author himself; the others were by other amateurs. It was quite the rage with all the people of fashion, who crowded nightly to see the gratuitous performance.

About this time I changed my singing-master, and was placed under Signor St. Giorgio, who was engaged at the Rotunda; his voice was not powerful, but he possessed exquisite taste. He was an honest man, and married a widow with large property, previously to which, he, Signor Carnevali, Signor Micheli, and Signor Sensi, got a £.30,000 prize in the lottery, a piece of good fortune of which he was very deserving, and I believe is still living to enjoy.

Trifling occurrences during childhood often influence our future lives. I recollect once, when returning from a visit to a relation of my mother's, I saw Signor St. Giorgio enter a fruit-shop; he proceeded to eat peaches and nectarines, and at last took a pine apple, and deliberately sliced and ate that. This completed my longing, and while my mouth watered, I asked myself why, if I assiduously studied music, I should not be able to earn money enough to lounge about in fruit-shops, and eat peaches and pine apples, as well as Signor St. Giorgio. I answered myself by promising that I would study hard; and I really did so;—and, trifling as this little anecdote may appear, I firmly believe it was the chief cause of my serious resolution to follow up music as a profession; for my father had other views for me. His intention was to place me under Surgeon Neale, one of his oldest and most intimate friends, who, independently of his profession, ranked as one of the first violin players of his time; he had a most powerful hand, and his tone, expression, and taste, nothing could surpass.

His celebrity for playing Correlli's and Geminiani's music was so great that, singular to say, in the year 1787 he was commanded by King George III. to go to London, where he had the honour of performing before His Majesty several times, and His Majesty expressed the greatest approbation of his extraordinary powers. He was a constant visitor at our house, and took great pains with me, particularly in the song of 'Prudenti mi chiede', in Metastasio's opera of Il Demofoonte, which was composed by Vento, and sung by the famous Mansoli, at the King's Theatre many years before.*

Dublin, in these days, had to boast of much musical excellence. The greatest performers in Europe, who came to London, were engaged there in the summer season by the governors of the principal charities, who were also managers of the Rotunda Concerts. I can remember at different times that Mr. and Mrs. Barthelemon, (Barthelemon was a fine performer of the old school, on the violin,) Le Vacher, Pepe, La Motte, Cramer, Salomon, Pinto, and all the most celebrated violinists of the day; not forgetting two Irishmen, honest Sam Lee (father to Mr. Lee, who now keeps a music shop in Dublin), and Mr. Mountain, who also kept a music shop, and was an excellent violin player, and a very worthy man.†

They also brought Ritter, the finest bassoon player I ever heard; Crosdil, on the violoncello, who was unrivalled on that instrument, and is still alive and merry; and though last, not least, Fischer, the great oboe player, whose minuet[1] was then all the rage; he was a man of singular disposition, and great professional pride. Being very much pressed by a nobleman to sup with him after the opera, he declined the invitation, saying, that he was usually very much fatigued, and made it a rule never to go out after the evening's performance. The noble lord would, however, take no denial, and assured Fischer that he did not ask him professionally, but merely for the gratification of his society and conversation. Thus urged and encouraged, he went; he had not, however, been many minutes in the house of the consistent nobleman, before his lordship approached him, and said, 'I hope, Mr. Fisher, you have brought

* When I was first at Florence, I had the gratification of hearing that great and celebrated performer sing it, which he did at the particular request of Signor Veroli and myself. I also sang it to him with the English words, 'Oh, talk not to me of the wealth she possesses', and he seemed much pleased. Having returned to Italy with a princely fortune, Mansoli purchased an estate within a few miles of Florence, where I dined with him: he spoke of England with admiration, and expressed great gratitude for the attention and applause he received at the Opera House, and in concerts.

† Mr. Mountain, who formerly led the Covent Garden Band, and at present leads that of the English Opera with so much ability, is a son of this gentleman. His wife, Mrs. Mountain, was for many years a principal singer at Covent Garden and Drury Lane, where she was deservedly a great favourite. Mrs. Billington was an ardent admirer of hers, and spoke of her talents with unfeigned praise. She has retired from the stage, I sincerely hope with competence and happiness. A son of Mr. and Mrs. Mountain is in the service of Government, in the Admiralty.

your oboe in your pocket.'—'No, my Lord,' said Fischer, 'my oboe never sups.' He turned on his heel, and instantly left the house, and no persuasion could ever induce him to return to it.

The singers, or, as they are now called, vocalists, at these concerts were numerous; among them were a Miss Jameson, a pupil of Doctor Arne, who sung 'The Soldier tired'[1] with much applause; and Mrs. Cramer, (first wife of the celebrated leader, and mother of John Cramer and F. Cramer, the esteemed successor of his father, celebrated for his performance on the piano-forte, and compositions for that instrument;) a beautiful woman, a charming singer, and a distinguished professional favourite of Tenducci, Leoni, and Rauzzini.

Speaking of Signor Rauzzini, whose name is familiar to all who have lived in the musical world, it may not perhaps be considered irrelevant to say a few words of his early career. He was a native of Rome, and made his first appearance on the stage there, at the Teatro della Valle. He was a great musician, had a fine voice, was very young, and so proverbially handsome, that he always performed the part of the Prima Donna;—at that period no woman was permitted to appear on the stage at Rome.* His reception was highly flattering, and he afterwards performed in all the principal theatres in Italy. The Elector of Bavaria, who expended immense sums on his Italian opera, invited him to Munich. His success at that court was, as usual, unqualified. But, alas! his beauty was his bane! an exalted personage became deeply and hopelessly enamoured of him, and, spite of his talents, it was suggested to him that a change of air would be for the benefit of his health. He took the hint, and left Munich: he then engaged himself at the Italian opera in London, where he attained the highest reputation both as a singer and composer; and his acting in Pyramus, in the opera of Pyramus and Thisbe, was so fine, that Garrick has often complimented him on it.

I was now taking lessons from Doctor Cogan† on the piano-forte. His execution on that instrument was astonishing, and his compositions, although not generally known in this country, possess great merit. The whole phalanx of musical talent which I have mentioned, frequently visited at my father's house, and I was so fortunate as to be taken great notice of by Rauzzini during his stay in Dublin. He gave me lessons, and

* The present Pope has, I perceive, issued a *veto* against the performance of women on the stage, to take effect after the 1st of January, 1826.

† Doctor Cogan is still living in Dublin; he has good health and independence, and is an hospitable worthy fellow, highly esteemed by all his connexions.

taught me several songs, particularly that beautiful air of his own, which he sang divinely, 'Fuggiam da questo loco, in piena libertà',[1] which the late Mr. Linley introduced into the Duenna, with Mr. Sheridan's words, 'By him we love offended'.

Rauzzini was so kind to me, and so pleased with the ardent feeling I evinced for music, that, previously to his leaving Ireland, he called upon my father, and said, 'My dear Sir, depend upon it your son will never follow any profession but that of a musician; and as there is no person in this country who can give him the instruction he requires, you ought to send him to Italy. He is now at the time of life to imbibe true taste, and in Italy only is it to be found. If you send him to Rome, let him study under Latilla; if to Naples (the better place of the two) send him to either of the Conservatorios;—the head master at St. Onofrio is Monopoli,* at the other, La Madona di Loreto, Finaroli is master. This celebrated Conservatorio produced Scarlatti, Duranti, Porpora, (at that time the greatest of all singing masters,) Pergolesi, Jomelli, Cimarosa, Paesiello, and a long list of celebrated men: let him go there, and depend upon it he will one day repay you for it.'

This advice made a deep impression on my father, particularly as a similar opinion had been given by Sir William, then Mr. Parsons, the late musical composer and magistrate of Bow Street, who had studied music in Italy, and was, at the time I speak of, in Ireland on a visit to his friend and patron, Mr. Henery.

My father consulted my mother, who would not hear of such a proposal. She had but a few months before, parted with my brother Patrick, for whom my father had procured a cadetship in India—and I cannot but think of my mother's kind feelings towards me, with affection and gratitude—as for my brother, poor fellow, we never saw him more. He was esteemed a brave soldier; and was much beloved for his goodness of heart and companionable qualities, for he sang sweetly, and with great taste; but poor Patrick was cut off in the flower of his youth,—he was killed at the storming of Seringapatam when a captain in the East India Company's service.

About the period at which Rauzzini gave my father the advice I have mentioned, Mr. Ryder, the comedian, brought over a singer, of the name of Webster, to Smock Alley Theatre; with him came a lady whom he called his wife, but who was really the wife of Battershill, a musical

* Monopoli was a sound musician; his church music was in great repute in Italy. Stephen Storace was one of his favourite pupils.

composer, from whom she had eloped with Webster. She was a fine-looking woman, and played Lucy, in the Beggar's Opera, and Jenny, in Lionel and Clarissa; but however, charming as she was, she soon left Webster, and Mrs. Baddely came to supply her place.

My father had a private box at the theatre, and my mother, passionately fond of theatricals herself, often took me to the play. From the time I first saw him act, nothing ran in my head but Webster, unless, indeed, it was the desire of going on the stage. I used to look at him with wonder, when he was performing Macheath; and those who recollect him in that character will agree with me that it certainly was a masterly performance. He had a fine figure, with a marked and rather handsome countenance; his voice was a fine baritone, with a sweet falsetto,[1] of which, being a good musician, he made a judicious use, particularly in 'The Charge is prepared'; indeed, I think it impossible that his performance of this character can be surpassed. Whatever little credit and indulgence I received when I performed Macheath, at Drury Lane, I owe, in a great measure to my recollection of him in the part; and I avow the same obligation to his Lionel, which was a *chef-d'œuvre*.

About the time of which I am now speaking, a third theatre sprang up in Fishamble Street, under the Lord Mayor's licence; the managers were Vandermere and Waddy, who had deserted from Smock Alley, and taken with them a large portion of the company. To oppose them, Ryder brought over Michael Arne to produce Cymon: his wife performed in it, and it brought great houses. But Arne, not content with being one of the greatest musical geniuses the world ever produced, wished also to possess the philosopher's stone; and, fancying himself a great alchymist, actually took a house at Richmond, near Dublin, and, neglecting all his pupils, gave himself up to a scientific search after gold. The consequences were ruin and a spunging-house. He was under articles to compose an opera[2] for Covent Garden; and my father, knowing this, sent him in his confinement, a piano-forte, supplied him with wine, &c. and while in 'durance vile', he composed some beautiful music. In return for this kindness, he gave me a lesson every day, and, after his release, continued particularly attentive to me.

It was also about this period that a Portuguese, who called himself Il Cavaliero Don Pedro Martini, came to Dublin: he played the Spanish guitar delightfully, and succeeded in ingratiating himself with the Duke of Leinster, Earl of Westmeath, Lord Belmont, and most of the leading people. He persuaded them that Dublin and Edinburgh were the only capitals where there was not an Italian opera, and proposed to engage Smock Alley Theatre, and bring a comic Italian company, to give operas twice a week. He consulted my father on the subject, who, conceiving the scheme likely to succeed, gave him encouragement, and promised him all the assistance in his power.

The Portuguese procured a large subscription, took the theatre, and brought over the company, amongst whom were La Sestini, the best buffo[1] of the day, Signor Pinetti, a Venetian, a most excellent actor; Signor Fochetti, a powerful primo buffo, with a fine bass voice; Signors Savoy, Peretti, &c. &c. and a second and third woman. Signor St. Giorgio conducted at the piano forte, and Signor Georgi led the band, which was strengthened by many performers from London. The etiquette was, that the band in the orchestra, as well as the company in the boxes and pit, should be full dressed. Bags and swords were then the order of the day: the prices were, boxes and pit, half-a-guinea; first gallery, five shillings; and the upper one, three shillings.

The first opera was L'Isola d' Alcina, composed by Gazzaniga; there was some beautiful music in it. Pinetti, who in Italy was celebrated for his performance of French characters, played the Frenchman in the opera admirably.

The next opera was Paesiello's La Frascatana; the houses were unusually crowded. La Buona Figliuola,[2] Piccini's popular opera, was put into rehearsal at the express desire of some of the old cognoscenti, who had seen it performed in London. Lovatino was the cavalier, (and I am informed, never was equalled in singing 'E pur bella è la Cecchina';) Morigi, the German soldier; Micheli, the gardener; Savoy, the Count; La Samperini, Cecchina, &c. &c.

Expectation was on tiptoe to hear this opera in Dublin, as it had been quite the rage in London; when a circumstance occurred which threatened its being laid aside; namely, the severe illness of Signor Savoy, who was to have performed the Count, a part of the greatest importance to the opera, and written for a high soprano voice. As there was no professional man to do it, the Portuguese turned his thoughts towards me, and offered my father his own terms, for I was well versed in the Italian language. He was backed in his application by the Duke of Leinster, Mr. Conolly of Castle Town, and several others, who were ever kind and partial to me. They all seemed to feel assured that if I undertook the part, I should gain both credit and emolument. This induced my poor father to listen to them; particularly, as he had made up his mind to send me to

Naples, and was actually in treaty with the captain of a Swedish vessel, bound thither, to take me as a passenger.

I was delighted when I found that I was to perform on the Italian stage, and counted every tedious moment while studying the part. At length, however, the awful night arrived! The house was crowded, and I received great applause. I had a powerful treble voice, pronounced Italian well, and was tall for my age, and acquitted myself beyond the most sanguine expectations of my friends. The opinion the foreign musical men gave of my abilities, of course, weighed greatly in my favour.

A circumstance now took place, which had nearly terminated my theatrical career. Il Cavaliero Portuguese, who had given the company to understand that he had all Peru and Mexico at his command; turned out to be a needy Chevalier d'Industrie, and would not pay them. They all struck; 'point d'argent, point de Suisse', was their motto. Pinetti, when he found he could get no money, set off for England with Fochetti, and without those two principals, it was impossible to get up an opera; so the rest of the Italians followed their leaders, dispersing, some to England, others to Scotland, &c. &c.

Ryder, who then had Crow Street Theatre, had entered into a fresh engagement with Michael Arne for three nights, to receive Cymon. Mrs. Arne, (his second wife), was a sweet singer, and being also a very pretty, petite figure, was very popular in Silvia.* They thought that I might be an additional attraction, and proposed to my father that I should play Cymon the three nights, and choose any character I pleased for the fourth, which should be given to me free of all expense, as a remuneration.

My father considered very wisely that, as every thing was arranged for my voyage to Naples, it was as well for me, or rather for him, (for *I* thought of nothing but the rapture of again shewing myself on the stage,) to accept the proposal.

I played Cymon three nights, and on the fourth, Lionel, (or, properly speaking, Master Lionel,) for my own benefit. The house was crowded

* The first wife of Michael Arne was a scholar of Doctor Arne's, at the same time with Miss Brent, for whom the Doctor composed the character of Mandane, in Artaxerxes. It is said that Doctor Arne translated Artaxerxes from the Italian of Metastasio into English; if he did, it was highly to his credit, for some of the thoughts are rendered beautifully; one for instance, from Mandane; in Italian it is,

'Si piange di piacer come d'affanno.'

which is translated thus,

'Pleasure may start a tear as well as grief.'

Dibdin composed his Leonora in the Padlock for the first Mrs. Arne, when Miss Wright.

in every part. I was successful in my songs, and acted the part decently, recollecting well all the points Webster had given in it.*

On the first of May, 1779, with an aching heart, I parted with my father, mother, and family, and sailed on board a Swedish merchantman, accompanied by a young Irishman, intended for the Roman Catholic church; and with a fair wind, left the kind and hospitable shores of my native country, and I may safely say quitted it with no little fame; for although not fifteen,[1] I had earned sufficient money to pay for my voyage to Italy, and for my maintenance and musical education for some time, after my arrival there.

I was so fortunate as to have letters of recommendation to Sir William Hamilton, at that time English *chargé d'affaires* at the Court of Naples, and to Father Dolphin, a Dominican friar, who was to be my 'guardian, protector, and guide.'

As good piano-fortes were in those times scarce every where—in Italy particularly, my father bought a grand one, made by one of the first London makers, which turned out in every respect excellent, and which, with a few books, English and Italian, he gave me. My mother furnished me with plenty of good sea store, ten guineas in my pocket, and a gold watch. I had besides, a letter of credit, which I was to deliver to Father Dolphin, who had instructions to pay my allowance according to circumstances.

The following occurrence which took place during my voyage, I would omit, if it could not be well authenticated both in Naples and Dublin.

* The opera was cast thus:—[2]

Lionel,	Master KELLY,
(Being the last night of his appearing on the stage previous to his going to Italy.)	
Sir John Flowerdale,	Mr. HEAPHY.
Jessamy,	Mr. O'KEEFE,
(The celebrated dramatic writer.)	
Harman,	Mr. GLENVILLE.
Colonel Oldboy,	Mr. WILDER.
Jenkins,	Mr. BARRETT.
Lady Oldboy	Mrs. HEAPHY.
Diana	Miss JAMESON.
Jenny,	Miss TISDAL.
Clarissa,	Mrs. ARNE.

The Band:—At the piano-forte, Michael Arne; Leader, the celebrated Pinto. First oboe, Mr. Bartlett Cooke, father of my friend, Mr. T. Cooke, of Drury Lane Theatre, whom I greatly esteem for his private worth, and high and diversified talents.

My father had a small country house near Drumcondra, with an extensive garden; his gardener, whose name was Cunningham, had a son, a very fine young man, who was a great favourite with all the family, and received many marks of kindness from my father, which he repaid to me when a child, by continued acts of affection. Poor Jack, however, degenerated, became a drunkard, associated with depraved companions, and left my father's service; shortly after, he was implicated in a burglary, tried, and transported to America. This made a grievous impression on me at the time, as I recollected, with gratitude, the apples and plums which had been gathered for me by poor Jack Cunningham.

My voyage took place during the American war, but the ship I was on board of, being a Swede, was under a neutral flag; yet, in the Bay of Biscay we were hailed by an American privateer. Our captain lay to, while a set of the greatest ragamuffins my eyes ever beheld, boarded us. They swore the vessel was under false colours, and proceeded to overhaul the captain's papers, and seize every thing they could lay hands on. A sturdy ruffian began to break open my piano-forte case with a hatchet, which, when I saw, I *manfully* began to weep, and cry out, 'Oh! my dear piano-forte,' &c. &c. The cabin boy, who was about my own age, called out, 'For God's sake, don't cry, MASTER KELLY.' The chief mate of the privateer, who was quietly perusing some of our Captain's papers, on hearing these words, turned round, and looking stedfastly at me, said, 'Is *your* name Kelly?' I answered, 'Yes.' 'Do you know any thing of a Mr. Thomas Kelly, of Mary Street, Dublin?' said he.—'He is my father,' was my reply. The young man immediately started up, ran to me, clasped me in his arms, and with tears in his eyes, said, 'Don't you remember me? I am Jack Cunningham, who, when you were a little boy, nursed you and played with you.' He seemed quite overcome by the unexpected meeting, and made the most affectionate inquiries about my family, when, after examination, the Captain finding that our vessel was really a neutral, left us. Jack again embracing and blessing me, took leave of me, and we soon lost sight of them. I never heard of him more. The next day we were boarded and examined by an English sloop of war, and our Captain gave information of the route of the American, which I honestly confess, if I had fancied it could have hurt poor Jack Cunningham, I should have been mightily sorry for.

To those whose health would be benefited by sea-sickness, I can safely recommend the ungentle exercise of the Bay of Biscay;—there is little chance of failure. After we left it, however, we had very fine weather for some time, and the islands of Minorca, Majorca, and the coast of Africa, though at a great distance, were noble objects.

When we had passed the Island of Ischia, we encountered a tremendous storm: actually alarmed by the violence of the tempest and appearance of the sea, which ran mountains high, I retired to my cot, and spite of terror and sea-sickness, fell fast asleep. I was awakened by the cabin-boy on the following morning, the 30th of May, 1779, who, to my great joy, told me that we were in the Bay of Naples.

The astonishment and delight I experienced when I got on deck, can never be effaced from my recollection. The morning was beautiful; I was restored to health, and safe in the wished-for port.

The Bay, full of shipping, the Island of Caprea where Augustus and Tiberius once held their revels; to the West the Isles of Procida, and Ischia, the picturesque and varied scenery of Pozzuoli, Posilipo, so celebrated for La Grotta del Cane and Virgil's Tomb, the King's Palace at Portici, the Campagna Felice, the Castle and fort of St. Elmo,* the terrific Vesuvius, the delightful coast of Tarrentum, the Castel a Mare, and the City of Naples, with its numerous palaces and convents, have beauties far, far beyond my feeble powers of description.

Before we entered the Mole, the officers of health came on board, and gave us the pleasant information, that as there was a report that the plague was raging on the African coast, we must perform quarantine before we were suffered to land.

An old tarrerdemallion was put on board our vessel, to prevent our escaping to the shore: he was an inexhaustible source of amusement to me; for although his clothes were all in tatters and patches, and spoke 'variety of wretchedness,' he wore his hair in an enormous bag, and carried a tremendously long sword by his side, of which I now almost wonder he did not give me a taste; for, if the truth must be told, I was very mischievous, and he, a particularly good subject for my mirth.

When Father Dolphin heard of my arrival, he came alongside,

* The Castle of St. Elmo is the strongest fortification the Neapolitans have. It stands on an eminence, said to command the finest view in the world; near it, lower down, stands the Carthusian convent of St. Martino. The fraternity are supposed to be very rich, and are celebrated for the excellence of their gastronomy. Their confectionary, wines and dinners are of the first order, but only to be got at by a card of admission from the Prime Minister; this is delivered to a lay brother, who shews the bearer the chapel and all that is curious, after which, he is invited to an excellent repast, for which they are forbidden to receive any remuneration.

In consequence of the great height of the Castle of St. Elmo, vessels can be distinguished at an immense distance. This is rendered of great utility to the mercan-

accompanied by another Friar, and a Mr. Fleming, a cadet in the Irish brigade, a worthy good Irishman. He was my daily visitor; and, what with the wines which we purchased from the boatmen, the delicious fruits, and good society, our bondage was not altogether unpleasant. Added to all the other *agrémens*, was the beautiful prospect around us; alongside of us was a Venetian vessel also under quarantine, on board of which were several Italian singers, dancers, &c. on their way to the theatre at Palermo, and two brothers, very fine French horn players; besides many other passengers. In the evening they danced or sang on deck, and played duets on the French horns, while the Mole was crowded with all ranks of people to enjoy the sea breeze; so that the whole scene was delightful.

At length the time of our release arrived; and my friend, accompanied by another Irish gentleman, called Plunket, also a cadet in the Irish brigade, (in one of the regiments of which his elder brother was Colonel,) took me on shore to an hotel near the Largo di Castello, kept by an Irish woman, married to a Neapolitan, an egregious rogue, but who possessed the pleasing art of speaking English very well.

I ordered a hair-dresser, at that period an indispensable appendage to a man's establishment; and shortly a very well-dressed person, with his hair in a bag, and a sword by his side, entered my room; on inquiring his business, he informed me he was the barber, come according to order, to adorn me alla moda di Napoli. I at first felt abashed at the idea of employing so fine a gentleman in such a capacity, but I soon became reconciled to the national gaiety; for the very beggars, with hardly any clothes to their backs, had ragged bags tied to their hair.

Accompanied by Fleming and Plunket, I went to hear mass at the church of San Giacomo, and after this, made my first visit to the worthy Father Dolphin. He was Prior of the Convent of St. Dominick, a fine pile of building, close to the gate through which runs the road to Capua, and also to the Conservatoiro of La Madonna di Loreto. I found him in his study, which opened into a spacious garden, and every thing around

---

tile part of the community, by means of signals made, according to the custom of all sea-ports, from the Castle on the approach of any vessel; these signals consist of balls of great size, projected into the air, the number of which signifies the description of vessel, whether frigate, sloop of war, merchant-man, &c. &c. at the same time the colour of the nation to which she belongs is hoisted. Thus, a merchant, while transacting business in any part of Naples, may know what ships, and of what nations, are entering the Bay, long before they reach the Mole. 'The first object of my attention every morning, was the signal station, and my first walk was on the Mole. The sight of an English vessel was a reward for days of watching.'

him breathed piety, benevolence, and content; he was about seventy years old, but full of health and activity.

He received me with the greatest kindness, and after reading my letter of credit, introduced me to two Friars of his order; one of them, called Plunket whom I often see in London even now; the other, named M'Mahon, whom I saw the last time I was in Dublin, at the Friary in Denmark Street; they were both Irishmen, as I need hardly mention, considering their names.

The first advice the Father gave me, after taking some chocolate and snow water, was to present my letter to Sir William Hamilton, and to make up my mind in which Conservatorio I should like to be placed. He gave me the choice of three, St. Onofrio, La Pietà, or La Madonna di Loreto. At St. Onofrio, Signor Monopoli was the head master; at La Pietà, Signor Sala, who had never produced a melody worth hearing, though the first counterpointist of the day; and at La Madonna di Loreto, Finaroli, a first-rate composer of church music. He had also written several serious operas, and several great composers were his scholars, amongst them was Cimarosa.

Having heard Rauzzini speak of him as a great master, I gave the latter the preference; but Father Dolphin desired me to ask the opinion of Sir William Hamilton, and be guided by it.

I immediately waited on Sir William, and presented my letters; when he had read them, he received me most kindly, and assured me that he should be happy to give me any advice as to the line I ought to pursue, and render me every service in his power.

Sir William having invited me to dinner that day, I returned, and was introduced to the first Lady Hamilton. The taste and partiality for music of this highly-gifted person, are too well known to need a remark from me. At that period she frequently gave concerts, to which all the best performers were invited. She was herself considered the finest piano-forte player in Italy.

After dinner, at which I had the honour of being introduced to the late Duke of Bedford; there was music. The celebrated Millico accompanied himself on the harp in the charming canzonetta, 'Ho sparso tante lagrime'; his singing was enchanting. I was asked, and sang Rauzzini's song, 'Fuggiam da questo loco', and 'Water parted from the sea',[1] accompanying myself on the piano-forte. I seemed to give general satisfaction, and Signor Millico, in particular, said many kind things. He told me he had often heard Tenducci sing 'Water parted', in England.

—Signor Borghi, who was afterwards stage-manager at the Pantheon, when the Opera House was burned down, had just arrived from England, and was also of the party.*

At parting, Sir William desired me to call upon him at eight o'clock the following morning; I did not, however, arrive till a quarter before nine. On entering the breakfast-room, I found with him Mr. Drummond, his physician, and a couple of antiquaries; his table was covered with cameos, intaglios, and lava. As soon as I entered the apartment, he said, 'My good boy, you were to have been here at eight; it is now three quarters of an hour past;' and added, looking very seriously at me, 'if you do not learn to keep time, you will never be a good musician.' Through life, I have recollected that hint.

When we were alone, he desired me to give him a candid detail of my views and intended pursuits, and which way my own inclinations lay. I told him all the circumstances which had preceded my leaving Ireland, and that my father's wish and intention were, that when I had finished the study of composition in Naples, I should return to England, and become a composer and teacher. I also told him that I feared the profession, towards which my own inclinations strongly led, the stage, would be my father's aversion. With respect to money, I informed him that my annual allowance, while pursuing my studies was to be two hundred Neapolitan ounces, (80*l.* English) to be paid monthly by Father Dolphin.

When we spoke of music, I mentioned my wish, that Finaroli should be my master; he said, 'My good lad, it is impossible to choose a more able instructor, or a better man. I know him intimately, and will introduce you to him, and recommend you to his care; but when you begin, you must bear in mind that nothing is to be done without steady application: your inclination for the stage you must smother for the present; your youth, and the unsettled state of your voice, should preclude all thoughts of that; a year or two may do much for you.'

'However,' he continued, 'as it is natural for you to wish to see the sights of Naples, take a fortnight's pleasure. Your friend Fleming is a worthy man; he speaks the language, and knows where every thing remarkable is to be seen, and no doubt will take care of you. Give my compliments to the worthy prior, and ask his permission; and recollect, as Gay says, "to-day for pleasure, to-morrow for business;" when once we begin, we must work hard.'

* The operas at the Pantheon were conducted by the Duke of Bedford, Lord Salisbury, and Mr. William Sheldon, an eminent solicitor, and a worthy man.

He shook me by the hand, and saying, 'be prudent', gave me a purse of twenty ounces, to pay, as he said, for my calashes.[1]

I repeated this conversation to Father Dolphin, who entirely approved of Sir William's advice; and giving his consent for a fortnight's pleasure, with his blessing and best wishes, advanced me *six ounces*, which *he* thought an ample disbursement for my *menus-plaisirs* during that period. Mr. Fleming consented to accompany me in my rambles, and I was as happy as an emperor.

To commence;—we dined at the St. Carlino tavern, opposite the King's palace; we had an excellent dinner of maccaroni stufato, bouilli, stewed veal, fried calamara,* a roasted chicken, salad, cheese, fruit, biscuits, two bottles of wine, a cup of coffee each, and a glass of chasse caffé, with iced lemonade &c. for eighteen-pence each. But, as George Colman says in his Mountaineers, 'Those days are past, Floranthe.' If they were not, what a delicious place of residence would Naples be for my old friend Pope, who joins to his talents as an artist and an actor, a share of judgment, experience, and taste in culinary matters almost unequalled.

The next morning we went to Portici, and slept. We saw the theatre at Herculaneum, which had been buried sixteen centuries; and passed under vaults to view it by torch-light;—while wandering about the galleries, I was of course obliged to express surprise and pleasure; but in truth I wished myself away, for there were neither singers nor dancers, nor pretty women there, and I never had any taste for antiques.

We returned to sleep at Portici; the next morning, we had an excellent breakfast of ham, fresh figs, and a bottle of lagrima Christi.† After discussing which, Fleming and myself mounted our donkies, and, accompanied by our guides, began the ascent of Mount Vesuvius. We passed through fields covered with fig and mulberry trees, and our guide

* The Calamara, or Ink Fish, is as great a favourite with the Neapolitans, as it was with the ancient Romans. An Italian told me that he had once eaten it many years before at Brighton; I was for several seasons inquiring for it there in vain. At length an old fisherman brought me one;—even *he* had never heard of its being eaten, or eatable, for when caught there it is always thrown away. It is quite black, but when washed, near a pint of ink comes from it, and it appears like snow; when fried, it eats like a veal cutlet, and is a great luxury. On the 25th of September, 1819, I had one, and my friends, who partook of it, said it was delicious.

† As I was brought up a rigid Roman Catholic, I was shocked at the name given to this delicious wine, but in time my scruples were overcome, and now often take a bottle with my esteemed friend, Mr. Savory of Bond Street, who has some of a superior flavour, imported by himself from Naples.

pointed out the favourite retreat of Pergolesi, the great composer. Here he was said to indulge his fatal tendency to melancholy; yet, perhaps, had he not been of that melancholy temperature, he would not have composed his celebrated 'Stabat Mater dolorosa', or his intermezzo, 'La Serva Padrona', both of which I heard with such delight at Naples.

He died at the early age of twenty-seven; it was supposed by poison,[1] given by a brother composer, jealous of his transcendent talents.*

We had some conversation with the hermit who lived on the mountain; he was a Frenchman, and said to have been formerly a hair-dresser in London; whether this be fact or not, I cannot say; the subject was much too delicate to touch upon with a recluse in such a situation. The mountain seemed in a most villainous humour, emitting flames and large bodies of lava. I soon had enough of it, and was right glad to find myself once more at Portici, with a supper of red mullet, &c. before me:—the next morning we returned to Naples.

2

The two following days we dedicated to Baja, and its burning sands. The view of Naples, and indeed every thing except the people, was luxurious and beautiful;—they were wretched. One miserable object pointed out the different situations of the villas of Cæsar, Mark Antony, and Cicero. All this was, I knew, very fine, and very classical; but to me, at that period, a complete bore: it was not my *gusto* to 'shun the busy haunts of men', nor of women; and a petticoat in a populous street in Naples, was to me the finest sight in the world; but I had no wish to

* I never heard the following truly poetic lines written by Mr. Rogers, author of the Pleasures of Memory, set to music and sung with exquisite pathos by my ever-lamented friend Mrs. Crouch, without thinking of poor Pergolesi's untimely death.

'Go, you may call it madness, folly,
You cannot chase my gloom away,
There's such a charm in melancholy,
I would not, if I could, be gay.

'Ah! did you know what pensive pleasure
Bends my bosom when I sigh,
You would not rob me of a treasure
Monarchs are too poor to buy.'

accomplish the Neapolitan proverb,—Vedi Napoli e poi mori*; *i.e.* see Naples, and then die.

Our next visit was to Posilipo, and the Grotta del Cane.[1] The Grotta di Posilipo, which leads to it, is so dark, that even by daylight, torches are necessary; the peasantry, when driving their cattle through this subterraneous passage, which they are obliged to do when going to or leaving Naples, call out to each other, 'Keep to the rock side,' or 'Keep to the sea side,' to avoid coming in contact.

We ascend the mountain of Posilipo, and entered Virgil's tomb; saw the stoves, the sulphureous vapours of which rise from the earth, and are so hot that eggs may be boiled in them.

At a little distance from the stoves is the Grotta del Cane; the keeper of the dog, who is the great actor of the scene, orders the poor animal to lie down in the cave; the vapour acts on it almost instantaneously; the body swells, the creature falls into strong convulsions, and after a violent struggle, appears dead. The keeper then draws him out into the open air, which speedily restores him, and he very wisely takes to his heels. This paltry and cruel experiment astonished me exceedingly at the time.

We now went to the Capo del Monte, and dined there with a friend of Fleming's. We were told that the king's intaglios and cameos were kept there;—our host shewed us some fine pictures, by Schidoni (a pupil of Correggio). His passion and forte were to paint the Lazzaroni, who swarm about the Chiaja and Santa Lucia, and the Largo di Castello. They are a fine hardy race of men, and, it is calculated, amount to fifty thousand. It cannot be ascertained how the greater number of them find subsistence, as those who work at all will only do so to earn as much as will keep them from starving. With scarcely any covering, they sleep on the steps of the church doors, or in the street. Their favourite spot, however, is the Largo di Castello; there they literally swarm, and pass the whole day playing the game of *mora*; or, by way of variety, listening to some ragged fellow near the Mole, who recites lively stories from Boccaccio, in the

* This Neapolitan saying has two meanings attached to it:

'Vedi Napoli e poi mori,'
'See Naples, and then die.'
Again,
'Vedi Napoli e poi Mori,'
'See *Naples,* and then *Mori.*'

Mori is the name of a little island near Naples; which island the Neapolitans think so beautiful that no place after it is worth viewing.

Neapolitan jargon, and perhaps sings the verses of Tasso, or Ariosto, or details the feats of Masaniello[1] the rebel fisherman.

All the time he exhibits, they sit round him with fixed and mute attention. I have myself often stopped to listen to the half-naked improvvisatore, and have been delighted by his dry humour and inimitable gesticulation. After entertaining them for hours, he thinks himself repaid amply, when they give him a coin called a callo (about half a farthing) each.*

The Lazzaroni are dreadful thieves; but theft they mildly denominate sleight of hand. I once saw one of them pick a gentleman's pocket of a handkerchief at one end of the Largo di Castello, and offer it to him for sale at the other; yet, had the pillaged man, or any other person, spoken, or even made a motion expressive of displeasure at the bare-faced infamy of the action, it is a thousand to one but that he would have been stilletoed on the spot. They are indeed such a formidable and united body, that the King himself finds it politic to persuade them that he feels flattered by being called their *captain*.

It is remarkable, that notwithstanding the vices of these people, and the extraordinary cheapness of wine in Naples, I never, during my sojourn there, witnessed a single instance of intoxication.†

The Neapolitans are proverbial for their gesticulation: if you ask a man in the street what o'clock it is, he looks at the sun, and by his fingers makes you understand the hour, but does not condescend to speak. The natives of every part of Italy are perfect mimics; and the strongest indication of either menace or revenge you can receive from an Italian, is to see him bite his thumb at you. Our immortal Shakspeare was well aware of this, when he wrote the quarrelling scene between the servants

* The game of mora is played by two persons; they both hold out their right hands, with their fingers extended, then each contracts one, or as many of his fingers as he likes, calling out at the same time the number which he guesses will be the amount of his own and his adversary's contracted fingers, this they both do at the same moment, and very quick; whoever guesses rightly, scores one, which is done by holding out one finger of the left hand; the game may be five or ten, or more, as agreed upon.

† The Neapolitans in general hold drunkenness in abhorrence. A story is told there of a nobleman, who, having murdered another in a fit of jealousy, was condemned to death. His life was offered to him on the sole condition of his saying, that when he committed the deed, he was intoxicated. He received the offer with disdain, and exclaimed, 'I would rather suffer a thousand deaths than bring eternal disgrace on my family, by confessing the disgraceful crime of intoxication!' He persisted, and was executed!

What a pity this poor fellow had not lived a few years in England or Ireland—we manage those matters better!

in the tragedy of Romeo and Juliet; there, Gregory,[1] Capulet's servant, says, 'I will bite my thumb at him; which is a disgrace to them if they will bear it.'

Malone, the commentator, says, that this mode of quarrelling appears to have been common in England in our author's time; as Decker, describing the various groupes that daily frequented the walks of St. Paul's Church, says, 'What shouldering, what jostling, what jeering, what bitings of thumbs, to beget quarrelling;'—yet, I think it but fair, to suppose that Shakspeare knew it was also an action adopted to 'beget quarrels,' in Verona, where the scene of the play lies, otherwise the coincidence would be remarkable.

Another trait of national character, which Shakspeare has ably displayed, is in the Merchant of Venice. In former times, as in the present, a Neapolitan nobleman was extremely proud of his horses, and made them the principal topic of his discourse. In the scene where Nerissa recounts the names of her various suitors to Portia, she says, 'First, there is the Neapolitan prince;' Portia replies, 'Ay, that's a colt indeed, he doth nothing but talk of his horses.'

The mode of living of the Neapolitans at first was disagreeable to me. They are very early risers; and at noon flock to the coffee houses, shops, promenades, &c.; the streets are crowded with monks, abbés, mountebanks, and lawyers.* Twelve o'clock is their usual hour of dinner, after which they take the siesta, rising usually an hour or two before sunset, and repairing again to the coffee houses to eat ice, which is in Italy beyond conception fine. Their chocolate, melons, grapes, peaches, &c. are delicious; my favourite was the harlequin, which is a mixture of all, served up in a silver cup, piled like a pagoda, which cost then only twopence English.

Even the Lazzaroni have their cooling luxuries; at the corner of every street, there are stalls, belonging to venders of water melons, iced and lemonade water, crying out, 'Bella cosa è l'acqua fresca!' (What a beautiful thing is fresh water). For a novo callo (half a farthing), a man, at the time I am speaking of, could get a large glass of iced water, with the juice of a lemon, and a slice of water melon in it.

The favourite drives of the nobility are the Molo, and along the shore

* It is calculated that in the kingdom of Naples only, there are twenty thousand lawyers, most of them younger branches of the nobility, whom poverty condemns to the bar. There is no nation, however large, in which so many lawsuits are carried on.

to Posilipo; there they enjoy the sea breeze in their carriages. It is only the very commonest people who go on foot; a Neapolitan gentleman would be branded with disgrace, if he were caught committing the heinous misdemeanour of using his own legs.

Some of their equipages are very handsome; all had two running footmen, who ran before the carriages with incredible speed; many of the richer nobility had four.

My Lord Tylney, who had resided in Italy for many years, and spent his princely fortune between Florence and Naples, appeared on the drives on gala days, in great splendour; I have seen him drawn by six beautiful English cream-coloured horses! he had four men before his carriage, and a great number more behind.

His Lordship gave splendid dinners, concerts, and balls, which were frequented by all the English of consequence resident at Naples. I have seen there Sir William Hamilton, Lord Bristol, who was also Bishop of Derry, Lord and Lady Maynard, and a number of fashionables of different nations.

After having taken my full swing of sight-seeing, and having spent Sir William's money, in and out of calashes,* I thought it full time to wait upon him. I accordingly did so, and received his promise to introduce me the following day to Finaroli, which he did.

Finaroli was a light, sprightly, animated little man, about fifty: he heard me sing, and was pleased to say, I evinced promising abilities; he took me to see his Conservatorio, in which there were between three and four hundred boys; they studied composition, singing, and to play on all instruments. There were several rooms, but in the great school-room, into which I was introduced, there were some singing, others playing upon the violin, hautboy, clarionet, horn, trumpet, &c. &c. each different music, and in different keys. The noise was horrible; and in the midst of this terrific Babel, the boy who studied composition was expected to perform his task, and harmonize a melody given him by his master. I

* Calashes are to be found at the corners of all the principal streets in Naples. A calash is a small narrow gilt chair, set between two wheels, and without springs, drawn by one horse, which is guided by a cord tied round its nose, without bridle or bit. The driver, who usually wears his hair in a net, sometimes sports his night-cap, with a gold-laced hat over it, gets up behind, and, to do you honour, endangers your neck, driving helter-skelter through the streets, even through the Toledo Street, the longest and most populous one in all Naples, I think as long as Oxford Street, and actually swarming with friars, lawyers, and Lazzaroni. All the time he bellows, with the lungs of a stentor, 'Make way there for my Lord Anglais!'

left the place in disgust, and swore to myself never to become an inmate of it.[1]

I acquainted Father Dolphin with my feelings on the subject, and the dislike I had to walk in the processions after the host, and wear the dress, which all who enter the Conservatorio must do.*

On his representing this to Finaroli, he answered, 'I have taken a liking to the boy, and will receive him as an inmate: he shall have a small apartment on the ground-floor of the house where I live, and eat at my table. In addition to this, he will have the benefit of visiting the Conservatorio daily, and receive all the advantages of a scholar, without being obliged to put on the dress or perform the duties.'

My English piano-forte was of little use to me, as Finaroli had made it a *sine qua non,* that I should give up all thoughts of being a performer on it; indeed, all Italian masters think it highly prejudicial to the voice.

My master introduced me to the directors of the different theatres, and I had the *entrée* of them all.

At San Carlo's are performed grand serious operas, (the other three theatres are for the opera buffa,) the first I saw there was Metastasio's Olimpiade, the music by Metzlevisic, a German of great musical celebrity. I thought it very fine, and the performance exquisite.

The celebrated Marchesi, the first soprano, performed the part of Megacle; his expression, feeling, and execution in the beautiful aria, 'Se cerca se dice l' amico dov' è', were beyond all praise. Ansani, then the finest tenor voice in Europe, was there; and Macherini his wife, was the principal female singer; she had a very sweet voice, but small, and of limited compass; the Neapolitans called her 'La cantante con la parruca,' from her wearing a wig, in consequence of her head being shaved during illness, previous to her engagement; but they liked her in spite of her wig!

Nothing could surpass the splendour of the spectacles they produced, or the beauty of their ballets. Le Pique was their first ballet master, Rossi the second,—both great artists. Madame Rossi was the principal female dancer amongst a crowd of talent.

The first ballet I saw, was Artaxerxes. Le Pique, the Arbaces; Madame Rossi, Mandane; and Artabanes, by Richard Blake, an Irishman, who

* On or after the 17th of October, the boys of the three Conservatorios are obliged to attend morning and evening, for nine days, at the Franciscan Church in their dresses. It is by attending this festival, and performing without remuneration, that they are exempt, by the king's permission, from all taxes on provision and wine, which are paid by every other class of inhabitants.

went abroad very young, and had become a very fine pantomime actor, and was considered the best grotesque dancer of his day.

The decorations of this ballet were magnificent; one in particular struck me. In the opera of Artaxerxes, on our stage, in the scene where Artabanes makes Arbaces exchange swords with him, and receives the bloody one, he comes on at the side scene, which is very poor. In the ballet, the scene is placed in the middle of the stage, the galleries over each other, with apartments opening into them, are before you; you see Artabanes rush out of the chamber of Artaxerxes, having murdered him, and fly across the different galleries, pursued by the guards of Artaxerxes, with lighted torches; he makes his escape by a private door into the royal gardens, where he meets Arbaces.

The manner in which this scene was managed, was powerfully effective. I cannot conceive why, on our theatres, it might not be equally so, except, indeed, that the stage at San Carlo is of an immense size, capable of bearing and working any machinery, and besides, opens at the back towards the sea, and because it seems that the English theatres would not risk the expense.

The 'Rape of the Sabines', and 'Il Disfatta di Dario' (the defeat of Darius), were also splendidly got up, as ballets. In the latter, in the battle between the armies of Alexander and Darius, eighty horses were introduced, and the whole arranged with the greatest skill. There were four hundred persons employed in it. I recollect there was a comic ballet, called the 'Achievements of Don Quixote', in which my friend Blake shone conspicuously as Sancho Panza.

Four times in the year this magnificent theatre is illuminated; viz. on the evening of the birth-day of the King of Spain, and on those of the King, Queen, and Prince Royal of Naples.

In this vast edifice there are seven tiers of boxes; in the front of each box is a mirror, and before each of those, two large wax tapers; those, multiplied by reflection, and aided by the flood of light from the stage, form a blaze of splendour perfectly dazzling.

Each box contains twelve persons, who have commodious chairs, &c.; at the back of each of those, on the principal tiers, is a small room, where the confectioner and pages of the proprietor wait, and distribute sweetmeats and ices to the company in the boxes, and any of their friends in the pit, whom they choose to recognize.

There are sixteen rows of seats in the pit, forty seats in each row; they are fitted up with stuffed cushions and rests for the arms, like chairs. When any one takes a place for the night, he receives a key of it, and when he leaves the theatre, he locks the seat up again, and returns the key.

On all gala days, the King, Queen, and all the Court attend in full dress; at which times, the *coup d'œil* is magnificent.*

The Teatro di Fiorentino is the most fashionable for the comic opera; it is about the size of the little theatre in the Haymarket. The first opera I saw there was the 'Italian in London', (from Voltaire,) composed by Cimarosa. From this drama the elder Colman took the plot of his comedy of the 'English Merchant'.

They had at that time excellent performers. The celebrated Genaro Luzzio was the primo buffo, and the principal female, La Coltellini, was delightful, both as a comic actress and singer.

At the Teatro Nuovo, another comic opera house, but by no means as good as the former, acted the celebrated Cassaciello, the idol of Naples. Whenever he appeared on the stage, the house was in a tumult of applause, and though he gave his recitation in the Neapolitan jargon, there never was a greater favourite, nor one more deserving of favour.

There were also two principal female singers, the Benvenuti, sisters and beauties; one of them had to boast of having in her train, the young Marchese Sambuco, son of the then prime minister of Naples.

Here I saw the first representation of Paesiello's comic opera, 'Il Socrate Imaginario', (The imaginary Socrates). Cassaciello performed Socrates to admiration. I was informed that Garrick, having seen him in Naples, on his return to England said, that the best comic actors he had ever seen, were Cassaciello in Naples, Preville at the Comédie Française in Paris, and Sacchi, the harlequin, at Venice.

Another theatre, called Il Teatro del Fondo, had closed before my arrival in Naples. It is considerably larger than the two of which I have just spoken—the principal buffo, named Buonaveri, was an excellent actor as well as singer. He had lately returned from Russia, where he had amassed a large fortune. The tenor singer was Signor Mengozzi, a sweet voice, replete with science and great taste. But the delight of the Lazzaroni, and the common people in general, was Jean Cole, the famous Pulcinella. He performed twice a day in a little theatre called Saint Carlino, on the Largo di Castello. The house was always crowded, and even the King and Court frequented it, to enjoy his comic powers.

Whatever Jean Cole said was received with rapture. Once, when the

* This fine theatre has been since destroyed by fire; but I understand that one, if possible, more splendid is built on the same spot.

King was at the theatre he was performing in the piece called 'Pulcinella in Disgrace'; in the midst of a dialogue with another actor, he exclaimed, 'Oh, Naples! Naples! dear, dear Naples! beautiful Naples! I shall never see thee more! How happy I was in thee! My royal and gracious master, the King, used to order maccaroni, lagrima Christi, and other dainties, to be sent to me; but, alas! that is over! he has forgotten the good custom, and poor Pulcinella; oh! poor Pulcinella!'

The King laughed heartily, and taking the hint, the next morning sent Jean Cole a massive silver tureen filled with maccaroni.

Carlino, of the Comédie Italienne, in Paris, was an actor in Jean Cole's line, and equally celebrated and followed. He likewise performed twice a day. He had an extraordinary facility in seizing and introducing the flying gossip of the moment. The report of the day always found an evening circulation through Carlino.

But I apprehend that I am wandering a little from my subject; considering the subject to be myself, that, perhaps will be forgiven: however, to return to Naples—I continued to go on attentively receiving instructions. By day I studied with avidity and ambition, but in the evening followed my own devices, or was kindly introduced by my master to families of distinction. I was honoured by the patronage of the Princess Belmonte, Princess Ghigi, the Duchess of Castel Duoro, Marchese del Vasto, Marchese St. Marca, and a long list of nobility. In their houses every evening after a little music, a Faro, or Basetta bank, was held by the proprietor of the mansion. They also played at Berabis, or Lotteria. Indeed, the whole delight of the Neapolitans, high and low, seemed to be gambling of one sort or another.

The house I frequented with the greatest pleasure, was that of La Signora Moretti. She was a very charming person, and (which was not her least recommendation to *me*) an excellent judge of music, and a good singer and performer on the piano-forte. I frequently had the pleasure of meeting there the celebrated composer, Cimarosa, who had been the favourite scholar of my master, Finaroli. It was a great treat to hear him sing some of his comic songs, replete with humour and taste, accompanying himself. Amongst other professors frequently assembled there, I saw, one evening, Signor Di Giovanni, who many, many years afterwards, was my deputy stage-manager at the King's Theatre, and who had just then returned from Poland.

About the month of July the King and Queen usually went to Posilipo, and in fine weather had concerts in the open air. To one of those I was taken by Sir William Hamilton, who did me the honour to introduce me to their Majesties as a lad from Ireland, come to study music in Naples. The first question the King asked, was, 'Ne; siete Cristiano?' 'I say, are you a Christian?'—'I hope I am, Sire,' was my reply. Shortly afterwards he commanded me to sing an English song, and I put forth my strength in 'By him we love offended',[1] from the Duenna. Her Majesty, then ordered an Italian air, and I sung 'Ho sparso tante lagrime'; they seemed pleased, and her Majesty, after asking me with great affability, how I liked Naples, where I lived, who was my instructor, &c. invited me to take some ice and a glass of Maraschino. I need not say with what pleasure I obeyed the command, nor how much my young mind was elated at her Majesty's condescension.

Her Majesty had a fair complexion, and beautiful hair. It was said at Naples, that she bore a strong resemblance to her mother, Maria Theresa, Empress of Germany. I confess I did not think her particularly handsome. She had the character of a busy meddling woman, and the reputation of governing the King and kingdom completely; indeed, in all matters of business he was accustomed to refer to her, saying, 'Go to the Lady, she understands affairs better than I do;' and judging by all I ever heard on the subject, he *was in the right*!

The King was very tall, near-sighted, with very light eye-brows, and remarkably fair hair. He was very partial to theatricals, and when he went to Caserta,[2] (one of his palaces) in which there was a beautiful little theatre, he often condescended to act in burlettas with the Queen. They uniformly took the parts of the principal Buffo and Buffa; the graver and more important characters were filled by the Lords and Ladies of the Court.

His Majesty was a man of excellent heart, of which the following well-known, well-authenticated fact gives proof:—

When making a tour of Italy, his brother-in-law, Joseph II. Emperor of Germany, met him at Milan. Joseph's acuteness led him to suggest many alterations in the internal government of the kingdom, most of which would have been improvements; but some of them, although very advantageous to the revenue, threatened to press somewhat hardly upon the subject. 'I flatter myself I live in the hearts of my people,' was the king's reply, 'and I never will disturb their happiness by any thing which looks like oppression. I find in my dominions numerous natives of other countries, many poor and wretched; but in all the cities I have visited, I have neither seen nor heard of one Neapolitan in a similar situation,—a proof, as I think, that they find more comfort and encouragement in their own country than elsewhere, which illustrates the old Neapolitan proverb: "Chi sta bene non si muova", (Those who are well should not change)'.

Had this monarch possessed the advantages of a common education, he might have done much for his country; but it was with difficulty he could even write his name, and, consequently, he left every thing to the Queen, the Marquis Tanucci, his former and but too indulgent tutor, and the Chevalier Acton, an extremely clever man and minister, and, above all, as it was said, a great favourite with Her Majesty.

The King, uneducated as he was, was proportionably fond of field sports; he was perpetually hunting, shooting, or fishing, in which exploits he was usually accompanied by Sir William Hamilton, to whom he was very partial. Upon these occasions His Majesty would go out into the Bay, with a large escort of fishermen, and not return until a quantity of fish was caught, which was sent to Santa Lucia (the fish-market), for sale. The convents had the first choice, the remaining part went to the best bidder, and the money arising from the sale was distributed amongst the poor.

Another of his amusements was, the game of Pallone,[1] which he often played in a court built for that purpose, in the Largo di Castello, and any person decently dressed, was admitted to see him. One day, when I was amongst the spectators, he came to me, and asked whether I had ever seen the game played in England. But skilful as he was at this amusement, he performed one feat which surpassed all competition;—I mean, the eating of maccaroni, of which he was very fond. This exhibition, I honestly confess, surprised me most of any thing I had ever seen either of a king or a subject. He seized it in his fingers, twisting and pulling it about, and cramming it voraciously into his mouth, most magnanimously disdaining the use of either knife, fork, or spoon, or indeed any aid except such as nature had kindly afforded him.

In the month of August 1779, which will be remembered for their lives by all those who chanced to be in Naples at that period, happened one of the most terrific irruptions of Vesuvius that ever was recollected by man. At that time, a great fair was held in the Piazza St. Ferdinando, and the Largo di Castello; I was at the fair when the mountain first began to throw forth its lava, and, during the whole duration of the irruption, I was permitted to be near Sir William Hamilton, and this was indeed a most fortunate circumstance for me, for, independent of his scientific knowledge, he was respected by all the better classes, and a favourite with the Lazzaroni into the bargain, who often lamented that so good a man *must* be eternally punished, since he was a heretic.

Vesuvius continued to throw up such abundance of lava, that had the wind been in a different direction, Naples and Portici must have been swallowed up; for, on the opposite side, whole villages, vineyards, &c. were destroyed. During two days the scene was most appalling,—horror and dismay were in every countenance, and despair in every heart.

The Lazzaroni, as usual, appealed to their patron saint and protector, St. Gennaro, and went in a body to the palace of the Archbishop of Naples, to demand the keys of the church where the figure of the saint is kept, that they might carry him off, and place him *vis-a-vis* to the villainous mountain; well convinced, that at the bare sight of his wooden countenance, it would cease roaring! The Archbishop, however, having intimation of their approach, and thinking, with Falstaff, that 'the better part of valour is discretion,' retreated by a private way in his carriage, and set off for his palace at Capua, too far distant to be followed by the Lazzaroni on foot. Indeed, his Eminence had good reasons for supposing, that had those mirrors of integrity got possession of the saint, they might, when he had quelled the mountain, have carried their gratitude so far as to ease him of the weight of diamonds and other precious gems with which his head and body were covered; a species of toilette to which his Excellency was wisely unwilling to subject his Saintship.

The Lazzaroni finding themselves disappointed, held a council, and I saw them in an immense body march to Posilipo, whither the King and Queen had retired, determined to force the King to order the Saint to be given to them. The King appeared on the balcony to address them, but in vain; the Queen also (*enceinte*,) came forward, but without avail. The Royal guard and a Swiss regiment were ordered to disperse them; but they were not to be intimidated; neither entreaties nor menaces could divert them from their purpose. 'The Saint! the Saint! give us up our Saint!' was the universal cry. Just as popular fury was at its height, a man appeared, whom, the moment they saw, the wolves became lambs; the mob fell on their knees before him bareheaded and in total silence. He addressed them in the following conciliatory manner:—

'What do you come here for, ye infamous scoundrels? Do ye want to disturb your Saint, in his holy sanctuary, by moving him? Think ye, ye impious rascals, that if St. Gennaro had chosen to have the mountain silent, ere this, he would not have commanded it to be so? Hence! to your homes, ye vagrants! away! be off! lest the Saint enraged at your infamous conduct, should order the earth to open, and swallow you up!'

This soothing speech, aided by a kick to one, and a knock on the head to another, (fairly dealt to all within his reach,) dispersed them without a single murmur! So that what the supplication of their Sovereign, backed by the soldiery could not effect, was accomplished by one man, armed indeed with superstition, but with nothing else!

This man was Father Rocco, well known to have possessed the most unbounded power over the lower orders in Naples; of no Saint in the calendar (St. Gennaro excepted,) did they stand in such awe as of Father Rocco. He was a sensible shrewd man, and used the power he possessed with great discretion. He was much in the confidence of the Chevalier Acton, and the other Ministers.

Previous to his time, assassinations were frequent at night in the streets, which were in utter darkness; and the Government dared not interfere to have them lighted, lest they should offend the Lazzaroni; but Father Rocco undertook to do it. Before each house in Naples there is a figure of a Madona, or some saint, and he had the address to persuade the inhabitants that it was a *mortal sin* to leave them in the dark!

I was myself a witness of the following ridiculous scene. One evening a groupe of Lazzaroni were very attentively playing at their favourite game of *mora*; beside them was a puppet-show, in which Punch was holding forth with all his might. Father Rocco suddenly appeared amongst them. The first step the holy man took, was to sweep into his pouch all the money staked by the gamblers; then, turning to the spectators of Punch, he bawled out, 'So, so, ye rapscallions! instead of going out to fish for the Convents and support your families, ye must be loitering here, attending to this iniquitous Punch! this lying varlet!' Then lifting up a large wooden cross, suspended by huge beads round his waist, he lustily belaboured all within his reach, lifting up the cross at intervals, and crying out, 'Look here, you impious rogues!' 'Questo è il vero Pulcinella!' 'This is the true Punch, you impious villains;' and strange as this mixture of religious zeal and positive blasphemy may appear, they took their thrashing with piety, and departed peaceably like good Catholics. I got out of his way with great alertness, feeling no desire to become a disciple of such a *striking* school of religious instruction.

On the 8th of September, however, I saw a religious procession which was truly beautiful. The King and Queen, with the Court, attended by a large body of the military, crowds of monks, the boys of the Conservatori, &c. went, as they do annually, to pay their respects to La

Madona del Piè di Grotta. All the balconies of the houses in the streets through which they passed were hung with tapestry, rich silk, satins, &c. and the sight was really striking and magnificent.

Another interesting ceremony, la Festa della Nouvena, took place nine days previous. The peasantry and shepherds from Abruzzo, Calabria, and Apulia, upon this anniversary, come from the mountains in their sheepskin dresses, playing on their various instruments, some on the Zampogna, (a kind of bagpipe,) others on the Colascione. This instrument is the common one in the Neapolitan dominions, and is something like a guitar, having however only two strings, tuned fifths to each other. These shepherds visit all the churches, and play their famous *pastorale* there, and at all the principal noblemen's houses. During Christmas the processions are to be seen in which they perform; amongst their pageantry they have moveable stages, the machinery connected with which is admirable, representing the birth of our Saviour, the Virgin, &c. all as large as life. The expense of some of these processions is enormous; and the 'properties,' as they would be theatrically called, are constantly left in families as heir-looms.

As my master, whose church music was highly approved of, conducted the principal church festivals, I was allowed to sing at many of them, being a *Christian*, or, as I have before explained it, a Roman Catholic. I was delighted at this, not for the lucre of gain, (although they pay their singers liberally,) but because the nuns of the convents where the performances take place, send round trays full of delicious sweetmeats, made by themselves. Such traits of female attention were peculiarly gratifying to me at that period.

The profession of a nun, as indeed many travellers have described, is a most magnificent and impressive sight. If the lady be of a noble and rich family, the luxury displayed on the occasion is excessive; she is covered with diamonds, all of which, if she does not possess them herself, are borrowed or hired for the occasion.

Finaroli told me an anecdote so illustrative of the ridiculous punctilio and vanities which sometimes mix themselves with this solemn act, that I cannot forbear repeating it.

The young and beautiful daughter of the Duke de Monteleone, the richest nobleman in Naples, was destined by her family to take the veil; she consented without a murmur to quit the world, provided the ceremony of her profession was performed with splendour; and a *sine qua non* was, that Cafarelli, the great soprano singer, should perform at it. It was represented to her that he had retired with a fine fortune to his estate, in the interior of Calabria, and had declared his determination never to sing again. Then said the reasonable young lady, '*I* declare *my determination* never to take the veil unless he does. He sang six years ago, when my cousin was professed, and I had rather die, than it should be said, that she had the first singer in the world to sing for *her*, and that I had not!' The fair lady was firm, and her glorious obstinacy was such, that her father was obliged to take a journey into Calabria, when, with much entreaty, and many very *weighty* arguments, he prevailed on Cafarelli to return with him to Naples. He sang a *salva regina* at the ceremony; and the Signora having gained her point, cheerfully submitted to be led, like a lamb to the sacrifice, to eternal seclusion from the gay and wicked world.

In justice, however, to her taste it must be said, that Cafarelli was one of the greatest soprano singers Italy ever produced. He was a Neapolitan, and the Neapolitans were very proud of him. He amassed a great fortune, and purchased the Dukedom of Dorato, for his nephew, and built a magnificent palace for himself; over the entrance to which, was inscribed—

AMPHYON, THEBAS,
EGO, DOMUM.

3

At the period of which I am now speaking, there were amongst the English at Naples, a Mr. Stewart and family. He had taken a house for three years; but he and his family were going to spend the ensuing carnival at Rome. On my accidentally saying that, had my means permitted, I should have rejoiced at the opportunity of seeing that city in their company, Mr. Stewart most generously offered me a seat in his carriage, and a cover at his table, and to bring me back, free of all expense. I confess, my heart beat with joy at the proposal! I flew to my master and the good Father Dolphin, to obtain permission for this delightful journey, which was granted, and with a few zecchinos *on account*, from the latter, completed my happiness. My friend Fleming went with me to the Molo*

* Near the Molo is the money market, where there were stalls, in which the owners sat with wooden bowls before them, filled with the coin of every nation in the world; there, for a small premium, the traveller might obtain the current cash of the nation he was about to visit; and this in many instances was more convenient than a letter of credit.

to get my Neapolitan ducats exchanged for Roman scudi; and on the following morning, December 26th, with a heart as light as my pocket, I found myself seated in an excellent travelling carriage, with the worthy Mr. Stewart, his amiable wife and sister; a courier before, and a Neapolitan carriage with the servants and luggage behind us:—and truth to say I never felt more perfectly happy in the whole course of my existence.

We passed the first night at Terracina, a dangerous place to sleep at during the summer months, as it is then rendered dreadfully unwholesome, by what the Romans call the '*mal aria.*' All the inhabitants who have the means of doing so, leave it during that period. We however escaped, and arrived in Rome the following evening, and drove to the Piazza di Spagna,[1] where the English usually took up their abode. The Spanish Ambassador always resided there, and it was so completely his territory, that he could grant protection, even in cases of murder! Whether in compliment to the Spanish Embassy, or the English society, I know not, but *unprejudiced ladies* were, in those days, not suffered to live in any other quarter of the city!

The day after our arrival, we went to the Corso, where the sports of the carnival were going on. There was to be seen the whole population of Rome, high and low, rich and poor, *en masque*; the nobility and ladies in their most splendid equipages all masqued, throwing sugar-plums to the motley groupe below, which was composed of mountebanks, pulcinellas, cardinals, harlequins, &c. with music, dancing, singing.—In short, I was in a delirium of pleasure! Every evening, we visited the theatres:—there are two for serious operas, the Aliberti and the Argentina, where the best performers are always found; indeed, should the manager attempt to introduce any thing inferior, woe be to him! and, as these theatres are only allowed to be open during the carnival, he is obliged to pay enormous salaries to procure the first singers; for the Romans will have the best or none. There are also two theatres for comic operas, La Capranica and La Valle.

The Romans assume that they are the most sapient critics in the world; they are certainly the most severe ones:—they have no medium,—all is delight or disgust. If asked whether a performance or a piece has been successful, the answer, if favourable, is, 'è andato al settimo cielo,'—'it has ascended to the seventh heaven.' If it has failed, they say, 'è andato all' abbisso del inferno,'—'it has sunk to the abyss of hell.' The severest critics are the Abbés, who sit in the first row of the pit, each armed with a lighted wax taper in one hand, and a book of the opera in the other, and should any poor devil of a singer miss a word, they call out, 'bravo, bestia,'—'bravo, you beast!'

It is customary for the composer of an opera, to preside at the piano-forte[1] the first three nights of its performance, and a precious time he has of it in Rome. Should any passage in the music strike the audience as similar to one of another composer, they cry, 'Bravo, il ladro,'—'bravo, you thief;' or, 'bravo, Paesiello! bravo, Sacchini!' if they suppose the passage stolen from them, 'the curse of God light on him who first put a pen into your hand to write music!' This I heard said, in the Teatro Aliberti, to the celebrated composer Gazzaniga, who was obliged to sit patiently at the piano-forte to hear the flattering commendation.

Cimarosa, who was their idol as a composer, was once so unfortunate as to make use of a movement in a comic opera, at the Teatro della Valle, which reminded them of one of his own, in an opera composed by him for the preceding carnival. An Abbé started up, and said, 'Bravo, Cimarosa! you are welcome from Naples; by your music of to-night, it is clear you have neither left your trunk behind you, nor your old music; you are an excellent cook in hashing up old dishes!'

Poggi, the most celebrated buffo singer of his day, always dreaded appearing before those stony-hearted critics; however, tempted by a large sum, he accepted an engagement at the Teatro della Valle. He arrived in Rome some weeks previous to his engagement, hoping to make friends, and form a party in his favour; he procured introductions to the most severe and scurrilous, and thinking to find the way to their hearts, through their mouths, gave them splendid dinners daily. One of them, an Abbé, he selected from the rest, as his bosom friend and confidant; he fed, clothed, and supplied him with money; he confided to him his terrors at appearing before an audience so fastidious as the Romans. The Abbé assured him, that he had nothing to fear, as *his* opinion was looked up to by the whole bench of critics, and when *he* approved, none dare dissent.

The awful night for poor Poggi at length arrived; his *fidus Achates* took his usual seat, in his little locked-up chair, in the pit. It was agreed between them, that he was to convey to Poggi, by signs, the feeling of the audience towards him;—if they approved, the Abbé was to nod his head; if the contrary, to shake it.—When Poggi had sung his first song, the Abbé nodded, and cried, 'Bravo! bravissimo!' but in the second act, Poggi became hoarse, and imperfect; the audience gave a gentle hiss, which disconcerted the affrighted singer, and made him worse: on this,

his *friend* became outrageous, and standing up on his chair, after putting out his wax-light, and closing his book, he looked Poggi in the face, and exclaimed, 'Signor Poggi, I am the mouth of truth, and thus declare, that you are decidedly the worst singer that ever appeared in Rome! I also declare, that you ought to be hooted off the stage for your impudence, in imposing on my simple and credulous good nature, as you have done.' This produced roars of laughter, and poor Poggi retired, never to appear again, without even exclaiming, 'Et tu, Brute,' which he might most appropriately have applied to his guardian crony.

A circumstance something like this, took place at the Teatro Argentini. A tenor singer of the name of Gabrielli, brother of the great female singer of that name, was engaged there. Before he had got through five bars of his first song, the critics began to hiss and hoot, (and very deservedly so, for he was execrable,) saying, 'Get away, you cursed raven!' 'Get off, you goat!' On which he came forward and addressed the audience very mildly, 'You fancy you are mortifying me, by hooting me; you are grossly deceived; on the contrary, I applaud your judgment, for I solemnly declare to you, that I never appeared on *any* stage without receiving the same treatment, and sometimes much worse!' This appeal, though it produced a momentary laugh, could not procure a second appearance for the poor fellow.

A description of the magnificent buildings of Rome is not what is expected perhaps in memoirs such as these; yet it is impossible to speak of that magnificent city without noticing the splendid structures which every where strike the eye of a stranger.

The Church of St. Peter appeared to me so magnificent, that our St. Paul's seemed but an epitome of it, though built on the same plan. When the Pope chaunts the Te Deum, assisted by the choir, and in some parts by the whole congregation, (generally possessing good voices and fine ears,) the effect produced is certainly sublime; but it is in the Pope's chapel only, one can hear in perfection the divine music of Palestrina.

Like all strangers, I of course visited the Coliseum, the Palazzi Corsini and Borghese, with their magnificent gardens, the Villa Albani, the Vatican, the Pantheon, and all its superb antiquities. Before I left Naples, I was so fortunate as to procure a letter from a Dominican friar to Father M'Mahon, a Capuchin, and a very worthy countryman of mine; who kindly became my guide, and explained every thing to me. He conducted me to see the house where Raphael had resided in the Via Cornari—to the Via Gregorina, where Salvator Rosa and Gaspar Poussin both had lived, and also to the Trinità del Monte, where Taddeo Zucchero died. He had begged his way to Rome, but was rich enough before his death to build some of the most superb palaces in that city. On the Trinità del Monte, Mengs had also dwelt, and painted the walls of his own bedchamber. His apartments were afterwards inhabited by Angelica Kauffman, when she finally left England.

We went to the church of the Saint Onofrio convent, where lie the remains of Tasso, whose incomparable genius produced his Jerusalem Delivered before he was thirty years of age; and who, it is said, composed verses at seven years old! The sight of the beautiful palace, Via Colonna, the dwellings of Propertius and Virgil, near Porto St. Lorenzo, and the gardens of Mecænas, finished our researches.

Amongst the living sights, I frequently saw in his carriage his Eminence Cardinal York, brother to the Pretender, but whom the Romans called brother of the King of England! He bore an excellent character, and was charitable in the extreme, particularly to any English who claimed his protection.*

Mr. Stewart, his family, and myself, in our way back from Rome, passed a day at Frascati. I was delighted with this village, the scene of Paesiello's beautiful comic opera, called La Frascatana, particularly as it was the first Italian opera I had ever seen in Dublin.[1]

4

We returned in safety to Naples, Mr. Stewart proceeding to his house in the Chiaja, and myself to my worthy master, Finaroli. He seemed

* Father M'Mahon told me a comical story of a countryman of ours, a Mr. Patrick O'Flanagan, who having been wrecked at Genoa, travelled on foot to Rome to beg assistance of Cardinal York, and got the Cardinal's porter, who was a Scotchman, to present his Eminence with the following conciliatory letter.

May it please your Sanctity,

I was cast on shore at Genoa—travelled on foot to Rome. Hearing of your Holiness's humanity to poor Irishmen—for thirteen years I served his Britannic Majesty, King George the Third in the navy. God bless and prosper him to boot. I hate and detest the Pope and the Pretender, and I defy them and the devil and all his works, and am,

Your Sanctity's obedient servant,
PAT. O'FLANAGAN.

Pat waited until the Cardinal was going out to take his morning's ride, when he threw himself on his knees before his Eminence, who laughed heartily at his elegant epistle, and ordered him twenty Roman crowns.

pleased to see me, and expressed a hope that I would now attend steadily to my studies. My mornings were devoted to the Conservatorios and festivals which were daily celebrated in the different churches. My passion for music amounted to adoration, and as at my time of life, good or bad taste was easily imbibed and fixed, I was fortunate in never hearing any but of the most superior kind, and performed by the first professors of the age. My evening I passed generally at one of the theatres, if not so fortunate as to be engaged to Sir William Hamilton, or at some of the great houses, where I had been introduced. I must say, that at the time I speak of, to be a native of Great Britain, was a *passe partout* all over Italy! indeed, the name of Englishman was held in such reverence, that if two Italians were making a bargain, it was clenched by one saying, 'I pledge myself to do so and so on the honour of an Englishman.' This was considered more binding than any oath they could swear. I am sorry to say that the feeling which then existed towards my countrymen has become almost extinct; and am still more sorry to be obliged to admit, that in the many disgraceful scenes I have witnessed, the Italians were not always in fault.

Amongst the many great musical professors at this time at Naples, was the celebrated Schuster. He was the favorite scholar of the renommé Hasse, Maestro di Cappella to the then Elector of Saxony. Schuster, though a very young man, had been sent for, from Dresden to compose for Pachierotti, at the theatre St. Carlo. The opera chosen was Metastasio's 'La Didone abbandonata'. I recollect his taking me to a rehearsal, which was a crown and sceptre to me in those days. The opera was received with enthusiasm, particularly the rondo, sung divinely by Pachierotti, 'Io ti lascio, e questo addio', which was afterwards introduced in the musical entertainment of 'The Flitch of Bacon', with the English words, 'No 'twas neither shape nor feature', adapted to it by my worthy friend Shield. La Didone drew crowded houses, but the rondo was the magnet; indeed, Pachierotti's singing it, was supposed to have raised a flame in the bosom of La Marchesa Santa Marca, one of the most beautiful women of the Neapolitan court. She was said to be of a very *susceptible* nature, and to have fallen desperately in love with the pious Eneas, which love he honestly returned; this, though very pleasant to the parties themselves, was by no means relished by a certain Cavalier Ruffo, who had been cavalier servente to the Marchesa, but was fairly dismissed by the rondo. He did not choose to lose his mistress to that tune, and meeting Pachierotti one evening on the Molo, (the fashionable promenade of the

Neapolitans to taste the sea-breeze,) he overwhelmed him with abuse, and struck him! Pachierotti drew his sword, and being as good a swordsman as a singer, soon wounded and disarmed il Cavaliere. He immediately reported the affair to the minister il Marchese Sambuco, who submitted the matter to the King. His Majesty was pleased to approve of Pachierotti's conduct, and it was hinted to il Cavaliere, that if he attempted further outrage, himself and family might find cause for repentance in the loss of their places at Court. This was decisive, and the affair dropped. But Pachierotti, who lived in perpetual fear of assassination, though engaged for two seasons, gave in his resignation on the score of ill health at the end of the first, and acting Eneas for the last time, left the fair Marchesa to play Didone at her leisure!

But to return to myself.—It is really curious to observe upon what trifling circumstances the greatest and most important events of our lives depend. I was walking one evening, with my friend Blake, through the Strada di Toledo; and when passing some billiard-rooms, he recollected that he was likely to find a person in them whom he wished to see. We went up stairs, and in the room found the famous soprano singer, Signor Giuseppe Aprile, who was allowed to be the greatest singer and musician of the day. He was called by the Italians, and indeed every where, 'Il padre di tutti i cantanti,'—the father of all singers. Blake introduced me to him, and he very kindly invited us to take chocolate with him the next morning. When we went, he received us with great cordiality, and after hearing me sing, said, 'This boy has both taste and expression, and I think so well of his abilities, that if his friends approve of it, I will take him with me to Palermo, and instruct him without any remuneration; indeed, I have no doubt but that in a short time I can make him capable of earning his bread any where.'

Blake was delighted at my receiving through his means such an offer from so great a man. I was charmed at the prospect of seeing the capital of Sicily, and Sir William Hamilton and the good Father Dolphin were as pleased as either at the happy prospect opening before me, and cheerfully gave their consent to my going. Our departure was to take place in four months. In the interim, Aprile made me solfeggiare with Signor Lanza, (father to the Lanza, who was said to be the instructor of Miss Stephens.) He was an excellent singing master, and was afterwards brought into this country, with his family, by the Marquis of Abercorn, for the purpose of instructing his daughters, and lived with his Lordship's family at the Priory.

Previous to our going to Palermo, Aprile went to see his family at Abruzzo; and at the same time to conduct a musical festival at Gaeta, and took me with him. The best professors in the kingdom were engaged, and I had the honour of singing a salve regina. The festival was most splendid, and had Aprile been the greatest potentate on earth, he could not have been more caressed by his townsmen than he was.

Gaeta is four days' journey[1] from Naples, and as we slept each night at a convent, I had a good opportunity of witnessing the luxurious mode in which the monks of Abruzzo lived. It beggars all description; they and their convents are proverbially rich, and their country abounds in all good things, especially wines, which are indeed excellent. After the festival was over, and we had remained a week at Gaeta, we returned to Naples, not forgetting in our way back our nocturnal visits to the holy fathers, who repeated their hospitalities.

On our return, I continued my attention to Aprile, who gave me a lesson every day, and almost every day an invitation to dinner; he seemed much entertained by my boyish mimicry, a talent which I possessed at that time in no mean degree. I went with him to visit the miracle of St. Gennaro or Januario, in the Cathedral; the King and Queen, in state, attended his saintship. There were two immense orchestras erected in the church, and all good professors, vocal and instrumental, were engaged to perform upon these occasions. The Archbishop prays, or appears to pray, while the Te Deum is sung. He then displays a phial, which contains the congealed blood of St. Gennaro; towards this he holds up a large wax taper, that the people may perceive it is congealed. The miracle consists, as every body knows, in this blood dissolving before the congregation, and is supposed to be performed by the saint himself. As soon as it is liquified, the Archbishop roars lustily, 'the miracle is accomplished!' The Te Deum is again sung, and the whole congregation prostrate themselves before the altar of the saint with gratitude and devotion, and every face beams with delight.

On one of those miraculous days, I witnessed a ludicrous scene. It happened by some accident, that the Archbishop could not make the miracle work. The Lazzaroni and old women loudly called on the Virgin for assistance. 'Dear Virgin Mary! Blessed Madona! Pray use your influence with St. Gennaro! Pray induce him to work the miracle! Do we not love him? Do we not worship him?' But when they found the Saint inexorable, they changed their note, and seemed resolved to abuse him into compliance. They all at once cried out, 'Porco di St. Gennaro!'—'You pig of a Saint!'—'Barone maladetto!'—'You cursed rascal!'—'Cane faccia gialutta!'—'You yellow-faced dog!' In the midst of this, the blood (thanks to the heat of the Archbishop's hand,) dissolved. They again threw themselves on their knees, and tearing their hair, (the old ladies particularly), with streaming eyes, cried, 'Oh! most holy Saint, forgive us this once, and never more will we doubt your goodness!' Had I not been an eye-witness of this scene of gross superstition and ignorance, I really could not have given credit to it.

Time, which flies the faster the longer we live, wore on rapidly even in my young days, and the period approached at which I was to leave enchanting Naples, where, 'Wit walks the street, and music fills the air.' Sir William Hamilton continued his kindness towards me, and procured many letters of introduction for me, in addition to those which he himself gave me to the Prince Villa Franco Paternò Budera, and Petrapersía his son, the Duke of Verdura, and the Duke St. Michele. I was greatly grieved at quitting the friends I had acquired, particularly my faithful companion Fleming, and a Mr. Cobley, a young man who was in a mercantile house in Naples. Many years after I had the pleasure of meeting him at the house of his brother-in-law, Mr. Haydon,[1] of Plymouth, when we talked of our youthful pranks and 'fought all our battles o'er again,' not forgetting the innumerable bowls of punch we had drunk on the Mole, at the house of the pretty widow Mac Mahon, who had one great attraction in my eyes, in addition to those of her person. She let me score, and I did 'score, and spared not,' and the consequence was, that being born with a natural genius for drinking punch, I got pretty deep into her books; not into her bad books, however, for I paid her honourably before I left Naples.

Aprile, his brother, Guiseppe, a valet de chambre, and myself, embarked on board a polacre,[2] commanded by a Trapani Capitano, and set sail for Palermo, at which place, after a tolerable passage, we arrived on the evening of the third day; though we suffered much by sea sickness, it was two days before we were allowed to go on shore. While enduring this delay, a number of young men swam near our vessel, while bathing. The Sicilians are reckoned the most expert swimmers and divers in Europe; consequently it is their favourite amusement, and they are so accustomed to it, that they are able to remain several hours in the water. The Captain of our polacre told me, that swimming actually formed part of the education of a Sicilian, and that with them it was an acquirement of equal importance to reading or writing.

When we were released we went to the only tolerable hotel in Palermo, kept by a Madame Montano, a saucy old French woman. However, we were soon released from her den, and conducted to an excellent house taken for Aprile, in the Strada del Cassaro, near La Porta Felice.

La Strada del Cassaro is a beautiful street, and four others leading from it, called Le Strade dei Quattro Cantoni, are also very fine, and contain the palaces of the first nobility. At one end of the Cassaro is the Palace of the Viceroy, a ponderous piece of architecture; and at the other are Flora Gardens, and the Porta Felice itself, which opens to the Marino.

Aprile had the goodness to appropriate a comfortable apartment in his house to my use, and I determined to make the best of my time, and the favourable opportunities which presented themselves. I studied between five and six hours every day, with the greatest assiduity; my voice fell gradually into a tenor, and in a short time I could execute several songs which had been composed for two celebrated tenors of that day, Ansani and David. I delivered the letters of introduction which I brought from Naples, and was generally well received by those to whom I delivered them, particularly by the Duke St. Michele, and the Prince Val Guarniera; with these noble and kind friends, I was permitted to pass much of my time. The Duchess St. Michele was accomplished and beautiful, and sang delightfully. The Duke spoke English fluently, and was an enthusiastic admirer of Shakspeare, and our old dramatic authors. Indeed, I was surprised to find so many of the Sicilian nobility had studied English. They had a Casino, called the 'English Casino,' to which none were admitted who could not, at least, make themselves understood.

The Palermitans are all fond of music, and every evening there was an Accademia di Musica held at some private house. I was usually invited to these: to be the scholar of Aprile, and an Irishman, were sufficient; but I was besides considered a christian.

Every good has more or less of evil to counterbalance it, and amongst all my comforts, I found the climate of Sicily warmer and more oppressive than that of Naples; indeed, when the sirocco blows, it is almost insupportable. As a proof that this is actually the case, the indolence and torpitude of the people during its continuance may well be adduced; they are perfectly dreadful, and are greatly increased by the seclusion in which every body necessarily live; the doors, window shutters, and verhandas being almost hermetically sealed, and all business and visiting at an end. Such is the opinion which the natives have of its baleful influence, that I once heard a Palermitan dilettante say, when obliged to allow that some music composed by his favourite Pigniotti, was bad—'Well, I suppose I must admit it is bad; but perhaps he composed it during the sirocco!'

When the tramontane or north wind returns, every thing resumes its gay and beautiful appearance, not excepting the ladies, who in general have brilliant black eyes and eye-lashes, and a fine, energetic, vivacious expression of countenance. Their costume is very becoming, and in the street they wear the black veil, after the Spanish fashion; in the evening, they dress much in the French and English style, that is, the higher orders, who on their gala days wear a profusion of diamonds. All ranks, however, are fond of ornament, the very poorest loading their throats with gold chains, &c. &c. In no country in the world are the women more fascinating. In their hospitality, and liveliness of conversation, they reminded me of the ladies of old Ireland! but when they dance, their attitudes and movements are—what shall I say?—inspiration itself. I soon began to find myself too susceptible to their winning ways, and my young heart resembled a target, in which almost every shot told.

I was astonished at not finding any female servants in Palermo; and when I expressed my wonder, an Irish friend of mine accounted for the fact by stating, that all the *maid* servants in that part of the world, were *men*. It is said, that if the girls were suffered to go out as servants, they could not procure husbands:—all Italians, the Sicilians in particular, being very jealous *before marriage*.—This is hardly to be wondered at in Palermo, for there are a number of beautiful women among the lower order, which, 'I am ashamed and sorry, sorry and ashamed' to say, made me every Sunday very religiously pay a visit to the tomb of Santa Rosalia, on Mount Pellegrino, where these good Christians go dressed 'in all their best,' to pay their respects to their sanctified protectress!

But while I am retracing the beauties of the ladies, I am forgetting my pursuits and my master. The opera chosen by Aprile for his début, was Sarti's[1] Allesandro nell' India, (the jealous Poro being a favourite character of his.) The Prima Donna, La Signora Agatina Carara, was much dissatisfied with his choice, and the result was, *bella! horrida bella!* Parties ran high! Aprile, justly considered as the greatest of all artists, had a strong faction; La Carara, one of the most beautiful women of her day, and a fine singer, had abundance of partisans, besides being protected by the committee of noblemen, five in number, (for there was a committee *there*). With them she played her cards so cleverly, that each supposed himself the favoured lover; but in all these little delicate arrangements she had an able and experienced, if not very respectable ally, in her husband! He, worthy soul, had but one weakness; an inordinate love of gold, and the bearer of such arguments had every thing to hope from the sweetness of his disposition. I never knew any man who could bow so gracefully, or quit a room with a better air, when a nobleman called upon his cara sposa:—fortunately he was fond of taking long walks, and never was known to return home at an unseasonable hour.

The theatre being closed every Friday evening, Aprile was usually invited to concerts at private houses, and, as a matter of course, I went with him. At these parties, *playing* was almost as popular an amusement as singing, for a Faro bank was always held after the music was over. There was frequently very high play at many houses. Suppers are also introduced, of which fish formed a very important feature. Their moreau, a species of eel, is delicious, and only to be procured in this part of the Mediterranean; their tunny fish and pesce spada (sword fish) are very fine; and their ices, which they serve up in all shapes, are exquisite, as well as their Malavisa wine, the produce of the Liparian Isles. Since I am touching on the subject, I must say, the best suppers were given by the Princess Villa Franca, and the Prince her husband, an old man, who was good tempered and affable, while his consort was young and perfectly beautiful; their palace at the Seven Hills, a short distance from Palermo, was magnificent, and always crowded with visitors during the vintage, when all is life and pleasure.

Aprile had an invitation to pass a few days at the country residence of his patron, Prince Val Guarniera, in the neighbourhood of La Bageria; near it, amongst many other noblemen's houses, was one, I sincerely hope, the only one of its kind in Europe, belonging to Prince B——,[1] a sort of maniac; the impression it made upon me will never be effaced. On entering the hall, I saw the heads of beautiful women, and the bodies of the most frightful animals; and the body of a man with the head of a mastiff. The family statues were all fancifully clad in suits of different coloured marble, with red stockings and black shoes. The roofs of the apartments were lined with looking glass, so that if five or six persons were moving about a room, it appeared as if an hundred were walking on their heads. Each pane of glass in the windows was of a different colour, and even the clock in the hall was stuck into a giant's body! yet the rooms themselves were beautiful, paved with fine marble, and containing a profusion of china, and objects of taste and *virtù*. The prince's dressing-room was filled with figures of snakes, scorpions, and other disgusting animals; in short, his whole life seemed devoted to the study of the horrible and disgusting.

I was particularly taken notice of by Prince Paternò, a man of superior wit and talent; as well as by the Duke of Verdura. The Prince Petrapersía also favoured me with his patronage and friendship; he was a very handsome man, famous for his strength and activity, and spoke excellent English. When he was going to visit his estates in Catania, Aprile gave me permission to accompany him, on condition that I returned in a fortnight; we set out with a great retinue of servants, and six of his Highness's body-guards, who, I verily believe, were banditti! However, they were faithful to *us*, and conducted us safely to the palace of the Prince Budero, his Highness's father. After remaining there three days, we continued our journey to Catania, to see the Prince Biscaria, who resided in one of the most superb palaces in all Sicily. I was astonished to see such a structure built nearly at the foot of Mount Etna, liable, at all times, to be swallowed up by an eruption. The Prince wished me to ascend the mountain, which, however, no persuasion could induce me to do. I was content to view it at an humble distance. I had no ambition to be deified, like the heathen philosopher, for throwing myself into the great crater; nor had I even curiosity enough to visit Il Castagno di centi Cavalli; I was more anxious to see Syracuse, Dionysius' Ear,[1] and the scene of the Transformation of Acis; but, however, we contented ourselves, after enjoying the Prince Biscaria's hospitalities for a few days, with returning to Palermo, where we found the whole population alive, making preparations for the grand fête of Santa Rosalia, which was to take place in a few days.

On the 12th July, the saint's natal day, the annual festival commenced. From Aprile's house, in the Strada del Cassaro, we had a fine view of the procession, which commenced at five in the evening, and passed from the Marino to the Porto Felice: all the military in and about Palermo were assembled to protect it. Among them, on the present occasion, were a Swiss regiment and the Irish brigade, a fine set of men. The car on which the saint was carried, was an enormous machine, drawn by forty mules, richly caparisoned, with twenty postilions in blue and silver: near the bottom of the car was a large orchestra; the musicians placed in rows above each other, the whole interspersed with a precious assortment of angels, saints, artificial trees of coral, orange, lemon, &c. and surmounting all, on the dome of the car, and as high as the houses themselves, stood a large silver statue of the saint herself. The procession lasted till eight o'clock, when the illumination on the Marino commenced, the whole chain of which continued a mile in length. Imagination can picture nothing so splendid as the fire-works, which were then displayed. On the sea stood an immense palace of fire, and all the shipping, gallies, &c. were brilliantly lighted up.

The second day commenced with horse racing, of a nature to an Englishman extremely strange. The horses, eight or ten in number, have no riders, but stand in a row, held by their fine manes by grooms; they are almost covered with ribands of different colours: the grooms find it difficult to restrain them till the signal is fired from the Corso.

At the sound of the cannon, they start with the fleetness of the wind, and the sight is really beautiful. The conqueror is led back in triumph, and hailed with trumpets, kettle drums, and the shouts of the populace, who vociferate, with all their might, 'Viva il bel cavallo! viva mille anni!' (May the beautiful horse live a thousand years!) All this time, the noble animal stalks majestically through the Corso, as if conscious of his triumph, and the applause bestowed upon him. I have seen races in many countries, but none which gave me such true delight as those in Palermo. On the third night, the Marino, the Flora Gardens and the four gates of the city were illuminated. There was music in the Chiesa Grande, where four large orchestras were erected, which contained all the principal musicians in the island, and many from the kingdom of Naples, both vocal and instrumental; the whole was under the direction of Aprile, and there was my first regular appearance. I sang a mottetto, composed by the celebrated Genario Mano. Aprile had taken great pains with me in it, and appeared fully satisfied with my execution of it.*

I think when the church was completely illuminated, the walls, pillars, and roof ornamented with artificial flowers, gold and silver paper, interwoven with the lights, nothing earthly could surpass the *coup-d'œil*; the eye absolutely shrank from the splendour of the blaze.

I continued my old routine with my master; and going to the parterre of the theatre one evening, on seeing an empty seat, I sat down. A very pretty woman sat next to me, with whom I entered into conversation. At the end of the first act of the opera, a young gentleman, who, I afterwards found, was the Marchese St. Lucia, and the professed cicisbeo

* It may not be thought unworthy of remark, that the first and only native of Great Britain that ever sang at that festival, or indeed, in any church in Sicily, was myself. The circumstance was considered so extraordinary, that Aprile had my name and country inserted in the archives of the church.

of the lady I was speaking to, came to me, and said, 'How dare you, you insolent fellow, place yourself in a seat that belongs to me?' I answered truly, that had I known the seat to be his, I would not have taken it. His reply to this pacific speech, was a thump on the head, which I repaid with interest. But in an instant, I was seized, and, for the heinous crime of returning a blow, was hurried to prison, and left there amongst culprits of every description. My entrée seemed to create a bustle amongst them, and I felt myself a personage of importance.

About a dozen of them messed together, and invited me to sup with them, and I can say, with justice, I never passed a more jolly night in my life! They had some good pesce spada for supper, and plenty of wine. They sang and told laughable stories. One of them had been a captain of Calabrian banditti, previous to which, he had been the hero of the pickpockets on the Largo di Castello at Naples. He told us many of his exploits, and something of his education. When a boy, he had been placed at a school, where his trade was regularly taught. A large figure, made of straw, was placed in the middle of a room, about which were arranged watches, trinkets, pocket-handkerchiefs, &c. &c. The master of the school (and a very great master of arts he was), stood by and gave instructions. No one was allowed to be an adept, or fit to take the field, till he could rob the figure without being observed, or deranging a single straw.

They recounted many anecdotes; the following one of the celebrated Gabrielli, though well known, I cannot refrain from repeating, as she had, in consequence, remained several days in the very room we then occupied. Gabrielli, though beautiful, generous, and rich, had a most capricious temper. She was the idol of the Palermitans; notwithstanding, one evening, on which a new opera was to have been performed, as they were going to begin, the house being crowded, and the Viceroy and court present, she sent word she had a head-ache, and could not perform. Every endeavour of the manager and her friends to induce her to fulfil her duty, only rendered her the more obstinate; and even the threat of a dungeon, from the Viceroy, had no effect; at length, after exhausting every other method to restore her to reason, a guard seized and conducted her to prison. She told the captain of the guard, with the greatest sang froid, 'Your Viceroy may make me cry, but he shall not make me sing.' After remaining two days in confinement, she was released. But while in prison, she feasted the prisoners sumptuously, and on her departure, distributed a large sum amongst the poorer class of them. It was said that she never would have returned to the theatre had she not entertained a penchant for the manager.

This affection of her's commenced in rather a strange manner. When she was performing at the theatre St. Carlo, at Naples, and living in great splendour with Count Kaunitz; the manager wrote to her, requesting to know what terms she would accept for singing one season at his theatre at Palermo. She answered, 'If you will build a bridge that will reach from Naples to Palermo, I will sing for you, not else;' to which he replied, 'Madame, if you can recollect, and will give me a list of ALL those on whom you have bestowed favours, in the course of your life, I will build the bridge you mention; not else.' She was puzzled, and the negotiation dropped; however, when they met, shortly after this free and easy beginning, they became excellent friends.

I was detained in prison for three days, and was only liberated through great interest. I returned to my master, who received me with his usual kindness, and applauded my spirit for not receiving a blow without returning it. The termination of his engagement approached, when he proposed returning to Naples. He called me to him one morning, and after hearing me sing half a dozen songs, in which he had taken great pains in my instruction, said,—'The time of our separation is approaching; your talent will now procure you an engagement in any theatre in Europe. I have written to Campigli, the manager of the Pergola theatre in Florence (he was also a sort of agent, and was, at that time, in correspondence with, and furnished every Italian opera in Europe, with singers, dancers, composers, &c.) he will be glad to see you, and under his care and patronage you cannot fail of success, because you have the peculiar distinction of being the only public scholar I ever taught. A Syracusan polacre will sail in a few days for Leghorn, in which I will procure you a passage, and will give you several letters of recommendation; and so, God bless you, my good boy!'

I was overwhelmed with melancholy at the thought of leaving my kind, liberal, and great master. He was a man of the most honourable and independent mind I ever met, and considered an excellent scholar. He took great pains to explain Metastasio, and other great Italian poets to me, and particularly inculcated a love of truth, and a horror of committing a mean action; I may truly say, with Nicodeme, in the French play,[1] '*Le maître qui prit soin de former ma jeunesse, ne m'a jamais appris à faire une bassesse.*'

I prevailed on him to accept, as a remembrance, the piano-forte I brought from Ireland;—it was my only possession, but I declare that had it been worth thousands, it would have been his; my love and gratitude to him were so strong.*

The day arrived when I was to leave my beloved master. He amply provided me for the voyage, and paid my passage, giving me, at the same time, thirty Neapolitan *ounces,* which were sufficient to take me to Florence, where I might expect an engagement. After taking an affectionate leave of me, he sent his faithful Giuseppe, a Milanese, who had lived with him several years, in the boat with me, to see me safe on board. Giuseppe was a worthy creature, but as vain of his hair-dressing as the elder Vestris was of his dancing, and flourished his comb with as much grace and dignity as *le Dieu de dance* moved the *minuet de la cour*. Poor fellow, he shed tears at parting with me, and said,—'Farewell, Signor! remember your attached Giuseppe; in whatever part of the world you may be, if embarrassed, write to me, and I will go to you. *I* can live any where, for in classical hair-dressing I will yield to none, however illustrious; and thank heaven! in these days, the comb takes the lead of every thing.'

5

The wind was fair, and we set sail from beautiful Sicily, 'where Ceres loves to dwell.' I was dreadfully sick during the first day and night, and obliged to keep below. The second, I went on deck, and had a view of the Lipari Islands, famous for their delicious wines; Stromboli, their chief, was out of humour, for it poured forth volumes of flame. It is said that this mountain discharges a greater quantity of lava than either Etna or Vesuvius, and never ceases roaring! On the third morning, I was roused by a dreadful noise on deck; when I went up, all was uproar; at last the captain told me we were pursued by a Turkish galera; the crew, instead of working the vessel and endeavouring to escape, were on their knees,

* Many years afterwards, when dining with my dear and lamented friend, the late Lady Hamilton, at Merton, I had the pleasure of hearing of this circumstance from the illustrious Lord Nelson, near whom I had the honour of being seated at table. He said, 'Mr. Kelly, when in Naples, I have frequently heard your old master, Aprile, speak of you with great affection, though he said, that when with him, you were wild as a colt. He mentioned, also, your having given him your piano-forte, which, he said, nothing should induce him to part with.' I confess I was much gratified by the repetition of this trifling anecdote.

each praying to his patron saint! some one of which, however, was propitious, for a stout breeze springing up, we got close in shore, and lost sight of the terrible galera. After being six days at sea, during the last of which it blew a complete hurricane, at eight o'clock in the morning we arrived in the bay of Leghorn, and lay close to the Lazzaretto; it is a beautiful building, and was then used as an hospital for seamen. After we had been visited by the officers of health, I went on shore to shew my passport at the Custom-house; I had on a Sicilian capote,[1] with my hair (of which I had a great quantity, and which, like my complexion, was very fair) floating over it: I was as thin as a walking stick. As I stepped from the boat, I perceived a young lady and gentleman standing on the Mole, making observations; as the former looked at me she laughed, and as I approached, I heard her say to her companion in English, which, of course, she thought I did not understand, 'Look at that girl dressed in boy's clothes!' To her astonishment, I answered in the same language, 'You are mistaken, Miss; I am a very proper *he* animal, and quite at your service!'

We all laughed till we were tired, and became immediately intimate; and these persons, my acquaintance with whom commenced by this childish jest on the Mole at Leghorn, continued through life the warmest and most attached of my friends. All love and honour to your memories, Stephen and Nancy Storace! *He* was well known afterwards, as one of the best of English composers, and *she* was at that time, though only fifteen, the prima donna of the Comic Opera at Leghorn. They were Londoners, and their real name wanted the *t*,[2] which they introduced into it. Their father was a Neapolitan, and a good performer on the double bass, which he played for many years at the Opera House, when the band was led by the celebrated Giardini. He married one of the Misses Trusler of Bath, celebrated for making a peculiar sort of cake, and sister to Doctor Trusler, well known in the literary world as a chronologist.

The elder Storace, Doctor Arnold, and Lowe, the singer, opened Mary-le-bone Gardens for the performance of burlettas, &c. &c. Owing to the attraction of the music, and Miss Trusler's plumcakes, the Gardens were successful for a time, but, disagreeing among themselves, the proprietors closed them, I believe, with loss.

When Mr. Sheridan married Miss Linley, and brought her from Bath, their first lodging in London was at Mr. Storace's house, in Mary-le-bone, and from that time a strong friendship existed between the families. Nancy, the only daughter, could play and sing at sight as early as eight years old; she evinced an extraordinary genius for music, and Stephen the son, for *every thing*! He was the most gifted creature I ever met with! an enthusiast and a genius. But in music and painting he was positively occult! I have often heard Mr. Sheridan say, that if he had been bred to the law, he thought he would have been Lord Chancellor.

His father sent him, when very young, to the Conservatorio St. Onofrio at Naples, to which he became a great ornament. Nancy Storace had the singular good fortune to be instructed by Sachini, and Rauzzini, in England; and after making prodigious progress under them, her father took her to Naples, where she sang at some of the Oratorios given at the theatre St. Carlo, during Lent. She was very well liked, and afterwards went to Florence, where the celebrated soprano singer, Marchesi was engaged at the Pergola theatre. He was then in his prime, and attracted not only all Florence, but I may say all Tuscany. Storace was engaged to sing second woman in his operas; and to the following circumstance, well known all over the Continent, did she owe her sudden elevation in her profession.

Bianchi had composed the celebrated cavatina 'Sembianza amabile del mio bel sole', which Marchesi sung with most ravishing taste; in one passage he ran up a voletta[1] of semitone octaves, the last one of which he gave with such exquisite power and strength, that it was ever after called 'La bomba di Marchesi!' Immediately after this song, Storace had to sing one, and was determined to show the audience that she could bring a bomba into the field also. She attempted it, and executed it, to the admiration and astonishment of the audience, but to the dismay of poor Marchesi. Campigli, the manager, requested her to discontinue it, but she peremptorily refused, saying, that she had as good a right to shew the power of her bomba as any body else. The contention was brought to a close, by Marchesi's declaring, that if she did not leave the theatre, *he* would; and unjust as it was, the manager was obliged to dismiss her, and engage another lady, who was not so ambitious of exhibiting a bomba.

From Florence she went to Lucca, and from thence to Leghorn, where I met her, and where she was a very great favourite. I dined with her and her brother the very memorable day of my landing; and Stephen, who had a wonderfully quick conception, intuitively, as it were, inquired into the state of my finances. I honestly told him that they were not in a very flourishing condition; 'We must endeavour to recruit them,' said he. I mentioned, that I had a letter from Aprile to a Signor Chiotti, an opulent jeweller, who was an amateur and director of the concerts. He told me that Chiotti could be of great use to me if I took a concert, and he had no doubt the opera people would sing for nothing for me. Ever warm and active, my dear Stephen introduced me the next day to the British Consul, and the Messrs. Darby, eminent mercantile men, residing at Leghorn, brothers of Mrs. Robinson, the beautiful Perdita, and two Scotch families, the Grants and Frazers, patronized me, and I had a crowded concert room,—the nett produce, eighty zecchinos; and above all, to me, my singing was very much approved.

My time passed delightfully while I remained in Leghorn. The Russian fleet were at anchor in the Bay, commanded by Admiral O'Dwyer, a distinguished seaman, and an Irishman by birth. The Storaces and myself often went on board his ship, and were delighted by hearing the Russians chaunt their evening hymn. The melody is beautifully simple, and was always sung completely in tune, by this immense body of men. There was at the same time, in the harbour, a privateer from Dublin, called the Fame, Captain Moore: he and his first officer, Campbell, were Irishmen, and had a fine set of Irish lads under them. When Storace's benefit took place, the officers and crew, who could be spared from their duty, to a man (and a famous sight it was), marched to the theatre, and almost filled the parterre. At the end of the opera, Storace sung the Irish ballad, 'Molly Ahstore', on the conclusion of which, the boatswain of the Fame gave a loud whistle, and the crew, en masse, rose and gave three cheers. The dismay of the Italian part of the audience was ludicrous in the extreme. The sailors then sang 'God save the King' in full chorus, and when done, applauded themselves to the very skies: nothing could be more unanimous or louder than their self approbation.

At length, Stephen Storace took his departure for England, and I for Lucca. I was very much affected when I saw him sail, and set out on my journey with a very heavy heart. At Lucca I remained two days. The country of this little commonwealth is delightful: the oil of Lucca is the best in Europe; the inhabitants are industrious, and call their country the garden of Europe. They were then governed by a Doge, whom they choose every two months. They always dressed in black, to save expense, though living is remarkably cheap. The baths are considered highly salutary, and are a few miles out of the town. They have a grand musical festival for the feast of the Holy Cross. An old lady, a native of Lucca, left a large sum of money to be disposed of in the following manner:—every musician who came to the festival of the Holy Cross, (and at that time they pour in from all parts of Italy,) was to be paid a stated price, at so much a mile, be the distance what it would! Her ladyship's executor had no sinecure. Pachierotti once sang at this festival, and was also engaged at the theatre. The common people of Lucca have the reputation of being great tricksters. They have a saying, 'Sono un Luchese, ma vi sono dei buoni e cattivi al mio paese.'—'I am a Luchese, but there are good, as well as bad, in my country.' Aretin the satirist, 'yclept 'the Bitter Tuscan', and who hated Lucca for some slight shewn to him, said, that when their best actress was acting with energy, she always threw one, or both of her arms, out of the republic; meaning it was so contemptibly small. In my time there was a custom of sending presents of sweetmeats, for which they are famous, and oil, to all foreigners of distinction, who visit their town. I wished much to remain there longer, but was obliged to hurry on to Pisa, where I arrived the following day.

On my arrival I immediately sought out Viganoni, the charming tenor singer, so well known in this country. He was decidedly the best mezzo carattere in Italy; he was engaged at the theatre, and his prima donna was Signora Clementina Bagliona. When I delivered my letter of introduction to him, he took me to see her. They both behaved with great kindness to me, and invited me to stay a week at their house; an invitation which I was the more inclined to accept, as, during that particular week, the festival of the Battle of the Bridge,[1] so renowned and so extraordinary, was appointed to take place.

It would hardly be believed, if it were not generally known, that upon this occasion, two armies of citizens, accoutred *cap-à-pie,* the one representing the army of St. John the Baptist, the other, that of St. Antonio, meet to dispute the passage of a bridge across the Arno, and do not separate till one or other has conquered. The battle is real, and contested with the most inveterate obstinacy, many of the combatants being desperately wounded, and sometimes killed.

Surely this barbarous custom is unworthy a civilized nation.

Previous to the exhibition of this extraordinary spectacle, Viganoni took me to see the baths, which are considered extremely efficacious in pulmonary complaints. They are admirably constructed, and are visited by invalids from all parts of Europe, amongst whom are many English. While there, a man was pointed out to me, whose head was shaved, and who wore the dress of a galley-slave, sweeping the baths. He did the most laborious work by day, and at night was chained on board a Tuscan galley, which lay in the Arno. This man was the well-known Giuseppe Afrissa, who had visited and been received at all the courts of Europe;

and at Vienna, had been in such favour with the Emperor Francis I. and his Empress, Maria Theresa, that he sat at their table, and was appointed Master of the Revels at Schoënbrunn and all the royal palaces! He was banished from Vienna for some disgraceful act, but not before he had contrived to lose at the gaming-table every shilling of a large fortune, which he had originally acquired there. He returned to Turin, his native place, where he joined with four notorious swindlers, who travelled into various countries, committing forgeries. In England and Holland they were particularly successful. At length Afrissa was arrested in his career at Pisa, by a Dutch merchant, on whom he had committed a forgery to an immense amount; he was tried, and condemned to hard labour as a galley-slave for life. When seized, he was in company with one of his associates, a Genoese, who instantly took a small phial from his pocket and swallowed the contents. He died in great agonies. Of the fate of the rest of the gang, I never heard any thing.

I remember well, that the day on which I saw this man, I dined with Signora Bagliona, and Signor Soderini, who had just returned from England, where he had been for several years one of the violin players at the Opera House, while Giardini was leader. He was one of the ugliest men I ever saw. When M. Favar was first ballet-master, Soderini went on the stage, after the rehearsal, and said to him, 'Allow me, my dear Sir, to introduce myself to you;—you are the dearest friend I have on earth,—let me thank you a thousand times for the happiness you have conferred on me by coming amongst us;—command me in any way, for whatever I do for you, I can never sufficiently repay you!'

The ballet-master, who had never seen or heard of Soderini before, was astounded; at last, he said, 'Pray, Sir, to what peculiar piece of good fortune may I attribute the compliments and professions with which you favour me?'

'To your unparalleled ugliness, my dear Sir,' replied Soderini: 'for before *your* arrival, I was considered the ugliest man in Great Britain.'

The ballet-master, (strange to say, since he really was so ugly,) took the joke in good part, and they became extremely intimate; but, amiable as they were to each other, they were universally known as the ugly couple! This anecdote Soderini told me himself.

I was very much stricken at Pisa with the resemblance which the quays of that city bear to those of Dublin. The cathedral and leaning tower are beautiful and curious; yet, of all places in Italy, I left Pisa with the least regret; its sombre appearance, and want of amusement, did not at all suit my mercurial spirits, and, although extremely grateful to my friend Viganoni for his hospitality, I confess I felt almost pleased when I quitted it.

The following evening I reached Florence;—Florence too, that was to make my future fortunes, or un-make them quite. I went direct to an English hotel, kept by an Englishman of the name of Meggot, where I had a very good bed-room and board, at the rate of three shillings English per day. Immediately upon my arrival, I called upon Signor Campigli, a rich jeweller, who was also manager of the Pergola theatre: he was besides, a *sensale*, (a broker,) and furnished theatres with performers, for which he received a per centage from both manager and singer. He was very rich, and his influence supposed to be so great, that no performer dare risk making him an enemy, Pachierotti alone excepted, who has declared to me, that he never would have dealings with a man whom he considered, half jokingly, a trafficker in human flesh. But Pachierotti was at this time immensely wealthy, and could do what he chose. Independent of the fortune which his talents secured him, he was supposed to have received large sums from an English lady of high birth, who was said to be fervently attached to him.

The shop of this Campigli was on the Ponte di Trinità. I found him at home, and delivered my letter from Aprile: after reading it, he told me, that I had just come in the nick of time, as he could offer me an engagement as first comic tenor, at the Teatro Nuovo, which was to be opened for the first time, the week after Easter. If I accepted it, I should have to perform from the middle of April till the end of June, for fifty zecchinos, about 23*l.* sterling, which I was glad enough to get, considering that the engagement was on the spot.

I next delivered my letter of recommendation to Lord Cowper, who received me with the greatest kindness. His Lordship had most pleasing and affable manners. He spent his princely fortune with the greatest liberality, patronizing the arts and artists nobly; and indeed, had more influence in Florence than the Grand Duke himself. His Lordship invited me to dinner. Sir Horace Mann, our minister at the court of Tuscany, then very old, and Mr. Merry, the Della Cruscan,[1] who afterwards married the elder Miss Brunton of Covent Garden Theatre, sister of the present Countess of Craven, were of the party.

In the evening, Lady Cowper gave a concert to a large party. There I had the gratification of hearing a sonata on the violin played by the great Nardini; though very far advanced in years, he played divinely.

He spoke with great affection of his favourite scholar, Thomas Linley,[1] who, he said, possessed powerful abilities. Lord Cowper requested him to play the popular sonata, composed by his master, Tartini, called the Devil's Sonata. Mr. Jackson, an English gentleman present, asked Nardini whether the anecdote relative to this piece of music was true, for Mr. de la Lande had assured Dr. Burney that he had it from Tartini's own mouth.

Nardini answered, that he had frequently heard Tartini relate the circumstance, which was neither more nor less than this:—He said that one night he dreamed that he had entered into a contract with the devil, in fulfilment of which his satanic majesty was bound to perform all his behests. He placed his violin in his hands, and asked him to play; and the devil played a sonata so exquisite, that in the delirium of applause which he was bestowing, he awoke, and flew to the instrument to endeavour to retain some of the passages, but in vain! they had fled! yet the sonata haunted his imagination day and night, and he endeavoured to compose one in imitation, which he called 'the Devil's Sonata:' but it was so inferior to the sonata of his dream, that he has been heard to say, that if he had had any other mode of gaining a living, he would have left the musical profession. I hope my being able to add the additional authority of Nardini himself, as to the truth of this anecdote, will be my excuse for repeating what has been so ably related by Dr. Burney. Nardini was the favourite scholar of Tartini, and was allowed to possess more of his master's excellence than any other.

The opera in which I was to make my appearance at Florence was 'Il Francese in Italia'—the Frenchman in Italy. I was to play the Frenchman, and as it was a good part, Lord Cowper advised me to take some lessons in acting, for which purpose he introduced me to Laschi, who had been the greatest actor of the day, but was at that time living in retirement at a country-house near Florence. He undertook to instruct me, and did it *con amore*; nothing could exceed the pains he took with me, and I endeavoured by rigid attention to reap the full benefit of his instruction.

Campigli advised me to leave my lodging at the hotel, and placed me in the house of one Signor Cechi, his stage-manager, a very good sort of man, who took in theatrical people.—(If I might be allowed a pun, I should say, more managers than one do *that*.) At his house I had a good bedroom, the use of a large drawing-room, in common with other boarders, with breakfast, dinner, coffee, supper, and as much of the wine of the country as I chose every day, for 1*l.* 15*s.* British money, per month!

Amongst the boarders was Signor Andreozzi, who was then composing an opera for the Pergola theatre. He was an eccentric man and a great genius, and his language was always technical. He told me one morning that he had just called upon Morichelli, the prima donna in his opera, for whom he was composing a song. 'I found her,' said he, 'in a *motivo penseroso*. I approached her in *andante Siciliano*, followed by a movement *allegretto vivace*, when she ran up a division of abuse *con spirito*, and came out with two false fifths and a change of key so discordant, that I was obliged to quit the house in a *molto prestissimo*, to *volti subito* and ran down stairs, leaving her screaming *in tempo furioso*!'

The rehearsals began; we had a fine orchestra and a good company. My prima donna was Signora Lortinella, a native of Rome: she was called Ortabella, from her extraordinary beauty; indeed, I never saw any thing more lovely than she was; she was also a very fine singer. Signor Morigi, the primo buffo, who had been so popular in London in the part of the German Soldier, in Piccini's La Buona Figliuola. He was still a great actor, though infirm. He never sung his old song, 'Paterno Giudizzio', without applause; for if the audience failed, he never failed to applaud himself. He would make his exit, clapping his hands loudly, and saying, 'Well! if they want taste, I do not!' One thing I must say of him, poor fellow! during the whole time I knew him I never once saw him guilty of ebriety! yet, having been a great favourite, the sober Tuscans laughed at him and with him, and found an excuse for his failing in his misfortunes; they said he was driven to the last and worst resource of the unhappy by the death of his only child, a beautiful girl, full of talent and promise, who lost her senses, and died in a madhouse in Bologna in her twenty-third year!

The eventful night fixed for my first appearance at length arrived. I made my *début*, and received a most flattering reception. I was encored in two of my songs and a duet. Though, at that time, I would not have exchanged situations with the Grand Duke himself, I was so elated by my success; yet I could not avoid attributing it, in a great measure, to my extreme youth, and the strong party made for me by Lord and Lady Cowper, and all the English that were in Florence; besides, I was the first British male singer who had ever sung in Italy, or indeed on the Continent. Several other persons of distinction also patronized my first appearance, which was honoured by the presence of the Pretender, who entered his box before the opera began. He was at that time very old and infirm, yet there appeared the remains of a very handsome man. He was very tall, but stooped considerably, and was usually supported by two of his suite, between whom he hobbled; in this state he visited one of the theatres every night (he had a box in each); in a few minutes after he was seated, he fell asleep, and continued to slumber during the whole performance. The Italians always called him the King of England, and he had the arms of England over the gates of his palace, and all his servants wore the royal livery. The order of the Garter, which he wore when I saw him, he left to his wife,[1] Princess Stolberg.

The magnificent theatre, La Pergola, was open at this time; during the spring season, it was considered the first in Italy. Here I first saw our old favourite, Rovedino, perform with the prima donna La Morichelli, and excellent they both were, in Anfossi's comic opera, 'Il Viaggiatore Felice'. There was another theatre, a small one, La Via del Cocomera, in which Morelli had often delighted the Florentines with his magnificent bass voice, which, take it for all in all, was the finest I have ever heard.

It is perhaps not generally known, that, in the early part of his life, Morelli was Lord Cowper's volante, or running footman. One night, when going to bed, his Lordship's attention was attracted by some one singing an air, from an opera then in vogue; the person was seated on the steps of a church, opposite to his Lordship's palace: the prodigious quality of the voice, the fine ear and excellent taste displayed, astonished his Lordship. He ordered his valet to inquire who the extraordinary performer could be; the valet replied, 'that he knew very well; it was young Giovanni, one of his Lordship's volantes. His ear for music is so perfect,' said the valet, 'that whatever he hears, he catches instantly: he often sings to the servants, and is the delight of us all.' The following morning, Giovanni was ushered into his Lordship's breakfast room, where he sang several songs, in a style and with execution to surprise him still more! His Lordship ordered Signor Mansoli, Signor Verolli, and Camparini, Maestro di Capella to the Grand Duke, to hear him: they all declared it the finest voice they had ever heard, and that he only wanted instruction to become the very first bass singer in the world! 'Then,' said Lord Cowper, 'that he shall not want long,—from this moment I take him under my protection, and he shall have the best instruction Italy can afford.'

His Lordship kept his word; and for two years, Morelli had the first masters that money could procure. At the end of that time, he was engaged as primo buffo at Leghorn. He then went the round of all the principal theatres with great éclat. At the Teatro della Valle in Rome, he was perfectly idolized, often singing at the Carnival. He was engaged at the Pergola theatre; and his success, on his return to Florence, was triumphant indeed! I have often heard him say, that the proudest day of his life was that on which his former master, Lord Cowper, invited him to dine with him. This must, indeed, have been gratifying to him; but what honour does it not reflect on the liberality of his noble and generous patron!

I had the good fortune to be noticed by Signor Giuarduci, the celebrated soprano, and he gave me a few lessons. He had been the first cantabile singer of his time, and his sostenuto singing was still admirable. I went to pass a few days with him, at a villa which he had built, on his retirement from public life, at Montefiascone, his native town. From the house, there were beautiful views of the Lake of Balseno, and the Hills of Viterbo; but the prospect most interesting to me, was the vineyard! The wines of Montefiascone are considered exquisite, and I must say, I proved my opinion of them by copious libations! Fortunately, Signor Giuarduci was a liberal and hospitable landlord; and I shall ever retain a grateful sense of his kindness.

While performing at Florence, I received a letter from Mr. Linley, the father-in-law of Mr. Sheridan, and joint patentee with him in Drury Lane Theatre, offering me an engagement for five years, as first singer; and I was on the point of replying to him, when I received another letter from him, stating, that he must reluctantly decline entering into any engagement with me for the present, as he had received a prohibition from my father, who even threatened to take legal means to prevent it; which my being under age allowed him to do. I thought this both hard and unaccountable, but, as there was no remedy, I was obliged to submit. I afterwards learned that this gave great mortification to Stephen Storace, who was in England, and the originator of the offer to me.

At the latter part of June, my engagement ended at Florence; but my friend Campigli told me, he could offer me an engagement for the Teatro Saint Moïse, at Venice, as first tenor singer in the comic opera. This pleasing intelligence I received most graciously, and gladly accepted the engagement.

During July and August, I was on the *pavé*, without an engagement; but I had youth, health, and high spirits, with certain zecchinos remaining in my pocket to give them play: add to these, that I had very good friends in Florence; Lord Cowper's house was always open to me, as was that of our Ambassador; and the Polish Prince, Poniatowski, a fine young man, who spoke English fluently, invited me to his concerts and dinners, and gave me frequent marks of his esteem. There was also a Mr. Faulkner, who was very kind to me, and who feasted the Florentines sumptuously.

Florence is a delightful place to live in, the climate is pure, the country charming, and the city magnificent. In my time, the Trinità Bridge (the most beautiful bridge in the world, built entirely of white marble, and adorned with four fine statues, representing the Seasons,) was the constant place of resort for serenaders of all description. Every square, street, indeed every corner of this superb city, is filled with statuary, architecture, and paintings, by Michael Angelo, Bandinelli, Benvenuto Cellini, &c. &c. In the fifteenth century, a rich merchant called Pitti, built the fine palace which still bears his name; but overwhelmed by the expense, he became a bankrupt, and the palace was purchased by the Medici family. It has continued ever since the residence of the Grand Dukes of Tuscany.

The Dominican church was richly hung with striped silk, red and yellow. The monks of the convent had in it an apothecary's shop, in which they made up medicines of the best quality, and sold them at a very cheap rate: they also sold all kinds of perfumery. The church of St. Marc is a very fine structure; the remains of the celebrated Politian are buried there.

The Casano Wood, something resembling our Hyde Park, is a delightful ride, where the nobility drove their own carriages; on the holidays particularly, the whole population of Florence assembled there; and there Il Commandatore Pazzi, a nobleman of immense fortune, used to exhibit his coachmanship, driving his phaëton with six cream-coloured horses, which he managed with great dexterity. The Boboli Gardens were much frequented in the evening, and were very beautiful. The peasantry of the environs of Florence are considered rich, and all, in a greater or less degree, gifted with a talent for poetry. No young man would dare to approach his mistress if he were not able to declare his passion in verse, or *improvvisare* on her beauties!

During my idle time, I went with a large party to Forligani, about twenty-five miles from Florence, in the Upper Val di Arno, to witness the grand festival, in honour of Santa Massinina. It is a curious fact, that for months sixteen or seventeen thousand of the peasantry are kept in training to represent the story of David and Goliath. They form two grand armies, the Philistines and the Israelites. Their kings, princes, &c. are all dressed magnificently in ancient costume, with ancient martial instruments, &c. on both sides. The programme was very clearly made out, and well executed. The whole of the challenge, David's acceptance of it, his breaking his adversary's head with a stone, and then cutting it off with his own sword, were all performed in very excellent pantomime. After the general battle and route of the Philistines, the Israelites return, and place David in a triumphal car; his prisoners following, amidst the clang of martial instruments, and the shouts of between twenty and thirty thousand people.

From this extraordinary fête, I went for three days to Sienna, a very pretty city, remarkable for the beauty of its women. The natives of this town have none of the coarse gutteral manner of speaking which prevails in Florence, and other parts of Tuscany; indeed, they speak the purest Italian, and in the most common conversation fall into poetry. Ask a Siennese the way to the town,—he answers,

'Varca il fiume,
Passa il monte,
Averà Sienna
Nella fronte.'[1]

The landlord of the inn where I put up, took me to see a tomb in the cathedral, bearing the following epitaph,—a hint to wine-bibbers: 'Wine gives life! it was death to me. I never beheld the morning sun with sober eyes; even my bones are thirsty.—Stranger! sprinkle my grave with wine; empty the cup, and depart.'

While I staid at Florence I had the honour of being intimate with a rich Jew, of the name of Jacobs; he had two beautiful daughters, fine musicians, and lived amongst his tribe with splendid hospitality. The Jews enjoy more privileges in Florence than in any other catholic country I ever was in.

When I quitted Florence, wishing to pass a short time at Bologna, on my way to Venice, I made an agreement with a vetturino,[2] who had three excellent mules, to take me to Bologna; and set out, under his guidance, upon my journey. We travelled rather slowly; but the roads over the Appenines were rugged and steep. The beauty and sublimity of the prospects, however, compensated amply for the difficulty, or even danger, of crossing their snow-covered summits. On the top of one was a convent, where we slept the first night, and found a good supper and a hospitable welcome. My vetturino, I must confess, was somewhat of a convivalist, and, to beguile the time, sang Tasso and Ariosto's beautiful verses, with Stentorian lungs, even up to the very gates of Bologna.

Bologna la Grassa, so called from the luxurious country in which it stands, its plenty and cheapness, is a very fine city. There are piazzas on each side of the street, which guard passengers equally from sun and rain; those in the city of Chester resemble them in an inferior degree. The principal curiosities are the leaning tower, so often described.

The morning after my arrival, I sought out the house of Signor Passerini, to whom I had a letter, the purport of which was, to request he would place me in a cheap and convenient boarding house for the short time I had to remain in Bologna. To my surprise I found he was a hair-dresser, but it gave me great pleasure to find in him the father of my respected singing-master, Signor Passerini, who, as the reader will remember, was one of my first instructors. The old man was delighted to hear me repeat anecdotes of his son, whom he had not seen for many years; and I was so gratified to find something like an acquaintance in the old man, that I took lodgings in his house, where I had a neat first floor, three meals a day, and wine at discretion, (as the French say of bread,) for 1*l.* 8*s.* British per month. His shop was in a central situation, and the high temple of gossip. Numbers of theatrical and literary people frequented it. There I was introduced to Lovatini, whose fame was so great in England, and to Signor Trebi also a very popular singer: they were natives of Bologna, and had retired from public life with very ample means.

One morning, sitting very quietly in my dressing gown in the shop, to have my hair dressed, I suddenly heard 'The Pope! the Pope!' cried out from every quarter. His Holiness had arrived the day before from Rome, and was now on his way to visit Cardinal Buona Compagnia. Regardless of my appearance, my hair half dressed, my face covered with powder, my dressing gown the same and flying open, I rushed out of the shop, and ran after the carriage of his Holiness, even to the very gates of the Cardinal's palace. I was not a little flattered at seeing how completely I divided public attention with his Holiness. Fancying myself to be 'a marvellous proper man,' I placed this to the score of my personal attractions; but certain symptoms of laughter, which ended in roars, referred me to my dressing gown for an explanation, and I retired at full speed, laughing, too, I confess, although rather mortified to find that I had given more entertainment than I received.

The theatre, which is one of the largest in Europe, was open, and I saw Cimarosa's beautiful opera, 'Il Falegname', ably performed by three great buffo singers—Mandini, Blassi, and Leperini. At this period, Bologna was the mart (the carnival being over in all other places) to which actors from all parts of Italy resorted, to make their future engagements. The large Café dei Virtuosi was filled with them from morning till night, and it was really amusing to see them swarm round a manager the moment he entered. I passed much of my time there, and there first saw and heard the two extraordinary blind brothers, called 'Le bravi Orbi.' They were natives of Bologna, and during the spring and summer travelled to Rome, Naples, Venice, &c.; their talents were everywhere held in the highest estimation: the one played the violin with exquisite taste, the other the violoncello with such wonderful execution, as to have obtained from the Bolognese the additional cognomen of 'Spacca note'—'Split note.' I never missed an opportunity of hearing them.

Signor Lovatini took me to see the Specola Museum, which the Bolognese consider the finest in the world. I was astonished to hear that the wax figures there, were the work of a female, a native of the town. I also saw the church of La Madonna della Santa Lucia, where she is to be seen as large as life; the church stands on a hill, and, to guard La Madonna from bad weather, when she is carried in procession, a covered way, nearly six miles in length, has been built as an approach to it.

I had a letter to deliver to a Bolognese nobleman, Signor Ferussini, a singular character, though a very worthy man; he was frightfully ugly and hump-backed, yet he was afflicted with the disease of supposing every woman who saw him in love with him; as he was rich, he spared no expense in adoring himself, in order to set off his *charms* to the best advantage. I was waiting for him one morning, when he came from his toilette, dressed in a new suit of the richest and most expensive quality—painted, patched, and made up in every possible way. He placed himself before a large mirror, and indulged himself thus:—'I am handsome, young, and amiable; the women follow me, and I am healthy and rich—what on earth do I want?'—'Common sense, you rascal,' said his father (who had just entered the room) in a fury, and immediately knocked him down. Even the immortal Liston might take a lesson in the ludicrous, from my astonished Adonis!

I found here by accident Signora Palmini, the prima donna, who was engaged to sing with me at Venice. We agreed to travel together. She was a very handsome woman, though on a large scale; her husband, *au contraire*, was a diminutive, shrivelled old man, and jealous in the extreme: he, with her mother (an ugly old body), a little black boy, a servant, and a lap dog, composed her suite. With these rational and pleasing companions did I embark in the canal passage-boat from Bologna to Ferrara; it was drawn by horses, and nearly half the time employed in getting through the locks. When we arrived at Ferrara, we determined on remaining there a day, to look about us: and accordingly left our boat, and went to the Hôtel de St. Marc; we had a very good dinner, and a very merry landlord. He told us many stories in his talkative way: amongst others, one of the *mad* poet, Ariosto, as he chose to call him.

It appears that Ariosto, one day passing a potter's shop in Ferrara, heard the owner singing a stanza of the Orlando Furioso. Attracted by his own poetry, he listened, and found that the potter mangled it most miserably, rendering a most beautiful passage rank nonsense. This so enraged the poet, that, having a stick in his hand, he laid about him lustily, and broke every thing he could reach. When the poor devil of a potter expostulated with him for destroying the property of a man who had never done him any injury, he replied—''Tis false, you have done me the deepest injury; you have murdered my verses;—I have caught you in the very fact.' When pressed to pay the poor man for some of his property, his only answer was—'Let him learn to sing my poetry, and I will leave alone his pottery.'

Ferrara, called Ferrara la Civile, had some noble buildings in it, and fine wide streets, but so thinly peopled that the grass actually grew in many of them. The greater part of the inhabitants wore long swords, which they still call Andrea Ferraras, and were in general expert swordsmen. The place was so miserably dull, that I was glad when the morning came, and we set of in a coach for La Ponte del Lago Scuro, where we arrived in the evening, and embarked again in an excellent barge on the river Po. We had a number of passengers on board—friars, Jews, singers, dancers, &c. &c. all mirth and jollity. A good dinner and supper were provided on board, and each found good spirits, dancing and singing. From the Po we got into the Adigo, and from that river entered the Laguno leading to Venice.

6

Venice! dear, beautiful Venice! never shall I forget the sensations of surprise and delight which I experienced when I first caught sight of thee!

Michael Kelly in 1792, by J Condé

Ann (Nancy) Storace in 1792, by J Condé

Castello dell'Ovo at Naples c. 1775, *by Paul Sandby*

thy noble palaces! thy magnificent churches, with their cloud-capt spires! appearing as if just arisen from the sea, and floating on its surface! Years and years have passed away, yet I still call thee, dear, beautiful Venice.

On our arrival, we anchored near the bridge of the Rialto; I and my travelling companions took up our abode at the Hotel, called the Queen of England. After dinner, the caro sposo of my prima donna went to inform the manager of our arrival. He soon returned with the face of him who 'drew Priam's curtains in the dead of night,' and told us that our manager, he by whom we 'were to live, or have no life,' was not to bc found! That not being able to make his deposit, he was unable to make his appearance, and that we had 'all the world before us where to choose.'

Here was a pretty *coup* for a man with five zecchinos in his pocket. To render the destruction of our hopes intelligible, I must explain, that so many needy speculators had taken the theatre, and failed, leaving their performers destitute, that the Senate had felt it necessary to interfere, and had appointed a person, under whom the following regulations were to be strictly observed:—The person proposing to take the theatre, was compelled to give in a list of his performers, their salaries, &c. together with every estimated expense attending his proposed arrangements; and then was forced to give security, or actually deposit money to the amount so stated, before he could procure a licence to open the doors!

My prima donna, her caro sposo, mamma, little black boy, lap-dog, &c. returned to Bologna, as the most likely place to procure another engagement. And here was I left in Venice with the cheering prospect of being six months, (the period for which I was engaged) without employment! I was pennyless! It is true I had a few good clothes, and a small stock of linen; but then I had a large stock of spirits, and felt no poverty in the article of *conceit*; there, indeed, I was affluent, and stood mighty well *with myself*, for hope, the 'nurse of young desire,' never forsook me. And I had a presentiment that something fortunate would turn up for me!

In the boat from Ferrara there came with us a young man of the name of Lampieri, a fine, generous-hearted fellow, the son of a silk-merchant at Florence, on his way to visit his uncle at Trieste. He was bound to Venice to take a passage for that place, and as we had formed a sort of friendship on board, and he wished to stay a few days to see what was to be seen, we agreed to live together. A friend of his, a good-natured fellow, who was to act as cicerone, procured me a lodging on a cheap scale, and we dined every day at a table d'hôte.

Morelli was then engaged at the Teatro St. Samuel. Lampieri, who had known him in Florence, introduced me to him, and he procured us the freedom of his theatre. He again introduced me to Signor Michael dell' Agato, manager of the theatre of St. Benetto, the first serious opera-house, (the Phenice theatre was not then built,) who politely gave the *entrée* before and behind the curtain to myself and companion. This was a source of great delight to me. The first opera I saw there was Orpheo and Euridice. Orpheus was performed by Rubinelli, a native of Brescia; his fine contre-alto voice has never been surpassed, and he was an excellent actor as well as a sound musician. The prima donna was Signora Banti, who had just then returned from London, where she had been engaged at the Opera House. As many of my readers doubtless remember, she had a finely-marked countenance, and a noble soprano voice, but was no musician. The difficulties arising from this deficiency she obviated by an extraordinary quickness and niceness of ear, perfect intonation and strong feeling. She played Euridice finely. The music of this opera was by Bertoni; one duet between Banti and Rubinelli was almost the most exquisite treat I ever received. Two such voices I never heard before nor since. When a superior contre-alto voice and a fine soprano unite in a duet, nothing can surpass the effect!

The Venetians are in general adorers of music, and Venice, one of the first cities in Europe for the cultivation of that art. It is famous for its female conservatories, of which there are four, which are in fact foundling hospitals, supported by wealthy citizens, &c. where the girls are maintained and educated; some are married from them, and those who display strong talent for music, are instructed by the very best masters. They gave concerts every Sunday evening, and on festival days; I heard two, one at La Pietà, the other at La Mendicanti—the former celebrated for its fine orchestra, the latter for its singers. At La Pietà[1] there were a thousand girls, one hundred and forty of whom were musicians: all the instruments were charmingly played by girls. The churches were crowded on those occasions; and while the performance was actually going on, the most perfect silence was observed; but, at the conclusion of a piece of music, which excited their approbation, the audience expressed it in the most extraordinary manner,—they coughed aloud, and scraped their feet on the ground, for some moments, but did not utter a word! which seemed to me a practical mode of pointing out the beauty of concord in opposition to the horrors of discord.

Michael dell' Agato, who was, as I said before, the manager of St.

Benetto, invited me to dine with him *tête-à-tête*. He expressed a friendly feeling for me, and gave me advice, which subsequently I found of the greatest utility to me. 'In this city,' said he, 'you will find innumerable pleasures; your youth and good spirits will lay you open to many temptations; but against one thing, and one thing only, I particularly caution you:—never utter one word against the laws or customs of Venice,—do not suffer yourself to be betrayed even into a jest on this subject. You never know to whom you speak; in every corner spies are lurking, numbers of whom are employed at a high price to ensnare the unwary, and report the language of strangers; but with no other protection than a *silent tongue*, you may do what you like, and enjoy every thing without molestation. I will relate an anecdote,' added he, 'which will give you some idea of our police.'

'A countryman of yours came to this city, accompanied by a Swiss valet; he took up residence at the Scuda di Francia. On his return home one evening, he found his writing-desk broken open, and a large sum of money taken from it. After making peaceable inquiries, without effect, he flew into a violent rage, charged the landlord and waiters, &c. with being thieves; but above all, he called them Venetian thieves, and cursed himself for having come into a country where the property of a traveller was not safe even in his own hotel. In the height of his wrath he dismissed his valet for going out and leaving the door of his apartment unlocked; and having thus vented his displeasure, thought the matter ended; but not so. On the third morning after this event, he was roused out of his sleep by the officers of the Inquisition, who informed him, that he must go immediately before the three grand inquisitors. His feelings were not to be envied when, hoodwinked, he was led on board a gondola, and thence into a room hung with black, where sat his judges. After due preparation and solemnity, and a severe lecture on the enormity of the abuse which he had uttered against the Venetian state, its laws, and subjects, he received a peremptory order to quit its territories in twenty-four hours; this he of course tremblingly promised to obey; but just as he turned to leave the tribunal, a curtain was suddenly drawn aside, behind which lay the strangled corpse of his Swiss valet, and the stolen bag of money by his side.' I confess this instance of the summary mode of administering justice in Venice, made a deeper impression upon me than all the good Signor's advice.

About this time I wrote to my father, acquainting him with the situation in which I was left, and requesting a remittance, and gave my address to the care of Signor Zanotti, at the Hotel La Regina d' Inghilterra.

Venice! dear beautiful Venice! scene of harmony and love! where all was gaiety and mirth, revelry and pleasure, with what warm feelings do I recal thee to my memory; day and night were the gondoliers singing barcarolles, or the verses of Tasso and Ariosto to Venetian airs; barges full of musicians on the Grand Canale, serenading their enamoratas; the Piazza of St. Marc brilliantly lighted up; ten thousand masks and ballad singers; the coffee houses filled with beautiful women, with their cicisbeos; or if alone, unmolested, taking their refreshment and enjoying themselves without restraint. Venice was the paradise of women, and the Venetian women worthy of a paradise at least of Mahomet's. They were perfect Houri; and the Venetian dialect, spoken by a lovely woman, is the softest and most delicious music in the world to him whom she favours. In short, a Venetian woman, in her zindale dress, well answers young Mirable's description in the play of the Inconstant; 'Give me the plump Venetian, who smiles upon me like the glowing sun, and meets my lips like sparkling wine; her person shining as the glass, her spirit like the foaming liquor.'

My friend Lampieri received a letter from his uncle at Trieste, desiring him to proceed thither immediately; this was bad news for me; for besides the loss of my agreeable companion, I felt that I should lose his pecuniary assistance, which, 'though somewhat of the smallest, Master Matthew,' as Bobadil says, was generously and frankly given. A Ragusan polacca was to sail in about a week, on board of which he took his passage; the intermediate time we resolved to pass in pleasure; the mornings we usually spent on the Rialto,—it was a favourite lounge, crowded with shops, where merchants of all countries meet. It is their exchange, and a scene of continual bustle, crowded with Christians, Turks, Armenians, and Jews. The latter enjoyed but little liberty in this city,—they were obliged to wear a piece of red cloth in the hat, by way of distinction, (which, considering how much the hand of nature has done for them in that way, seems superfluous,) and to live in a particular quarter called La Giudica,[1] and were obliged, under a heavy penalty, to be in their houses before sun-set.

When Lampieri was forced to go, I was unhappy enough; my finances were becoming deplorable, and I was obliged to part with a kind and dear friend. I saw him on board the polacca, and took leave of him with an aching heart. He had expended almost his last ducat, and I had but two zecchinos left wherewith to fight my way through this wicked world. My spirits, for the first time, deserted me: I never passed so miserable a night in my life, and in shame of my 'doublet and hose,' felt very much inclined to 'cry like a child.' While tossing on my pillow, however, I chanced to recollect a letter which my landlord of Bologna, Signor Passerini, had given me to a friend of his, a Signor Andrioli: for, as he told me, he thought the introduction might be of use to me.

In the morning, I went to the Rialto coffee-house, to which I was directed by the address of the letter. Here I found the gentleman who was the object of my search; after reading my credentials very graciously, he smiled, and requested me to take a turn with him in the Piazza St. Marc. He was a fine looking man, of about sixty years old. I remarked there was an aristocratic manner about him, and he wore a very large tie-wig, well powdered, with an immensely long tail. He addressed me with a benevolent and patronizing air, and told me that he should be delighted to be of service to me, and bade me from that moment consider myself under his protection. 'A little business,' said he, 'calls me away at this moment, but if you will meet me here at two o'clock we will adjourn to my Casino, where, if you can dine on one dish, you will perhaps do me the favour to partake of a boiled capon and rice. I can only offer you that; perhaps a rice soup, for which my cook is famous; and it may be, just one or two little things not worth mentioning.'

A boiled capon—rice soup—other little things, thought I,—manna in the wilderness! I strolled about, not to get an appetite, for that was ready, but to kill time. My excellent, hospitable, long-tailed friend, was punctual to the moment; I joined him, and proceeded towards his residence.

As we were bending our steps thither, we happened to pass a Luganigera's (a ham-shop) where there was some ham ready dressed in the window. My powdered patron paused,—it was an awful pause; he reconnoitred, examined, and at last said, 'Do you know, Signor, I was thinking that some of that ham would eat deliciously with our capon:—I am known in this neighbourhood, and it would not do for *me* to be seen buying ham—but do you go in, my child, and get two or three pounds of it, and I will walk on, and wait for you.'

I went in of course, and purchased three pounds of the ham, to pay for which, I was obliged to change one of my two zecchinos. I carefully folded up the precious viand, and rejoined my excellent patron, who eyed the relishing slices with the air of a *gourmand*; indeed, he was somewhat diffuse in his own dispraise for not having recollected to order his servant to get some before he left home. During this peripatetic lecture on gastronomy, we happened to pass a cantina;—in plain English—a wine cellar. At the door he made another full stop.

'In that house,' said he, 'they sell the best Cyprus wine in Venice,—peculiar wine,—a sort of wine not to be had any where else; I should like you to taste it; but I do not like to be seen buying wine by retail to carry home;—go in yourself, buy a couple of flasks, and bring them to *my Casino*, nobody hereabouts knows you, and it won't signify in the least.'

This last request was quite appalling; my pocket groaned to its very centre: however, recollecting that I was in the high road to preferment, and that a patron, cost what he might, was still a patron, I made the plunge, and, issuing from the cantina, set forward for my venerable friend's *Casino*, with three pounds of ham in my pocket, and a flask of wine under each arm, *sans six sous et sans souci*!

I continued walking with my excellent and long-tailed patron, expecting every moment to see an elegant, agreeable residence, smiling in all the beauties of nature and art; when, at last, in a dirty miserable lane, at the door of a tall dingy-looking house, my Mæcenas stopped, indicated that we had reached our journey's end, and, marshalling me the way that I should go, began to mount three flights of sickening stairs, at the top of which I found his Casino,—it was a little Cas, and a deuce of a place to boot,—in plain English, it was a garret. The door was opened by a wretched old miscreant, who acted as cook, and whose drapery, to use a gastronomic simile, was 'done to rags.'

Upon a ricketty apology for a table was placed a tattered cloth, which once had been white; and two plates; and presently in came a large bowl of boiled rice.

'Where's the capon?' said my patron to his man.

'Capon!' echoed the ghost of a servant— 'the——'

'Has not the rascal sent it?' cried the master.

'Rascal!' repeated the man, apparently terrified.

'I knew he would not,' exclaimed my patron, with an air of exultation for which I saw no cause; 'well, well, never mind, put down the ham and the wine; with those and the rice, I dare say, young gentleman, you will be able to make it out.—I ought to apologize—but in fact it is all your own fault that there is not more; if I had fallen in with you earlier, we should have had a better dinner.'

I confess I was surprised, disappointed, and amused; but, as matters stood, there was no use in complaining, and accordingly we fell to, neither of us wanting the best of all sauces—appetite.

I soon perceived that my promised patron had baited his trap with a fowl to catch a fool; but as we ate and drank, all care vanished, and, rogue as I suspected him to be, my long-tailed friend was a clever witty fellow, and, besides telling me a number of anecdotes, gave me some very good advice; amongst other things to be avoided, he cautioned me against numbers of people who, in Venice, lived only by duping the unwary. I thought this counsel came very ill *from him*. 'Above all,' said he, 'keep up your spirits, and recollect the Venetian proverb, Cento anni di malinconia non pagheranno un soldo dei debiti.'—'A hundred years of melancholy will not pay one farthing of debt.'

After we had regaled ourselves upon my ham and wine, we separated; he desired me to meet him the following morning at the coffee-house, and told me he would give me a ticket for the private theatre of Count Pepoli, where I should see a comedy admirably acted by amateurs; and in justice to my long-tailed friend, I must say, he was punctual, and gave me the ticket, which, however, differed from a boiled capon in one respect—he got it gratis.

Having obtained this passport, I dressed myself, and went to the parterre, which was filled with elegant company. The play was 'La Vedova Scaltra', in which the Count Pepoli displayed much talent. However, I had no heart, no spirit for amusement, and sat mournful and moneyless, in the midst of splendour and gaiety, without hope or resource, and careless of what became of me; I was contrasting the past with the present, and the prospect before me, and repeating to myself Dante's expressive lines, 'Non v' è nessun maggiore dolore che di ricordarsi del tempo felice quando siamo nella miseria,'[1]—when I perceived the eyes of a lady and gentleman, who were at the upper part of the parterre, fixed on me, as if they were speaking of me. At the end of the play, the gentleman approached me, and said, 'Sir, the lady who is with me, and who is my wife, requests to speak to you.' I went, and she said to me, 'I rather think, Sir, you are the young Englishman (which I was called in Venice), who was engaged at St. Moïse, as tenor singer.'

'I am that unfortunate personage, Madame,' said I.

She then introduced herself to me as La Signora Benini, a name well known all over Italy, as that of the first comic singer and actress of the day. She told me that she was going to set off for Germany in a few days, being engaged as prima buffa, for the autumn and carnival at Gratz, the capital of Styria. She had that morning received a letter from the manager, acquainting her that Signor Germoli, who was engaged as first tenor singer, had disappointed him, and eloped to Russia *sans cérémonie*; at the same time authorizing her to engage any person capable, in her opinion, of filling his place. 'Now, Signor O'Kelly,' (for, at Naples, Father Dolphin tacked an O to my name,) said the lady, 'I wish to offer you this engagement; come and take chocolate with us to-morrow morning, and we will talk the matter over.'

Here was a change! ten minutes before, a beggar, in a strange country, plunged in despair; now, first tenor of the Gratz theatre; at least it was as completely settled in my mind, as if the articles had been actually signed; and, with a bounding heart, I returned home to my late miserable bed, and slept—Oh, ye Gods, how I slept!

I was punctual the following morning; exactly at ten I was set down by a gondola at the house of Signora Benini, on the Canale Maggiore. The Signora received me at her toilette; where she was braiding up a profusion of fine black hair. I thought her handsome at the play the night before, but the Italian women all contrive to look well by candlelight; nature gives them good features, and they take care to give themselves good complexions. But Signora Benini wanted not 'the foreign aid of ornament;' her person was petite, and beautifully formed; her features were good, and she had a pair of brilliant expressive eyes. After breakfast, she requested me to sing. I sang my favourite rondo, 'Teco resti, anima mia'.[1] She appeared pleased, and said she had no doubt of my success. The terms, she said, were to be two hundred zecchinos for the autumn and carnival, and to be lodged free of expense; at the same time, she offered me a seat in her carriage, and to pay my expenses to Gratz. 'Hear this, ye Gods, and wonder how ye made her!' For fear of accidents, I signed the engagement before I left the house.

I passed a couple of hours with the Signora delightfully; she possessed all the Venetian vivacity and badinage, together with great good sense and much good nature. I related my adventure with my knight of the long-tail, told her of the capon, the Cyprus wine, &c.; which amused her greatly. It seemed she knew his character well: in his younger days he had been by turns, an actor and a poet, and was at that time supposed to be a spy in the pay of the police; one of those whom I had been specially advised most carefully to avoid; indeed, she counselled me to be cautious, but not to slight him; he might be a negative friend, but if offended, a positively dangerous enemy. 'Remember the proverb,' said the Signora, 'let sleeping dogs lie; they may rise and bite you.' While recounting the disbursements which I had made in the purchase of the repast, she observed that I was reduced to my last zecchino, and in the kindest manner advanced me some money on account.

I was not at the very summit of prosperity in my own opinion; but one cannot enjoy happiness alone; so when I left the Signora, I flew to the coffee-house, where I found the knight of the tail. I desired him to meet me at the Stella d' Oro tavern at three o'clock, where *I* would treat *him* with a capon. The innkeeper's poulterer was rather more punctual than my patron's, and we had an excellent dinner. I related my good fortune, and, in short, told him every thing that had occurred, except the advance which I had received; for, barring the importance of his tail, I thought the knight had a borrowing countenance.

7

The Signora, with her husband, her lap-dog, servant, and myself, set off in a gondola for Mestra, where we found her travelling-carriage, in which we proceeded day and night, till we reached Gorizia, where we remained a day to repose ourselves. The part of the Venetian states through which we passed abounds in beauties; as Goldsmith says,

> 'Could Nature's beauties satisfy the breast,
> The sons of Italy were surely blest.'[1]

I suffered greatly from the cold, as we proceeded into Germany; the roads were hilly and heavy, the cattle miserable, and the post-boys incorrigible. But what was all this to me? I was in a comfortable carriage, in pleasant society, and seated opposite to a beautiful woman of six-and-twenty. At length, we arrived at Gratz; Signora Benini's house was elegantly fitted up. The manager waited on her, and after dinner conducted me to the apartments which were taken for me. Before I quitted her, the Signora insisted on my accepting a cover at her table every day, and indeed evinced the greatest friendship and hospitality towards me.

A great number of nobility resided in this pleasant lively city, and many rich merchants; but which was far better for me, a great number of Irish officers, among whom were Generals Dillon, Dalton, and Kavanagh. General Dalton was commandant; and when I was introduced to him, I was delighted to find that he remembered my father, for whom he expressed the highest respect, and indeed said every thing that could gratify the feelings of a son; at the same time assuring me he would be happy to see and serve me at all times. He kept his word amply, for I found in *him* a father when I wanted advice, and his acquaintance was of course an introduction to the best society.

He was an enthusiast about Ireland, and agreed with me that the Irish language was sweeter and better adapted for musical accompaniment than any other, the Italian excepted: and it is true that, when a child, I have heard my father sing many pathetic Irish airs, in which the words resembled Italian so closely, that if I did not know the impossibility, the impression on my memory would be that I had heard him sing in that language.

To return to Gratz: the time at length arrived for opening of the operatic campaign. The company was good, the first comic man, Guglielmi, excellent; La Signora Benini was a great favourite. The first opera was 'La vera Costanza', the music by Anfossi. I had some good songs in it, and was in high spirits.

As it was the custom for the ladies, the first night of the opera, to go in grand gala, the boxes and parterre were a perfect blaze of diamonds, and every part of the house was crowded. I was supported by numbers of my countrymen, who were present; and, independently of them, the applause I received was beyond my expectations, and far beyond my merits.

The carnival at length arrived, with all its wonted jollity; and, to my astonishment, I found that the sober Germans understood masquerading and keeping up the frolic of the season as well as the inhabitants of any part of Italy, Venice excepted. On those occasions I was seldom 'lost in the throng;' indeed, I had nothing to do but to enjoy myself.

Amongst the distinguished persons to whom General Dalton's friendship introduced me, was the Governor of Gratz, a most highly-gifted nobleman, whose wife laboured under the extraordinary misfortune of not having seen her own face for many years! She was considered the most complete mistress of the art of enamelling in Germany!

> 'And all, save the' husband, 'could plainly descry,
> From whence came her white and her red.'

Independently of this little failing, she was an amiable, accomplished woman, though proud; and, what was more to my purpose, a good musician. When General Dalton introduced me to her, I had the pleasure of hearing her play very finely on the piano-forte. I recollect she found fault with the manner in which my hair was dressed, observing that it would become me better if combed off my forehead. I defended my mode, merely on the score of being used to it; on which she said, 'My good young man, bear in mind what I now say; while you live, eat and drink to please yourself; but in dress always study to please others.'

About this time, Grétry's opera of 'Selima and Azor' was sent from Vienna, and put into rehearsal. Signora Benini performed Selima; and I the Prince. It was brought out under the immediate patronage of the Governor's lady, who attended all the rehearsals herself. No expense was spared on the scenery and decorations. The second dress I wore, that of the Prince, after being transformed from the monster, was very magnificent, and, to render it more so, the Countess made my turban herself, and almost covered it with her own diamonds! I often thought, while bearing those shining 'honours thick upon me,' that I should be a lucky fellow, if, like Gil Blas,[1] I could make a bolt, merely for the sake of a *jest*! but had I been so inclined, it 'might not so easily be,' as the Countess, though she had the highest opinion of my *honour*, thought it not amiss to place her maitre d'hôtel behind the scenes, to support it, should it be inclined to make a slip with her diamonds! I was allowed this splendour only for three nights—at the end of the third, I sighed, and returning the turban to the lynx-eyed maitre d'hôtel, said, with Cardinal Wolsey, 'Farewell, a long farewell to all my greatness;'—'Addio a tutta la mia grandezza.'

The end of the Carnival was now approaching, and with it was to terminate my engagement. It was fortunate for the manager that his season was so near a close, for, returning one morning from a ball, where I had been heated by dancing, I caught a dreadful cold, which confined me to my bed, and an intermezzo opera was got up without me. In a short time I got rid of my fever, but my voice was deprived of all power, or rather of intonation. Although I was gifted by nature with a perfect ear, yet, when I attempted to sing, my voice was so sharp as to be near a note above the instruments, and though I could distinguish the monstrous difference, I could not by any effort correct it. I was obliged to give up singing at the theatre, and was completely wretched! My complaint baffled the skill of all the faculty at that time in Gratz, though the surgeon of an Irish regiment quartered there, a Mr. O'Brein, who stood high in his profession, assured me that it arose from great relaxation; but even in that case, it was impossible to account for the loss of ear and intonation, which nature had formed so perfect. He, however, expressed great hopes of my recovery, resting them on my youth and excellent constitution, and bade me look for the return of fine weather with good spirits. But, above all, he advised me, if possible, to return to the mild and genial air of Italy, that of Germany being too keen for me; so much so, as to render the return of my voice doubtful, notwithstanding his hopes. On his expressing the same opinion to General Dalton, the General sent for me, and in the most soothing terms desired me to prepare for an immediate return to Italy, as both my life and bread depended on it.

What a reverse of fortune! but a few weeks before I was the happiest of the happy! caressed by my friends! a favourite with the public! with every prospect of a renewed engagement; possessing health, spirits, and competence.

My kind patron, the General, gave me letters of recommendation to the Countess of Rosenberg, (an English lady, whose maiden name was Wynne,) to the Austrian Ambassador, Count Durazzo, Count Priuli, the Cornaro family, and to the senator Benzoni; besides these, I had a particular introduction to Mr. Strange, British *chargé d'affaires* in Venice.

The stage-manager of the theatre, an Italian, of the name of Melaga, was going to Venice for the express purpose of engaging a tenor singer to fill my situation. We agreed to travel together, and I felt happy in having such a *compagnon de voyage*, for he was merry and witty, a native of Bologna, and the very man to drive away low spirits! The second week in Lent, half heart-broken, I took a melancholy leave of my kind and dear friends, and set off for Venice. We had hired a German post waggon, which they call a chaiser, and a complete bone-setter it was! While undergoing its operations, nothing could have so ably aided its torments, as the unconquerable phlegm of the postilion; whatever one suffers,—whatever one says, there he sits, lord of your time; you may complain, but it is useless; his horses and his pipe are his objects, and his passengers are but lumber.

Besides this, the extortions on the road were insufferable; we were obliged to add an extra horse, or perhaps more, at the high and mighty will of the postmaster, to our bone-setter, and often to wait two or three hours for those. The ostlers are the greatest thieves in the world! they make no scruple of stealing any part of the luggage they can lay hold of. Our expenses in horses and postilions, till we got out of Germany, came to about one and sixpence a mile, including extortion! provisions were dear, scarce, and bad; we sometimes got good beer, and now and then a bottle of excellent hoffner (Hungarian wine). For my part, I lived chiefly on bread and eggs, but my companion was not so easily satisfied. Nature had gifted him with a voracious appetite, and an insatiable taste for drinking. He was good security for three bottles of wine a day! and for sleep he was unrivalled! as Prior says,[1]

> 'He ate, and drank, and slept,—what then?
> He slept, and drank, and ate again!'

but, when thoroughly awake, and his appetites satisfied, he was full of intelligence and anecdote, good natured, and communicative; and, heaven save the mark!—the ugliest fellow I ever beheld!

He had formerly been in the army, and, after running through a small patrimony, resided with an aunt in Alsace, on the very spot where Voltaire, when travelling, was taken seriously ill. In this part of the world, Voltaire was equally unknown, as a poet or a Deist; and the good people of Alsace, in whose house he was, and who spoke hardly any French, thought the best thing they could do for a dying man, would be to procure for him the consolations of religion. Every one is acquainted with Voltaire's hatred for priests and monks, and may conceive how he was disposed to religion by the introduction of one of the clergy into his bed-room, without his knowledge. The unconscious offender, a simple, pious man, walked up to the bed, with zeal and solemnity, and, drawing the curtains aside, said to Voltaire, in French, 'Sir, can you speak French?' What the emphatic reply of the philosopher was, I must be excused from mentioning; suffice it to say, it was accompanied by an order to his valet to kick the priest down stairs!

After going through the purgatory of German roads and German postilions, we arrived in the Venetian States, and remained a day at Palma Nuova, to refresh ourselves, and view its celebrated fortifications, considered to be amongst the strongest in Europe. My companion, as a military man, was delighted while the sergeant who accompanied us, gave a long and perhaps learned dissertation on the art of engineering; to me it was dreadfully tiresome, for, like Mungo, in the Padlock, 'What signify me hear, when me no understand!'[2]

My companion prevailed on me to accompany him to Padua, where he had business to transact. It was very little out of our way, and I had a strong desire to see that learned city. When we arrived, we went to an inn, called the Stella d' Oro. Padua was interesting to me, as the birth-place of Tartini, and the two greatest singers of their time were living there retired, Pachierotti and Guadagni. The latter was a Cavaliere. He had built a house, or rather a palace, in which he had a very neat theatre, and a company of puppets, which represented L'Orpheo e Euridice; himself singing the part of Orpheo behind the scenes. It was in this character, and in singing Gluck's beautiful rondo in it, 'Che farò senza Euridice', that he distinguished himself in every theatre in Europe, and drew such immense houses in London.

His puppet-show was his hobby-horse, and as he received no money, he had always crowded houses. He had a good fortune, with which he was very liberal, and was the handsomest man of his kind[1] I ever saw.

I never was in any place so over-run with mendicants as at Padua; they allow you no peace, but torture you in the name of their patron saint, Saint Anthony. We went to see his church, a very large, old building: the inhabitants call it, Il Santo (the Saint). The interior is superb, crowded with fine paintings and sculpture. There are four fine organs, and a large choir, consisting of celebrated professors, vocal and instrumental. I heard a mass there, composed by Il Padre Vallotti, and both the composition and performance were delightful. There seemed to be a great number of students, native and foreign, in the university; but altogether I did not like the place, and at the end of three days, I left it, with great pleasure, in the common boat, filled with passengers of all sorts, for Venice.

We landed at the Piazza. My companion took leave of me, and I returned to my worthy friend and host, Zanotti, of the Regina d'Inghilterra. Zanotti had formerly been in England, in the service of Il Cavaliere Pissani, Ambassador to St. James's, and spoke English very well, which made his house much frequented by the travelling English nobility. He had a handsome gondola, which he allowed me to make use of; his gondolier was one of the most lively and intelligent of those expert and witty fellows: they are a privileged caste, and say what they like to their masters and others, no person taking offence at the jest or repartee of a gondolier. In their style, they greatly resemble the lower order of Irish, and are faithful in the extreme, if you put trust in them. Gondoliers were usually called 'Momolo,' it being the diminutive of St. Girolomo, or St. Jerome, their patron saint. By the way, it is strange, that those gentry, who are, to a man, adorers of the fair sex, should have chosen *him*, of all the saints in the calendar, for their patron, who had declared, that 'a good woman was more rare than the phœnix.' On this saint's day they have a fête, and not a gondolier will handle an oar if he can avoid it.

The functions in Passion Week were carried on with great solemnity.

The Doge went in procession to St. Marc's, where there were six orchestras erected, and High Mass celebrated. There was also a function at St. Giovanni di Paulo. I visited both. The fair of the Ascension coming on, every one was in preparation for it. It lasted fifteen days: all the theatres were open, and, at night, St. Marc's was brilliantly illuminated. On the Day of the Ascension, the Doge went in grand procession to marry the sea. My host took me to see this truly singular and magnificent sight. The Doge left Venice in his beautiful Bucantore, which contained near three hundred persons. It was superbly adorned, and carried twenty-one oars on each side. There were several bands of music on board. On reaching a certain point, the Doge threw a plain gold ring into the sea; saying, 'We marry thee, O Sea! in sign of true and perpetual dominion.' He then returned to Venice in the same order; the sea covered with gondolas, barges, and boats, and the spectators rending the air with acclamations.

'Mine host' related a ridiculous circumstance, which took place at this curious marriage ceremony some years before. The celebrated and witty Lord Lyttleton, and several other English gentlemen, went in a barge to see the ceremony. They had on board with them, a *lacquais-de-place*, a talkative fellow, making a plaguy noise, explaining every thing that was going on. This unfortunate Cicerone was standing up in the barge, and leaning over it, at the moment the Doge dropped the ring into the sea; the loquacious lacquey bawled out with all his might and strength, 'Now, my Lord, look, look, the Doge has married the sea!'

'Has he,' replied Lord Lyttleton, 'then go you, you noisy dog, and pay the bride a visit;' and, giving him a push, into the sea went the poor prating valet; he was taken up immediately, without having received any injury beyond a ducking, for which he was well repaid.

Of all the foreign cities I had ever seen, Venice appeared to be the best lighted; to a stranger it seems to be in a general illumination; the shops are kept open until twelve o'clock at night, and most of them not shut at all; the blaze of light which they give is great, particularly those in the Piazza St. Marc and the Freseria, where all the chief milliners and haberdashers live; the taverns are also open the greater part of the night, and supper is always ready 'on the shortest notice.'

It is quite common for ladies and gentlemen, after they have spent their evening at the different casinos, which many of the noble Venetians have in the Piazza St. Marc, and in which they have concerts, conversaziones, and plays, to form different parties, and adjourn to the taverns to supper. I have often been at these delightful parties: the ladies particularly are fond of these banquets, where good humour, mirth, and pleasantry abound: but they make it a rule, which they never in any instance deviate from, to pay their share of the bill; nor will they allow their cicisbeos or relations to pay for them;—nothing would offend a Venetian lady more than any man of the party offering to pay for her upon one of their sociable expeditions.

Shortly after my arrival in Venice, I delivered the letter I had from my worthy friend, General Dalton, and was received by the Countess Rosenberg with great kindness; she was a widow, and resided entirely at Venice with an only daughter. The Countess was a native of Wales; her maiden name, as I said before, was Wynne, and she was considered by the Venetians a grand dilettante. I afterwards waited upon his Excellency Priuli, Cornaro, and the beautiful Benzoni, with my letters, and was received by them with equal affability. The Austrian Ambassador, Count Durazzo, who was an intimate friend of General Dalton's, said he should be happy to see me at his conversazione, which he held three times a week; at his house, foreigners of every nation then at Venice assembled, but no Venetian. There is a strict law or custom, that a Venetian senator or nobleman is not allowed to visit a foreign ambassador; not even are their servants permitted to have intercourse with each other, under a severe penalty. However, as I had the happiness to be a British subject, I went on amusing myself very well with the conversazioni, concerts, and suppers, and going to one theatre or another every night, having the freedom of them all: but the theatre with which I was most pleased was that of St. Angelo, where the inimitable actor, Sacchi, the speaking Harlequin, and his company performed.

There were at that time in Venice, solely for comedies, four theatres—St. Angelo, St. Cassan, St. Luke, and St. Giovan Chrisostomo; but at whichever Sacchi performed, that one was always the best attended. I saw him for the first time perform in Goldoni's comedy, called 'The Thirty-two Misfortunes of Harlequin;' he was then considerably turned of seventy years of age, but when he had his Harlequin's jacket and mask on, the vivacity of his manner and activity would have led one to suppose him not above fifty; he was esteemed a great wit, full of bon-mot and repartee: he was allowed to have the power of applying the thoughts and sayings of the best ancient and modern writers extemporaneously, even while assuming in manner and tone the simplicity of an idiot: nothing seemed to come amiss to him, and he was justly the delight of the Venetians.

Mrs Crouch, by George Romney, 1787

Mrs Billington as Mandane in Thomas Arne's Artaxerxes, *1787*

Amongst the theatrical pieces of the Venetians, the comedies of Four Masques are the most entertaining. These Four Masques are—Pantaloon, who is always supposed to be a rich old Venetian merchant; an old Dottore, supposed to be an old cunning Bologna lawyer; Harlequin and Brigella are two natives of Bergamosco, servants; the Brigella ought to be clever, acute, and witty,—a knavish intriguer; and the performer of this part, who is not able to retort with quickness and point upon every subject proposed, is not fit to represent the character.

The Harlequin is to represent (in appearance) a stupid, clownish fellow; but, under the mask of stupidity, he should possess superlative sharpness of repartee, to answer others without hesitation, and put the most puzzling questions to the Doctor, to Pantaloon, and Brigella. It is delightful to hear good actors of those characters, particularly when they chance to be in the humour, to badger each other; and as the dialogue in some of those plays (Goldoni's and some of Gozzi's excepted) is spoken mostly impromptu, it is truly astonishing. Goldoni was a charming writer; Voltaire called him the *Painter of Nature*; his muse was wonderfully prolific; he has written, as I have been told, above one hundred plays, and finished his dramatic career in Paris by writing, when he was upwards of seventy years of age, a comedy in the French language.

Another popular and prolific author was the one I have just mentioned, Conte Carlos Gozzi, a Venetian nobleman. I saw one of his comedies, which had been translated into German, performed at Vienna; it was a favourite stock piece there: indeed, at one period, Gozzi was the rival of Goldoni, and nearly beat him from the field; he took the theatre of St. Giovan Chrisostomo, and brought forward pieces full of show and pageantry. I saw his Mostro Turchino (the Blue Monster), Le Tre Corve (the Three Crows), L'Uccello Belvedere (the Beautiful Bird), &c. all pieces of enchantment, performed; there was, I thought, a great deal of stage effect in them: but his chief dependence at that period was upon gorgeous spectacle. He appeared to go upon the old Spanish proverb, that

> The eye never grows wise,
> All *have* eyes,
> And only few have understanding.

Be that as it may, the public flocked wherever his pieces were represented, and for a length of time, Goldoni's regular dramas were neglected.

I had the satisfaction, many times and oft (not on the Rialto, but in the very next street to it), to dine in company with the veteran Sacchi, at the house of his Excellency Il Conte Pissani. Nothing could be to me more delightful than the innumerable stories and anecdotes with which this old man's conversation abounded; he was as sprightly as a boy, full of good humour and good nature. I remember one day he told us a story, that a short time previous, he was passing near the church of St. Giovanni, with a nobleman of very singular character, who was of very obscure origin; but his father having made an immense fortune in the Levant trade, purchased an estate and barony in Friuli for his son. The inordinate pride of this novus homo, rendered him universally ridiculous; but he was much flattered with having the witty Sacchi in his train, who laughed at him even while loading him with adulation.

As they were walking along one day, some priests, carrying the host to a dying person, passed them; every one in the street, as it is the custom in all Roman Catholic countries, fell on their knees, with their heads bare, bowing to the ground; amongst the rest, the proud baron knelt with great devotion; Sacchi, who was close to him, only took his hat off, and slightly inclined his head as the host went by, and did not go on his knees. The baron, quite shocked at this apparent want of religion and respect, exclaimed with affected humility, 'Signor Sacchi, I am petrified; to a poor miserable mortal like myself you pay every obsequious homage; yet, when the holy host passed you, instead of prostrating yourself before it, you only made a slight inclination with your head.'

'Very true, my Lord,' replied Sacchi; 'I admit the fact, but the host must not be made game of, and that makes all the difference.'

Sacchi was an enthusiast in favour of his art, and its professors who had been celebrated before his time, and was always particularly pleased to recount any anecdotes which might redound to the credit of the profession. He said that the celebrated wit and harlequin, Dominic, was sometimes admitted to the high honour of dining at the table of Louis XIV.; and that Tiberio Fiorelli, who invented the character of Scaramouch, had been the amusing companion of the boyhood of the same great monarch, and that from him Molière himself had learnt much.

One morning, while I was enjoying myself in all the delights of a circle so gay and accomplished as that in which I was luckily placed, I received a visit from my friend and patron with the long tail. He came to tell me that the manager of the theatre at Brescia was in Venice, forming a company to open his theatre with a comic opera for the ensuing fair. The fair at Brescia is greatly frequented from all parts of Italy, by all descriptions of mercantile people; that fair, and the fair of Senegaglia, in the Pope's dominions (where Catalani was born), are the greatest in Italy. My patron proposed to introduce me to the manager, which I acceded to, and had an interview with him, which terminated by his engaging me as his tenor singer. He agreed to pay me eighty Venetian golden ducats; not much, to be sure; the time, however, to be employed was not quite two months, and those too in the summer season. But the engagement had advantages besides pecuniary ones; I was delighted to find that my prima donna was to be the beautiful Ortabella, my *first* and great *favourite*. My patron, Signor Bertini (the manager), and I dined together, and settled the engagement over our wine. My patron and the manager seemed to be old cronies, and I had heard much of Bertini myself, for he had gained a good deal of credit by a trick which he played off upon a celebrated singer whom he had engaged to perform at the last fair, in a grand serious opera; the Signor demanded an enormous salary, which the nobility of Brescia insisted upon it should be given to him, and Bertini was obliged to submit. The expensive Signor never performed any where without receiving, beyond his great salary, all his travelling expenses (let him come from whatever distance he would), and having, during his stay, apartments for himself, and a table provided for six persons; and these conditions were always included in the Signor's articles.

In pursuance of such an engagement, he arrived at Brescia, and invited three friends to dine with him; they came:—he ordered his servants to let the manager know that he was ready for dinner, and desired it might be put down. The Signor's servant returned, and said that there was no dinner prepared; the infuriated performer went down stairs to the manager, and inquired why his dinner had not been prepared in proper time?—'Sir,' replied the manager, 'you gave no orders about providing dinner.'

'How, Sir,' said the singer, 'is it not set down in my articles, that you are to provide a table for six persons?'

'Undoubtedly, Sir, such is my agreement, and I do not deny it; if you will walk into the dinner-room,' (in the middle of which stood a new table,) 'you will see that I have fulfilled it to the letter; there, Sir, is your table, and a handsomer piece of furniture for its purpose, I flatter myself you never saw; and you will find that it accommodates six with the greatest convenience.'

'The table is extremely good,' quoth the singer, 'but where is the *dinner*, Sir?'

'Oh!' replied the manager, 'as for the dinner, *that I know nothing about*; the words of the engagement are, that I am to provide you a table for six persons; I not only have provided one, but I have gone beyond my bargain, for that will hold *eight*; but not one syllable will you find in the articles which binds me to find you either *eatables* or *drinkables*; and to my engagement I will stick.'

'Then, Sir, I will not sing at your theatre,' said the Signor.

'With all my heart, Signor,' answered Bertini; 'you are under a penalty of a thousand zecchinos if you do not fulfil your agreement; I shall be ready to try in a court of law, whether I am bound to provide food for you, when the words in the articles distinctly are, a table for six persons, and nothing more.' The manager stuck to his point, and the enraged musician was obliged to submit; but was much more chagrined, it was said, at the trick so successfully played upon him, than at the loss of the dinner to which he thought himself entitled.

As I was not to be at Brescia before the third week in June, I determined to return to Padua to spend a few days during the fair at St. Anthony; for at that period every one who can afford it, resorts thither from Venice; so that during the fair time, Padua, which I found so dull, is crowded with noble Venetians, who vie with each other in the splendour of their equipages. A Venetian nobleman's establishment is very expensive, as he must have his gondolas and gondoliers in Venice, and when he goes to his country house, of course a land equipage.

I was exceedingly amused with what I saw in Padua; and amongst the *sights* which possessed the never-failing charm of novelty, were races on the Corso by running footmen, whose speed, I think, would astonish the English patrons of pedestrianism. I found, besides, the attraction of a charming opera, and above all, I there first heard the afterwards celebrated singer, Crescentini. I was delighted. David, the popular tenor of his day, I remember, performed the character of Iarba, the Moorish king, in the opera of 'La Didone abbandonata;'[1] and the prima donna, although she sang and acted extremely well, was, since the truth must be told, extremely ugly. At the general rehearsal of the opera, where there were numbers of people assembled, David said, what shewed his want of good nature and gallantry. When Iarba is introduced to Dido, seated on her throne to receive him, his confidant asks him, 'Qual ti sembra, O Signor?'—'What do you think of her?' Iarba answers, 'Superba e bella.'—'Proud and beautiful.' Instead of saying this, David substituted the following agreeable exclamation, 'Superba e brutta!'—'Proud and ugly!' As Mathews says, 'it made a great laugh at the time;' but David was much blamed for his attempt at wit, which was reckoned extremely gross, particularly as the lady's homeliness was not to be made a joke of.

The theatre at Padua is handsome and commodious; it has two superb stone staircases, and five rows of boxes. During the fair, there was a grand room open for gambling, called La Sala di Ridotto, where immense sums were won and lost. I went two or three times to see the play, but never attempted to play myself; the bank is generally held by the proprietors of the theatre, who gain more profit by *that*, than they do by either their operas or ballets.

After staying in these scenes of gaiety and dissipation until their termination, I returned to my old quarters at the hotel in Venice, where I found a letter from my father, enclosing a letter of credit on a Venetian banker, together with a letter from Lord Granard to Mr. Strange, the English resident at Venice, which, however, was of no use to me, since Mr. Strange had returned to London about two months before its arrival.

I started in due time to Brescia, and put up at the sign of 'the Lobster', where Bertini came to meet me, and conducted me to a lodging which he had taken for me; it was a second floor of the house, the first floor of which was occupied by La Bella Ortabella herself. I was charmed to be under the same roof with her, and it was, besides, very convenient for me to practise the duets and concerted pieces. The day after she arrived we began our rehearsals; the first opera was 'Il Pittore Parigino'; the music, by Cimarosa, was beautiful;—the Painter was the character allotted to me;—the opera pleased very much. The town of Brescia was all alive, being fair-time, and the theatre was crowded; it was a very splendid building; the boxes, of which there were five tiers, were ornamented with glasses, like those of San Carlo, at Naples, and the seats in the pit turned up in the same way as in Padua. Independently of a very good company of singers, there was an excellent, and very expensive corps de ballet.

The proprietor, who was, in fact, our ostensible manager, was a most celebrated personage, Il Cavaliere Manuel, surnamed, 'Il Cavaliere Prepotente;' a man of inordinately bad character, and implacable in his revenge, wherever he took offence.—He was enormously rich, but never would pay any evitable debt, which, in some degree, accounted for his wealth; indeed, it was at the risk of life that any body pressed him for money;—he had in his pay a set of Sicari (assassins), who wore his livery, and when commanded by him, would shoot any person in the streets at noon-day;—woe to the man marked for his vengeance. The dress of these assassins, who were mostly mountaineers from his own estates, consisted of scarlet breeches and waist-coats, and green jackets,—their long hair was tied up in nets; they wore enormous whiskers, and large cocked hats with gold buttons and loops; in their belts were pistols, carbines at their backs, and large rapiers by their sides; and yet those ruffians walked the streets at liberty, and though known by all classes, none dare molest or take notice of them. The Venetian Senate, whose subjects they were, never could subdue them, though they used every means in their power to do so; and such was the state of society at the period of which I speak, that there was scarcely a noble Brescian who had not a set of them in his service, and rarely a week passed without an assassination.

While I was there, one of these fellows walked up to a coffee-house, tapped a gentleman on the shoulder, and begged of him to stand aside; he then levelled his carbine at a person who was sitting on a bench at the coffee-house door, and shot him dead on the spot; yet no one had sufficient courage to secure the murderer, who with the greatest *sang froid* walked unmolested to the church of the Jesuits, della Grazzie, where he was in perfect security.

Unfortunately for me, this Cavalier Manuel made proposals to the Prima Donna, La Ortabella, which she had the courage to reject. He attributed her coolness to a partiality which he suspected she had for me; and told her, that her refusal of the honour he offered of his protection, was owing to her preference of a vulgar singer, and swore that my interference should be the worst act of my life. She told me this, and felt alarmed for my safety. A foolish frolic increased his hatred towards me.

One day, looking at the frolic and fun going forward in the Fiera, with three or four of the opera singers, I saw a Neapolitan mountebank, mounted on a stage, holding forth to the crowd, telling their fortunes;—'Egad!' said I, to my companions, 'I have a mind to ask the mountebank a question which concerns us all:' they entreated me to do so. I accordingly made my way to the rostrum, slipped half a silver ducat into the mountebank's hand, and said to him, 'Most potent astrologer, my companions and myself, convinced of your great science, are anxious that you should resolve the question I shall put to you.'

The mountebank pocketed the half ducat, and with becoming gravity desired me to state the case.

'The question is,' said I, 'one which we, performers of the theatre in

Brescia, are most anxious to get answered: it is, whether the proprietor will pay us our salaries when they become due?'

The mountebank replied, 'Not one sou, if he can help it.'

I left him, and told my companions the prognostication, which they thought it extremely probable would be verified: this trifling circumstance was, of course, repeated by some of my good friends, to his Excellency, who was weak enough to take it as an offence, and told Bertini, that were it not to stop the performance of the theatre, he would annihilate me forthwith; but that, at all events, a day of retribution should come ere long.

My friend Bertini came and told me this, and advised me to be upon my guard whenever I went out. I went to wait upon Signor Conte Momelo Lana, the gentleman to whom Signora Benetti had given me a letter of recommendation, and told him what had passed, and the danger I thought I had to dread. He said he believed, from the well known implacable temper of my enemy, that I had every thing to fear; 'but,' said he, 'Manuel must know that you are under my protection, and I assure you, that if he *assassinates you, I will revenge you.*' I thanked the Count for his kind intentions, but told him, I would not trouble him, and that I thought the best thing I could do, was to beat a retreat.

The Count said I must be cautious how I did *that*, for if he got a scent of my intention, he would order his Sicari to despatch me. 'There is but one thing you can do,' said he, 'to get out of his reach: and I will give you every aid to accomplish it,—the grand ballet of the Siege of Troy, which is now performing, lasts an hour and a half at least, and is played after the first act of the opera; immediately before the ballet commences, go to your room, change the coat and waistcoat in which you perform, and put on your own; then lock your door, put your pelisse over you, watch your opportunity while they are in the bustle of preparing the ballet, slip out at the door at the back of the stage, and at the bottom of the street you will find my travelling carriage ready; my servant Stephano shall accompany you till he places you safe in Verona; *once there*, you are out of the reach of Manuel and his assassins; there he has no power to harm you. I will give you a letter of recommendation to my intimate friend and relation, the Count Bevi Acqua, who has interest sufficient to render you every service; he is a worthy man, and a great patron of the arts.' He then offered to accommodate me with the loan of money, which I refused, as I had my father's remittance untouched, which was most ample for all my present wants.

It was agreed that I should put his excellent project into execution the next night; he wrote me the letter for the Marquis Bevi Acqua, and the next evening I followed his directions implicitly, got to the end of the street, found the faithful Stephano, and, as fast as the horses could carry us on an excellent road, at full speed, escaped from Brescia and its threatened perils. I was full of terror till we got a few miles distant; we found horses ready at the first stage, and did not stop till we arrived at Desenzano, on the Lago di Garda, where we were beyond all dread of pursuit. I managed to send a small bundle of clothes the evening before I quitted Brescia to Stephano, which he put into his master's carriage; my trunks I left behind me, and requested my kind friend Count Momolo Lana to send them immediately after me to Verona, gave him the amount of what I had to pay for my lodgings, and begged him to write me an account of the sensation my escape made, and to give every publicity to the reasons why I quitted the place: I also left with him a letter to deliver to my kind and friendly Signora Ortabella, expressing the great regret I felt in quitting her, and hoping we should soon meet on safer ground than Brescia, where a man ran the risk, if only commonly attentive to a woman, of having half a dozen bullets put into his body.

I arrived safe at Verona, which I thought rather fortunate, as the greatest part of the road from Desenzano was infested by numerous banditti. I scarcely travelled a quarter of a mile without seeing a little wooden cross stuck by the road-side, as a mark that some one had been murdered on the spot. I put up at the sign of the Due Tori, and the day after my arrival hired a pair of horses, to take the Count Lana's carriage and his faithful Stephano back to Brescia. On the third day of my residence in Verona, I received a letter from the Count, together with my trunks:—he mentioned in his letter, that on the night of my departure, when the ballet was over, and the second act of the opera just about to begin, the greatest confusion prevailed amongst the performers; they searched every where for me, sent to my lodgings, where of course they could obtain no information, but they had not the slightest suspicion of my flight: an apology was necessarily made from the stage to the public, stating that I was not to be found; and, perforce, the opera was acted, omitting the scenes in which I was concerned.

8

Immediately afterwards, my friend the Count caused the letter I had written, explaining the reasons for my departure, and stating all that Count Manuel had told Bertini, of his intention to annihilate me, to be printed and widely circulated. In his letter to me, he mentioned, that he had a double motive for thus effectually giving publicity to my case; in the first place, he was anxious to exculpate me with the public, for breaking my engagement; and in the second, his object was, to deter my enemy from following up his revengeful threats, for that if any serious mischance should befal me, the world would, after such an exposition, naturally conclude him to be the author of it, and that he would consequently become responsible. He added, that the public considered me perfectly justified in my conduct.

Count Manuel, when the affair became known, publicly denied ever having had any intention to injure me; but those who knew him, weighing his general character in the scale opposite to that in which they placed the circumstances of the case, fully and clearly detailed as they had been, believed neither his assertions nor asseverations upon this point. I was, however, thank God, out of his reach before his *virtue* was put to the proof; the circumstance was talked of all over Italy, but in justice to myself, I ought to say, that I never heard of any blame attaching to me for my conduct.

In due season, after my arrival at Verona, I waited upon the Marquis of Bevi Acqua to deliver my letter of introduction. I found him at home in his magnificent house; he received me with marked kindness, and did me the honour to introduce me to his lady and three of her lovely daughters. The letter explained the particulars of my story, and the Marquis invited me the next evening to a concert at his house. Of course I accepted the invitation. I found an elegant assemblage of the first people of Verona. In the course of the evening, I sang two songs, and accompanied myself on the piano-forte, and the company seemed pleased with me. The story of my escape from Brescia, and its half-romantic cause, had created no small share of interest for me; and when I waited on the Marquis the next morning, I found that he and the Marchioness had planned a public concert for me under their patronage. I was introduced by them to Signor Barbella, the first piano-fortist and composer in Verona, who was directed by the Marquis to engage the concert-room and performers for me; all which he did with economy and punctuality.

The Marquis told me he was an enthusiastic admirer of Shakspeare, particularly of Romeo and Juliet, and took me to see the tomb of Juliet.[1] Indeed, the people of Verona are very proud of recounting the history of those ill-fated lovers, and taking foreigners to see their resting place. I felt great delight in visiting the spot. Juliet's tomb was in the church of St. Permo Magiani; its sides were a good deal mutilated, as strangers who visit it, are in the habit of breaking off pieces to keep as relics.

Verona, though not very large, is a very handsome city; the streets are wide, and generally well built. Sacchi and his company of comedians were performing at the amphitheatre, said to have been erected by Vitruvius. The arena of Verona is a stupendous fabric; forty-five rows of marble steps surround it; they will hold twenty thousand people, commodiously seated: in the centre of this place, in the summer, there are plays which are acted by day-light; a temporary theatre is erected, which is taken down every winter; there are no boxes; the enclosed space forms an immense pit, with chairs, where the fashionable and better sort of the audience are seated; the second best places are on the steps, twelve or fourteen deep, railed off from the rest of the steps; the seats are all of naked marble, and the whole is in the open air. This immense building, and the Coliseum at Rome, are the two most stupendous fabrics I ever beheld.

There was no city in Italy of its size, at the time I visited it, which could boast of so many good musical amateurs, vocal and instrumental, as Verona. Signor Barbella promised to take me to a concert, performed by one family only; to my very great surprise he took me to gaol, and introduced me to the gaoler: we were shewn into an apartment elegantly furnished, and after we had taken our coffee and chasse,[2] had really an excellent concert; the performers were the gaoler, who played the double bass; his two eldest sons, first and second violin; a third the violoncello; his youngest son, the viola; one of his daughters presided at the harpsichord, and his two youngest daughters executed some airs and duets extremely well. They had good voices, and sang like true artists: the whole of this gifted family were amateurs; the young men were in different trades, but had they been obliged to live by music, they could in my opinion have successfully adopted it as a profession in any part of Italy. They were all enthusiasts and excellent performers, and extremely courteous in their behaviour; and I returned to my hotel, after having supped with them, much gratified by the pleasant evening I had passed, *though it was in prison.*

The Sunday following this exhibition was appointed for my concert, and the room, owing to the popularity and interest of the Marquis and Marchioness, was crowded; Signor Barbella conducted the performance; Signor Salinbeni was first violin; and, luckily, La Signora Chiavaci, a very good singer, was passing through Verona on her way to the theatre at Bergamo at the time, and being an intimate friend of Signor Barbella, at his request, she agreed to stop a day and sing at my concert, which she did gratuitously, and was much and deservedly applauded.

The nett receipts of this concert were 71 zecchinos, (about 30*l.* British); in addition to which, the Marquis made me a special present for his own ticket. I was now *high* in spirits, and not *low* in cash; and, as good fortune never comes alone, on the morning after my concert, I received a letter, forwarded from Brescia to me, from Signor Giani, the manager of Treviso, offering me an engagement for six weeks, at 50 zecchinos, which I accepted, and promised to be in Treviso in three days after the date of my answer.

I waited upon my worthy friends, the Marquis and Marchioness of Bevi Acqua, to take my leave of them, and parted from them with grateful regret; they were all affability and condescension: indeed, I liked every thing about them, except their name, to which, Bevi Acqua, (in English, *Drinkwater,*) at no period of my life could I bring myself to be partial, although there are several very estimable persons so called in England at this present moment. The Marquis gave me a letter to Signora Marcello, a Venetian lady of consideration, who resided at Treviso, whose husband was a noble Venetian, and a descendant of the celebrated composer of sacred music, Benedetto Marcello. Before I set off, I went and took leave of the musical gaoler, and his harmonious family; and having made all due preparation for my departure, hired a valet and started for Vicenza, where I supped and slept. In the morning, I walked about the city, which I found extremely neat and pretty, and the country about it very beautiful. After breakfast, I set off for Treviso, and was delighted by the appearance of the elegant villas which surround it, belonging to noble Venetians, who, during the theatrical season, pass their vendemmias there, and have what they call their *cuganas* (*i.e.* revelries).

Treviso itself, during this period, is crowded with people of less exalted rank from Venice, which is within a few miles, and, as the canals at Venice are at certain periods very offensive, every one who can, quits it for Padua or Treviso.

I found engaged, as Prima Donna at Treviso, the celebrated Clementina Bagliona (to whom I had been introduced at Pisa by Signor Viganoni); and, for the first Buffo, her sister's husband, Signor Pozzi, who, when at Rome, met with the kind treatment from his patron and friend, the Roman Abbé, which I have already endeavoured to describe.

The theatre was crowded every night, and the opera, as well as the ballets, gave great satisfaction. I waited upon her Excellency La Signora Marcello, and delivered my letter of introduction given me by the Marquis Bevi Acqua. She gave me an invitation to her morning concerts, where I met all the beau monde of Treviso, and passed many delightful hours. In that very house, many years afterwards, lived my lamented friend the late Mrs. Billington, who has described to me the period of her residence in it, as the most miserable of her existence.[1]

At one of Madame Marcello's concerts, I had the pleasure of hearing the greatest reputed dilettante singer in Europe, La Signora Teresa de Petris. Nor was her reputation higher than her merits; she had one of the finest voices I ever heard, combined with great science and expression: in addition to this, she was very beautiful, and had about her all the Venetian fascination. She married a noble Venetian, Il Signor Veniera, but, for some reason, was separated from him. Her cavaliere servente was Count Vidiman, a handsome and rich young nobleman, who resided at Venice, and who was devoted to music and to her. He was also a great protector of the composer Anfossi, and so attached to his music, that he would scarcely listen to any other. He had fixed a performance to take place at Venice the beginning of Lent; an oratorio composed expressly for her Excellency La Signora De Petris, by Anfossi, was to be performed at Count Pepoli's private theatre. The Count called upon me one morning, and said, 'La Signora de Petris wishes that you should perform in the oratorio with her. If you think it worth your consideration, I offer you an engagement for four months.'

I was elated at the proposition, and accepted his offer. I was to be at his command for four months, to remain during that period at Venice, and to accept of no public engagement whatever. I could not have met with any thing so pleasing, as my delight was Venice, and its amusements were congenial to my taste and time of life.

We were now within a few nights of closing the theatre at Treviso, and Count Vidiman and Signora de Petris were going to Udina, the capital of Friuli, where he had large estates, and afterwards to spend a month or six weeks with his mother, the old Countess, with whom La Signora de Petris was a great favourite. The Count having heard me express a wish to visit Parma, said, he thought that the time he should be absent at Udina would be the most convenient whereat to satisfy my curiosity; and besides, I then might have a chance of uniting profit with pleasure, as the Arch-duchess, who was a lover of music, and a fine performer herself, gave great encouragement to musical artists who visited her court, and her private band was esteemed the choicest and best in Italy. The Count procured me a letter of recommendation to Her Royal Highness from Il Signor Cavaliere Giustiniani, who had been at the court of Parma, Ambassador from the Venetian State, and while there, was in the highest favour.

I set off post for the city of Modena, on my way to Parma, and on my arrival there, at the door of the post-house, recognised Fochetti, the bass singer, who had performed with me when I was so much younger in Dublin. I made myself known to him, and it was an agreeable surprise to us both to meet where we so little expected it. I passed a pleasant evening with him at the Inn, talking of old times, and Ireland; he told me he had retired from the stage, with a sufficient fortune to enable him to remain in his native city of Modena, where he held the situation of first bass singer at the reigning Duke's Royal Chapel.

At an early hour the next morning, he called upon me to shew me what was worth seeing. Modena stands twenty miles west of Bologna, and twenty-eight east of Parma. It is curious enough, although perhaps generally known, that carrier pigeons are constantly used here for the conveyance of letters. It is said that this custom had its origin in Hirtius the consul, who adopted the use of them while Decius Brutus was besieged by Marc Antony.

Fochetti took me to see the Ducal Palace. I thought it very superb. In it are a number of very fine paintings, particularly a nativity by Correggio. The inhabitants of Modena are not a little vain in having to boast that the divine poet Tasso was a native of their city. Of the churches, those of St. Domingo and the Jesuits are the worthiest of notice; we went also to view the College of St. Carlo Bremeo, in which upwards of one hundred noblemen are educated. Most of the houses in the city have porticoes, and covered walks; their chief trade, I understood, consisted in masks, which they are famous for making, and export in great numbers.

But to proceed:—After seeing the sights, I took an affectionate leave of my old friend; I confess that the parting made me quite melancholy, and brought to my mind the happy days I had passed with him at my father's house, where he was a constant and welcome guest. However, I dissipated my care by travelling, and about six in the evening got sight of the city, so famous for its truffles and its cheese; (of which, by the way, not one morsel is made in Parma, for what are called Parmesan cheeses, are made at Piacenza and Lodi); and was set down at the Osteria di Gallo, where I took up my residence.

In the morning I was informed that Her Royal Highness the Archduchess was at her villa at Colorno, a few miles from town. I therefore hired a carriage, and proceeded thither; I was struck with the magnificence of the palace, and the beauty of the grounds, as I approached the end of my journey; which having achieved, I announced myself to Her Royal Highness's Chamberlain, and informed him that I came to Colorno to present Her Royal Highness with some letters from Treviso; the Chamberlain conducted me immediately to Her Royal Highness's presence. I found her in her billiard-room, playing with some of her suite, (amongst whom were the favourite musicians belonging to her band,) and without appearing to possess the smallest pride, putting every person completely at his ease by her fascinating condescension. She seemed in perfect good humour with her game, at which she appeared a great proficient.

After it was concluded, she came up to me, inquired most kindly after Il Cavaliere Giustiniani, conversed with me for some time about Naples particularly, and asked me if I had ever seen her sister, the Queen of Naples. I replied that I had had the honour of singing before Her Majesty at Posilipo. 'Had you?' said Her Royal Highness, 'then you shall also sing before her sister at Colorno. Remain here a few days, if you have time to spare, and we will have a little music.' She then left the billiard-room, and desired Count Palavacini, her Chamberlain, to introduce me to the gentlemen of her private band; they were all great favourites with her. I dined with them, and they were particularly attentive to me, and had an excellent table kept for them, covered with the best viands and choicest wines. I paid my respects to the Burgundy, which, to be sure, was delicious.

In the evening there was a concert, which Her Royal Highness, attended by several Ladies of the court, honoured with her presence. She was perfectly affable to all the professors in the orchestra, and presided herself at the piano-forte; the whole band was worthy of its reputation. If there were any superiority amongst them, in my opinion, it was in the French horns, played by two brothers (whose names I have forgotten); such tones I never heard from the instrument as those which they produced, in a duet they played.

I sang Sarti's Rondo of 'Teco resti, anima mia', and accompanied myself on the piano-forte. Her Royal Highness did me the honour to approve, and asked me who was my instructor; when I mentioned Aprile, she said that I certainly had had the advantage of the best of singing masters.

At ten o'clock the concert finished, and I retired to supper with the rest of the professors, and in the morning, two gentlemen of the band took me in a court carriage to see some of the beauties of the neighbourhood. At twelve o'clock we attended Her Royal Highness at the billiard table, where she appeared in a morning dress, with a large apron before her, with pockets, in which she kept a quantity of silver coin; she always played for some trifling stake, and was very anxious to be the winner. She asked me if I was fond of billiards, and if I played; I said I had always been partial to it. 'Come,' said she, 'you shall try a game with me:' I had the honour of doing so, but Her Royal Highness beat me hollow.

She possessed a very fine person, very tall, and rather large; her features were masculine, but still there was a likeness between her and her sisters, the Queens of France and Naples. But I was told by Count Palavacini that she was much more like her mother the Empress Maria Theresa, than either of them. The Arch-duke of Parma, her husband, and herself, were upon good terms, but seldom together; either of them had pursuits diametrically opposite to the other's taste: she, a clever acute woman, was fond of pleasure;—on the contrary, he was esteemed very weak, a great bigot, and half a madman; his chief amusement and delight was, at different periods of the year, accompanied by some of the favourite noblemen of his court, to go every step of the way on foot, to the different cities and towns of his dukedom; to visit the different churches, and hang up tapestry; and this too, let the distance be what it would from his capital. He was said never to be happy but in a church, mounted on a ladder, with a hammer in his hand. This mania was spoken of in all parts of Italy, insomuch, that he was nicknamed the *Royal Upholsterer*; but, with the exception of this strange propensity, he was thought harmless and good-natured.

I stopped a week at Colorno, where there was music every night, and had great pleasure in hearing the Arch-duchess's performance. On my taking leave of Her Royal Highness, she gave me a rouleau of fifty zecchinos, and a beautiful little enamelled watch, set round with small diamonds, and a gold chain; on my kissing her hand for her liberality and condescending kindness, she was pleased to compliment me, and wished me every success. I took my dutiful leave of her, and bade adieu to the gentlemen of the orchestra, whose kindness and attention were so marked during my delightful stay at Colorno.

I returned to Parma, and the Grand Theatre not being open for representations, I got permission the next morning to see it. I was much pleased at having an opportunity of viewing so fine an edifice, it being much larger than the theatre of St. Carlo at Naples; or, indeed, than any other in Europe. There was a small theatre open at the time, where plays were representing. I went one evening to see Goldoni's Comedy of Il Padre di Famiglia. The celebrated Petronio's acting of the Father, was a fine performance. The house was crowded, and some very beautiful women graced the boxes. The next day, at the Cathedral, (one of the finest in Europe,) I heard a mass of Jomelli's chaunted; the singers and band were numerous and excellent. I remained two days longer there, seeing what was worth viewing, and then, without delay on the road, posted to Bologna, and took up my abode at my old friend Passerini's, who was as kind as ever to me.

While at Bologna, Signor Tambourini, the great theatrical broker, offered me two engagements for the autumn and carnival; one for Barcelona in Spain, and the other for Warsaw; both of which I was obliged to decline on account of my engagement at Venice, to which place I shortly proceeded; and, in a few days, the Count Vidiman, and La Signora de Petris returned thither from Udina. It was then the month of October, all the theatres open, and the Piazza St. Marc in all its revelry, crowded with masks, &c. &c. I paid my respects to the Count and the Lady; the Count desired I should quit my Hotel, and, for the term of my stay at Venice, reside at the house of La Signora de Petris, where he said it would be more comfortable and economical for me. I had an excellent apartment there; she kept a table which would have gratified Apicius himself. Count Vidiman had an elegant Casino in the Piazzo St. Marc, where, every night, he saw a number of friends; after they came from the theatres, there was always a little music, at which the Lady presided; and afterwards a supper. La Signora de Petris had boxes at all the theatres, whither I used to accompany her whenever she went to them.

At the Theatre of St. Marc, I used to sit at the piano-forte as an amateur, and accompany the comic operas;—it was amusement, as well as improvement, to me. At the Theatre of St. Samuel there was a powerful comic opera;—at the head of it was my old friend Madame Storace;[1] her success was great indeed. Signor Vicenzo Martini, the celebrated Spanish composer, composed the opera; his was a soul of melody, and melody is the rarest gift a composer can possess, and one which few attain to. I may with safety aver, from my own knowledge, that I have met with ninety-nine good theorists to one melodist; nature makes the one, study the other. Two of the greatest theorists I ever met with were, Friar Padre Martini of Bologna, and Sala, the master of the Conservatorio della Pietà, Naples; yet neither of these ever produced a remarkable melody that I recollect; I mean, not such a one as our justly celebrated composer, Dr. Arne, used to say, 'would grind about the streets upon the organ.'

I cannot omit here quoting what the immortal Haydn has mentioned on the subject of melody; he said,—'It is the air which is the charm of music, and it is that, which is most difficult to produce;—patience and study are sufficient for the composition of agreeable sounds, but the invention of a fine melody is the work of genius; the truth is, a fine air needs neither ornament nor accessories, in order to please,—would you know whether it really be fine, sing it without accompaniments.'

Storace drew overflowing houses, she was quite the rage;—she announced a benefit, the first ever given to any performer at Venice; but, being an Englishwoman, it was granted to her. The house overflowed; her mother stood at the door to receive the cash; the kind-hearted and liberal Venetians not only paid the usual entrance money, but left all kinds of trinkets, watch chains, rings, &c., to be given to her; it was a most profitable receipt for her, and highly complimentary to her talents; but, notwithstanding those honours were heaped upon her, a circumstance occurred, which gave her the most poignant annoyance, as well as her mother and her friends.

I have already stated that Stephen Storace was her brother, and that she had no other brother, or a sister; yet, an unprincipled woman came to Venice, and gave out that she was the sister of Signora Storace, took up her abode in a street called La Calla di Carbone, (a quarter of the town where ladies of her description were obliged to reside,) where she had her portrait hung out of her window, and under it written,—Questo è il ritratto della sorella della Signora Storace—(*i.e.* this is the portrait of

Signora Storace's sister). It is almost incredible that people should be so duped; but it is an absolute fact, that the woman's apartments were daily crowded by all ranks, to see the supposed sister of their favourite songstress, and the impostor gained a large sum of money by the price paid for admission to see her. The game was carried on for some time, but on some of Storace's friends making application to the police, the imposture was detected, and its contriver imprisoned, and subsequently banished the Venetian Republic.

It had been an ancient custom in Venice for personages of this lady's vocation, to have their portraits painted, and hung out of the windows of their apartments, to attract notice and visitors. In Mrs. Behn's comedy of 'The Rovers', which was revived and altered by Mr. Kemble, and successfully produced at Drury Lane under the title of 'Love in many Masks', is a character drawn of one of those women, whose portrait is seen hanging out of a balcony on the stage.

I was one morning sitting in the Rialto coffee-house with my long-tailed patron, and stating that Storace never had a sister, and wondering that the people of Venice could be so imposed upon, when an Abbé, who was sitting close to us, said,—'Your observation may be very true, Sir, that the people of Venice, in the instance of which you speak, have proved themselves credulous, but, surely not more so than your own countrymen;—when I was in London, I was told that they had been taken in by a mountebank, who advertised that he would, at one of their theatres, creep into a quart bottle. The house was crowded to witness this incredible exhibition, but the cunning mountebank, after pocketing the money received at the doors, made off with it, and was on his way to Dover before the humbug was found out.—Now, Sir, I beg to ask you, which of the two nations, English or Venetian, proved itself the greatest dupe?' The question was a puzzler, and I was glad not to proceed further with the subject, remembering, a little too late, the saying, that those who live in glass houses should not throw stones.

I continued, until the end of the Carnival, passing my time with very little variation, living in the lap of luxury, and in a vortex of pleasure. We began the rehearsal of Anfossi's oratorio, and the first week in Lent the performance commenced. I had a song which had been composed purposely for me, and sent from London by Anfossi to Count Vidiman. Nothing could exceed the brilliancy of Signora de Petris' execution and feeling; she sang divinely, and we repeated the oratorio eight nights to the fashionables invited by the Count and the Signora. There was a particular friend of her's, Signor Gioacino Bianchi, then an amateur, a man of very good family, and a sweet singer; but, owing to some circumstances of a tender nature, he quitted Venice, and went to England, where he became a singing-master of eminence, esteemed by all his friends for urbanity and talent, and highly patronized by the Earl and Countess of Harcourt.

One morning I received a message from His Excellency the Austrian Ambassador, desiring me to go to him in the evening. I waited on His Excellency, who informed me that he had received a letter from Prince Rosenberg, Grand Chamberlain of His Majesty Joseph the Second, Emperor of Germany, directing him to engage a company of Italian singers for a comic opera, to be given at the Court of Vienna; that no expense was to be spared, so that the artists were of the first order; that no secondary talent would be received amongst them, and that characters were to be filled by those engaged, without distinction, according to their abilities; and the will of the director appointed by the Emperor.

9

The Italian opera had for a length of time been discontinued at Vienna, and a first rate French company[1] of comedians substituted. The Emperor and his Court were at Schoënbrunn, and the French company were performing there; apartments in the palace had been appointed for them, and a plentiful table allotted to their exclusive use. One day, while they were drinking their wine, and abusing it, the Emperor passed by the *salle à manger,* which opened into the Royal Gardens. One of the gentlemen, with the innate modesty so peculiarly belonging to his nation and profession, jumped up from table with a glass of wine in his hand, followed His Majesty, and said,—'Sire, I have brought your Majesty some of the trash which is given us by your purveyor, by way of wine; we are all disgusted at his treatment, and beg to request your Majesty to order something better, for it is absolutely impossible for us to drink it;—he says it is Burgundy—do taste it, Sire, I am sure you will not say it is.'

The King, with great composure, tasted the wine: 'I think it excellent,' said His Majesty, 'at least, quite good enough for *me*, though, perhaps, not sufficiently high-flavoured for *you* and your companions; in France,

I dare say, you will get much better.' He then turned on his heel, and sending immediately for the Grand Chamberlain, ordered the whole corps dramatique to be discharged, and expelled Vienna forthwith. They repented their folly, but His Majesty would never hear more of them, and their audacity caused the introduction of an Italian opera at Vienna.

Count Durazzo read the letter containing this anecdote to a numerous party assembled at his house, who were much amused at it. His Excellency then asked me if I should like to go to Vienna; if I did, he would enlist me into the service. I thanked His Excellency, and answered that I should not desire better. The Countess Rosenberg kindly promised, that if I went there, she would give me some letters which might be of great service to me; and His Excellency desired me to consider of it for a day or two, and then return and bring my proposals to him. The term of my engagement with Count Vidiman having just expired, I mentioned to him the offer which had been made me, which he considered highly advantageous. Decided by this disinterested advice, I waited upon His Excellency the Ambassador, and concluded an engagement for one year, my salary being at the rate of 400 Venetian golden ducats (200*l.*); to be lodged free of expense, fuel found me, and four large wax candles per diem, which was the customary allowance. I signed the agreement with His Excellency, and was highly contented with it, and thought myself most lucky in having made it. Madame Storace was also engaged,[1] and the two best comic singers in Europe, Bennuci and Mandini.

When the time for my departure arrived, the Countess of Rosenberg gave me, as she had promised, a letter to her noble relative, the Grand Chamberlain; one to Prince Charles of Lichtenstein, Governor of Vienna, and one to Sir Robert Keith, His Britannic Majesty's Minister at Vienna. From Count Durazzo I had one for Grand Marshal Lacy, one for Marshal Laudon, and a third for the illustrious and witty Prince de Ligne; more powerful recommendations no young man perhaps could boast; and, as in my road to Vienna I had to pass through the city of Udina, my kind friend Count Vidiman gave me also a letter of introduction to the Countess his mother, as well as one to the Venetian Count Manini, both of whom resided at Udina.

Thus prepared, I set off from Venice in a calassetto, accompanied by my servant, for Udina; and it was with a heavy heart I quitted dear Italy, in which I had been so warmly patronized, and found such kindness and hospitality. I proceeded, however, on my journey, and alighted at a very comfortable inn, on the sign of which was written, in capital letters, 'No trust to-day, but to-morrow.' I was a good deal amused at the flying promise, never to be fulfilled.

Udina is twenty-two leagues from Venice; the town is very neat and pretty, the suburbs particularly so; the language of the inhabitants is a Patois, a mixture of Italian, French, and German; the Venetians ridicule them for a singular mode they have of calling *night, evening,* and *evening, night*. When the Venetians speak of them, they say, 'Gente cui si fa notte inanzi sera.'—(*i.e.* People to whom night appears before evening.) I lost no time in delivering my credentials to the Countess Vidiman, and afterwards went to present my letter to Count Manini, who was residing at a magnificent country seat of his, called Pascan;—he made me quit my inn, and stay with him for a couple of days. He entertained me splendidly and hospitably, and, on my departure, ordered some delicious wine, made on his own estate, called Picolet, (the taste of which resembled Tokay, but less sweet,) to be put into my calassetto.

After a tedious journey, I arrived at Vienna, and put up at the sign of the White Ox, and, on the following morning, waited upon Signor Salieri, to deliver my letter of recommendation from Signor Bertoni. Salieri was a Venetian, and a scholar of the celebrated composer Guzman; Salieri, himself, indeed, was a composer of eminence.—He was Maestro di Cappella at the Court of Vienna, and a great favourite with the Emperor. He presided at the harpsichord at the theatre, and was subdirector under Prince Rosenberg, Grand Chamberlain of the Court. He was a little man, with an expressive countenance, and his eyes were full of genius. I have often heard Storace's mother say, he was extremely like Garrick. He received me politely, and informed me that his opera of 'La Scuola dei Gelosi', was the first to be performed, in which I was to make my début. He accompanied me to the apartments which had been taken for me, and which consisted of an excellent first and second floor, elegantly furnished, in the most delightful part of Vienna. I was found, as usual, in fuel and wax candles, and a carriage to take me to rehearsals, and to and from the theatre, whenever I performed.

After having been duly installed in my new residence, I delivered all my recommendatory letters, and was delighted with the reception I met with, from those to whom they were addressed; particularly from Marshals Laudon and Lacy, and Sir Robert Keith,—the affability of the last was highly flattering to my feelings. I was altogether delighted, and thought Vienna a delightful city, and a charming place of residence. In a fortnight after my arrival the theatre opened. Storace and Bennuci's receptions were perfectly enthusiastic, and I may perhaps be permitted to say, that I had no reason to complain of my own.

The Emperor, Joseph II. accompanied by his brother Maximilian, the Archbishop of Cologne, were present at the performance, and evinced their approbation by the applause they bestowed. At the period I speak of, the Court of Vienna was, perhaps, the most brilliant in Europe. The theatre, which forms part of the Royal Palace, was crowded with a blaze of beauty and fashion. All ranks of society were doatingly fond of music, and most of them perfectly understood the science. Indeed, Vienna then was a place where pleasure was the order of the day and night.

The women, generally speaking, are beautiful; they have fine complexions, and symmetrical figures, the lower orders particularly. All the servant-maids are anxious to shew their feet, (which are universally handsome,) and are very ambitious of having neat shoes and stockings. Vienna, in itself, then contained between 80,000 and 90,000 inhabitants, and is surrounded by fortifications, which served for pleasant walks;—the ramparts are picturesquely beautiful. There are two Faubourgs[1] at Vienna, which contain 170,000 inhabitants of all descriptions. That superb river, the Danube, borders the central town, and separates on one side the Faubourg of Leopoldstadt, from the Prater, reckoned the finest promenade in Europe. There are many splendid palaces in the Faubourgs. Among the most conspicuous, are those of Prince Schwartzenberg, and Prince Adam Ausberg, &c. I had the honour of being patronized by Prince Ausberg. His Highness employed a great number of workmen at his own expense in a manufactory for steel, and all kinds of hardware, which he had established. I have seen some things from his fabrique, which would not lose by comparison with the excellent workmanship of Mr. Bolton's manufactories at Birmingham. His Highness also was a great patron of musical performances. He had a beautiful theatre in his palace, at which I saw the Countess Hatzfield perform inimitably well, in Gluck's serious opera of 'Alceste.'—She was a charming woman, and full of talent.

The Prater, as I said before, I consider the finest public promenade in Europe, far surpassing in variety our own beautiful Hyde Park. It is about four miles in length; on each side of the road are fine chesnut trees, and a number of avenues and retired drives. These roads, on spring and summer evenings, are thronged with carriages. On all sides, as in our Hyde Park and Bushy Park, deer are seen quietly grazing, and gazing at the passing crowds. At the end of the principal avenue is an excellent tavern, besides which, in many other parts of this enchanting spot, there are innumerable cabarets, frequented by people of all ranks in the evening, who *immediately after dinner* proceed thither to regale themselves with their favourite dish, fried chickens, cold ham, and sausages; white beer, and Hoffner wines, by way of dessert; and stay there until a late hour: dancing, music, and every description of merriment prevail; and every evening, when not professionally engaged, I was sure to be in the midst of it.

The Danube runs through part of this charming retreat. One evening, Salieri proposed to me to accompany him to the Prater. At this time he was composing his opera of Tarrare, for the Grand Opera House at Paris. At the back of the cabaret where we had been taking refreshments, near the banks of the Danube, we seated ourselves by the river side; he took from his pocket a sketch of that subsequently popular air which he had that morning composed. *Ah! povero Calpigi*. While he was singing it to me with great earnestness and gesticulation, I cast my eyes towards the river, and spied a large wild boar crossing it, near the place where we were seated. I took to my heels, and the composer followed me, leaving '*Povero Calpigi*', and (what was worse) a flagon of excellent Rhenish wine behind us, which was to me a greater bore than the bristly animal, whose visit seemed intended for us. The story was food for much laughter, when we were out of danger. Salieri, indeed, would make a joke of any thing, for he was a very pleasant man, and much esteemed at Vienna; and I considered myself in high luck to be noticed by him.

Shortly after I had presented my letter to him, Marshal Lacy did me the honour to invite me to dine with him; and amongst other great men who were his guests, I had the honour to meet Marshal Laudon. I looked upon it as a great event in a young man's life, to be seated at the same table with these two heroes; rivals in the art of war, though attached friends. Marshal Lacy was a fine looking man; free, convivial, and communicative; he was about seventy years of age, of Irish extraction, but himself a Russian born. He had amassed a splendid fortune, and lived in a princely style, and was in high favour with the Emperor.

Marshal Laudon was a very different kind of personage; he appeared to be the soldier only, and spoke very little; he seemed about the same age as Marshal Lacy, but they were very different. Marshal Laudon was of Scotch extraction, but a Livonian by birth. Such were his military talents, that he rose from the ranks in the Imperial Guard to the highest military command in the service; and was, as all the world knows, a rival of the great Frederick; yet, although they had often contended with varied success, either admitted the splendid talents of the other. As a proof of this, an anecdote was told me, by the celebrated and witty Prince de Ligne, who indeed said he could vouch for its truth from personal knowledge.

In an interval of peace between Austria and Prussia, Frederick the Great was at Silesia, at the same time with the Prince de Ligne, Marshal Brown, Marshal Laudon, and many Austrian officers. The king gave them a grand dinner, to which several Prussian officers were invited. Marshal Laudon was placed at table *vis-à-vis* to Frederick. The king rose, and said, 'Marshal Laudon, I request you will quit your seat; come hither and sit by me, for believe me (and with sincerity I speak it) I always prefer having you at my side to having you opposed to me.' The Prince de Ligne said, that Laudon was highly gratified by this elegant compliment from so great a warrior.

The people of Vienna were in my time dancing mad; as the Carnival approached, gaiety began to display itself on all sides; and when it really came, nothing could exceed its brilliancy. The ridotto rooms, where the masquerades took place, were in the palace, and spacious and commodious as they were, they were actually crammed with masqueraders. I never saw, or indeed heard of any suite of rooms, where elegance and convenience were more considered; for the propensity of the Vienna ladies for dancing and going to carnival masquerades was so determined, that nothing was permitted to interfere with their enjoyment of their favourite amusement—nay, so notorious was it, that for the sake of ladies in the family way, who could not be persuaded to stay at home, there were apartments prepared, with every convenience for their accouchement, should they be unfortunately required. And I have been gravely told, and almost believe, that there have actually been instances of the utility of the arrangement. The ladies of Vienna are particularly celebrated for their grace and movements in waltzing, of which they never tire. For my own part, I thought waltzing from ten at night until seven in the morning, a continual whirligig; most tiresome to the eye, and ear,—to say nothing of any worse consequences.

One evening, at one of these masquerades, a well-turned compliment was paid to the Emperor, by a gentleman who went in the character of Diogenes with his lantern, in search of a man. In going round the room he suddenly met the Emperor. He immediately made a low obeisance to

His Majesty, and, opening his lantern, extinguished the candle, saying, in a loud tone, 'Ho trovato l'uomo' (I have found the man); he then took his departure, and left the ball room. He was said to have been a courtier, but none of the courtiers would admit that he was.

Another favourite amusement, going forward at this period of the year, is a course des traineaux, or procession of sledges. These sledges are richly ornamented, and carved with figures of all kinds of monsters, and inlaid with burnished gold, &c. A vast number of carrettas and carts, on the day previous to this singular spectacle, gather snow, and distribute it along the principal streets of Vienna, in order that the sledges may be drawn with perfect security. The effect at night, by torch-light, is like enchantment. I have seen forty or fifty sledges drawn up, one behind the other; in every sledge was a lady seated, covered with diamonds, in furs and pelisses; behind each was a gentleman, as magnificently dressed, driving; before every sledge, were two running footmen, having long poles, with knobs of silver at their ends. The Hungarian Prince Dietressteen, the Grand Master of the Horse, was always the first to lead the traîneaux. The immense velocity with which these things are drawn is perfectly astonishing: they go on for three or four hours, and the procession, at its close, draws up before the Emperor's palace. The running footmen have costly liveries, and the horses are caparisoned with rich trappings, and large plumes of milk-white feathers, and the spectacle, upon the whole, is very magnificent.

I was quite charmed with my situation at Vienna; nothing could exceed the gaiety of that delightful place. I was fortunate enough to get introduced to the best society; my salary amply supplied my wants and wishes, and the public were kind and indulgent to me when I appeared on the stage. The kind countenance of Sir Robert Keith was not a little conducive in advancing me in the good opinion of the Directors of the theatre.

As the theatre was in the palace, the Emperor often honoured the rehearsals with his presence, and discoursed familiarly with the performers. He spoke Italian like a Tuscan, and was affable and condescending. He came almost every night to the opera, accompanied by his nephew, Francis, then a youth. He usually entered his box at the beginning of the piece, but if not there at the precise moment, the curtain was to be drawn up; he had given orders that he was never to be waited for. He was passionately fond of music, and a most excellent and accurate judge of it.

His mode of living was quite methodical. He got up every morning, winter and summer, at five o'clock, wrote in his *canceleria* (study) until nine, then took a cup of chocolate, and transacted business with his ministers till one. He was very partial to the *jeu de paume*, and a good player. He had a fine racket-court, and when not in it, he usually walked or rode from one till three: punctually at a quarter after three, his dinner was served; he almost always dined on one dish—boiled bacon, which the people, from his partiality to it, called kayser fleische, *i.e.* the Emperor's meat; sometimes he had a dish of Hungarian beef bouilli, with horse radish and vinegar, but rarely, if ever, any other: his beverage at dinner was water; and after dinner one goblet of Tokay wine. During dinner, he allowed only one servant to be in the room; and was never longer at the meal than half an hour.

At five, he usually walked in the corridor, near his dining room, and whilst there, was accessible to the complaints of the meanest of his subjects: he heard them with complaisance, and was ever ready to redress their grievances. He generally wore either a green or white uniform faced with red; nor did I ever see him that he was not continually putting chocolate drops, which he took from his waistcoat pocket, into his mouth. When he walked out, he took a number of golden sovereigns with him, and distributed them personally among the indigent. He was an enemy to pomp and parade, and avoided them as much as possible; indeed, hardly any private gentleman requires so little attendance as he did. He had a seat for his servant behind his carriage, and when he went abroad in it (which was hardly ever the case in the day time) he made him sit there. I was one day passing through one of the corridors of the palace, and came directly in contact with him; he had his great coat hanging on his arm: he stopped me, and asked me in Italian, if I did not think it was very hot; he told me that he felt the heat so oppressive that he had taken off his great coat, preferring to carry it on his arm.

To the Princesses Lichtenstein,[1] Schwartzenberg, Lokowitz, and the Countess Thoun, he was particularly partial, and often paid them evening visits, but always retired unattended to his carriage, which stood in the street, for he never allowed it to be driven into the court yards, where other carriages were waiting. His desire was, never to have any fuss made about him, or to give any trouble, which was all mighty amiable; but as there is, and ought to be, in all civilized countries, a marked and decisive distinction between the Sovereign and the subject, this did not appear particularly wise, even if it were not particularly affected; and of all prides, that is the most contemptible, which, as Southey says, 'apes humility.'

The present Emperor Francis, at the period of which I am writing, was as thin as possible. I do not think I ever saw so thin a youth; his uncle was very rigid with him, and made him enter the army, mount guard, clean his horse, and go through the duties of a common soldier, until he progressively rose to the rank of an officer.

The Emperor Joseph had a strange aversion from sitting for his portrait, although the greatest artists were anxious to have the honour of taking it. Pelegrini, the celebrated painter, solicited to be allowed the honour, but in vain.—The Emperor said to him, 'There can be no occasion for taking up your time and mine by my sitting to you; if you are anxious to have a likeness of *me*, draw the portrait of an ill-looking man, with a wide mouth and large nose, and then you will have a facsimile.' The reverse, however, was the fact; for his majesty had an intelligent countenance, a fine set of teeth, and when he laughed and showed them, was rather handsome than otherwise.

There was a wide difference between the habits of Joseph the Second, and those of his prime minister Prince Kaunitz, who was a most eccentric personage, but reckoned nevertheless a great statesman. He was said to be very proud of having made up the match between Louis XVI. and the unfortunate Marie Antoinette. For several months in the year he kept open house for all strangers, provided they had been presented to him by their respective ambassadors; he kept a splendid table, and those who were by their introduction entitled to dine with him, had only to send their names to his porter before ten o'clock in the morning. For my own part, I have wondered how he could get any persons to be his guests, so extraordinary was his mode of receiving them. He rose very late in the day, and made a point before dinner of taking a ride in his riding-house, which he never commenced until the whole of his company were assembled for dinner: after having deliberately ridden as long as he thought fit, he proceeded, without making any excuse, to make his toilette.

Though a very old man, he was very fond of adorning his person, and remarkably particular in having his hair well dressed, and *bien poudré*.—In order to accomplish this object, he had four valets with powder puffs, puffing away at him until his hair was powdered to his satisfaction, while he walked about his dressing room in a mask. Another of his eccentricities was, that at all times, when he had at his table ambassadors, foreigners, and ladies of the first distinction, he would, immediately after dinner, have all the apparatus for cleaning his teeth put down upon the table; literally tooth brushes, basons, &c.; and, without the least excuse to his company, would go through the whole process of cleaning his teeth; a ceremony which lasted for many minutes. It was justly said of him, that he first made his guests sick by making them wait so long for their dinner, and that after they had dined, he made them sick again by this filthy custom. But in every thing else he was a strict observer of etiquette, and piqued himself on it; thinking, with Lord Chesterfield, that etiquette was the characteristic excellence of good society.

The Italian operas were performed at Vienna only three times a week, the other four nights (including Sundays), were appropriated to German plays, which I made a point of attending, as there were two large boxes always kept for the Italian company, on one side of the theatre, and on the other, two for the German company. I have with delight seen there the great actor Schroëder, who was called the Garrick of Germany. His Sir Peter Teazle was an excellent performance, and his Lord Ogleby not inferior to King's, and, in my opinion, those two were the best representatives of the old eccentric nobleman I ever saw. Schroëder was also very great in King Lear: The scene where he asks after his fool was one of the most exquisite pieces of acting I ever beheld, and indeed, he was very great in most of Shakspeare's plays which had been translated into German.

His performance of Sir Benjamin Dove, in Cumberland's play of 'The Brothers', was also an exquisite piece of acting; as was the Captain Ironsides of Brockman, who was an excellent comedian, as well as tragedian. When Brockman went, by permission of the Emperor, to act for a limited period at Berlin, his performance of Hamlet was reckoned by the Prussians such a masterpiece, that there was a medallion struck of him in that character. He gave me one of them, which, I am sorry to say, I lost. All the cities in Germany wished to have this great performer, but he would not leave Vienna, though tempted by offers of great emolument, and would only occasionally go to Hamburgh; for, although that theatre could not pay half so well as many others, he preferred it beyond all the rest; and the reason which he gave me for this predilection was, that in Hamburgh he could get fresher herrings (in which he delighted) than in any other place.

He was a very studious man, but absent and indolent; indeed, proverbially so. To one trait of his indolence, I was myself a witness.

Shakspeare's Othello was brought out for the first time on a Saturday night; he personated the Moor, which part he did not wish to act, though, he said, he was delighted with it, because the trouble of blacking his face was to him accumulated horror; however, the Emperor issued his commands, and there was no appeal; he, of course, acted it, and so finely, that His Majesty commanded it to be repeated on the Sunday, announcing that he would again honour the performance with his presence. I had been engaged previously to dine with Brockman, on that day, with some other friends. We went accordingly, and to our great surprise, Brockman presided at table, with his face as black as it had been the night before. He excused his strange appearance by telling us that he had gone through so much fatigue and trouble in blacking his face for the Saturday's performance, that he would not wash it off, as, if he had done so, he should have had to undergo the same painful process on the following evening, rather than which, he had sat up all the preceding night in an arm-chair. This curious instance of innate laziness produced much laughter and surprise amongst us.

When my old and valued friend Charles Kemble went to Vienna, I gave him a letter of introduction to Brockman, and I am sure he will corroborate my encomia of his acting. Schroëder, who was an excellent dramatic writer, translated 'The Constant Couple' into German, and acted Alderman Smuggler himself, and Brockman played Sir Harry Wildair: this comedy had a great run. Schroëder told me, that he went to London for the purpose of seeing the School for Scandal, previously to translating it. He understood English perfectly, and spoke it with fluency. I was told by those whose judgment I could depend on, that his translations into German were very good. I was not sufficiently acquainted with the language to be a judge of their literary merits, but still I understood German quite enough to be delighted with the representations.

It was rather singular that Schroëder, while in England, never made himself known to any theatrical person. During the time he was in London, he went (as he told me) every night the School for Scandal was performed, and placed himself in the middle of the pit. He gave the most unqualified praise to the English actors, as being true to nature. He regretted not having had the good fortune to see Garrick; but he had a very fine picture of him, which he shewed me: it was the first I had ever seen of him, and I had not the good fortune to see the original; but the portrait certainly bore a great resemblance to the composer Salieri.

Schroëder produced a dramatic piece, of which I witnessed the first representation, called 'The Freemasons'. Great curiosity was excited by the title: there were, at that time, a number of Lodges in Vienna, and parties were formed to condemn the piece, should any thing transpire in the representation to ridicule the masonic ceremonies; but there was nothing in the piece which was not perfectly allowable and respectful to the craft. The most rigid mason could not find any thing to censure, for every thing was complimentary to their useful and respected society. The consequence was, the piece was received with rapturous applause, and represented for a number of nights.

Cumberland's West Indian was a favourite, and always received great applause; Schroëder was the representative of Major O'Flaherty.—I was well acquainted with the play from my childhood.—In Dublin, many times and oft, I had seen Ryder in the Major, Mrs. Sparkes in Charlotte Rusport, and the Prince of all Belcours—Lewis. I considered Lewis, in his line, a perfect actor; but, candidly speaking, I thought his best days were past before my friend, Frederick Reynolds, made him a dramatist. The Vienna Belcour was Langé,[1] esteemed the most perfect representative of the lover and gentleman on the German stage. He was a fine performer, and, like my friend and countryman, Pope, considered an excellent miniature painter, as well as an ornament to the stage. He spoke English very well, and had the reputation of being a good scholar. —His society was much courted.

How a Vienna audience could relish a national Irish character like O'Flaherty, was to me a matter of great surprise, as I never heard, *but once,* that the Irish brogue was translatable; to be sure, that was from pretty good authority.—I happened one morning to meet the Right Honourable John Philpot Curran in Pall Mall, and, in the course of conversation, he told me that he had been the night before to Drury Lane, to see the West Indian.—'Well,' said I, 'did you not think that my friend Jack Johnstone was an inimitable Major O'Flaherty?'—'Why, indeed,' said he, 'I thought it an able representation of the Irish gentleman, but not of the Irish brogue—our friend Jack Johnstone does not *give* us the brogue, Sir, he *translates* it.'

I told Mr. Curran that I was sorry to differ in opinion with such an excellent judge as his Honour, but that, through the earlier part of my life in Italy, Sicily, and Germany, I had associated with a number of Irish officers, and it appeared to me that nothing could be more like their manner than my friend's performance; indeed, I thought him unique, and suspected, that had his brogue been broader, it might have been unintelligible to an English audience.

Schroëder's representation of this part appeared, by the applause he received, and the laughter he produced, to delight his auditors. The Emperor Joseph was partial to his performance of it. Another favourite part of Schroëder's was Gradus, in Mrs. Cowley's 'Who's the Dupe?' That celebrated, and most excellent low comedian, Widman, the great pet of the good people of Vienna, acted Old Doiley, and convulsed the house with laughter. I knew him well; he was a singular character, and, like the celebrated Italian Harlequin at Paris, a prey to hypochrondriacal affection, always fancying, from one hour to another, he should *breathe his last,* and continually taking medicine to avert the impending calamity. In the characters of 'Corbachio' in the 'Comedy of the Fox', and the 'Tartuffe' of Molière, he was super-excellent.—He was one of the committee of five actors who were directors of the drama; the other four were Brockman, Langé, and the two brothers Stephani,[1] both excellent comedians in their line. The elder Stephani was reckoned a man of considerable literary talent. It was his province to read all the new pieces that were presented, and send his opinion of their merits to Prince Rosenberg, the Grand Chamberlain.

There was a law amongst the committee of five actors, that one of them, in full dress, bag, and sword, &c. should be in attendance during the performance every evening, to announce the entertainments of the following night, and make any appeal to the audience which might be necessary, always being one of the actors not otherwise concerned in the business of the evening. The leading female of the company was Madame Sacqui, considered as a rival in talent to the celebrated Clairon, so much praised by Garrick. Madame Sacqui was a fine woman, but I should think turned of forty when I saw her; she had a sweet countenance, and the rays of beauty still lingered about her. I have seen her with great delight in the 'Widow of Malabar.'[2]

There was a species of drama at that time much in vogue at Vienna, and indeed all over Germany, called a *Monologue*,[3] and which has since been occasionally introduced upon the English stage. The person who performs is accompanied between the different speeches by music, made to accord with the different passages of the recitation. Madame Sacqui performed 'Medea,' in 'Jason and Medea.'—Her representation of the part was truly terrific, and the music, the composition of the celebrated Bendar, sublime. Another Monologue, entitled 'Ariadne and

Theseus', was divinely acted by Mademoiselle Jacquet, the sister of the lovely Ademberger, of whom, it was said, that she united the elegance of the Graces with the talents of the Muses; nothing could be more affecting than her grief and despair when abandoned by Theseus. I never missed her representation of Ariadne, and each time I saw it, I fancied I discovered new beauties in it: the music of the piece, composed by Graun, the favourite composer of the King of Prussia, was very beautiful and appropriate.

Melpomene might well be proud of her two great followers, as might Thalia of the incomparable and matchless Madame Ademberger,[1] wife of a tenor singer who performed at the Opera House in London. She was called Nature's darling child. I never then had seen Mrs. Jordan; but Stephen Storace, who had just come to Vienna from London, had repeatedly seen her, and told me that Madame Ademberger was her very prototype in figure, voice, action, and genius. Her performance of Peggy, in the 'Country Girl', was a treat; and when I came to England, and saw Mrs. Jordan at Drury Lane in the same character, had I not been convinced that they never could have seen each other, I should have sworn that one of them copied the other, so great was their resemblance. Brockman's acting in 'Moody' was a masterpiece, and, strange to say, (for *they* neither could have seen each other,) very much in the style of King's representation of that part.

In the midst of my devotion to tragedy and comedy, I did not forget what I owed to music; and what more favourable opportunity could offer for evincing my devotion to the science of harmony than that which presented itself, of visiting the immortal Haydn. He was living at Eisenstadt, the palace of Prince Esterhazy, in whose service he was, and thither I determined to go and pay my respects to him; accordingly, accompanied by a friend of mine of the name of Brida, a young Tyrolese merchant, I set off post to fulfil my intentions.

I had the pleasure of spending three days with him, and received from him great hospitality and kindness. The Prince Esterhazy lived in regal splendour; his revenues are enormous, and His Highness spent his great fortune with munificence and noble liberality. He was particularly fond of music;—his band was formed of great professors;—Haydn was his maître de chapelle. There was at Eisenstadt, merely for the amusement of the Prince, his family, suite, and vassals, an Italian Opera, a German and a French theatre, and the finest Fantoccini[2] in Europe.

At this delightful place Haydn composed the greatest part of his immortal works. I saw and admired the different artists employed by the Prince, who unanimously gave His Highness an enviable character for generosity and exalted goodness. His vassals absolutely adored him.

The country about Eisenstadt is delightfully picturesque, abounding in wood and water, and all kinds of game. The Prince had the goodness to desire Haydn to take one of his carriages, that we might drive about and see all the beauties of this terrestrial paradise, for such I thought it. His Highness was very partial to shooting, hunting, and fishing.

We took our departure on the evening of the third day, delighted and flattered with the gracious kindness we had received, and with light hearts arrived at Vienna.

Upon my return, my servant informed me that a lady and gentleman had called upon me, who said they came from England, and requested to see me at their hotel. I called the next morning, and saw the gentleman, who said his name was Botterelli, that he was the Italian poet[1] of the King's Theatre in the Haymarket, and that his wife was an English woman, and a principal singer at Vauxhall, Ranelagh, the Pantheon, &c. Her object in visiting Vienna was to give a concert, to be heard by the Emperor; and if she gave that satisfaction, (which she had no doubt she would,) to accept of an engagement at the Royal Theatre; and he added, that she had letters for the first nobility in Vienna.

The lady came into the room; she was a very fine woman, and seemed sinking under the conscious load of her own attractions.—She really had powerful letters of recommendation. Prince Charles Lichtenstein granted her his protection; and there was such interest made for her, that the Emperor himself signified his Royal intention of honouring her concert with his presence. Every thing was done for her;—the orchestra and singers were engaged;—the concert began to a crowded house, but, I must premise we had no rehearsal.

At the end of the first act, the beauteous Syren, led into the orchestra by her caro sposo, placed herself just under the Emperor's box, the orchestra being on the stage. She requested me to accompany her song on the piano-forte.—I of course consented. Her air and manner spoke 'dignity and love.' The audience sat in mute and breathless expectation. The doubt was, whether she would melt into their ears in a fine cantabile, or burst upon them with a brilliant bravura. I struck the chords of the symphony—silence reigned—when, to the dismay and astonishment of the brilliant audience, she bawled out, without feeling or remorse, voice or time, or indeed one note in tune, the hunting song of 'Tally ho!'[2] in all its pure originality. She continued shrieking out Tally ho! tally ho! in a manner and tone so loud and dissonant, that they were enough to blow off the roof of the house. The audience jumped up terrified; some shrieked with alarm, some hissed, others hooted, and many joined in the unknown yell, in order to propitiate her. The Emperor called me to him, and asked me in Italian (what tally ho! meant?)—I replied I did not know, and literally, at that time, I did *not*.

His Majesty, the Emperor, finding, that even *I*, a native of Great Britain, either could not, or would not, explain the purport of the mysterious words, retired with great indignation from the theatre; and the major part of the audience, convinced by His Majesty's sudden retreat that they contained some horrible meaning, followed the Royal example. The ladies hid their faces with their fans, and mothers were heard in the lobbies cautioning their daughters on the way out, never to repeat the dreadful expression of 'tally ho,' nor venture to ask any of their friends for a translation of it.

The next day, when I saw the husband of 'tally ho,' he abused the taste of the people of Vienna, and said that the song, which they did not know how to appreciate, had been sung by the celebrated Mrs. Wrighton at Vauxhall, and was a great favourite all over England. Thus, however, ended the exhibition of English taste; and Signora Tally ho! with her Italian poet, went *hunting* elsewhere, and never returned to Vienna, at least during my residence.

I went one evening to a concert of the celebrated Kozeluch's, a great composer for the piano-forte, as well as a fine performer on that instrument. I saw there the composers Vanhall and Baron Dittersdorf; and, what was to me one of the greatest gratifications of my musical life, was there introduced to that prodigy of genius—Mozart. He favoured the company by performing fantasias and capriccios on the piano-forte. His feeling, the rapidity of his fingers, the great execution and strength of his left hand, particularly, and the apparent inspiration of his modulations, astounded me. After this splendid performance we sat down to supper, and I had the pleasure to be placed at table between him and his wife, Madame Constance Weber, a German lady of whom he was passionately fond, and by whom he had three children. He conversed with me a good deal about Thomas Linley, the first Mrs. Sheridan's brother, with whom he was intimate at Florence, and spoke of him with great affection. He said that Linley was a true genius, and he felt that, had he lived, he would have been one of the greatest ornaments of the musical world. After supper the young branches of our host had a dance, and Mozart joined them. Madame Mozart told me, that great as his genius was, he was an enthusiast in dancing, and often said that his taste lay in that art, rather than in music.

He was a remarkably small man, very thin and pale, with a profusion of fine fair hair, of which he was rather vain. He gave me a cordial invitation to his house, of which I availed myself, and passed a great part of my time there. He always received me with kindness and hospitality.—He was remarkably fond of punch, of which beverage I have seen him take copious draughts. He was also fond of billiards, and had an excellent billiard table in his house. Many and many a game have I played with him, but always came off second best. He gave Sunday concerts, at which I never was missing. He was kind-hearted, and always ready to oblige; but so very particular, when he played, that if the slightest noise were made, he instantly left off. He one day made me sit down to the piano, and gave credit to my first master, who had taught me to place my hand well on the instrument.—He conferred on me what I considered a high compliment. I had composed a little melody to Metastasio's canzonetta, 'Grazie agl' inganni tuoi',[1] which was a great favourite wherever I sang it. It was very simple, but had the good fortune to please Mozart. He took it and composed variations upon it, which were truly beautiful; and had the further kindness and condescension to play them wherever he had an opportunity. Thinking that the air thus rendered remarkable might be acceptable to some of my musical readers, I have subjoined it.

Encouraged by his flattering approbation, I attempted several little airs, which I shewed him, and which he kindly approved of; so much indeed, that I determined to devote myself to the study of counterpoint, and consulted with him, by whom I ought to be instructed.—He said, 'My good lad, you ask my advice, and I will give it you candidly; had you studied composition when you were at Naples, and when your mind was not devoted to other pursuits, you would perhaps have done wisely; but now that your profession of the stage must, and ought, to occupy all your attention, it would be an unwise measure to enter into a dry study. You may take my word for it, Nature has made you a melodist, and you would only disturb and perplex yourself. Reflect, "*a little knowledge* is a dangerous thing;"—should there be errors in what you write, you will find hundreds of musicians, in all parts of the world, capable of correcting them; therefore do not disturb your natural gift.'

The Poetry by METASTASIO. *The Melody composed by* MICHAEL KELLY, *and arranged by* MOZART, *with variations at* VIENNA *in the year* 1787.

GRAZIE AGL'INGANNI TUOI.

Published by Henry Colburn, London, July, 1825.

2.nd

Odi se Io Son Sincero
Ancor mi sembri Bella
Ma non mi sembri quella
Che paragon non ha'
E non ti offenda il vero
Nel tuo Leggiadro aspetto
Or Scopro alcun difetto
Che mi Parea Belta

Da Capo

Grazie agl'Ingann i tuoi &c.

3.rd

Io Lascio un incostante
Tu perdi un Cor Sincero
Non so di Noi primiero
Chi s'abbia a Consolar.
Un si fido amante
Non trovera Piu Nice
Che un altra Ingannatrice
E facile a Trovar

Da Capo

Grazie agl'Ingann i tuoi &c.

Eng.d by Sid.l Hall, Bury Str. Bloomsb.y for Kelly's Memoirs. Vol. I page 224

'Melody is the essence of music,' continued he; '*I* compare a good melodist to a fine racer,[1] and counterpointists to hack post-horses; therefore be advised, let *well alone*, and remember the old Italian proverb —"Chi sa più, meno sa—Who knows most, knows least".' The opinion of this great man made on me a lasting impression.

My friend Attwood (a worthy man, and an ornament to the musical world) was Mozart's favourite scholar,[2] and it gives me great pleasure to record what Mozart said to me about him; his words were, 'Attwood is a young man for whom I have a sincere affection and esteem; he conducts himself with great propriety, and I feel much pleasure in telling you, that he partakes more of my style than any scholar I ever had; and I predict, that he will prove a sound musician.' Mozart was very liberal in giving praise to those who deserved it; but felt a thorough contempt for insolent mediocrity. He was a member of the Philharmonic Society of Bologna and Verona; and when at Rome, the Pope conferred on him the Cross and Brevet of Knight of Lo Sprone[3] d'Oro.

At the time of which I am speaking, music was in the highest state of perfection at Vienna; for, independent of the great talents that were stationary, there was a number of the most celebrated artists passing from Italy to Poland, Prussia, and Russia, most of whom gave concerts at Vienna. The Emperor usually attended them, and amply rewarded the performers. The celebrated Marchesi came from Venice to Vienna, on his road to Petersburg, where he was engaged for the Italian opera. He gave a concert, and was honoured by the Emperor's presence, and a brilliant audience; he was a great singer, and in the prime of his abilities. During his stay at Vienna, he was on a visit to the Venetian Ambassador, who, in compliment to him, gave a grand dinner to the Italian performers, amongst whom, I had the honour of being invited;—the banquet was splendid. His Excellency was a great gourmand, and was a good deal ridiculed for his attention to the gastronomic art; he gave his cook five hundred zecchinos per annum, but he was rich, and had a right to please himself. For my own part, though not much of an epicure, I think a good cook an essential personage in an establishment, and in the end, an economical one; and there is no place, generally speaking, where the art of cookery is better understood than at Vienna.

During my stay, I had the pleasure of hearing two of the first performers on the violin, perhaps in the world; both gave concerts, and their performance was truly exquisite, although in different styles. The first was Giornovick, who was on his way from Russia to Paris, and had been many years first concerto player at the court of Petersburg. He was a man of a certain age, but in the full vigour of talent; his tone was very powerful, his execution most rapid, and his taste above all alluring. No performer, in my remembrance, played such pleasing music. He generally closed his concertos with a rondo, the subject of which was some popular Russian air, to which he composed variations with enchanting taste; his performance reminded me strongly of the celebrated La Motte, whom I had often heard at the Rotunda in Dublin.

Janewitz, the other, was a very young man, in the service of the King of Poland; he also touched the instrument with thrilling effect, and was an excellent leader of an orchestra. His concertos always finished with some pretty Polonaise air; his variations also were truly beautiful.

But the Apollo, the Orpheus of the age, was the redoubted and renowned Baron Bach, who came to Vienna to be heard by the Emperor. He (in his own conceit) surpassed Tartini, Nardini, &c. &c. This fanatico per la musica had just arrived from Petersburg, where he went to make his extraordinary talents known to the royal family and court. Now I have often heard this man play, and I positively declare, that his performance was as bad as any blind fiddler's at a wake in a country town in Ireland; but he was a man of immense fortune, and kept open house. In every city which he passed through, he gave grand dinners, to which all the musical professors were invited; at Vienna, myself among the rest. One day, having a mind to put his vanity to the test, I told him that he reminded me of the elder Cramer. He seemed rather disappointed than pleased with my praise—he acknowledged Cramer had some merit, that he had played with him out of the same book at Manheim, when Cramer was first violin at that court; but that the Elector said that *his* tone was far beyond Cramer's, for Cramer was tame and slothful, and *he* was all fire and spirit; and that, to make a comparison between them, would be to compare a dove to a game cock. In my life, I never knew any man who snuffed up the air of praise like this discordant idiot.

After he had been heard by the Emperor (who laughed heartily at him) he set off for London, in order that the King of England might have an opportunity of hearing his dulcet strains. When he had taken his departure, another violin player arrived from Russia, a Doctor Fisher, a most eccentric man, possessing some merit in his profession, but a bit of a quack, and an inordinate prattler; he related strange things of himself, and was particularly tenacious of his veracity. The harmonious Doctor, however, (who by the bye was a very ugly Christian) laid siege to poor

Nancy Storace; and by dint of perseverence with her, and drinking tea with her mother, prevailed upon her to take him for better for worse,[1] which she did in despite of the advice of all her friends; she had cause, however, in a short time to repent of her bargain, for instead of harmony, there was nothing but discord between them; and it was said he had a very striking way of enforcing his opinion, of which a friend of her's informed the Emperor, who intimated to him, that it would be fit for him to try a change of air, and so the Doctor was banished from Vienna.

Storace was the second wife of the discordant Doctor. His first wife was one of the daughters of Mr. Powell, the proprietor of Covent Garden Theatre. The Doctor had a sixteenth share of the Covent Garden Theatre property, in right of his wife; but was such an inordinate coxcomb, that the other proprietors had a great contempt for him and his opinion. I have heard Moody say that he came one evening into the green room when he was present, and abused an actress for having torn her petticoat; and when questioned by her as to his right to do so, he replied, with great pomposity,—'All the right in the world, Madam, I have to look after my property; for know, Madam, the sixteenth part of the petticoat which you have destroyed belongs to me, and is mine, to all intents and purposes.' When his wife died, he parted with his share, to the great joy of the other partners in the concern.*

10

The same year, 1784, the city of Vienna was honoured with the presence of His Royal Highness the Duke of York, then Bishop of Osnaburgh. On his entry into the city, he was received by the populace with acclamations, and welcomed by brilliant fêtes and rejoicings. The

* The first Mrs. Fisher had two sisters; the one married, first, Mr. Warren, an actor, and secondly, Mr. Martindale, who kept one of the club houses in St. James's Street, who also left her a widow: upon her death, she bequeathed her share of Covent Garden Theatre to Francis Const, Esq. the worthy and excellent chairman of the Middlesex and Westminster Sessions. The other married Mr. White, one of the clerks of the House of Commons, in right of whose daughters, (to whom they are married,) Mr. Willett and Captain Forbes of the navy, now hold each similar shares of Covent Garden Theatre to that which the veracious Doctor Fisher possessed by a similar tenure at the time to which I have just alluded, and have, of course, if they chose to exercise it, a similar right to the sixteenth part of every actress's petticoat at the present moment.

condescension and kindness, for which His Royal Highness ever has been distinguished, thus early gained him the hearts of all ranks of society: he was in his one and twentieth year, and allowed to be a model of manly beauty. I have seen him often walking in the streets of Vienna dressed in the Windsor uniform, with his hair platted behind, attended by one or two of his aides-de-camp, visiting the different shops, and conversing with the most amiable familiarity with the concourse of people that flocked around him. The Emperor paid him great and marked attention.

His Royal Highness's first visit to the theatre[1] attracted a crowded and brilliant assemblage. The Emperor, accompanied by his brother Maximilian, the Archbishop of Cologne, was present. A new opera, composed by Stephen Storace, was produced on the occasion; Signora Storace and myself had the two principal parts in it. In the middle of the first act, Storace all at once lost her voice, and could not utter a sound during the whole of the performance; this naturally threw a damp over the audience as well as the performers. The loss of the first female singer, who was a great and deserved favourite, was to the composer, her brother, a severe blow. I never shall forget her despair and disappointment, but she was not then prepared for the extent of her misfortune, for she did not recover her voice sufficiently to appear on the stage for five months.

As proof of the retentive memory of His Royal Highness, the circumstances of which I speak are now one and forty years old; and yet, His Royal Highness recollected, and repeated them to a friend of mine very recently. To have lived so long, in his Royal remembrance, is to me high honour and gratification.

During the continuance of Storace's illness, three operas were produced, in which Signora Cortellini, Madame Bernasconi, and Signora Laschi performed. The last of these operas was composed by Signor Rigini, and written by the poet of the theatre, the Abbé da Ponte, by birth a Venetian. It was said, that originally he was a Jew,—turned Christian,—dubbed himself an Abbé,—and became a great dramatic writer. In his opera, there was a character of an amorous eccentric poet, which was allotted to *me*; at the time I was esteemed a good mimic, and particularly happy in imitating the walk, countenance, and attitudes of those whom I wished to resemble. My friend, the poet, had a remarkably awkward gait, a habit of throwing himself (as he thought) into a graceful attitude, by putting his stock behind his back, and leaning on it; he had also, a very peculiar, rather dandyish, way of dressing; for, in sooth, the Abbé stood mighty well with himself, and had the character of a consummate coxcomb; he had also a strong lisp and broad Venetian dialect.

The first night of the performance, he was seated in the boxes, more conspicuously than was absolutely necessary, considering he was the author of the piece to be performed. As usual, on the first night of a new opera, the Emperor was present, and a numerous auditory. When I made my *entrée* as the amorous poet, dressed exactly like the Abbé in the boxes, imitating his walk, leaning on my stick, and aping his gestures and his lisp, there was a universal roar of laughter and applause; and after a buzz round the house, the eyes of the whole audience were turned to the place where he was seated. The Emperor enjoyed the joke, laughed heartily, and applauded frequently during the performance; the Abbé was not at all affronted, but took my imitation of him in good part, and ever after we were on the best terms. The opera was successful, had a run of many nights, and I established the reputation of a good mimic.

Storace had an opera put into rehearsal, the subject his own choice, Shakspeare's Comedy of Errors.* It was made operatical, and adapted for the Italian, by Da Ponte, with great ingenuity. He retained all the main incidents and characters of our immortal bard; it became the rage, and well it might, for the music of Storace was beyond description beautiful. I performed Antipholus of Ephesus, and a Signor Calvasi, Antipholus of Syracuse, and were both of the same height, and strove to render our persons as like each other as we could.

About the time of which I am now speaking, the celebrated poet, L'Abbate Casti, came from Italy to Vienna, on a visit to Prince Rosenberg. He was esteemed by the Literati, the severest satirist since the days of Aretin. The *Animali Parlanti,* for its wit and satire, will always be

* I often mentioned (after I came to England) to Mr. Sheridan, how much I thought introducing Storace's music into the Comedy of Errors would do for Drury Lane: he approved of it, and said he would give directions to have it done, but he never did. It is singular, that more than thirty-six years after I had suggested the idea, the proprietors of Covent Garden should bring the play forward as an opera; yet, had it been produced at Drury Lane at the time I mentioned it, my friend Prince Hoare would not have had in his excellent afterpiece, called 'No Song no Supper', the beautiful sestetto, 'Hope a distant joy disclosing', for that piece of music and the trio, 'Knocking at this time of day', were both in the Equivoci; or, Italian Comedy of Errors. The music used, where Antipholus seeks admittance into his house, and his wife calls the guard, was that fine chorus in the Pirates, 'Hark the guard is coming', and was certainly one of the most effective pieces of music ever heard. Both the songs sung by me in the Pirates,[1] at Drury Lane, I had sung at Vienna, in the same opera of the Equivoci: Storace certainly enriched his English pieces, but I lamented to see his beautiful Italian opera dismantled.

remembered. Just at the same period, the celebrated Paesiello arrived at Vienna, on his way to Naples, from Petersburg, where he had been some years, and amassed very great wealth. I had the pleasure of seeing him introduced to Mozart; it was gratifying to witness the satisfaction which they appeared to feel by becoming acquainted; the esteem which they had for each other was well known. The meeting took place at Mozart's house; I dined with them, and often afterwards enjoyed their society together.

The Emperor hearing that Casti and Paesiello were in Vienna, wished to have them presented to him on the first levee day; they were accordingly introduced to his Majesty by the Great Chamberlain. The compositions of Paesiello were always in high favour with the Emperor. His Majesty said to them, with his usual affability, 'I think I may say, I have now before me two of the greatest geniuses alive, and it would be most gratifying to me, to have an opera the joint production of both, performed at my theatre;' they of course obeyed the flattering command, and the greatest expectations were excited by the union of such talents.

One day, during the stay of Paesiello, I heard him relate an anecdote illustrative of the kindness of the Empress Catherine of Russia towards him. She was his scholar; and while he was accompanying her one bitter cold morning, he shuddered with the cold. Her Majesty perceiving it, took off a beautiful cloak which she had on, ornamented with clasps of brilliants of great value, and threw it over his shoulders. Another mark of esteem for him, she evinced by her reply to Marshal Beloselsky. The Marshal agitated, it is believed, by the 'green-eyed monster,' forgot himself so far as to give Paesiello a blow; Paesiello, who was a powerful athletic man, gave him a sound drubbing. In return, the Marshal laid his complaint before the Empress, and demanded from her Majesty the immediate dismissal of Paesiello from the court, for having had the audacity to return a blow upon a marshal of the Russian Empire. Catherine's reply was, 'I neither can nor will attend to your request; you forgot your dignity when you gave an unoffending man and a great artist a blow; are you surprised that he should have forgotten it too? and as to rank, it is in my power, Sir, to make fifty marshals, but not one Paesiello.'

I give the above anecdote as I heard it, although I confess it is rather a strange coincidence, that a similar circumstance should have occurred to Holbein, when a complaint was made against him to Henry VIII. by a Peer of Great Britain.

Casti was a remarkably quick writer; in a short time he finished his drama, entitled 'Il Re Teodoro'.[1] It was said, Joseph II. gave him the subject, and that it was intended as a satire upon the King of Sweden, but the fact I believe was never ascertained. The characters of the drama were Teodoro, Signor Mandini; Taddeo, the Venetian innkeeper, Bennuci; the sultan Achmet, Bussani; his sultana, Signora Laschi; Lisetta, daughter to the innkeeper, Signora Storace; and Sandrino, her lover, Signor Viganoni; all these performers were excellent in their way, and their characters strongly pourtrayed; but the most marked part, and on which the able Casti had bestowed the most pains, was that of Gafferio, the king's secretary. This character was written avowedly, as a satire on General Paoli, and drawn with a masterly hand. Casti declared, there was not a person in our company (not otherwise employed in the opera) capable of undertaking this part. It was decided, therefore, by the directors of the theatre, to send immediately to Venice, to engage Signor Blasi, at any price, to come and play it. This delayed us a little, and in the interim, Storace gave a quartet party to his friends. The players were tolerable; not one of them excelled on the instrument he played, but there was a little science among them, which I dare say will be acknowledged when I name them:

The First Violin	HAYDN.
„ Second Violin	BARON DITTERSDORF.
„ Violoncello	VANHALL.
„ Tenor	MOZART.[2]

The poet Casti and Paesiello formed part of the audience. I was there, and a greater treat or a more remarkable one cannot be imagined.

On the particular evening to which I am now specially referring, after the musical feast was over, we sat down to an excellent supper, and became joyous and lively in the extreme. After several songs had been sung, Storace, who was present, asked me to give them the Canzonetta. Now thereby hung a tale, new to the company! The truth was this:—There was an old miser of the name of Varesi living at Vienna, who absolutely denied himself the common necessaries of life, and who made up his meals by pilfering fruits and sweatmeats from the parties to which he was invited; the canzonetta for which Storace asked, he was particularly fond of singing with a tremulous voice, accompanied by extraordinary gestures, and a shake of the head; it was, in fact, this imitation which I was called upon to exhibit, and I did so. During my performance, I perceived Casti particularly attentive, and when I had finished, he turned to Paesiello, and said, 'This is the very fellow to act the character of Gafferio, in our opera; this boy shall be our old man! and if he keep old Varesi in his eye when he acts it, I will answer for his success.' The opera was brought out, the drama was excellent, and the music was acknowledged the *chef-d'œuvre* of Paesiello. Overflowing houses, for three successive seasons, bore testimony to its merits. I played the old man, and although really little more than a boy, never lost sight of the character I was personating for a moment.

After the first night's performance, his Majesty, the Emperor, was pleased to have it signified to me, through Prince Rosenberg, that he was so much surprised and pleased with my performance, that he had ordered an addition to my salary of one hundred zecchinos per annum, (about fifty pounds British,) which I ever after enjoyed, during my stay at Vienna: in short, wherever I went I was nicknamed Old Gafferio.

Paesiello was particularly kind to me, during his stay at Vienna, and was much diverted with my monkey antics. When at Naples, he wrote to me, to say that the king of Naples had commanded him to put the opera of 'Il Teodoro' in rehearsal, and wished me to ask the Emperor for six months leave of absence to go to Naples and perform in it; and I should have my journey paid, and a most ample remuneration given me. This offer, liberal as it was, for private reasons not worth recording, I refused. The song in Old Gafferio's part, which I may say was the lucky star of my professional career, strange as it may appear, I had the folly to refuse to sing, thinking it too trivial for me. I sent it back to Paesiello; he desired to see me—I went—and he played me the beautiful accompaniment for it which he had written, but which was not sent me, I having received only the voice part. When I was going away, this great man gave me a gentle admonition, not to judge of things rashly; a piece of advice not thrown away upon me.

The Emperor, this season, had a number of gala days, both at Vienna and at Schoënbrunn, the gardens of which very much resemble those of Hampton Court, but on a larger scale. There were several balls and fêtes given there, and fireworks of the most brilliant description, all open to the public. I remember one evening, seeing there Lord and Lady Buckley, Sir Robert Williams, Lord and Lady Granard, Colonel and Mrs. Doyle, and a great number of English nobility, who were then at Vienna, and whom I had the honour of meeting at Sir Robert Keith's, the English ambassador.

There were a number of fêtes also given at the Hantz Garden, which the people of Vienna frequented, particularly on Sundays: several of the alleys and walks are like those in Kensington Gardens. In the Gardens there was an excellent restaurant where dinner parties continually met; and the accommodations were excellent.

An event happened to me in returning to Vienna, from that place, which, at the time, made a terrific impression on me. There was a young nobleman at Vienna, whose name it would be improper to publish (though the transaction was perfectly notorious). The son of Prince P——, who had been governor of Gratz; five and twenty years of age, very affable and accomplished, although wild and dissipated. Remembering me at Gratz, he often called upon me at Vienna. He was a great musical amateur, and a constant attendant at the Italian Opera House. One morning, he called, and asked me to meet him at three o'clock at the Hantz garden, and dine with him there afterwards. I kept my appointment; we had an excellent *tête-à-tête* dinner, and passed an extremely pleasant day. It was in the summer season, and about nine o'clock we returned to Vienna in a hackney coach. As we were entering the Graben Street, the coach was stopped and surrounded by a crowd of police officers; both the doors were instantly opened, and the Count and myself dragged into the street. Mr. Wivse, lieutenant of police, came to me, and desired me not to be alarmed. 'Mr. O'Kelly,' said he, 'you have nothing to fear, but we have a warrent against your companion, Count P——, for forgery, to a large amount: you are at liberty to go where you please, but *he* must be taken to prison.'

They accordingly took him away, and I was not allowed to follow him. In a few days he was tried, and condemned to sweep the streets of Vienna. Often, as I have been walking, I have met this unfortunate man, with his head shaved, wearing a paper cap, and a jacket of coarse cloth, chained, with a large log tied to his leg, and a broom in his hand, actually sweeping the crossways with other felons.

Those unfortunate wretches, after they have swept the streets for a limited period, as an example, are chained in couples, and compelled to drag barges on the Danube. Every interest was made to save him; the Princess L——n, to whom he was nearly related, then in a most critical state of health, threw herself upon her knees before the Emperor, to procure his pardon; but his Majesty was inflexible, and said that, 'If he had a son who had been guilty of the same crime, he should undergo the same punishment.' This event made an awful impression on me, and it was long before my spirits recovered the shock.

Just after this startling event, the Italian company were ordered to prepare to follow his Majesty to his palace at Luxemburgh,[1] and to remain there for the summer months. The palace is only a few miles from Vienna, and nothing can be more magnificent; it is surrounded by forests full of all kinds of game; the park, gardens, and grounds, truly beautiful, and in the centre of a rich and luxuriant country. The theatre was very pretty, and very well attended; for all had their *entrée* to it gratis, including the surrounding peasantry.

Italian operas were performed three times, German plays twice, and German operas twice in each week. I passed the time here most delightfully. Every performer of the Italian opera had separate apartments allotted to him, and his breakfast was sent thither. There was a magnificent saloon, in which we all met at dinner. The table was plentifully and luxuriantly supplied, with every delicacy of the season; with wines of all descriptions, as well as all kinds of fruits, ices, &c.; and every night, after the spectacle, an excellent supper. In the mornings I had nothing to do (there were no rehearsals,) but to amuse myself. The Emperor and his court went often in chase of the Airone[2] bird—an amusement he was very partial to. Prince Dichtrestein, the Master of the Horse, was very friendly to Signora Storace, and did her the kindness to send her one of the court barouches to view the chase. I always accompanied her on these excursions.

One day, the Emperor rode up to our carriage on horseback, and asked us, if we were amused, and if he could do any thing for us. Storace, with her peculiar characteristic bluntness, said, 'Why, Sir, I am very thirsty, will your Majesty be so good as to order me a glass of water?'—The Emperor with his usual affability smiled, called to one of his attendants to grant the request, and the glass of water was brought.

I have another instance to record of the condescension and urbanity of the Emperor. He one day reviewed twenty thousand of his finest troops: it was a glorious sight, and one that I shall never forget. Signora Storace, her mother, Bennuci, and myself, were on the ground at six o'clock in our barouche. The Emperor, who had a very military appearance, was surrounded by his staff, and accompanied by his nephew and heir, Grand Marshals Prince De Ligne, Prince Charles Lichtenstein, Prince Schwartzenberg, Prince Lokowitz, &c. &c. Marshals Lacy's and Laudon's regiments were on the ground, as well as some fine Hungarian regiments and the Emperor's Hungarian and Polish Guards, who made a magnificent appearance. To me it was enchantment. Our barouche was within view of the Emperor; and he sent one of his Aides-de-camp to us, to order the carriage to be drawn up nearer to himself.

At the close of the review, he rode up to us, and said, 'Has not this been a fine sight? this place is my stage; here I am the first actor.' And when General O'Kavanagh's regiment passed before him, with their colonel at their head, he condescended to say to me, 'Look there, O'Kelly; look, there goes your countryman O'Kavanagh, and a fine old soldier he is!' I never spent a more delightful day than that, which never has been effaced from my recollection.

Three delicious months did we pass at Luxemburgh, living in luxury and pleasure; at the end of which the Emperor returned to Vienna, and we received orders to follow him.

The theatre was opened immediately after our arrival. I was situated in every respect to my heart's content, living a life of gaiety and pleasure, and, thanks to the kindness and patronage of Sir Robert Keith, mixed with the best English society. A Mr. Stratton, a native of Scotland, who was Secretary to the British Embassy, was also kindly attentive to me. At Sir Robert's, I often had the honour of meeting the young Polish Prince Poniatowski, then in the service of Joseph the Second; he was remarkable for his elegance of manner and riding, and great partiality to almost unmanageable horses. I received many marks of friendship from him; he entered subsequently into the service of Buonaparte, and was unfortunately drowned in fording a river.

At this period of my life I was rather vain, and very fond of fine clothes; indeed my greatest expense was the decoration of my precious person. I wore every evening, full dress embroidered coats, either gold, silver, or silk. I wore two watches (as was the custom of the country), and a diamond ring on each of my little fingers; thus decked out, I had not of course the least appearance of a Paddy. While sitting one evening in the Milan coffee house, reading the Vienna Gazette, two gentlemen entered, and seated themselves opposite to me to take their coffee. One of them said to the other, with a most implacable Irish brogue, 'Arrah, blood and thunder! *luke* at that fellow sitting opposite to us (meaning me); did you ever see such a jackdaw?'

'Really,' answered his companion (who I perceived was an Englishmen), 'the fellow does not seem to be on bad terms with himself.'

'Look at his long lace ruffles,' said my countryman; 'I suppose he wears ruffles, to mark his gentility.'

I continued reading my gazette; but when the critique upon my long lace ruffles was ended, I laid down the paper, and tucked them up under the cuffs of my coat, not looking at the gentlemen, or seeming to take any notice of them.

'But now do *luke*,' continued the persevering brogueneer; 'what a display he is making of his rings; I suppose he thinks he will dazzle our eyes a bit.'

Upon this, I deliberately took off my rings, and put them into my pocket; at the same time fixing a steady look at my critics, I told them, in English, that 'If there were any other part of my dress at all disagreeable to them, I should have the greatest pleasure in altering it in any way they might suggest.'

The Irishman (improbable as it may appear) blushed; and the Englishman said, 'He hoped I would not feel an offence, where none was meant.' I said, 'Certainly not;' and, to prove my sincerity, requested them to take part of a bowl of punch, and drink our Sovereign King George's health, and towards our better acquaintance; and thus, in despite of laced ruffles and diamond rings, we introduced ourselves to one another.

My Irish friend, I found, was a Doctor O'Rourke, from the county of Down, who had only the day before arrived from Prague, where he had been for many years a medical practitioner; and, in my new English acquaintance, I had the pleasure to find the eccentric Walking Stewart,[1] so named from having walked almost all over the world, and whose pedestrian exploits were universally spoken of.

After taking our punch, we separated, and agreed to meet and dine together the next day at the French house, kept by the famous Monsieur Villar, celebrated, though a Frenchman, for giving excellent beef steaks, and dressing them to perfection *à l'Anglaise*. Stewart, though a great oddity, was a well informed, accomplished man; a true lover of the arts and sciences, and of a most retentive memory. The last little walk he had taken was from Calais, through France, Italy, and the Tyrol, to Vienna, and in a few days he was going to extend it as far as Constantinople. He was partial to most things in England, except the climate; he said, 'Sir, I am perfectly of opinion with Addison, that, in nature, there is nothing more inconstant than the British climate, except the humour of its inhabitants.'

He was a great enthusiast about music, although not about beef steaks; for, of the most tender, and dressed in Monsieur Villar's best manner, he would not touch a morsel; he lived entirely upon vegetables: but my friend, the Irish Doctor, was in truth a beef-eater.

In a few days Stewart left us to take his sauntering walk to Constantinople, and I very much regretted the loss of his society; but as the doctor had come to reside at Vienna, we passed a good deal of our time together.

I had the pleasure, about this time, to be introduced to Monsieur Martini.[1] He was a very old man. His sister, nearly his own age, kept his house for him. She was reckoned a deep blue, and very well versed in all the arts and sciences. The great poet Metastasio had lived *sixty years* in her brother's house, upon the most friendly terms, and died in it. The colleges of Bologna and Pavia gave her the title of Dottoressa, and deputations came from both those places, with her diploma. When I was admitted to her conversaziones and musical parties, she was in the vale of years, yet still possessed the gaiety and vivacity of a girl, and was polite and affable to all. Mozart was an almost constant attendant at her parties, and I have heard him play duets on the piano-forte with her, of his own composition. She was a great favourite of his.

At one of her parties I had the pleasure to be introduced to Mrs. Piozzi, who, with her husband, was travelling on the Continent; there appeared to me a great similarity in the manners of these two gifted women, who conversed with all around them without pedantry or affectation. It was certainly an epoch, not to be forgotten, to have had the good fortune, on the same evening, to be in company with the favourites of Metastasio and Dr. Johnson, and last, not least, with Mozart himself.

There was a very excellent company of German singers at the Canatore Theatre; it was more spacious than the Imperial Court Theatre. The first female singer was Madame Lange, wife to the excellent comedian of that name, and sister to Madame Mozart. She was a wonderful favourite, and deservedly so; she had a greater extent of high notes[2] than any other singer I ever heard. The songs which Mozart composed for her in L'Enlèvement du Sérail, show what a compass of voice she had; her execution was most brilliant. Stephen Storace told me it was far beyond that of Bastardini, who was engaged to sing at the Pantheon in London, and who, for each night of her performance, of two songs, received one hundred guineas, an enormous sum at that time; and (comparatively speaking) more than two hundred at the present day.*

A number of foreign Princes, among whom were the Duc de Deux

* Storace was then a boy, studying music under his father, who gave him a bravura song of Bastardini's to copy. Storace was so astonished that fifty guineas should be paid for *singing a song,* that he counted the notes in it, and calculated the amount of each note at 4*s*. 10*d*. He valued one of the divisions running up and down at

Ponts, the Elector of Bavaria, &c., with great retinues, came to visit the Emperor, who, upon this occasion, signified his wish to have two grand serious operas, both the composition of Chevalier Gluck;—'L'Iphigenia in Tauride,' and 'L'Alceste,' produced under the direction of the composer; and gave orders that no expense should be spared to give them every effect.

Gluck was then living at Vienna, where he had retired, crowned with professional honours, and a splendid fortune, courted and caressed by all ranks, and in his seventy-fourth year.

L'Iphigenia was the first opera to be produced, and Gluck was to make his choice of the performers in it. Madame Bernasconi was one of the first serious singers of the day,—to her was appropriated the part of Iphigenia. The celebrated tenor, Ademberger, performed the part of Orestes, finely. To me was allotted the character of Pylades, which created no small envy among those performers who thought themselves better entitled to the part than myself, and perhaps they were right;—however, I had it, and also the high gratification of being instructed in the part by the composer himself.

One morning, after I had been singing with him, he said, 'Follow me up stairs, Sir, and I will introduce you to one, whom, all my life, I have made my study, and endeavoured to imitate.' I followed him into his bed-room, and, opposite to the head of the bed, saw a full-length picture of Handel,[1] in a rich frame. 'There, Sir,' said he, 'is the portrait of the inspired master of our art; when I open my eyes in the morning, I look upon him with reverential awe, and acknowledge him as such, and the highest praise is due to your country for having distinguished and cherished his gigantic genius.'

L'Iphigenia was soon put into rehearsal, and a corps de ballet engaged for the incidental dances belonging to the piece. The ballet master was Monsieur De Camp, the uncle of that excellent actress, and accomplished and deserving woman, Mrs. Charles Kemble. Gluck superintended the rehearsals, with his powdered wig, and gold-headed cane; the orchestra and choruses were augmented, and all the parts were well filled.

The second opera was Alceste, which was got up with magnificence and splendour, worthy an Imperial Court.

For describing the strongest passions in music, and proving grand dramatic effect, in my opinion, no man ever equalled Gluck—he was a

£.18 11*s*. It was a whimsical thing for a boy to do, but perfectly in character; his passion for calculation was beyond all belief, except to those who witnessed it.

great painter of music; perhaps the expression is far fetched, and may not be allowable, but I speak from my own feelings, and the sensation his descriptive music always produced on me. For example, I never could hear, without tears, the dream of Orestes, in Iphigenia: when in sleep, he prays the gods to give a ray of peace to the parricide Orestes. What can be more expressive of deep and dark despair?—And the fine chorus of the demons who surround his couch, with the ghost of his mother, produced in me a feeling of horror, mixed with delight.

Dr. Burney (no mean authority) said, Gluck was the Michael Angelo of living composers, and called him the simplifying musician. Salieri told me that a comic opera of Gluck's being performed at the Elector Palatine's theatre, at Schwetzingen, his Electoral Highness was struck with the music, and inquired who had composed it; on being informed that he was an honest German who loved *old wine,* his Highness immediately ordered him a tun of Hock.

Paesiello's Barbiere di Siviglia, which he composed in Russia, and brought with him to Vienna, was got up; Signor Mandini and I played the part of Count Almaviva alternately; Storace was the Rosina. There were three operas now on the tapis, one by Rigini, another by Salieri (the Grotto of Trophonius), and one by Mozart, by special command of the Emperor. Mozart chose to have Beaumarchais' French comedy, 'Le Mariage de Figaro', made into an Italian opera, which was done with great ability, by Da Ponte. These three pieces were nearly ready for representation at the same time, and each composer claimed the right of producing his opera for the first. The contest raised much discord, and parties were formed. The characters of the three men were all very different. Mozart was as touchy as gun-powder, and swore he would put the score of his opera into the fire if it was not produced first; his claim was backed by a strong party: on the contrary, Rigini was working like a mole in the dark to get precedence.

The third candidate was Maestro di Cappella to the court, a clever shrewd man, possessed of what Bacon called, crooked wisdom; and his claims were backed by three of the principal performers, who formed a cabal not easily put down. Every one of the opera company took part in the contest. I alone was a stickler for Mozart, and naturally enough, for he had a claim on my warmest wishes, from my adoration of his powerful genius, and the debt of gratitude I owed him, for many personal favours.

II

The mighty contest was put an end to by His Majesty issuing a mandate for Mozart's 'Nozze di Figaro', to be instantly put into rehearsal; and none more than Michael O'Kelly, enjoyed the little great man's triumph over his rivals.

Of all the performers in this opera at that time, but one survives—myself. It was allowed that never was opera stronger cast. I have seen it performed at different periods in other countries, and well too, but no more to compare with its original performance than light is to darkness. All the original performers had the advantage of the instruction of the composer, who transfused into their minds his inspired meaning. I never shall forget his little animated countenance, when lighted up with the glowing rays of genius;—it is as impossible to describe it, as it would be to paint sun-beams.

I called on him one evening; he said to me, 'I have just finished a little duet for my opera, you shall hear it.' He sat down to the piano, and we sang it. I was delighted with it, and the musical world will give me credit for being so, when I mention the duet, sung by Count Almaviva and Susan, 'Crudel perchè finora farmi languire così.' A more delicious morceau never was penned by man, and it has often been a source of pleasure to me to have been the first who heard it, and to have sung it with its greatly gifted composer. I remember at the first rehearsal of the full band, Mozart was on the stage with his crimson pelisse and gold-laced cocked hat, giving the time of the music to the orchestra. Figaro's song, 'Non più andrai, farfallone amoroso', Bennuci gave, with the greatest animation, and power of voice.

I was standing close to Mozart, who, *sotto voce*, was repeating, Bravo! Bravo! Bennuci; and when Bennuci came to the fine passage, 'Cherubino, alla vittoria, alla gloria militar', which he gave out with Stentorian lungs, the effect was electricity itself, for the whole of the performers on the stage, and those in the orchestra, as if actuated by one feeling of delight, vociferated Bravo! Bravo! Maestro. Viva, viva, grande Mozart. Those in the orchestra I thought would never have ceased applauding, by beating the bows of their violins against the music desks. The little man acknowledged, by repeated obeisances, his thanks for the distinguished mark of enthusiastic applause bestowed upon him.

The same meed of approbation was given to the finale at the end of the first act;[1] that piece of music alone, in my humble opinion, if he had never composed any thing else good, would have stamped him as the greatest master of his art. In the sestetto, in the second act, (which was Mozart's favourite piece of the whole opera,) I had a very conspicuous part, as the Stuttering Judge. All through the piece I was to stutter; but in the sestetto, Mozart requested I would not, for if I did, I should spoil his music. I told him, that although it might appear very presumptuous in a lad like me to differ with him on this point, I did; and was sure, the way in which I intended to introduce the stuttering, would not interfere with the other parts, but produce an effect; besides, it certainly was not in nature, that I should stutter all through the part, and when I came to the sestetto speak plain; and after that piece of music was over, return to stuttering; and, I added, (apologizing at the same time, for my apparent want of deference and respect in placing my opinion in opposition to that of the great Mozart,) that unless I was allowed to perform the part as I wished, I would not perform it at all.

Mozart at last consented that I should have my own way, but doubted the success of the experiment. Crowded houses proved that nothing ever on the stage produced a more powerful effect; the audience were convulsed with laughter, in which Mozart himself joined. The Emperor repeatedly cried out Bravo! and the piece was loudly applauded and encored. When the opera was over, Mozart came on the stage to me, and shaking me by both hands, said, 'Bravo! young man, I feel obliged to you; and acknowledge you to have been in the right, and myself in the wrong.' There was certainly a risk run, but I felt within myself I could give the effect I wished, and the event proved that I was not mistaken.

I have seen the opera in London, and elsewhere, and never saw the judge pourtrayed as a stutterer, and the scene was often totally omitted. I played it as a stupid old man, though at the time I was a beardless stripling. At the end of the opera, I thought the audience would never have done applauding and calling for Mozart; almost every piece was encored, which prolonged it nearly to the length of two operas, and induced the Emperor to issue an order on the second representation, that no piece of music should be encored. Never was any thing more complete, than the triumph of Mozart, and his 'Nozze de Figaro', to which numerous overflowing audiences bore witness.*

* I was not aware at that time of what I have since found to be the fact, that those who labour under the defect of stuttering while speaking, articulate distinctly in singing. That excellent bass, Sedgwick, was an instance of it; and the beautiful Mrs. Inchbald, the authoress, another.

One morning while we were rehearsing in the grand saloon of the palace, His Majesty, accompanied by Prince Rosenberg, entered the saloon, and addressing himself to Storace, Mandini, and Bennuci, said, 'I dare say, you are all pleased, that I have desired there shall be no more encores; to have your songs so often repeated, must be a great fatigue, and very distressing to you.' Storace replied, 'It is indeed, Sir, very distressing, very much so;' the other two bowed, as if they were of the same opinion. I was close to His Majesty, and said boldly to him, 'Do not believe them, Sire, they all like to be encored, at least I am sure I always do.' His Majesty laughed, and I believe he thought there was more truth in my assertion, than in theirs. I am sure there was.

In the midst of all this gaiety and splendour, I received a letter from my father in Dublin, stating, that my mother was in a declining state of health, and that it was her earnest wish, that I should return to Dublin, if only for a few months; at the same time I got a letter from Mr. Linley, to say, that he and Mr. Sheridan would be very happy to treat with me for Drury Lane Theatre; that Stephen Storace would be soon at Vienna, and that he would have a *carte blanche* to close an engagement with me, on their parts. I confess, I had a great desire to see my mother; but for the present it was out of the question, as it was the very height of the season.

In the summer, the Emperor went to Luxemburgh, and I, with the other performers of the Italian opera, was of course obliged to follow: we remained there three months, in the usual enjoyment of every thing pleasant and luxurious; nothing of any particular interest occurred, and at the close of the summer, we again returned to our post at Vienna.

In the spring of 1787,[1] there was a great number of English at Vienna; amongst whom, were Lord Belgrave, now the Earl of Grosvenor, with his tutor, Mr. Gifford, one of the greatest ornaments of the literary world; Lord Bernard, now Earl of Darlington; Lord Dungarvan, now Earl of Cork; Lord de Clifford; Lord Carberry; Earl of Crawford; Sir John Sebright; Colonel Lennox; Mr. Dawkins; Mr. John Spencer; and many other fashionables; who were all young and full of vivacity—perhaps rather too lively to suit the temper of the phlegmatic Germans, who never heard of such a thing among themselves as a row; but at this period, they were initiated. The English noblemen and Gentlemen formed themselves into a club, took a house in the Graben Street, and generally dined together. I had often the honour of dining with them, and will venture to say, there were more corks drawn at one of their dinners, than during the same day all over Germany. There was another place frequented by many of them after the opera was over, which was neither more nor less than a grocer's shop in the same Street. This grocer was supposed to have the finest champagne and hock in the country; I was his constant visitor. Behind the shop was a room, where he admitted a chosen few, but it was not open to the public. There we always found excellent Parmesan cheese, anchovies, olives, and oysters. No table cloth was allowed, but each person had a large piece of brown paper presented to him by way of napkin.

I wish I had now in my cellar the excellent wines I have seen, during my sojourn at Vienna, drank in that room. Every thing was good except the oysters, which were somewhat of the stalest; none could be procured nearer than Trieste, which was so far from Vienna, that they never arrived sweet;—but the Germans liked them just as well when stale.

I heard an anecdote, which I was assured was authentic, of King George the First, touching oysters. When His Majesty went from Hanover to England, the Royal Purveyor having heard that the King was very fond of oysters, had a dish put down every day; of course, they were the finest that could be procured, but the King did not like them. This being mentioned to one of the pages who went over with him from Hanover, he told the Purveyor that the King did not find the same *relishing taste* in the English oysters, which he admired so much in those which he had in Hanover.—'Endeavour,' said the courtier, 'to get His Majesty some that are stale, and you will find he will like them.'—The experiment was tried, and actually succeeded, for His Majesty constantly ate them, and said they were delicious.

Several of the English gentlemen wished to introduce horse-racing. The Emperor kindly consented to their having any piece of ground near Vienna that they chose; and they fixed upon a spot in the Prater. They were to ride their own matches. I perfectly recollect that the Earl of Darlington, Earl Grosvenor, Lord Carberry, Lord de Clifford, and Sir John Sebright, &c. were the riders. It was quite a novel spectacle to the good people of Vienna,—and gentle and simple, high and low, crowded to the Prater to see my Lord Anglais turned jockey. The people seemed enchanted. The Emperor ordered his Polish Guards to keep the ground, that the riders might meet with no interruption; every thing was order and regularity, and the day passed off, to the content and enjoyment of all parties.

Stephen Storace at length arrived at Vienna from England,[1] and brought with him an engagement for his sister, from Gallini, the manager of the Opera House in London, as prima donna for the comic opera. Her engagement at Vienna was to finish after the ensuing carnival, and she accepted it; and I wished much to accompany her, and go to Dublin to see my family. I procured an audience of the Emperor at Schoënbrunn. I found him with half-a-dozen General Officers, among whom were Generals O'Donnell and Kavanagh, my gallant countrymen; the latter said something to me in Irish, which I did not understand, consequently, made him no answer. The Emperor turned quickly on me, and said, 'What, O'Kelly, don't you speak the language of your own country?'—I replied, 'Please your Majesty, none but the lower orders of Irish people speak Irish.' The Emperor laughed loudly. The impropriety of the remark, made before two Milesian[1] Generals, in an instant flashed into my mind, and I could have bit my tongue off. They luckily did not, or pretended not to hear my unintentionally rude observation,—it was, it must be confessed, a most unlucky *impromptu.*

I told His Majesty that I came to implore, after the approaching Carnival, His Royal leave of absence, to go and see my mother, in Dublin, for six months. He replied, 'Six months will not be sufficient, take twelve, and your salary shall be continued for that period;—I will give the necessary orders to Prince Rosenberg.' I asked permission to perform in London for a few nights, if I found it my interest to do so. 'Certainly,' he replied, 'you are right to make the best use of your time and talents; accept of any engagement that may be conducive to your interest, and if you do not better yourself, come back to my theatre, and you shall be received.' He further condescended to ask me how I intended travelling, and pointed out the best roads and accommodations between Vienna and Paris. I had the honour of kissing his hand, and returned to Vienna.

I remember that night a singular incident occurred to me.—At the Ridotto Rooms, there was some play going forward. I never, in the course of my life, had been addicted to that fashionable amusement, but, on that unlucky evening, rebellion lay in my way, and I found it. I lost forty zecchinos to a gallant English Colonel; I had only twenty about me, which I paid, and promised to pay the other twenty in the course of the week. I went home to bed, repenting of my folly.

In the morning, Nancy Storace called on me,—'So, Sir,' said she, 'I hear you were gambling last night, and not only lost all the money you had about you, but are still in debt—such debts ought not to be left unsatisfied a moment; you may one day or other go to England, and, should the transaction of your playing for more money than you possessed become known among Englishmen, it might give you a character which I know you do not deserve;—it must be settled directly.' She instantly produced the money, and made me go and discharge the obligation. Such an act of well-timed disinterested friendship was noble, and never has been forgotten by me.

About two months after this, an unlucky circumstance happened to me, which might have marred all my future prospects in life. A young Bohemian officer, of high rank in the Imperial service, chose to take it into his head that I had supplanted him in the affections of the Countess of S——. Though I assured him to the contrary, he did every thing in his power to degrade and injure me. He condescended to have me watched, go where I would;—and even bribed my own servant to betray my secrets. Heedless of menaces and threats, however, I went my own way.

One night, after having played the part of the Cavalier, in Paesiello's opera of 'La Frascatana', I slipped off my coat, keeping on the rest of my theatrical dress, threw my pelisse over me, and went to supper at the house of a friend. The opera finished at a later hour than usual, and the entertainment at my friend's house was prolonged till between four and five in the morning. At the time I set out to return, it was rather dark, but I could perceive two men following me; when I was turning round the Italian Street, they came behind me, and pushed me against a wall. They were muffled up in cloaks;—in one of them I recognised Count U——, and in the other, his companion, Baron S——, an officer in the same regiment. I asked them to let me pass, in the Emperor's name, in whose service I was, as well as themselves. The reply was, 'No, scoundrel! until you confess the justice of my suspicions, you shall not escape me with life.' I firmly persisted in not having the slightest knowledge of the lady in question. The Baron said, 'You lie, you rascal,' and struck me in the face. On receiving the blow, I returned it with such force, as made my opponent reel backwards from me. Finding myself at liberty, I seized the opportunity, and took to my heels, thinking my life was only to be saved by flight.

I had not ran far, before I was met by the police, who patrolled the streets every night; who, presenting their swords to my breast, commanded me to stop,—while my pursuers were close at my heels, ready to cut me down with their sabres. These two gallant officers represented me to the police as a robber; and the guardians of the night were in the act of dragging me to the guard-house, but, in doing so, they pulled open my pelisse, and saw the richly embroidered dress in which I had been acting. I had my two watches in my pocket, and my diamond rings on my fingers. On perceiving these, one of the policemen said to the other,—'This cannot be a thief.'—I informed them that I was a singer belonging to the Court, and requested them to conduct me to my lodgings, where they would find that I was telling them the truth. I wished, from principles of delicacy, to compromise the affair, in which the reputation of an individual was concerned; but my heroic opponents, (who still followed me,) swore they would be the first to publish the whole transaction, and though I had escaped them now, revenge they would have some other time, and that then I should bite the dust. I told them that, 'finding they were dead to all sense of honour, I should prevent all their attacks as assassins; but I was perfectly ready, notwithstanding their cowardly conduct, to meet them as men.' Full of bluster and threats, they took their departure, and the police conducted me in safety to my apartments, for which I amply rewarded them.

The first visit I had, on the following day, was from my friend Dr. O'Rourke, who informed me that he was told of the whole transaction the night before at the Military Coffee-house, and that, before four and twenty hours elapsed, my life would atone for my conduct. The Doctor begged me, by all means, to wait upon my kind friend and patron, Marshal Lacy; upon Prince Charles Lichtenstein, Governor of Vienna. Those exalted persons advised me, by all means, to lay the whole transaction before the Emperor; and Prince Lichtenstein promised he would prepare His Majesty for the recital.

As the Emperor was free of access to all, I sought an audience, and was honoured with the following gracious reception:—'So, O'Kelly,' said His Majesty, 'I hear that a disagreeable circumstance befel you last night. Prince Lichtenstein has told me all about it. I do not wish to hear any thing about the lady, keep that in your own breast, and, upon that point, you have acted as a man of honour; I only want to know from yourself how the quarrel began with my officers.'

I related the whole of the circumstances as they occurred, except one. The Emperor assured me I should have full satisfaction, and gave directions for the two heroes to be sent for. They were brought before him, and he inquired of them how they had dared to violate the laws. The Count said that I was the aggressor, by standing in the way of his pretensions to a lady for whom he had conceived an affection, which, but for such interference, would, in all probability, be returned.

The Emperor, to the best of my recollection, made the following remarks, verbatim:—'So, Sir, because you love a lady, to whom you are indifferent, you think you are justified in behaving ill to those on whom she chooses to bestow her attentions;—my laws, Sir, are not to be sacrificed to your malice, nor is the honour of my army to be sullied by any man who chooses to act in a manner unworthy of his rank. The duty of my officers is not only to keep peace themselves, but to preserve it inviolate against the attempts of others. What you both have done will justly stigmatize you in the eyes of the whole army. On my highway you attacked this young man, whose life you had meanly sought, at a moment when he was unarmed, and with odds, which baffled his making resistance.'

They attempted to justify their conduct, by observing, that they should degrade their birth and rank in society, by suffering themselves to be imposed on by a player, whom they considered so much beneath them. The Emperor said, 'The player whom you affect to despise is a man of honour; but, as for you, you have acted like assassins, and, from this moment, I consider you unworthy to continue in my service; I shall therefore give orders for removing you from the army.' The next day they were publicly degraded.

The whole of the above, nearly as I have written it, was inserted in all the public prints, and circulated throughout Germany.

I had the pleasure to hear from all quarters that the Emperor's decision was hailed as an act of justice; and the first night I afterwards appeared on the stage, I was received with repeated plaudits, which implied, I flattered myself, that the audience generally approved of my conduct.

The Carnival was now fast approaching. I informed Stephen Storace of the leave of absence I had obtained from the Emperor, and that I would accompany him and his sister, and mother, to London, at the close of the festival, and that he might let the proprietors of Drury Lane know, that I should be ready to try my fortune at their theatre about the beginning of April, but that I would not stipulate for any fixed terms;—those, I told him, I would arrange upon my arrival in London, and I had no doubt but we should agree.

The Carnival was kept with more than common splendour. Vienna was crowded with foreigners of all nations, and a number of British, in addition to those I made mention of. The ridotto balls were fully attended, and all was revelry and pleasure. The English were particularly respected and beloved—but, alas! there were some half-dozen amongst them (who shall be nameless) who occasionally sacrificed to the jolly god, and, when heated with wine, would sally out into the street, and shew a great inclination to encourage the trade of *lamp-mending*, which, one night, they did so effectually, that they did not leave a lamp unbroken in the Graben-street, or the street adjoining.

The art of lamp-smashing was not understood by the unaccomplished young men of Vienna, and great was their wonder and dismay that they should have lived so long in a state of ignorance; but the police, not wishing to have the science cultivated amongst their countrymen, intimated to the professors of the novel art that they must pay for what they had demolished, or, upon a repetition of their valorous exploits, they should be sent to prison.

I was very sorry that the affair happened, although not more than half-a-dozen were concerned in it, for, with this exception, no set of gentlemen could have conducted themselves with greater propriety. It was understood, however, that the Emperor was very much displeased, and had given orders, that the first person found committing any breach of the peace, should be put into confinement.

Four days before my departure for England, a little *contre-temps* had nearly broken up our travelling arrangements. We were supping at the Ridotto Rooms, and my poor friend, Stephen Storace, who was proverbially a sober man, and who had a strong head for every thing but drinking, had swallowed potent libations of sparkling Champagne, which rendered him rather confused. He went into the ball-room, and saw his sister dancing with an officer in uniform, booted and spurred. In twirling round while waltzing, his spurs got entangled in Storace's dress, and both she and the officer came to the ground, to the great amusement of the by-standers. Stephen, thinking his sister had been intentionally insulted, commenced personal hostilities against the officer: a great bustle ensued, which was ended by half-a-dozen policemen seizing Storace, and dragging him to the Guard-house, to which several English gentlemen followed him. The officer of the guard was very good-natured, and allowed us to send for some eatables and Champagne;—we remained with him all night, and a jovial night we had. In the morning we departed, but Storace was obliged to tarry in durance vile till further orders. He was not, however, the least discomfited; he thought of the Italian proverb, as he told me,—

'Non anderà sempre così; come diceva

Il piccolo cane, quando menava
Il rosto, alla fine la carne sarà cuccitta.'[1]

I was determined to make a bold push to get him released in the evening.—I placed myself in the corridor through which the Emperor passed after his dinner, to his study. He saw me, and said, 'Why, O'Kelly, I thought you were off for England?'—'I can't go, Sire,' was my answer; 'my friend, who was to travel with me, was last night put into prison.' I then told His Majesty who it was, and how it happened.—He laughed at the tipsy composer's wanting to fight, and said, 'I am very sorry for Storace, for he is a man of great talent; but I regret to observe that some of your English gentry who travel, appear much altered from what they used to be. Formerly, they travelled after they had quitted College,—it appears to me that now they travel before they go to it.' His Majesty then left me, saying, 'Bon voyage, O'Kelly,—I shall give directions that Storace may be set at liberty.'

The next morning he was liberated. I waited upon my kind patron Sir Robert Keith; Marshals Lacy and Laudon, and all those friends who had honoured me with their hospitality and protection. I went to take leave of the immortal Mozart, and his charming wife and family; he gave me a letter to his father, Leopold Mozart, who was at the Court of Saltzbourg. I could hardly tear myself away from him, and, at parting, we both shed tears. Indeed, the memory of the many happy days which I passed at Vienna will never be effaced from my mind.

In the first week of February 1787, I quitted it with a heart full of grief and gratitude. Storace, her mother, her brother, Attwood, and myself, not forgetting Signora Storace's lap-dog, filled the travelling carriage, and with four horses we started for England Ho!

12

Were I to recount the *désagrémens* of a German journey, my task would be endless. I shall therefore content myself with mentioning the different places at which we stopped: the first, worthy of observation, was Saltzbourg, which would be celebrated, if for nothing else, as the birth-place of Mozart, who was born there in the year 1756. As I viewed its lofty spires from a distance, I felt a kind of reverential awe. The morning after our arrival, escorted by a *lacquais de place*, I waited upon Mozart's father, and delivered his son's letter.[1] I found him a pleasing intelligent little man; he called upon Signora Storace, and offered to be our guide to every thing worth noticing; he was, as I have before mentioned, in the service of the reigning Sovereign, the Archbishop, who was passionately fond of music, and a distinguished amateur; he had also in his service, Michael Haydn, brother of the celebrated Haydn, who was by many competent judges reckoned even superior to his brother in the composition of church music. Saltzbourg is well built: the Archbishop's palace is positively magnificent; in the area before it is a fountain, esteemed the largest in Germany.

I was taken to see another palace, belonging to the Archbishop, called Mirabella, where there is a beautiful garden; we were told that twenty thousand oranges were annually gathered from the trees in his Holiness's orangery. The riding-school is a noble structure; the Archbishop was said to be particularly fond of horses; his stud, at the time I speak of, consisted of two hundred; his income was calculated at half a million sterling. The cathedral is a superb building: the inhabitants of the city have a most whimsical custom (I mean those who have the means of satisfying their caprice); when in good health and spirits they fix on their future burial-places, and having selected snug and suitable spots, have their portraits painted, and placed over their graves; to me it seemed as if this absurdity could not be surpassed.

The Archbishop sent one of his attendants to invite Signora Storace and her party to hear a concert at his palace; we felt ourselves highly honoured, and, of course, went. The Archbishop was a very fine-looking man, particularly gallant and attentive to the ladies, of whom there was a splendid shew; it was conceived that he was very partial to the English, and English manners. The music was chiefly instrumental, admirably performed; the band numerous and excellent.

After the concert we returned to supper at our inn, and after supper got into our carriage to continue our journey; but of all the roads I ever travelled, the Archbishop's was the worst; I was jolted to a jelly, and so irritated, that when we got to the barrier, and were stopped to have our passports examined, I said to the centinel, 'Comrade, it would be much better if your Archbishop, instead of spending so much money upon music, would appropriate part of it to mending his ways.' This ill-timed observation, which I confess was rather ungracious on my part, did not seem to please the centinel; however, he let us pass, merely muttering, that the English had more money than manners. Stephen Storace, in a well-timed moment, slipped a florin into his hand, which soothed the Cerberus, and made me think with Macheath, that 'money, well-timed, and properly applied, will do any thing.'

Nothing can exceed the beauty of the country between Saltzbourg and Munich; it is rich by nature, and highly cultivated. We arrived in due time at Munich, the capital of the Electorate of Bavaria, and put up at the best inn, where I had the pleasure to find Lord Bernard stopping, on his way to England. I had been gratified by meeting his Lordship at Vienna, where his affability and elegance of manner had gained him the esteem and respect of those who had the honour of his acquaintance. As all our party were known to his Lordship, he invited us to dine with him; he had an English landau, and travelled with one servant only. As he, like ourselves, was going to Paris, he proposed that we should all travel together, and that he would give a seat in his carriage to one of us, 'turn and turn about,' as the phrase goes; we were flattered by the proposal, and accepted it.

We agreed to remain at Munich three or four days to see the lions. We went over the Elector's palace, a magnificent building, consisting of several galleries, furnished superbly, and abounding with paintings, statues, &c. &c.; the chamber of the Elector, we were told, cost above one hundred thousand pounds; it contained a profusion of velvets, gold tissue, and old-fashioned carved work; the bed was immense, groaning with splendour; the great staircase is of marble and gold; from the garden of the palace we were shewn a secret passage, leading to the churches and convents of the town. The streets are regular and broad, and most of the houses painted on the outside; the market place is extremely beautiful. We were taken to see the Niemptenburg palace. The gardens are laid out with great taste; in one of the avenues, I remember Attwood and myself ran a race, and I won it; at that time I was as light as a feathered mercury; but alas! '*non sum qualis eram*.'

The country around this spot is pretty, and the public baths excellent. The Storaces and myself, by appointment, went to pay our respects to Raff, the justly celebrated tenor, esteemed by far the finest singer of his day, and for many years the delight of Naples and Palermo. He was by birth a Bavarian, and had retired to Munich with an ample fortune; he was past seventy, and did us the favour to sing to us his famous song, composed by Bach, '*Non so donde viene*';[1] though his voice was impaired, he still retained his fine voce de petto and sostenuto notes, and pure style of singing.

While staying at Munich, we were asked to assist at a grand concert, at which the Elector, the Electress, and their court were present; the band consisted of several eminent performers, among whom was the famous violin player, Frantzl, who performed a concerto in a masterly manner; and a most excellent female singer of the name of Dussek; and the next morning we set off for Augsbourg.

Lord Bernard's *avant-courier* was taken so ill that he was obliged to remain at Munich, and another could not at the moment be procured; it was agreed that we should, by turns, mount a post horse, and ride on before the carriages to the post-house, and get horses ready, without which precaution we might have been frequently detained on the road. I thought it a pleasant arrangement, although we travelled always in the night.

We arrived at Augsbourg early in the morning, and intended to pass the day there. There seemed to be a swarm of Israelites in this old town, which is renowned for wig-makers, pits, water-works, and dancing ladies, who are by no means scrupulous on the point of exhibiting their legs. It being Sunday, we did not visit their sulphureous water-works, but looked in at one of the balls which are given every Sunday evening, where were some very prettily-dressed servant girls, labouring assiduously at the dance, accompanied by a dulcimer, a violin, pipe and tabor. Having gratified our curiosity by this exhibition, we set off for Ulm, in which there is nothing very remarkable, except its cathedral. From Ulm, Storace and her mother, accompanied by his Lordship, went straight on to Strasbourg, where they agreed to wait for Stephen, Attwood, and myself.

Previous to his going to Vienna, my friend Attwood had been staying at a friend's house at Stutgard, and wished to spend a couple of days with him on his return; Stephen and I agreed to accompany him; but, in the execution of the design, we lost our way in the Black Forest: we were driven by a lad, the deputy assistant ostler at the inn where we had changed horses, all the regular post-boys being unluckily out of the way; the poor fellow was unacquainted with the road, the night was dark, and, considering the place we were in (famous for banditti), our situation was not the most enviable in the world. We wandered on, we knew not where, for some hours; at last we saw a distant light; we dismounted, and walked across the forest towards it, the carriage slowly following; at length we got to a gate, at which we knocked; a man within asked us what we wanted at that time of night. I was the spokesman, and, in bad German, said, 'We were English travellers, who had lost our way, and were benighted in the Forest.'—The young man immediately opened the gate, and invited us in, and told us he was sure his mother would make us welcome.

We were ushered into a large parlour, where was seated in an arm-chair, an elderly lady, with eight of her grandchildren, placed round a supper table; she gave us a most hospitable reception, told us we had strayed widely from the right road, made us sit down and partake of her supper, which consisted of some cold roasted veal, chickens, salad, and an excellent omelet, and gave us some of the finest old hock I ever tasted. She said she was very happy in administering to our comforts, for she had a high respect for the English. She was a very agreeable old lady, and her charming family very attentive. She insisted upon sitting up with us until day-break, as she could not accommodate us with beds, and told us, that her eldest son should accompany us to the next post town, on the road to Stutgard.

In the morning we took leave of her, and changed horses at the next stage—the country around Stutgard is very picturesque; at the entrance to the city we were impeded by an immense crowd of people, chiefly military, attending the funeral of a field marshal. The ceremony was grand and impressive.

Upon making inquiries in the place, we found that as the reigning Duke of Wirtemberg was absent on a visit to the King of Prussia, the theatre was closed; but in the morning I went to look at the stage, on which had been exhibited the most magnificent and splendid spectacles ever produced; indeed, it has been said, that the expense of this very theatre was so great that it materially injured the finances of the Sovereign, and that he was obliged to relinquish it: at one period, the Italian opera flourished at Stutgard more than at any court in Europe. The first soprano singer was the celebrated Caferelli;[1] for its tenor singer, the Cavaliere Hectore; and the prima donna, the great Gabrielli; Jomelli, Hasse, and Graun, the composers; with a corresponding orchestra, culled from all parts of Germany and Italy. The ballets were magnificent; the ballet master the celebrated Noverre; it was on this stage he produced his Armida, and Jason and Medea; the expense for the production of which, in scenery, machinery, and decorations, was said to be enormous; the elder Vestris, Le Picque, Duberval, and the first dancers from Paris were engaged; and the whole together formed a theatrical exhibition perfectly unique; but it was, I have before said, found necessary to put a stop to their gaiety.

Having seen what was to be seen at Stutgard, we proceeded on our journey; and barring bad roads, lazy post-boys, vile horses, wretched inns, and two or three overturns, our journey was pleasant enough; at length we found ourselves at the gates of Strasburg, renowned for its savory and goose-liver pies, and at the Hôtel de l'Empereur we found Storace and her party waiting for us; we sat down to an excellent *déjeûner à la fourchette,* quite happy at being released from our bone-setter:—we remained two days at Strasbourg, and liked it much.

One evening we went to a concert, which was crowded with military men and beautiful women, where I had the pleasure of being introduced to the justly popular composer Pleyel; he was engaged as director of the concerts; he came to the hotel and supped with us, and seemed delighted to hear that we had left his old master Haydn in good health and spirits. In the morning I went with him to the top of the spire of the cathedral, reckoned the highest in Europe; a foolish fellow, a week before, disappointed and crossed in love, had thrown himself from the top of it, and been dashed to pieces. In the body of the church, lie the remains of the famous Marshal Saxe, to whose memory there is a fine monument; and its clock is a curious piece of machinery.

In the evening I heard the celebrated French actress and comic singer, Madame Dugazzon, who sang the popular ballad of 'Mon bon André, mon cher André',[1] charmingly. The house literally overflowed with elegant company. Next day we set off for Nancy, the last stage of our journey, Storace and myself having ridden forwards to order breakfast, came to a place where four roads met:—which was the right one we knew not; I luckily thought of the expedient of throwing the reins over our horses' necks, and, as I foresaw, they mechanically brought us safe and sound into Nancy, which I thought a very pretty town.

13

The country all through Champagne is delightfully cultivated and picturesque; nothing, however, happened worth noticing until we reached Paris, where we took up our quarters at an hotel in the Faubourg St. Germain, at that time the most fashionable part of the town, and generally frequented by the English. We remained there a few days, and I believe saw every thing worth seeing, visited Versailles, and saw the King and Queen, and the royal family dine in public, apparently adored by the populace.

At that time there existed a ceremony, to which all foreigners were obliged to submit; I mean that of being actually compelled to receive the chaste salutes of the *dames de la halle* (fish women), who besieged, in those days, the residences of strangers, and presented them with nosegays, nor would they quit their post until they had obtained both money and kisses; but, I must say, that these amatory advances were to me a horrid nuisance.

My object while in Paris, was to see all the theatres, and I therefore visited one or other of them every evening. I went, first, to the grand opera, and was delighted with the magnificence of the scenery, decorations, and dresses, and, above all, with their choruses; in that department they decidedly bear away the palm from every other country: the orchestra was most minutely attended to, and more numerous than even that of San Carlos at Naples; but the principal singers (God save them) made a shriek louder than I thought any human beings capable of producing. The opera was Gluck's Iphigenia, which we had performed at Vienna; but for decorations and effect, Paris beat us out of the field. The chorus and procession, where Pylades and Orestes in chains, were dragged on by Gardel, Vestris, and a host of first-rate dancers, were beyond any thing I could have conceived. I went the next night to the same theatre, and saw the first representation[1] of the grand serious opera of 'Œdipe à Colon'; the music by Sacchini, was delightful and enchanting. I there heard, for the first time, the celebrated bass singer, Cheron, who played the part of Œdipe, and sang in a delightful style; it was quite different from the performance of the night before, indeed I could scarcely imagine myself in the same theatre. I saw, too, the opera of Phedra, and had great pleasure in seeing Madame St. Auberti perform the part of Phedra; she was a great actress, and when she sang in a *demi* voice, was quite charming. This unfortunate lady and accomplished actress subsequently married, and with her husband, the Count d'Entraigues, was robbed and murdered by their servant when in England.

In this opera I felt much gratified by hearing Monsieur Laïs, possessing a fine baritone voice, with much taste and expression; but his greatest praise, in my opinion was, that he was very unlike a French singer. The next theatre I visited, was the Français. Their great tragedians at the time were on leave of absence in the provinces; I had not, therefore, an opportunity of seeing a tragedy, but I was amply compensated by their excellent comedians; their comic acting is always natural. I saw Molé act the part of Duretête, in Farquhar's Inconstant, admirably. Fleury was inimitable in Le Pupile (the guardian), and Madame Contare in Susan, Beaumarchais' Marriage of Figaro, exquisite. Dugazzon was a fine low comedian; indeed, I thought all the actors good; but my favourite theatre of all was, the Théâtre Italien, in the Rue Favart, where French comic operas were performed; the orchestra was very good, and the actors and singers equally so; a Mademoiselle Renard had a most delightful voice, and was a sweet singer.

I saw there 'Richard Cœur de Lion', and enjoyed its charming music. I thought it always Grétry's masterpiece. Clairval, the original Blondel, gave the air of 'O Richard! O mon Roi!' with great expression. His acting in the scene when he heard the voice of Richard from the prison, was electrifying: his joy, his surprise, at having found his king, the trembling of his voice, his scrambling up the tree to let Richard hear his voice, and the expression altogether, made an impression on me that never can be effaced; and while I remained at Paris, I never missed going to see him. Monsieur Philippe played Richard remarkably well, and gave the bravura air, 'L'univers que j'ai perdu',[1] with great skill and animation.

Having at length satisfied our curiosity at Paris, we took our departure, and never halted until we got to Boulogne; when we arrived there, we went to the hotel kept then by Mrs. Knowles (now Parker's), and a very good house it was. The old lady herself went over with us in the packet to Dover; in it also was Pilon, who wrote 'The Fair American',[2] and 'He would be a Soldier'; a thoughtless, extravagant, hair-brained fellow, who had been a long time at Boulogne, where he had been much noticed by the principal people. When we got in sight of Shakspeare's Cliff, he expressed his surprise at Shakspeare's referring to it as particularly high, and found great fault with our immortal bard's judgment of altitude, and with the spot itself, which he considered wholly unworthy of his notice. We landed at Dover, and went to the York Hotel, and agreed to dine together, and travel to London the next day.

After dinner we went to the custom-house, in order to have our trunks examined; but poor Pilon had, in the hurry of leaving Boulogne, left his trunk behind him: he seemed absolutely paralyzed with horror; and told us, on our return to the inn, that he must set off to Boulogne in the packet; which was to sail that night, and get his trunk at all hazards. We thought it particularly silly for him to do so, especially as he suffered greatly from sea-sickness, and there was a stiffish breeze blowing. We advised him to dispatch a messenger for it, but all would not do; he persisted in going himself, and took such copious draughts of hot brandy and water, that the poet's head became considerably confused.

At length, as the effects of his numerous potations became more powerful, he opened his heart to us; 'Gad, my friends,' said he, 'If I don't get my trunk, I shall be ruined,—it will be opened, and in it, will be found the bitterest satire I could write, upon all the people with whom, and upon whom I have been living, during the whole of my stay at Boulogne; and if they should see it or hear of it, I shall never be able to shew my face amongst them again.' At midnight the packet sailed, and in it the grateful playwright, in order to save his reputation.

We, having neither written lampoons, nor left our trunks behind us, set off in the morning, breakfasted at Canterbury, and dined at Rochester, and an unlucky dinner it was for me; I had purchased some prints and trinkets at Paris, which, by the aid of the steward of the packet, I got safe across the water; and on leaving Dover, I had them packed in the bottom of the chaise, and fancied them quite secure; but no; a lynx-eyed custom-house officer, of the name of Tancred, while we were at dinner, stepped into the chaise, and spoiled me of my smuggled purchases. I strove to bribe, but the hard-hearted searcher was inexorable; and I was obliged to submit to the laws of my country, which, at the time, I thought very hard: however, cares were but trifles then, and I laughed away the loss; and on the 18th of March, 1787, arrived in London for the first time in my life. On the same evening, Stephen Storace and myself called upon Mr. Linley, at his house in Norfolk Street in the Strand, where I found his accomplished daughters, Mrs. Sheridan, and Mrs. Tickell. Mrs. Sheridan asked me if I had seen 'Richard Cœur de Lion' in Paris; and on my telling her that I had, only four evenings before, she requested me to go and see it at Drury Lane that evening, as she was most anxious to know my opinion of the relative merits of the French and English pieces. General Burgoyne had translated it, and Mrs. Sheridan adapted it to the English stage.

I and Storace, accompanied by a young gentleman, set off for the theatre, but the piece was nearly half over. I must premise, that I was then totally uninformed as regarded the actors and actresses at Drury Lane. Just as we entered the boxes, Richard was singing the romance from his prison, most loudly accompanied from behind the scenes by two French horns; I was astonished to hear an accompaniment so completely at variance with the intention of the composer, and which entirely spoiled the effect of the melody, nor did I think much of the vocal powers of the royal captive; and turning to Storace, said, 'If His Majesty is the first and best singer in your theatre, I shall not fear to appear as his competitor for public favour.' Storace laughed, and told me that the gentleman who upon that special occasion was singing, was Mr. John Kemble, the celebrated tragedian, who, to serve the proprietors, had undertaken to perform the part of Richard, as there was no singer at the theatre capable of representing it. However, as I was not gifted with intuition, my mistaking him for the principal vocalist of the theatre was natural enough, having a few days back seen Philippe, the first singer at the French theatre, perform the same part.

My friend Kemble laughed heartily when he was told that I had mistaken him for the Drury Lane Orpheus. By the way, I heard that when Kemble was rehearsing the romance, sung by Richard, Shaw, the leader of the band, called out from the orchestra, 'Mr. Kemble, my dear Mr. Kemble, you are murdering time.' Kemble, calmly and coolly taking a pinch of snuff, said, 'My dear Sir, it is better for me to murder time at once, than be continually beating him as you do.'

Mrs. Jordan's acting in this drama was delightful, and the Laurette of Mrs. Crouch most interesting. I was struck with admiration of her wonderful beauty, and delighted to hear that she was to be my prima donna in the opera in which I was to perform. She seemed to me to aggregate in herself, like the Venus of Apelles,[1] all that was exquisite and charming. I agreed with Mr. Linley for the remainder of the season at Drury Lane, and to make my début in the part of Lionel, on Friday, the 20th of April, 1787.

There were oratorios performing at Drury Lane, under the united management of Mr. Linley, Doctor Arnold, and Madame Mara, who were joint proprietors. One evening, after the first act of the oratorio, I went into the green-room, where, amongst other ladies, was Madame Mara, to whom I had never spoken. Doctor Arnold said, 'Pray, Mr. Kelly, tell us what sort of singer is Signora Storace?' I replied that, in my opinion, she was the best singer in Europe. I meant, of course, in her line; but, as it proved afterwards, Madame Mara was highly offended at the praise which I had given to my friend, and said to a lady, when I quitted the green-room, that I was an impertinent coxcomb. I then knew nothing of Madame Mara, nor at that time valued her good opinion; however, she carried her resentment so far against me, that she afterwards declared she would not sing where I did, if she could avoid it.

In selecting the opera of Lionel and Clarissa for my first appearance, I was guided in my choice by the circumstance of knowing all the songs, which, besides, were much in my style of singing. When the opera was produced, I sang all the original music, and introduced an Italian air of Sarti's, with English words, written for me by Mr. Richard Tickell, brother-in-law to Mr. Sheridan; and a duet written by the well-known Doctor Lawrence, the civilian. I composed the melody, and Stephen Storace put the instrumental parts to it. This duet was his first introduction to Drury Lane theatre.—That eminent actor, King, who had been a friend of my father's in Dublin many years before, took a great deal of pains to instruct me in the dialogue of the part.—To Mr. Linley I was also much indebted for his able tuition, and from all the performers I experienced the most kind and friendly attentions.

At the time of my début, my friend Jack Johnstone was engaged at Covent Garden as first singer. I saw him play Young Meadows, in 'Love in a Village'; he acted the part well, and sang the songs with good taste, and a peculiarly fine falsetto voice. Mrs. Billington was the Rosetta. I thought her an angel in beauty, and the Saint Cecilia of song.

I remember one day, shortly after my first appearance, dining with my friend Jack Johnstone, in Great Russell Street, I met an eccentric Irishman, well known in Dublin, of the name of Long, who was, by turns, an auctioneer and dramatist; he wrote a play called 'The Laplanders,' which was, at first, very coolly received by the audience, and afterwards very warmly condemned. He came to England to propose to Government a plan for paying off the national debt, or some such thing. He was, however, full of anecdote, and had a happy knack of telling stories *against himself*; one, I recollect, was, that, in his auctioneering capacity, amongst other schemes, he offered for sale, woollen cloths at a farthing a yard; yet, so completely was his character known, and so well appreciated, that he could not advance a bidding even upon that price. At one time, he told us his patience was actually worn out, and, in anger towards his auditory, he said, he thought they would treat him with the same inattention, if he were to offer a guinea for sale. He then literally took a guinea out of his pocket, and put it up; there were certainly advances, shilling by shilling, until it reached seventeen shillings and sixpence, at which price he knocked it down, and, handing it to the buyer, wished him luck of the bargain; the purchaser went immediately to try the value of his lot, when it appeared, being weighed, to be of eighteenpence less value than he had paid for it.

He mentioned another anecdote of a Mr. Lennan, a saddler in Dublin, who was seriously stage-stricken, and volunteered to act Major O' Flaherty, in which he was execrable; after this was over, however, he exhibited himself at the Cockle Club, where the facetious[1] Isaac Sparks presided, and Jack Long was vice-president; they made him extremely tipsy, and then gave him in charge to the watch for having murdered Major O'Flaherty, and left the poor saddler all night in durance vile, who afterwards stuck to making saddles, and never again was found guilty of murdering majors, even on the stage.

I had the pleasure also to be introduced to my worthy countryman, the Reverend Father O'Leary, the well-known Roman Catholic Priest; he was a man of infinite wit, of instructive and amusing conversation. I felt highly honoured by the notice of this pillar of the Roman Church; our tastes were congenial, for his Reverence was mighty fond of whiskey punch, and so was I; and many a jug of St. Patrick's eye-water, night after night, did his reverence and myself enjoy, chatting over that exhilirating and national beverage. He sometimes favoured me with his company at dinner; when he did, I always had a corned shoulder of mutton for him, for he, like some others of his countrymen, who shall be nameless, was ravenously fond of that dish.

One day, the facetious John Philpot Curran, who was also very partial to the said corned mutton, did me the honour to meet him. To enjoy the society of such men was an intellectual treat. They were great friends, and seemed to have a mutual respect for each other's talents; and, as it may easily be imagined, O'Leary, versus Curran, was no bad match.

One day, after dinner, Curran said to him, 'Reverend Father, I wish you were Saint Peter.'

'And why, Counsellor, would you wish that I were Saint Peter?' asked O'Leary.

'Because, Reverend Father, in that case,' said Curran, 'you would have the keys of Heaven, and you could let me in.'

'By my honour and conscience, Counsellor,' replied the divine, 'it would be better for *you* that I had the keys of the other place, for then I could let you out.'

Curran enjoyed the joke, which he admitted had a good deal of justice in it.

O'Leary told us of the whimsical triumph which he once enjoyed over Dr. Johnson. O'Leary was very anxious to be introduced to that learned man, and Mr. Murphy took him one morning to the Doctor's lodgings.

On his entering the room, the Doctor viewed him from top to toe, without taking any notice of him; at length, darting one of his sourest looks at him, he spoke to him in the Hebrew language, to which O'Leary made no reply. Upon which, the Doctor said to him, 'Why do you not answer me, Sir?'

'Faith, Sir,' said O'Leary, 'I cannot reply to you, because I do not understand the language in which you are addressing me.'

Upon this the Doctor, with a contemptuous sneer, said to Murphy, 'Why, Sir, this is a pretty fellow you have brought hither;—Sir, he does not comprehend the primitive language.'

O'Leary immediately bowed very low, and complimented the Doctor with a long speech in Irish, of which the Doctor, not understanding a word, made no reply, but looked at Murphy. O'Leary, seeing that the Doctor was puzzled at hearing a language of which he was ignorant, said to Murphy, pointing to the Doctor, 'This is a pretty fellow to whom you have brought me;—Sir, he does not understand the language of the sister kingdom.'—The Reverend Padre then made the Doctor a low bow, and quitted the room.

At the time when I met Jack Long, I was in the highest spirits; I had played Lionel, and been received with all the kindness and indulgence with which a British audience invariably encourages a new performer, and I had been successful beyond my warmest hopes.

On the following Tuesday, (the 24th,) I remember I went to the Opera House to see my friend Signora Storace make her first appearance, and was much gratified at her enthusiastic reception. The opera was Paesiello's 'Schiavi per Amore'. The whole of the music of this charming opera buffa is delightful. The opening of it is a masterpiece of harmony, and was warmly applauded by His Royal Highness the Prince of Wales, who honoured the theatre with his presence, and was in the house before the commencement of the opera. Amongst the audience were the late Duke of Cumberland (in the pit), and the Duchess (in her box) with the present Marquis of Conyngham. The 'Schiavi per Amore' was a great favourite for the remainder of the season.

While my friend Storace was earning laurels in the Haymarket, I was most kindly treated at Drury Lane. My performance, which succeeded Lionel, was that of Young Meadows, in 'Love in a Village'. In addition to the original songs, I introduced one of Gluck's to which Mrs. Sheridan did me the honour to write English words, 'Love, thou maddening power'; this was a great favourite, as also the duet, 'Each joy in thee possessing', both of which were always encored.

Daly, the patentee of the Theatre Royal, in Crow Street, sent over an offer of an engagement to perform at his theatre, with Mrs. Crouch, for twelve nights; the terms I demanded, and which were acceded to, were to share the house with Mr. Daly, he first deducting fifty pounds per night for his expenses; and the thirteenth night I was to have a benefit clear of all expenses.

It was during the summer of this year, that the commemoration of Handel took place. The last grand performances given at Westminster Abbey, were on the 28th and 31st of May, the 1st and 4th of June: upon those four mornings, I sang there, but to give an idea of the effect of that magnificent festival is far beyond my power; indeed, it has already been described most elaborately by those more competent to the task. I can only endeavour to express the effect which it produced on *me*. When I first heard the chorus of the Hallelujah, in the 'Messiah', and 'For unto us a child is born', my blood thrilled with rapturous delight; it was sublime; it was, in the inspired words of the chorus, 'Wonderful'. The orchestra was led by the Cramers; the conductors were Joah Bates, Esq. father of the present secretary of the Tax Office, Drs. Arnold and Dupuis. The band consisted of several hundreds of performers. The singers were Madame Mara, Storace, Miss Abrams, Miss Poole, Rubinelli, Harrison, Bartleman, Sale, Parry, Norris, myself, &c. and the choruses were collected from all parts of England, amounting to hundreds of voices.

The King, Queen, and all the royal family sat opposite the orchestra; the body of the church, the galleries, and every corner crowded with beauty, rank, and fashion:—such was the rage to procure seats, that ladies had their hair dressed the night previous, to be ready to get to the Abbey in good time. The performers unanimously exerted their great talents to admiration; but what made an everlasting impression on me was, the powerful effect produced by Madame Mara, in the sublime recitative, 'Sing ye to the Lord,[1] for he hath triumphed gloriously;' in that

> Her voice was heard around,
> Loud as a trumpet with a silver sound.

I have often sung with her the recitative tenor part, 'And Miriam the Prophetess took a timbrel in her hand'; and never heard her but with increased delight.

No place could be more appropriate to give effect to the divine strains of Handel than the spacious Abbey. His Majesty's partiality for Handel's music was generally spoken of; but I believe it was not universally known what an excellent and accurate judge he was of its merits. The fine chorus of 'Lift up your heads, O ye gates', was always given in full chorus, and indeed intended to be so given by Handel. The King suggested that the first part of it should be made a semi-chorus and sung only by the principal singers; but when it came to the passage, 'He is the King of Glory!' he commanded that the whole orchestra, with the full chorus, should, with a tremendous forte, burst out; the effect produced by the alteration was awful and sublime.

A strange coincidence happened at one of the performances: the morning, during part of the grand selection, was cloudy and lowering; but when the grand chorus struck up 'Let there be light,[1] and light was over all!' the sun burst forth, and with its rays illuminated every part of the splendid edifice. Every one was struck with the coincidence, and the effect produced by it.

About this time I received the melancholy news of my poor mother's death; she had died a few weeks before, but the event had not been divulged to me; however, I was anxious to see my father and family, and set off for Dublin, the 8th of June, having previously entered into an engagement with the proprietors of Drury Lane for the ensuing season, stipulating not to perform more than three times a week. Mr. and Mrs. Crouch and myself hired a travelling carriage, had a most pleasant journey, and I arrived in Dublin on the 12th of June,[2] at my father's house in Abbey Street. Mr. and Mrs. Crouch went to lodgings taken for them in College Green.

My father was, of course, delighted to see me, and I equally so to see him; for the lapse of so many years had made no alteration in my affection for him. I was most happy to see my sister, and my brothers, Joe and Mark, and on the 22nd made my first appearance in Lionel, to a crowded house; my reception was highly gratifying, and the plaudits I received from my warm-hearted countrymen, and in my native city, were ever most congenial to my feelings.

During my twelve nights' performance, I never shared less, upon an average, than fifty pounds per night; my benefit, a clear one, overflowed in every part, and the greater part of the pit was railed into boxes: two of our nights' performances were by the command of his Grace the Duke of Rutland, then the Lord Lieutenant of Ireland, who was accompanied to the theatre by his Duchess, a most beautiful woman. Holman was then acting in Dublin; the Masque of Comus was got up; he played Comus, I, the principal Bacchanal, and sang, 'Now Phœbus sinketh in the West', and all the principal songs. Mrs. Crouch was the Euphrosyne, and looked as lovely as if she had been bathed in the fountain of the Graces; her acting in the song of 'The Wanton God', and singing 'Would ye taste the noon-tide air?' and 'Sweet echo', were indeed a treat.

It struck me that there was a good opportunity to introduce, in the first act of the Masque, between the principal Bacchanal and Bacchante, a duet; and I fixed upon the celebrated Italian duet of Martini, 'Pace, cara mia sposa',[1] which created a great sensation at Vienna, but much greater in Dublin. The English words put to it, 'Oh, thou wert born to please me', were very good, and chimed in well with the scene; no piece of music every produced a greater effect; it was always called for three times, and no performance was allowed to go on in which it was not introduced; it was sung about the streets by the ballad-singers, and parodied by the news-boys, who used to sing to each other, 'Oh thou wert born to tease me, my life, my only love;' in short, it was completely the rage all over Ireland, England, and Scotland, for many, many years.

During my engagement in Dublin, I passed many happy days in the delightful and hospitable society of numerous and kind friends. We took frequent excursions to Clontarf,[2] Black Rock, Dunleary, Hill of Howth, and the Dargle, an enchanting spot. At Bray there was an inn, where every accommodation could be had; the red trout are delicious; and at Lord Powerscourt's place, the Dargle, the views are beautiful and picturesque, bearing a strong resemblance to many parts of Sicily, particularly about the environs of Palermo. However, these joys, like all others, were but transitory; and, in due time, I finished my profitable and pleasant engagement in Dublin, and sailed for Holyhead, on our way to the York theatre, where Mrs. Crouch and myself were engaged by the eccentric Tate Wilkinson, its proprietor, to perform during the race week. Mrs. Crouch was perfectly acquainted with the eccentricities of Tate, and told us many anecdotes of him; he was a great epicure, very fond of French cookery, and small dishes; large joints he never allowed to come to his table, and above all, had the most sovereign contempt for a round of beef; hearing this, it came into my head to play him a trick, and I got Mr. and Mrs. Crouch to aid me in my frolic.

14

We got to the inn at York just at supper time. I saw in the larder a huge round of beef; I ordered it up, and had it put on the table before me; I pulled off my coat and waistcoat, and tucked up the sleeves of my shirt, unbuttoned my collar, took off my cravat, and put on a red woollen nightcap; thus disrobed, and with a large carving-knife in my hand, I was gazing with seeming delight on the round of beef, at the moment Manager Wilkinson, to whom Mrs. Crouch had previously sent, entered the house.—He had never seen me; he went up to Mrs. Crouch, and congratulated her on her arrival in York; turning from her, he espied me, and starting back, exclaimed,

'Ugh! Ma'am, who is that, with the enormous round of beef before him!—How the devil came he here, Ma'am?' Mrs. Crouch said, with a serious countenance, 'That is Mr. Kelly, whom you have engaged to sing with me.'

'What, that figure!' said Tate,—'what, that my Lord Aimworth,—my Lionel,—my Young Meadows!—Ugh! send him away, Ma'am! send him back to Drury Lane! send him to Vienna! I never can produce such a thing as that, to a York audience, Ma'am.'

While he was abusing the bad taste of the Drury Lane managers and those of Vienna, I slipped out of the room, dressed myself, and in *propriâ personâ,* was introduced to Tate, who participated in the joke, and laughed heartily, and ever after we were the greatest friends.

On the 22nd of August we began our engagement with Lionel and Clarissa. Tate was the Colonel Oldboy, and Mr. Betterton (Mrs. Glover's father) Jessamy:—being the race week, York was crowded with company, and the theatre always full. This was the first place at which I saw Miss Farren, who was then on a visit to Sir William and Lady Milner. My worthy friend, that excellent actor Fawcett, then belonged to the York theatre, and was the Douglas of the company.

The week after the races Mrs. Crouch took her benefit, a great house; Mrs. Crouch played Clara, and I Carlos, with Comus; our duet, 'Oh, thou wert born to please me', was wonderfully well received. On Wednesday, the 29th, we commenced a four nights' engagement at Leeds, in the 'Maid of the Mill'; Patty, Mrs. Crouch; Lord Aimworth by myself. 'Love in a Village', 'The Duenna', and 'Lionel and Clarissa', to excellent houses.

Wilkinson proposed to us to perform four nights more at Wakefield, to which we consented: we arrived there on Wednesday, the 5th of September, and appeared in 'Love in a Village'; the house was thinly attended, but in the stage-box sat a lady, who made such a terrible noise, throwing herself into all kinds of attitudes, indulging ever and anon in horrid laughing, that she disconcerted every person who came upon the stage; but, above all, I in particular appeared to be the object of her ridicule, and I confess I felt extremely hurt at her pointed rudeness.

In the third act, when Young Meadows resumes his real character, and comes into the garden to meet Rosetta, I took out my watch to look at the hour, and sang, 'I wonder this girl does not come'; the fat lady in the stage-box instantly set off in a horse laugh, and said to those around her, loud enough to be heard in the gallery, 'Why, look there; la! the fellow has got a watch.'

I could not bear this; I admit I lost my temper; but I walked up to the box, and said, 'Yes, Madam, it is a gold watch, and reckoned one of the best in England,' putting it close to her;—my friend Fawcett was standing at the side of the stage at the time, and often since has spoken of it: the lady was violently hissed, and ever after, when she came to the theatre, conducted herself with becoming decency. The same lady, I was told, behaved one night so rudely to Mr. John Kemble, that he was obliged to address her from the stage, and say that he could not proceed with his part unless she would cease interrupting him with her noise; the audience insisted on her leaving the box; a party of her friends took her part, and wanted Kemble to apologise to her, which he refused to do, and left the theatre.

Our four nights ended; we consented to play one night more, by the express desire of the Earl of Scarborough, who, during our stay in Yorkshire, shewed us many marks of polite attention. On the 12th of September we left Wakefield, to commence the winter campaign on the 15th at Old Drury; and on the 23rd of September, 1787, Mr. Linley revived his musical piece of 'Selima and Azor',[1] with splendid scenery and decorations. Mrs. Crouch was inimitable in Selima—she looked and acted the character to admiration, and sang the favourite rondo of 'No flower that blows, is like the rose', in a manner to secure a nightly encore.

The music, though in a different style from Grétry's, so renowned all over the Continent, was very appropriate and pleasing. One night, during its run, I went to the Italian Opera House; it was a dreadful stormy night, and rained incessantly. I was lucky enough to get a hackney coach, and while waiting for its drawing up to the door, I heard two very handsome young women lamenting that they could procure no conveyance: after apologizing for my presumption, I told them that I had one in waiting, and should be happy to have the pleasure of offering them seats in it,—an offer which, with many thanks, they accepted.

We got into the coach, and the coachman was directed to drive to John Street, Fitzroy Square; the ladies, naturally enough, began to speak about the opera and public places; amongst other things, one of them asked me if I had seen Mr. Kelly, the new singer at Drury Lane: I replied, very often.

'My sister and I went to see him the other night,' said the young lady, 'and we have set him down as one of the most affected, conceited fellows we ever beheld; he strutted about the stage like a peacock; and as to his singing, how an audience could applaud it I cannot imagine. Do you not think him execrable, Sir?'

'Most certainly,' said I; 'I have a very mean opinion of him.'

'And then the puppy,' continued my fair friend, 'is so ugly, he is a perfect fright. Do you not think so, Sir?'

'Indeed,' said I, 'I do not think that, for I am rather partial to his personal appearance, and like his countenance as well as I do my own—but pray,' continued I, 'in what character might you have seen this frightful fellow?'

'In Selima and Azor, I think they called it,' said her sister; 'but we were so tired and disgusted with it, that we came away at the end of the first act.'

'Well, ladies,' said I, 'if you had stopped until the end of the piece, and seen Mr. Kelly with his mask off, you would have seen him assume the appearance of a prince, and perhaps not have thought him so very frightful.'

By this time, the coach had reached their door; and returning many thanks for my civility in seeing them home, they told me they should be very happy, if any morning I would favour them with a call, and asked me for my address. I gave it, upon which they both actually shrieked with horror, and asked a thousand pardons for the rudeness of which they had been innocently guilty. I laughed heartily at the little *contre-temps,* and took my leave; but returned the next day, and formed an intimacy with them which lasted many years, during which, I received the greatest hospitality and kindness from them:—one of them was the wife of a wealthy merchant, the other unmarried, but both were charming and agreeable women.

During this season, Storace introduced me to Mr. Cobb, the late secretary to the East India Company, who had written two successful farces for Drury Lane,—'The Humourist', and 'The First Floor', in which Bannister played admirably. Cobb was adapting, with Storace, Baron Dittersdorf's 'Doctor and Apothecary', for Drury Lane; they wished to consult me upon the kind of songs I should wish to be written for me: we proposed to dine together next day, at the Orange Coffee House, opposite to the Opera House. I agreed to meet Cobb in St. James's Park before dinner; and while we were seated on one of the benches (for it was then allowable to sit upon them) we were joined by Pilon, whom I had not seen since he set off to Boulogne to recover his trunk and his satire. He seemed very well acquainted with Cobb, and taking him aside, borrowed a couple of guineas of him; he then wished us a good morning. In about half an hour afterwards, we went to the Orange Coffee House, where we saw the borrowing author sitting in a box; he asked leave to join us. We had our dinner and wine; and after dinner, Pilon went to the bar, and insisted on paying the whole of the bill, with the money which, three hours before, he had borrowed of Cobb; this of course we would not allow, but we had a hearty laugh at the expense of both borrower and lender.

Most of my theatrical readers remember, and all have heard, of that exquisite actor, Parsons; to him I was particularly partial, and he, I may venture to say, was very partial to me. I have repeatedly dined with him, in a band-box of a house which he had near the Asylum, at Lambeth; it was an odd place for an asthmatic comedian to live in, for it was opposite a stagnant ditch; he called it Frog Hall. In his little drawing-room were several beautiful landscapes, painted by himself; he was reckoned a very good artist. Amongst his little peculiarities, was a fondness for fried tripe, which almost nightly, after the play, he went to enjoy, at an eating-house in Little Russell Street, nearly opposite the stage-door of Drury Lane Theatre, whither I used very often to accompany him; and night after night have we been *tête-à-tête* there. I was anxious to acquire what theatrical information I could, and he was very communicative and full of anecdote.

One evening I was expressing a wish to see him act the character of Corbachio, in 'The Fox', as it was one of his great parts.

'Ah,' said he, 'to see Corbachio acted to perfection, you should have seen Shuter; the public are pleased to think that I act that part well, but his acting was as far superior to mine, as Mount Vesuvius is to a rushlight.'

Parsons, when on the stage with John Palmer and James Aickin, used to make it a point to set them off laughing, and scarcely ever failed in his object. One evening, over our fried tripe, I was condemning them for indulging their laughing propensities on the stage, and said I thought it was positively disrespectful to the audience. 'For my own part,' said I, 'I enjoy your comicalities and humour as much as any one, when in the front of the house; but were I on the stage with you, nothing that you could do would make me so far forget the character I was acting, as to indulge in misplaced mirth.'

'Do you think so?' said he; 'well, perhaps you are right.'

Five or six nights after this conversation, we were acting in 'The Doctor and the Apothecary'.[1] I was to sing a song to him, beginning, 'This marriage article, in every particle, is free from flaw, Sir'. A full chord was given from the orchestra to pitch the key; just as it was given, and I was going to begin the song, he called out to Shaw, the leader, 'Stop, stop,' and putting his head into my face, and kicking up his heels (a favourite action of his) he drove me from one end of the stage to the other, crying out all the time, 'I'll be hanged if you shall ever have any more fried tripe, no more fried tripe, no more fried tripe,' and completely pushed me off the stage. I could not resist this unexpected attack, and naturally burst out laughing. The audience were in a roar of laughter too, for it was enough that he held up his finger or his heel to make *them* laugh. When we got off, he said, 'I think you must own, my serious lad, that I have conquered;' then taking me by the hand, he dragged me upon the stage to the spot whence he had before driven me, and looking down into the orchestra, said, 'Now, Sirs, begin,' which they did, and I sang my song, which was much applauded; but the audience were, of course, ignorant of the joke of the fried tripe, or what he meant by it: however, he is gone, poor fellow, and many a pleasant hour have I enjoyed in his society.

In the summer of this year I and Mrs. Crouch went to Liverpool, Chester, Manchester, and to Worcester races. The theatre there was most fashionably attended; we received much kindness, particularly from Mr. Walsh Porter and his lady. We took Birmingham for a fortnight in our way back, and our trip was pleasant and profitable. My leave of absence from Vienna had expired; and I had received my yearly salary punctually, from the Secretary to the Austrian Embassy in London. I wrote to Prince Rosenberg a respectful letter, requesting him to lay before his Majesty the Emperor, my humble duty and grateful thanks for the many bounties bestowed upon me, but that my father's state of health, and his wish for me to stay in England, induced me to remain there,—this was my excuse; but there were other reasons more potent than filial duty for my not returning to dear Vienna: had I gone, and remained ten years, I should have had half my salary for the remainder of my life, and have been allowed to retire with ease and comfort; but, as his Grace of Bedford's motto sayeth, 'Che sarà, sarà;'[1] and I cannot be expected *now* to account for my conduct *then*.

The oratorios[2] were this year carried on under the direction of Doctor Arnold and Mr. Linley, and they wished to engage me; but Madame Mara, who was their great prop, as I have before mentioned, had an aversion to my singing wherever she was, for reasons before stated; of course, they were obliged to submit to the caprices of the Queen of Song, and I cared little about the matter at the time. I went one oratorio night into the green room to speak to Mrs. Crouch, but the only persons in the room were Madame Mara and Monsieur Ponté, first French horn player to the King of Prussia, and a very fine performer; he was an intimate friend of Madame Mara, and engaged to play a concerto at the oratorio that night. He said to Madame Mara in German, 'My dear friend, my lips are so parched with fear, that I am sure I shall not make a sound in the instrument; I would give the world for a little water or beer to moisten my lips.'

Madame Mara replied in German, 'There is nobody here to send; and yet if I knew where to get something for you to drink, I would go myself.'

During their dialogue, I was standing at the fireside; and addressing Madame Mara in German, I said, 'Madame, I should be sorry for you to have that trouble, and I sit lazy by; I will, with great pleasure, go and get Monsieur Ponté some porter.' I instantly despatched a messenger for a foaming pot; and as soon as it arrived, I presented it to the thirsty musician, in the nick of time, for he was called on to play his concerto just at this moment. Madame Mara desired me to accept her best acknowledgments for my attention, and gave me an invitation to call at her house in Pall Mall the next day, at two o'clock. I accordingly went; and she then told me honestly, that upon her first knowledge of me, she had taken a violent dislike to me, which my kindness to her timid friend on the preceding evening, convinced her was ill-founded; she apologised, and concluded this *amende* (*très-honorable*) by asking me if I took a benefit at the theatre that season.

I answered in the affirmative: she then said, 'It was my intention never to appear on the English stage; yet if you think my playing for your benefit for the first and only time will be of service to you, I beg you will command me.'

I was thunderstruck at her kindness and liberality, and thankfully accepted it. She fixed on Mandane, in Artaxerxes, and brought the greatest receipt ever known at that house, as the whole pit, with the exception of two benches, was railed into boxes. So much for a little German proficiency, a little common civility, and a pot of porter.

The cast of Artaxerxes, upon this occasion, stood thus:—

Arbaces	MRS. CROUCH.
Artaxerxes	MR. DIGNUM.
Artabanes	MR. KELLY.
Semira	MRS. FOSTER.
Mandane	MADAME MARA.

June 11th, I played at the Opera House, Count Almaviva, in the Italian opera of 'Il Barbiere di Siviglia', for the benefit of Signora Storace; and on the 17th of the same month that theatre was destroyed by fire. I was an eye-witness to the dreadful conflagration; it was said to have been caused purposely, and I knew the person suspected. He was an Italian, who had been in the employ of Gallini, but having disagreed with him, it was reported that he set fire to his theatre; for my own part, I never believed it; but such was the report; certain it is, at all events, that the suspected incendiary was coolly supping at the Orange Coffee House, watching the progress of the flames.

The Opera company went to Covent Garden, and finished the remainder of the season, where I played six nights.

'Shakspeare's Jubilee' was revived this year, and acted five nights to crowded houses; all the performers walked in the procession, as the different characters of his plays. Mrs. Siddons personated the Tragic, and Miss Farren the Comic Muse. I had to sing the following lines, written by the present worthy Alderman Birch, author, amongst others, of three very popular musical pieces:—'The Mariners'; 'The Adopted Child'; and 'The Smugglers':[1] they were received with unqualified approbation.

AIR—*'The Mulberry Tree.'*

'The cypress and yew tree for sorrow renown'd,
And tear-dropping willow shall near thee be found;
All nature shall droop, and united complain,
For Shakspeare in Garrick hath died o'er again.'

In the procession I walked, or rather danced down, as Benedick, and Miss Pope as Beatrice, in 'Much Ado about Nothing'; both masked. Moody came to me one evening, and requested I would lend my domino and masque to a friend of his, who wished to see the audience from the stage, and who would do exactly as I did, having frequently seen me and Miss Pope. On he went, but appeared instantly planet struck, and stood perfectly still; nor did he move until pushed off; the rage and disappointment of Miss Pope, who was an excellent dancer, (and I not a very bad one,) at not receiving the applause which she had always brought, was very great; she stormed, and raged, and vowed vengeance against poor me. I wrote to her in the morning, asking her pardon, and signed myself '*The Fair Penitent*;' she took the letter in good part, and wrote me a friendly answer, admonishing me to be guarded against bad advisers: and to the day of her death was kindly attentive to *me,* but she never forgave Moody, by whose advice I had transgressed.

In the summer of 1788, I went to Liverpool, Manchester, Chester, and Birmingham;[1] Mrs. Crouch was also engaged at those places; our reception was most flattering, and we reaped a plentiful harvest. From Birmingham, we returned to Drury Lane. The first novelty was Dryden's alteration of Shakspeare's 'Tempest', which was received with marked applause for many nights. I composed a duet for myself and Mrs. Crouch, as Ferdinand and Miranda, which was a favourite: the whole of the delightful music by Purcell,[2] was well got up by Mr. Linley; the accompaniments by himself.

The next operatical novelty at Drury Lane was the 'Haunted Tower',[3] written by Cobb, the music by Stephen Storace. On the first night of this opera, Signora Storace made her first appearance on the English stage; and the piece was thus performed, Nov. 24th, 1789.

Lord William	Mr. Kelly.
De Courcy	Mr. Whitfield.
Edward	Mr. Bannister, Jun.
Baron of Oakland	Mr. Baddely.
Hugo	Mr. Moody.
Robert.	Mr. Dignum.
Lewis	Mr. Suett.
Martin	Mr. Williams.
Hubert	Mr. Webb.
Charles	Mr. Sedgwick.
Lady Elinor	Mrs. Crouch.

Cicely	Miss Romanzini.
Maude	Mrs. Booth.
Adela	Signora Storace.

The success of this opera was never surpassed; it was a lasting favourite for many years: the first season it was played fifty nights. The under plot was taken from an Italian intermezzo opera; the entire scene of the Baron of Oakland reading a letter, was taken from it. Storace was greatly received in Adela, both as a singer and an actress. Bannister and Baddely were excellent in the comic parts; Mrs. Crouch, as Lady Elinor, was in the full bloom of beauty, and the richest voice. I had two fine songs allotted to me, 'From Hope's fond dream', and 'Spirit of my sainted sire', one of the most difficult songs ever composed for a tenor voice; indeed, all the music was beautiful: the admiration of the audience of the sestetto, 'By mutual love delighted', I can never forget; certainly, nothing could exceed the composition or the execution of it; both were perfect.

This season I was engaged by the noble Directors of the Ancient Concerts, as principal tenor. The night of my début, the Earl of Uxbridge was the Director; the songs allotted to me by his Lordship, were 'Jephtha's rash vow',[1] and the laughing song from L'Allegro, 'Haste thee, nymph, and bring with thee'. The late Mr. Linley heard me sing it over and over again, and to his masterly instructions I owed the indulgence which I received. In singing sacred music I was aware of its value, and fagged at the tenor songs of Handel with unremitting assiduity. Mr. Joah Bates conducted those concerts, and was supposed to understand Handel perfectly; he was an excellent performer on the organ; Cramer was the leader, and Cervetto principal violoncello. The concerts were then held in Tottenham Street, and their Majesties and the royal family were constant attendants; but, although it was difficult to become a subscriber, the room was always crowded.

I was lucky enough to meet with the approbation of Mr. Bates, in the recitative of 'Deeper and deeper still'; my next song was the laughing one. Mr. Harrison, my predecessor at those concerts, was a charming singer: his singing 'Oft on a plat of rising ground';[2] his 'Lord remember David'; and 'O come let us worship and fall down', breathed pure religion. No Divine from the pulpit, though gifted with the greatest eloquence, could have inspired his auditors with a more perfect sense of duty to their Maker than Harrison did by his melodious tones and chaste style; indeed, it was faultless; but in the animated songs of Handel he was very deficient. I heard him sing the laughing song, without moving a muscle;

and determined, though it was a great risk, to sing it my own way, and the effect produced justified the experiment: instead of singing it with the serious tameness of Harrison, I laughed all through it, as I conceived it ought to be sung, and as must have been the intention of the composer: the infection ran; and their Majesties, and the whole audience, as well as the orchestra, were in a roar of laughter, and a signal was given from the royal box to repeat it, and I sang it again with increased effect.

Mr. Bates assured me, that if I had rehearsed it in the morning, as I sang it at night, he would have prohibited my experiment. I sang it five times in the course of that season by special desire.

There was at this time a subscription concert, held at Freemasons' Hall, called the Academy of Ancient Music, under the direction of Dr. Arnold; I was engaged also at that concert for the season. The subscribers were chiefly bankers and merchants from the city; I think I hardly ever saw a greater assemblage of beautiful women. In the summer of 1789, Mrs. Crouch and I went to Dublin, Cork, Limerick, and Liverpool, and had a pleasant and profitable campaign. We performed 'The Haunted Tower', in Dublin,[1] with complete success.

The morning after the first night's performance of that opera, I was at my father's, and heard a news-boy bawling about the street, 'Here is the high-born Hibernian Journal! the Freeman's Journal! and Saunder's Great News, and more to come!' Anxious to hear what the papers said of my performance of the night before, I opened the street door, and calling the news-boy to me, asked him for Freeman's Journal; 'Sir,' said the ragged urchin, 'I've sold the last I had.'

'Then,' said I, 'you stupid dog, if you have sold them, why are you crying them about the street?'

With an arch look, scratching his head, and looking me full in the face, he replied, 'Practice makes perfect, Mr. Kelly; I do it just to keep myself in voice;' and away he ran.

From Cork we went to perform a few nights at Waterford, and spent some very pleasant joyous days at Youghal, the seat of our worthy friend Mr. Robert Uniacke. His hospitable mansion was full of company; amongst whom were the Marquis of Waterford and family, and Mr. Newport the banker, now Sir John Newport.

In the month of October, there was a grand musical festival at Norwich. Madame Mara was engaged there, and so was I, as principal tenor singer. The first performance, was 'The Messiah', which I was to open on the Thursday morning. I was to quit town on the Tuesday, but on

Monday night I received an order not on any account to leave London; for Mr. Sheridan had sent a peremptory message to have Richard Cœur de Lion performed; and against his decree there was no appeal. John Palmer, the excellent comedian, was with me when I received the message; he said to me, 'My valued friend, Richard will be over by eleven o'clock; if you choose to have a carriage and four horses at the door, you will get with ease to Norwich by twelve, on Thursday, in time to open "the Messiah".—Norwich is the city that first cherished me, and where I married my beloved wife;—how I should like to accompany you, if you would give me a seat in your chaise.'

I said it would make me very happy to have the pleasure of his company. He told me he was perfectly acquainted with every inn on the road, and would write immediately to those where we were to change horses, to have relays prepared for us, that we might not meet with any delay on the road. I was much pleased with the promised arrangement, and wrote to Madame Mara that I should be at Norwich on Thursday in time, requesting her to secure two beds at the Hotel where she was; one for my friend Palmer, and one for myself.

On Wednesday evening, as I was dressing for Richard, my friend Palmer came to me, with the countenance of Joseph Surface,[1] and sighing, said, 'My best of friends, this is the most awful period of my life; I cannot leave town; my beloved wife, the partner of my sorrows and my joys, is just confined.'

I said, under such circumstances, of course I could not expect him to leave Mrs. Palmer, but I hoped there would be no mistake about the horses, which were ordered to be ready at each post; he sat down, and deliberately wrote down the names of all the places where he had ordered them to be in readiness.

About eleven o'clock, having merely taken off my Richard's dress, I got into the carriage; and accompanied by a Scotchman, who was my valet and hair-dresser, rattled off full speed to Epping, where we were first to change, at the inn marked down by my excellent friend; we knocked and bellowed for Mr. Palmer's horses; at last out came the ostler;—Mr. Palmer had no horses there; he had not sent any orders; nor did they even know who Mr. Palmer was.

I never in the course of my life experienced a greater disappointment; in short, all the way down I had to wait for horses, as Palmer had not written to any one of the inns; however, the road was excellent, and by paying the boys well, I got on at a capital pace without the smallest accident. It was market-day at Norwich, and as I drove in, the good folks stared and wondered to see me getting my hair dressed in the carriage; however, I reached the church-door just as the overture to 'the Messiah', was on the point of commencing. I took my seat in the orchestra, opened the 'Oratorio', and never was in better voice, although naturally much fatigued.

We had two more morning performances in the church, and three evening performances in the grand assembly room. At the conclusion of the festival I returned to town, and when I charged Palmer with neglect and deception, he swore that he had ordered all the horses exactly as he had stated. I thought it of no use to be at variance with him, and pretended to believe him, which of course prevented a quarrel, though his neglect might have been of the most serious consequence to me; and although the fact was, that Mrs. Palmer had not been confined at all.

About two months afterwards he was engaged to go to Reading, to act for a benefit, but he did not go; and wrote to the poor actor, for whom he was to perform, that he could not leave town, because Mrs. Palmer was just brought to bed; his letter was read from the stage to the audience. When I heard of it, I congratulated him upon the possession of a partner, who increased his family every two months. But Plausible Jack, all his life, was blessed with inventive faculties.

I remember there was a new comedy to be performed at Drury Lane, the name of which I do not now remember, in which Palmer had the principal part; it was very long, and the day before, at rehearsal, he did not know a single line of it. On the day the play was to be acted, the boxes all engaged, and a crowded house expected, Palmer sent word that he was taken dangerously ill, and that it would be at the risk of his life if he were to play that night. His letter was not sent to the theatre until three o'clock, when all was confusion, from the lateness of the hour at which the intelligence was received. Mr. Sheridan was at the box-office, and I was with him, when Powell, the prompter, brought him the letter. When he had read it, he said to me,—'I'd lay my life this is a trick of Plausible Jack's, and that there is nothing the matter with him, except indeed not knowing a line of the part he has to act to-night. Let you and I call upon him, and I am sure we shall find him as well as ever.'

He lodged in Lisle Street, two doors from my house. As we were passing by, Mrs. Crouch happened to be at one of the windows, and beckoned Mr. Sheridan to walk in; he did so, and I went on to Palmer's; and finding the street-door open, walked up-stairs, where I found him seated at table, with his family, in the middle of dinner, in seeming excellent health and spirits. I told him to clear away the table, for Mr. Sheridan would be there, in two minutes, to see him; 'and,' said I, 'he swears there is nothing the matter with you, and that you have shammed sick, only because you are not perfect; if he find himself right in his surmises, he will never forgive you, for putting off the play.'

'Thanks, my best, my dearest, valued friend,' replied Palmer; 'I'm sure you'll not betray me.'

I assured him I would not, and in a moment he was in his bed-room, enveloped in his dressing-gown, with a large woollen night-cap on his head, and a handkerchief tied under his jaw, stretched on a sofa. As Mr. Sheridan entered the room, he began groaning, as if in the most excruciating torture from the tooth-ache. Never did he act a part better, on or off the stage. Mr. Sheridan was really taken in; advised him to have his tooth extracted, and then to study his part, and get perfect in the new play. We went away, and I kept his secret till the day of his death.

It was about this time that the well-known Chevalier St. George was in London, and with him Giornovick, the celebrated violin player. Giornovick, who was a desperate duellist, quarrelled with Shaw, the leader of the Drury Lane orchestra, at an oratorio, and challenged him. I strove all in my power to make peace between them; Giornovick could not speak a word of English, and Shaw could not speak a word of French. They both agreed that I should be the mediator between them; I translated what they said to each other most faithfully; but unfortunately, Shaw, in reply to one of Giornovick's accusations, said, 'Poh! poh!'

'*Sacre Dieu*!' said Giornovick, 'what is the meaning of dat Poh! poh?—I will not hear a word until you translate me, Poh! poh!'

My good wishes to produce harmony between them for some time were frustrated, because I really did not know how to translate 'Poh! poh!' into French or Italian; I, however, at last succeeded in making them friends, but the whole scene was truly ludicrous.

In April 1789, I played Macheath, for the first time,[1] for my benefit. Mrs. Crouch, Polly; and Mrs. Charles Kemble (then Miss Decamp), Lucy; both these ladies were inimitable. To play Macheath was the height of my ambition: I took all the pains I could, and no young man had greater pains taken with him. Mr. Linley remembered Beard and Vernon; John Kemble, Digges; they gave me imitations of these Macheaths: there was also then in London, the celebrated Irish Macheath, and worthy man, old Wildar, who had retired from the theatrical profession, and was living in London. Previous to his going on the stage, he had been a painter, and had a secret for cleaning pictures, which produced him a good income. His Colonel Oldboy will never be forgotten, and his Macheath was excellent. From his tuition I learnt much; but my great support was the perfect recollection I had of Webster, who was certainly the best Macheath in the world. I acted the part a number of nights, with by far the best acting Polly, and the best Lucy, I ever saw, or ever hope to see again.

I had the good fortune on my benefit night to produce, for the first time, the musical entertainment of 'No Song, no Supper'.[1] It will hardly be credited that this charming and popular opera, which has been acted hundreds of nights, was actually rejected by the Drury Lane management. Its author, my valued friend, Prince Hoare, and Storace, the composer of its enchanting music, gave it me for my benefit; the applause it received on that night, induced the managers to solicit it from the author and composer.

All the music is beautiful, but the finale to the first act is a most masterly composition; the drama is full of comic situations, and the whole, in my opinion, excellent. In the summer I went to Liverpool, Birmingham, Manchester, and Chester. The Italian Opera was performed at the little theatre in the Haymarket this year, which was the first of George Colman the younger's management.

On the 31st of October died that eccentric comedian, and great supporter of O'Keefe's muse, Edwin. I knew him well; he was the best English burletta[2] singer I ever heard; he had great rapidity of utterance, and was a competent musician; his Peeping Tom and Lingo were masterpieces.

I this season received a most flattering mark of attention from Mr. John Beard, the celebrated English tenor singer. He did me the honour to come from his house at Hampton (as he told me) to hear me sing 'Spirit of my sainted sire', in 'The Haunted Tower'; he sat in the Drury Lane orchestra box, with his trumpet to his ear, for he was very deaf; and after the opera was over, came upon the stage to me, and was pleased to express himself in high terms of approbation. I confess such a tribute from such a man was gratifying in the extreme.

In the beginning of June 1789, Doctor Arnold, for whose distinguished talents I felt a great regard, called upon me, to request that I would assist him in engaging Madame Mara, Signora Storace, and Mrs. Crouch, with several other eminent singers, to go down to Cannons, where he had kindly undertaken to conduct an oratorio, or rather a selection from Handel's works, for the relief of the poor of Stanmore. Cannons was formerly in the possession of the Duke of Chandos, and the house in which Handel composed some of his finest music. This beautiful place was purchased by Colonel O'Kelly, of turf celebrity, who, at his death, left it to his nephew, Colonel O'Kelly, a particular friend of mine. His father resided with him at Cannons, and was a good-natured, well-meaning Irishman, with a fine Connaught brogue, and a great crony of Father O'Leary's.

When Mrs. Crouch and myself were at breakfast, he called upon us, and said to me, 'Arrah, my jewel of a namesake, tell me what tunes are we going to hear at church this morning?'

I shewed him the printed bill of the performance, part of which he read, and made his comments on it. In act the first was to be sung, 'Lord what is man?'[1] by Madame Mara. 'Upon my honour and conscience', said he, 'I am mightily mistaken if Madame Mara don't pretty well know without asking.'

The next song announced, was 'Total Eclipse',[2] by Mr. Kelly. 'That is right, my jewel,' said the Colonel, 'I like that now; the more you talk about Eclipse the better, for wasn't it Eclipse that bought Cannons?'

15

This season, a singer, of the name of Bowden, made his appearance at Covent Garden in 'Robin Hood'. I remember going to see his début with Madame Mara, who had known him when he was in a mercantile house at Manchester, and was very much interested in his success: he was received with great applause, his voice was good, and he sang with taste. Johnstone played the part of Edwin, and their voices blended well together in the duet of, 'How sweet in the woodlands'. Mrs. Billington was the Angelica, looked beautifully, and sang the simple ballad, 'I travelled India's barren sands',[3] like a true Angelica. In the same box, with Madame Mara and myself, sat Charles Bannister, who had originally acted the same part of Robin Hood; a person next to him, who was vehemently applauding Bowden, had the bad taste to say to Bannister (purposely, I suppose, to mortify him), 'Ay, ay, Sir, Bowden is the true Robin Hood, the only Robin Hood;' on which Bannister replied,

'Sir, he may be Robin Hood this year, but next season he will be robbing Harris.' This *jeu d'esprit* produced some merriment.

In August 1790, Mr. and Mrs. Crouch, myself, and a very old friend of Mrs. Crouch, a Mr. M'Donnell, proposed to spend some time at Margate, and thence to go to Paris: Mrs. Billington was at Ramsgate at the same time. In the churchyard of St. Peter's[1] are interred the remains of that excellent scholar and actor, Mr. Thomas Sheridan, who died at Margate; his son, Richard Brinsley Sheridan, followed him to the grave, and during his illness paid him the most affectionate and dutiful attention, as I can testify.

The recollection of this place is indelibly stamped upon my mind by a circumstance which deeply interested us all at the time. A poor girl, an inhabitant of it, by an accident, was deprived of the use of her limbs, and reduced to the greatest distress. Mr. Phillips, the father of Mrs. Crouch, then lived at St. Peter's, and took great pains to forward a subscription for the poor sufferer, and drew up a petition to the inhabitants and visitors; the Honourable Wellesley Pole (now Lord Maryborough) and his lady; the Honourable Mr. Villiers and his lady (Mrs. Pole's sister), were then at Margate, highly esteemed for their kindness and philanthropy; and with their usual goodness, they undertook to promote the subscription; and not only made a liberal donation themselves, but in the public library one evening, when the room was crowded with visitors, they went round to every individual to request their charity for the poor girl, and collected an unexpected sum of money.

Mrs. Crouch and I were present; and when it came to our turn to bestow our mite, I said to Mrs. Crouch, that I thought our best donation would be to play a night at the theatre for the girl's benefit; and as neither of us had ever been seen on the stage at Margate, and the place was very full, I hoped we should bring her a good receipt. Mrs. Crouch most cheerfully acquiesced, and the night appointed by the manager was the Saturday week: in the course of the next day, the performance was announced,—'The Beggar's Opera';—Mrs. Crouch, Polly; myself, Macheath: every place in the house was taken, and the whole pit, one row excepted, railed into the boxes.

Two days afterwards, looking out of my window, who should I see, but my old friend and countryman, Jack Johnstone, who told me he had just returned from the Federation at Paris. I mentioned to him that the day after the girl's benefit my party and myself were going there; 'Egad,' said he, 'I should like to make one of your party, and go with you.'

I said, 'I should be delighted with your company; but you tell me, that you are only this day returned from Paris.'

'That,' said he, 'makes no difference; I shall be ready to accompany you at an hour's warning; and,' added he, 'if you think that my playing Mat-o'-the-Mint, for the poor girl, will be of any use or strength to the performance, you may command my services.'

The offer was most liberal and kind; for the high rank he held in his profession, made it a condescension in him to play such a trivial character. He introduced a song in the thieves' scene at the table, which he sang admirably, and was most loudly applauded,—a just tribute to his talents and good nature; indeed, the whole of the performance gave satisfaction to as crowded an audience as ever filled a theatre. The receipts of the house, and many liberal presents sent to the poor girl, were by her patronesses invested in an annuity, which produced her at least a comfortable subsistence for the remainder of her life.

While at Margate, Mr. and Mrs. Crouch, and myself, were staying at the Hotel, kept by a man whose manners were as free and easy as any I ever met with.—He was proverbial for his nonchalance, and a perfect master of the art of making out a bill. One day, Johnstone dined with us, and we drank our usual quantum of wine. In the course of the evening, our bashful host, who, amongst other good qualities, was a notorious gambler, forced upon us some Pink Champagne, which he wished us to give our opinions of. My friend, Jack Johnstone, who never was an enemy to the juice of the grape, took such copious draughts of the sparkling beverage, that his eyes began to twinkle, and his speech became somewhat of the thickest;—my honest host, on perceiving this, thinking, I suppose, to amuse him, entered our room with a backgammon table and dice, and asked Johnstone if he would like to play a game. Johnstone, at that time, was considered fond of play, of which circumstance mine host was perfectly aware. Mrs. Crouch and I earnestly entreated Jack to go to bed, but we could not prevail upon him to do so; he whispered me, saying, 'You shall see how I will serve the fellow for his impudence;' and to it they went.—The end of the business was, that before they parted, Johnstone won nearly two hundred pounds, and I retired to bed delighted at seeing the biter bit. It was, what the Cockneys call, quite refreshing.

On Sunday morning, in a post coach and four, Mr. and Mrs. Crouch, Mr. M'Donnell, Johnstone, and I, set off for Dover, and went to the York Hotel, where we were detained by contrary winds until the Tuesday morning following. We met a very pleasant fellow there, a friend of

Johnstone's, a Captain Barnes, who had been second to the noted Dick England, in the duel which he fought at Cranford Bridge with Mr. Nolles, the brewer, of Kingston, and in which Mr. Nolles was unluckily shot. The Captain was an Irishman, with a strong vernacular twang, a powerful man, and remarkably tall; he had a man-servant not quite nine years old, and very short for his age. He was dressed *cap-à-pie* like a horse-jockey:—nothing could be more diverting than to see the huge master and diminutive servant together, going along the beach to the boat, to get aboard the packet;—the master took long Bobadil-like strides, and Tom was ordered to walk behind him; every two minutes master would stop, and cry out,—'Tom, are you after me?'—Tom answered,—'Yes, Captain.' The Captain, turning to me, vociferating,—'By the pipe of Leinster, Sir, he is the first man-servant in Europe,'—went on a few steps further, then repeated,—'Tom, are you after me?'—'Yes, Sir.'—'He is the first rider and shaver on the face of the known universal world.' In short, the Captain thought that his Goliath was the first of all valets. It was such a truly laughable scene, that when I returned from France, and told Jack Bannister of it, it tickled his fancy so much, that many and many an evening, to please Lord Derby, Miss Farren, &c. &c., in the Green Room, did we enact it—Bannister, on his knees, representing Goliath; and myself, his master; Bannister, with a great vein of comic humour, made the dialogue truly amusing as, indeed, he did every imitation which he gave.

At Calais, we went to Dessein's, made an excellent dinner, and passed the night there. We took our route the next morning for Lisle, and got to dinner at St. Omer. At the hotel where we dined, the landlady told us that Madame la grande actrice Anglaise Siddons had just dined, and quitted the house not more than a quarter of an hour before our arrival. I asked the landlady what she thought of Mrs. Siddons?—She said, she 'thought her a fine woman, and thought she made it her study to appear like a French woman; but,' added the landlady, 'she has yet much to learn before she arrives at the dignity and grace of one.' After this speech I could find nothing palatable in her house.

We slept at Mount Cassel, and took the route to Lisle, through Belle-isle,—a pretty country all the way. I was much pleased with Lisle. At this period, part of the Irish brigade was quartered there; among whom were two worthy Irishmen, and distinguished officers, a Colonel M'Carthy, and Major Doran, who took us to view the whole of the fortifications, &c. There I saw Sir Watkin Lewes, of whom it was jocularly said, that he possessed so much military ardour, that he always slept in his boots. The Chevalier St. George occupied apartments in the same Hotel with us, and favoured us with some solos on the violin, of his own composition; he certainly possessed infinite skill on that instrument. The Chevalier St. George, of whom I have already spoken, was a Creole,[1] and a man of great abilities; he was reckoned the finest fencer in Europe, and an excellent equestrian: he had composed a great deal of music, and was esteemed a very fine violin player. When he came to London with Giornovick, they attempted to carry on concerts by subscription, but they failed. He was driven to many schemes to recruit his finances, and, amongst others, he had recourse to one which did not redound to his credit. A Mr. Goddard, a noted fencing-master, challenged him in the public newspapers to fence at the Pantheon, which was crowded, to witness the trial of skill; every one anticipated that St. George would be the victor, but the reverse was the case,—Goddard won the day.

I remember being present, and much mortified, as St. George and I were intimate friends. It, however, was supposed afterwards, that he permitted himself to be vanquished for the consideration of a large sum of money; and, like the apothecary in Romeo and Juliet, 'his poverty, and not his will, consented.' Poor St. George proved the old adage, that

'He, whom the dread of want ensnares,
With baseness acts, with meanness bears.'

There was an excellent company of French actors at the theatre at Lisle, to which we went both the nights we remained there.

On Friday (an ominous day for travelling, as Mr. Sheridan used to say), in a post coach and four we set off for Douay. Had time permitted, I should have liked to stop at the latter place, and visit the College, having a feeling of affection for that seat of learning; inasmuch as a half brother of mine was sent there to be educated for the Roman Catholic priesthood, as well as my friends Messrs. John and Charles Kemble, who studied there. My excellent friend, John Kemble, as is generally known, was intended for a priest, but Melpomene claimed him as her darling son, and snatched him from the holy church, where, perhaps, he might have become as good a Cardinal, in reality, (and mayhap a Pope) as on the stage. He was the best theatrical one I ever saw;—his Cardinal Wolsey, in Henry VIII., was a masterpiece. I have heard him often say, that he was much indebted for his personification of that character to his recollection of Digges. Of one thing I am persuaded, from having lived for a number

Music by Michael Kelly for a song from Blue Beard *sung by Mrs Crouch in 1798*

Blue Beard: *Title page of vocal score. Mrs Crouch as the heroine is on the balcony, while Miss De Camp on*

of years in habits of the strictest intimacy with him, that from his intellectual endowments, the extent of his mind, and the perseverance of his nature, to whatever profession he had turned his thoughts, he would have been a splendid ornament to it. From those who could appreciate his talents better than myself, he was held in the highest estimation.

We, however, were unable to stay at Douay, and jogged merrily towards Cambray, armed, not with pistols, but with bottles of sparkling Champagne, in the pockets of our carriage, and we drank the health of the inhabitants of every château which we passed; Johnstone and myself singing all the way, and repeating, while we quaffed, the translation of Dr. Aldridge's Latin epigram of Causæ Bibendi.

'If on my theme I rightly think,
There are five reasons why men should drink;
Good wine—a friend—or being dry,
Or, lest one should be by and by,
Or——any other reason why.'

We got to Cambray, visited the cathedral; a fine structure, and then pushed on to Chantilly—a most enchanting spot; the avenues are finely laid out. In going through one of them, Johnstone was delighted to see the partridges walking about, as if conscious of their security. As we got to Chantilly early in the evening, we went to view the stables, the pride of the Prince de Condé; our conductor told us he had been brought up in the Prince's stables from a child.—'But,' said he, 'thanks to our good citizens, he is no more a greater personage than myself, parbleu, *I* am now his equal.' The triumphant air of satisfaction which the scoundrel displayed in his republican countenance, when reciting the downfall of his great, good, and unhappy master, actually filled us with horror; it seemed the *ne plus ultra* of baseness, villainy, and ingratitude.

In the morning, we set off for Paris, where we had superb apartments taken for us in the Rue Neuve St. Marc. We hired two French valets-de-place, one called Giuseppe, and the other, Louis; both, though very communicative, were very respectful. Louis was a strong revolutionist, which I discovered in the following way:—The third day after our arrival in Paris, we dined at the Palais Royal;—I told Louis to bring me my great coat at ten o'clock to the Théâtre Montansier; he said he would be there punctually. After dinner, previous to going to the theatre, the ladies, with Johnstone and myself, were sauntering about the Palais Royal, and saw, opposite to the Café de Foix, a great crowd, listening attentively to an orator who was haranguing them. We mingled with the rest, to listen, and heard the orator uttering the most revolutionary language, in extremely well-turned periods, and with great fluency. Johnstone asked me if I ever saw so strong a likeness as between the orator and our valet-de-place, Louis? I confessed the resemblance; however, we passed on, and went to the play.

On leaving the theatre at ten o'clock, we found Louis at the door waiting for us, with our great coats. While he was waiting on us at supper, I turned to him, and said,—'In the Palais Royal, this evening, we heard a man addressing the crowd with force and eloquence, so like you, Louis, in person, that, had not his coat been of a different colour to yours, I could have sworn it had been yourself.'—'Sir,' said he, 'you would have sworn rightly; it was me, though in a different coat from that which I now wear; I changed it before I came to you to the theatre.'—'Indeed,' said I, with surprise, 'why, I engaged you as my valet-de-place, not as a *Palais Royal orator*.'—'Sir,' answered my valet, 'you told me you did not want me until ten o'clock, and to be at the theatre with your great coats, and there I was to the minute; in the interim, Sir, I considered my time was my own, and I made what use of it I thought proper.'

All things considered, I thought it prudent to say that he was in the right, and certainly, all the time he was in our service, he proved himself a most attentive servant; and, strange to say, not spoiled by fancying himself (when off duty,) as good a man as his masters.

We remained in Paris three weeks, and saw every thing worth seeing, and went every night to one of the theatres. The first night we went to the Grand Opera, Mrs. Crouch, who was seated in a box in a conspicuous part of the house, had the eyes of the parterre turned on her, the audience seemingly staring at her with displeasure, and whispering to one another. A gentleman in the box with us explained the cause; poor Mrs. Crouch, quite unconscious of the impropriety, wore a white rose in her hair, which was the royalist colour. She was on thorns until she quitted the box, but met with no insult, which was singular, considering how completely the dominion of anarchy and tumult had brutalized the people.

There was an Italian Opera in the Faubourg St. Germain.—Among the performers, were my friends, Mandini, his wife, Viganoni, Rovedino, &c. &c., who paid us every attention. We had most agreeable parties made for us, and amongst them, one given by the justly celebrated actor, Monsieur La Rive, at his house (or rather palace) in the Champs de Mars. His style of living was magnificent, and I never saw a finer dinner put on table than his. I sat next to him, and when I asked to be helped to any of the exquisite dishes, he would say, 'Pray, do not eat of it, there's something coming which I am sure will please you better than any dish now on the table.' This something at last appeared, in the shape of a small piece of half roasted beef, not warmed through. The good Monsieur and Madame La Rive were astonished to see that we did not touch it, as it was prepared purposely for us, by way of a bonne bouche. His wines were excellent, but the treat he gave us after dinner was delightful. This great tragedian played all kinds of tricks to amuse us. We adjourned from his dinner-parlour to his spacious library, which opened into a beautiful garden, crowded with orange and lemon trees, &c. &c.: in different parts of the library, hung various crowns of laurel with which he had been presented in the different theatres of France, where he had performed, accompanied by copies of verses, eulogizing his wonderful talents. He acted a scene of Romeo and Juliet, by Ducis; it was a scene where Montague (which seems to be a great character in their play) vows vengeance and hatred to Capulet.

Never shall I forget his recitation;—it was the very essence of the histrionic art. Johnstone, Mrs. Crouch, and myself, had not words to express our admiration. In his library, he had a print of Mrs. Siddons, as the Tragic Muse, from the picture by Sir Joshua. He lamented that he had not the gratification to be known to her personally, but begged of me to say to her, that if she would honour him by visiting him in Paris, he would, for the sole purpose of having her an inmate in his house, go to Calais and meet her; and added, that it would be a proud day for him to embrace so great a genius. He made me a present of a fine print of Le Kain, the great tragedian, his predecessor at the Théâtre Français, which, on my return to London, I gave John Kemble. I had the satisfaction of seeing La Rive in several of his best parts;—one, in particular, I admired, of his Guillaume Tell. His manner of shooting at the apple, and the strong contrast of passions which he exhibited, were masterly, and called down thundering plaudits from his delighted auditory.

One morning, Johnstone and I, walking in the Palais Royal, met with the well-known Richard England, whose name occurs before in these pages; he was an old acquaintance of Johnstone's, and was living in Paris, keeping a Pharo Bank, in conjunction with the celebrated Lady Worsley, which was frequented by the beau monde of Paris. He gave us a sumptuous dinner, and, at his table, for the first time, I met the notorious Dr. Jackson, better known by the name of Viper Jackson. It was said that he broke Foote's heart by the letters he wrote against him in defence of the Duchess of Kingston. I found him a well-informed, pleasant man, full of anecdote, particularly about theatrical people. He was the great friend and adviser of John Palmer, when he had the Royalty Theatre.[1] He was considered a great republican, and a great rebel. I confess I thought him, from his conversation, a dangerous man, and was fully on my guard before him; he put me very much in mind of the advice of my long-tailed patron at Venice, that a silent tongue maketh a wise head.

I went more than once to the National Assembly; Mrs. Crouch and Johnstone were present at a great debate there, when Mirabeau defended his brother, who was at Berlin, with great force and eloquence, from charges brought against him.

The time, however, was fast approaching, at which we were to quit Paris; for, before I left London, Le Texier, the French reciter, had translated Grétry's opera of La Caravane[2] into English. Mr. Linley had adapted the original French music to English poetry, and it was to be produced at the opening of Drury Lane.—As Mrs. Crouch and myself had principal parts in it, I was very anxious to see it performed on the Grand Opera at Paris, and to make observations how they got it up. I mentioned my wish to Monsieur Gardel, and he was so polite (though another piece was announced to be performed) to have 'The Caravan' performed for the purpose of gratifying our curiosity. We saw it finely acted, and the decorations and scenery were of the most splendid description; we saw also the opera of 'Blue Beard'. 'Racule Barbe Bleue', is the French title of it: the fine bass singer, Chenard, was famous in 'Barbe Bleue'; and Madame Dugazzon, in Fatima, and Mademoiselle Cretue, in Irène, were both excellent: the music by Grétry, was very good; but so different are the tastes of a French and English audience, that when I produced my 'Blue Beard' at Drury Lane, I did not introduce a single bar from Grétry. Mrs. C. was struck with the subject, and wrote down the programme of the drama, with a view to get it dramatized for Drury Lane; Johnstone got the music copied to bring to Mr. Harris, at Covent Garden, and it was got up at that theatre as a pantomime, I believe by Delpini; I never saw it in that shape, but have heard that it was not successful.[3]

After bidding adieu to all our kind friends, after a sojourn of six weeks, we left Paris, which I quitted with great regret, as I found it all gaiety and pleasure, and very different to Rousseau's description of it:—

> Oh, Paris! ville pleine de brouillard,
> Et couverte de boue,

Où les hommes connoisent pas l'honneur,
Ni les femmes la vertu.

We made the best of our way *viâ* Amiens, Abbeville, Montreuil, and got safe to Boulogne, where we were detained four days by contrary winds; at length we got away,—had a passage of four hours, and arrived at the York Hotel, at Dover; not displeased to find ourselves once more in this free and happy country, with good old English fare before us.

16

On January the 1st, 1791, was produced at Drury Lane, the opera of 'The Siege of Belgrade'. The drama was written by Cobb, the music by Storace. The under-plot of this opera was taken from the Italian piece of 'La Cosa Rara', which had been originally taken from a Spanish drama. There was a good deal of beautiful original music in it, by Storace, who, with his great taste and knowledge of effect, had also selected some from Martini. The opera was received with great applause, and was performed the first season sixty nights to overflowing houses. The acting of Mrs. Crouch, in the 'Letter Duet', with the Seraskier, was beyond all praise, and Palmer's bye-play was excellent. One night, during the performance, an accident occurred which gave me great uneasiness: in the battle scene, between Palmer and myself, when fighting with scimitars, he left his head totally unguarded, and received so severe a blow in the forehead, that the blood spouted all over the stage; luckily, the wound was not sufficiently serious to confine him, although he was obliged to wear a black patch on his forehead for a length of time. In justice to poor Palmer, I must say he bore his misfortune with the greatest good humour.

On the 17th of February, the Italian Opera company removed to the Pantheon[1] in Oxford Street, which was converted into a theatre. I went the first night: the house was very small, and the stage particularly so; but the company was extremely good. For the serious opera, the celebrated Pachierotti, who is just dead, was engaged as first soprano; the tenor, Lazzerini; the prima donna, Madame Mara. 'L'Armida', was the serious opera. For the comic opera, they had Signors Cipriani, Morelli, Leperini, and Signora Cassentini, who afterwards married Signor Bergi, then stage manager for the Committee, which consisted of the Duke of Bedford, Lord Salisbury, and Mr. William Sheldon.

This season, the Abbé Casti's 'Grotta di Trofonio' was translated, or rather adapted for the English stage, under the title of 'The Cave of Trophonius', by Prince Hoare, and liberally given by the author to Mrs. Crouch for her benefit. Storace furnished the music, chiefly selected from the original composer, Salieri;[1] but, though skilfully dramatized, and the whole strength of the Drury operatic company in it, it did not meet with the reception which I think it deserved.

On the 4th of June, the Old Drury Lane closed for ever, with the comedy of 'The Country Girl', and 'No Song, no Supper'. At the end of the play, Palmer came forward, and thus addressed the audience:—'Ladies and Gentlemen, on the part of the proprietors, manager, and performers, I have to express their gratitude for the unprecedented support with which you have favoured them, during the past season; when next we have the honour to appear before you on this spot, we trust it will be in a theatre better calculated for your accommodation, more deserving Royal countenance, and the patronage of this great metropolis.'

There seemed to me so much whimsicality in the following newspaper paragraph, which I took a copy of at the time, that I think it will not be unacceptable to my readers: the date is June 6th, 1791:—

'Died, on Saturday night, of a gradual decay, in the hundred and seventeenth year of her age, old Madame Drury, who lived in six reigns, and saw many generations pass in review before her. She remembered Betterton in age, lived in intimacy with Wilks, Booth, and Cibber, and knew old Macklin when he was a stripling; her hospitality exceeded that of the English character, even in its earliest days of festivity, having almost through the whole of her life entertained from one to two thousand persons of both sexes six nights out of seven in the week; she was an excellent poetess, could be gay and grave by turns, and yet sometimes catching disorder from intrusive guests, could be dull enough in all conscience; her memory was excellent, and her singing kept in such a gradual state of improvement, that it was allowed, her voice was better the three or four last years of her life than when she was in her prime. At the latter end of the last century, she had a rout of near two thousand people at her house the very night of her death; and the old lady felt herself in such spirits, that she said she would give them *no supper without a song,* which being complied with, she fell gently back in her chair, and expired without a groan. Dr. Palmer, one of her family physicians, attended her in her last moments, and announced her dissolution to the company.'

The little theatre in the Haymarket opened on June 25th, and brought out 'The Kentish Barons', a play in three acts, interspersed with music; the drama by the Honourable Francis North, second son of Lord North, the prime minister; the airs were composed by Miss Monk, a *dilettante,* and very *dilettante-like* music it was. The language was bold and poetical, and written in elegant blank verse; but, owing to the inferiority of the music, it did not meet with unequivocal success. On the first night, I went behind the scenes,[1] and was introduced to its witty author, who honoured me with the most marked friendship and regard during the remainder of his life. I was so much pleased with the poetry of one of the songs, that I requested a copy of it from the noble author, to which I composed the music, and often sang it to him and the kind, good Countess of Guilford, both now no more.

SONG.—*Written by Francis, Earl of Guilford.*

I.

No, Clifford, no, for six long years
I felt a lover's hopes and fears;
The raging frenzy now is past,
Peace dawns upon my heart at last.

II.

Think not that I'd inconstant prove,
Where once I vow'd eternal love;
My heart had still felt all its flame,
Had beauteous Laura felt the same.

III.

Doom'd absence-lingering pangs to try,
I felt a transport in each sigh;
My lot was happy, though severe,
And pleasure mingled in each tear.

IV.

In vain I tried each honest art
To fix her foolish fickle heart;
But since she's gone, e'en let her go;
I'll sigh no more, no, Clifford, no.

Mrs. Crouch, Madame Mara, and Mr. Harrison, were engaged with me in the August of this year, for the second summer assize week at York cathedral: we arrived there the 8th of August, and went to the theatre, to see Mrs. Jordan in the 'Trip to Scarborough', and 'The Devil to Pay'; and, the devil to pay there was with poor Wilkinson: Mrs. Jordan and he could not agree; she thought herself slighted by the audience, and, *sans cérémonie*, before she had gone through half her nights, quitted York, leaving Tate's fair side all unguarded. Mr. and Mrs. John Kemble were on a visit to their old friend, Mr. Wilson, then Lord Mayor of York, with whom I dined twice, when Kemble and Tate were of the party. The city of York was crammed with visitors to attend the festival. The performances at the Minster for three mornings, gave universal satisfaction to crowded audiences: Madame Mara, Mrs. Crouch, and Harrison, were in fine song. The performances were, the 'Messiah', and two grand selections from the most approved works of Handel. There were concerts given in the evenings, at the great assembly rooms.

One of the most awful accompaniments to the inspired music of Handel, was furnished by the hand of Nature.

On Monday night, the 15th of August, 1791, during the grand chorus, 'He gave them hailstones for rain',[1] a storm, almost unparalleled in the memory of man, burst in all its violence over the rooms; the flashes of lightning, and the loud peals of thunder, were magnificently awful. The great room, almost crowded to suffocation, being surrounded with windows, which were opened to admit what little air there was, appeared full of blue flame; never before or since did I behold such a tremendous night,—such bursts of Heaven's artillery, and such sheets of fire, combined with the sacred words and the majestic music of the mighty master, were altogether appalling and magnificent.

It was during our stay this time at York, that Mrs. Crouch and I had the pleasure of first seeing my worthy friend Elliston: he played Carlos with great judgment and feeling, considering his youth, and considering moreover that Kemble was the Zanga. He was particularly impressive in the speech of

> 'Hope, thou hast told me lies from day to day,
> For more than twenty years.'

I remember Mrs. Crouch said to me, 'Depend upon it that young man will be an excellent actor;' and her prophecy has been amply fulfilled.

From York we were engaged to go to Newcastle-upon-Tyne, for a grand musical festival, which was fixed for the week following the assize week; we had, in the interim, a few days to spare, and Wilkinson engaged Mrs. Crouch and myself to play at the theatre on the Monday and Tuesday in the race week, August the 25th and 26th, which allowed us full time to get to the Newcastle Oratorio. Tate called upon us, and we agreed to perform 'Lionel and Clarissa', 'Inkle and Yarico', and Henry and Louisa in the 'Deserter', which we did to crowded houses. We were to return from Newcastle to York, and take our benefit on the Thursday after the races. I cannot conscientiously say, that my worthy Tate had any opinion whatever of my musical abilities, but he took it into his head that my skill in the culinary art was great. He used to call me the Harmonious Apicius; indeed, we hardly ever discussed any subjects but those of cooking and eating; he had a small appetite, but was a great epicure. At one time, when I was making an agreement with him, I wanted twenty guineas more than he was willing to give; at length he said, 'Well, young Apicius, twenty guineas shall not part us; you shall have it your own way; but, confess now, honestly, didn't you think the ducks were over-roasted yesterday at my Lord Mayor's?'

Wilkinson was certainly one of the most eccentric men I ever met with; one of his whims was, to hide chocolate drops and other sweet-meats in different holes and corners of his house, his great pleasure consisting in finding them, as if by accident, some days after. When he had taken a few glasses of old Madeira, of which he was very fond, he would mix his conversation about theatricals and eatables together, in a manner at once ludicrous and incomprehensible. I was sitting with him one night, in high spirits, after supper, and we spoke of Barry, the actor: 'Sir,' said he, 'Barry, Sir, was as much superior to Garrick in Romeo, as York Minster is to a Methodist chapel,—not but I think, that if lobster sauce is not well made, a turbot isn't eatable, let it be ever so firm.—Then there's that Miss Reynolds; why she, Sir, fancies herself a singer, but she is quite a squalini, Sir! a nuisance, Sir! going about my house the whole of the day, roaring out "The Soldier tired of War's alarms,"[1] ah! she has tired me, and alarmed the whole neighbourhood;—not but when rabbits are young and tender, they are very nice eating.—There was Mrs. Barry, for example; Mrs. Barry was very fine and very majestic in Zenobia; Barry, in the same play, was very good;—not but that the wild rabbits are better than tame ones.—Though Mrs. Barry was so great in her day, yet Mrs. Siddons—stewed and smothered with onions, either of them are delicious.—Mrs. Pope was admirable in Queen Elizabeth—a man I had here, made a very good Oronooko;—not but I would always advise you to have a calf's head dressed with the skin on, but you must always bespeak it of the butcher yourself;—though the last bespeak of Lord Scarborough did nothing for me, nothing at all; the house was one of the worst of the whole season;—with bacon and greens,—not twenty pounds altogether,—with parsley and butter;' and on he went talking, until he talked himself asleep, for which I did offer my thanks to Somnus, with all my soul; yet when clear of these unaccountable reveries, he was an amusing companion.

I have heard my friend King assert, that such was the power of Wilkinson's mimicry, that ugly as he was, he could make his face resemble that of Mrs. Woffington, who was a beauty of her time. I once requested him to make Mrs. Woffington's face for me, which he good-naturedly did, and to my utter astonishment, really made a handsome one. He was very fond of talking of his Peg, as he called Mrs. Woffington, and avowed that, in his younger days, he was passionately in love with her.

Tate Wilkinson was not singular in mixing with whatever subject he was talking about, that of eating. I knew a countryman of mine, a captain in the Irish brigade, whose constant habit was always to bring in something or other about eatables. A gentleman praising the Bay of Dublin, and its similitude to the Bay of Naples, 'Dublin Bay, Sir,' said my countryman, 'is far and away finer than the Bay of Naples; for what on earth can be superior to a Dublin Bay herring?'

'I am told,' said the gentleman, 'that the Irish brigade, in the Empress Maria Theresa's service, are a fine set of men.'

'You may say that, Sir,' said my friend, 'and she has also in her dominions the finest beef and mutton I ever tasted any where.'

One winter there was a severe frost in Dublin, and such a scarcity of coals, that hardly any were to be got for love or money; a gentleman was lamenting the situation of the poorer orders from the severity of the weather.

'It's very true, they are much to be pitied, poor devils,' said the captain; 'and the cold is very shocking, but it will bring in the curlews.'

There is an evident similarity in the turn of the Irish captain's mind to that of Tate Wilkinson.

Our time for departure, however, arrived; and Mrs. Crouch, her maid, and I, left York at five o'clock in the morning for Newcastle, and got to Durham to a late dinner: while it was preparing, I amused myself by looking about me, and in the hall of the inn, I saw a large bill posted, announcing the performances of the Newcastle festival; reading which, with great attention, I perceived a man, whom I recognised as Mr.

Hobler, the chorus singer, who sang at the Abbey, the King's Concert, and the Academy of Ancient Music. The bill announced an uncommon number of choruses, and I remarked upon the fact to the chorister. 'Why,' said I, familiarly, concluding, that as I knew Hobler, Hobler must know me, 'You will have warm work, my master, with all these choruses.'

'Not I,' said the singer; 'the more choruses there are, the better I am pleased; I never tire of them.'

'Why,' said I, 'that is strange, too, considering how much you have had of them in your time.'

'Not at all, I assure you,' said Hobler; 'I have for many years regularly attended the ancient concerts and music meetings,—I have never had too much of Handel's choruses yet.'

'Egad,' said I, 'you are quite a *fanatico per la musica*. And pray, now, to which of Handel's choruses do you give the preference?'

'Why, my dear Mr. Kelly,' said Hobler, 'I cannot decide; but I candidly tell you what Cicero said, when he was asked which of the orations of Demosthenes he liked the best, he answered the longest; so say I of Handel's choruses.'

'Bravo,' said I; 'you are quite a learned Theban.'

'Not much of that either,' said he, 'but I am never disinclined to avow an opinion of what pleases me.'

Just at this moment, the waiter came to announce dinner, and I asked the enthusiastic chorister if he would take a glass of anything.

'No, thank you,' said he, 'I have had my wine and my tea; I am an earlier man than you.'

'Pray,' said I, 'how did you travel here?'

'I came down in my carriage,' replied Hobler.

'The devil you did,' cried I.

'Yes,' said he, 'I always do.'

The landlord of the inn at this juncture made his appearance, and bowing respectfully to Hobler, told him that his carriage was at the door. 'Good day, Mr. Kelly,' said Hobler, 'I hope we shall meet at Newcastle;' and away he went.

While we were at dinner, the landlord came into the room, and I asked him if the chorus singer to whom I had been speaking in the hall was an old customer of his.

'What, Sir, the gentleman you were speaking to?' said the landlord, 'he is no chorus singer, Sir; he is one of the oldest baronets in England,

and has one of the finest places in Yorkshire; nor is there a more noble or liberal gentleman on the face of the earth than Sir Charles.'

'Sir Charles,' exclaimed I; 'What, is Hobler turned baronet?'

'Hobler?' said my host, 'why, that, Sir, is Sir Charles Turner.'

It is impossible to describe how vexed I felt at the gross mistake I had made, but it was too late to remedy it. I solemnly assured the landlord that Sir Charles Turner and Hobler the chorus singer were so like one another, that they were undistinguishable apart.

Sometime after this unpleasant equivoque, I met Sir Charles at Lord Dudley's, and made him every apology in my power. The worthy baronet laughed heartily, and told me that he mentioned the circumstance wherever he had an opportunity, as a capital joke. The next Christmas he sent me a fine large Yorkshire pye. His son, who succeeded to his title and estates, continued my friend, to the day of his death; and many times and oft, when I have dined with him, or met him at Lord Mexborough's and elsewhere, have we talked of my having taken his father for a chorus singer.

The Newcastle festival was very productive, and the oratorios in the church in the morning (three), and three concerts, were attended by all the people of Newcastle and its vicinity. We went to see all that was curious, and were received with much hospitality. We returned to York, on Wednesday, the 1st of September, and had for our benefit 'The Haunted Tower', and 'Richard Cœur de Lion'. The house overflowed. The next day I dined with my friend Tate, who gave me a calf's head, with the skin on it, admirably cooked by Mrs. Wilkinson; and the day after, we set off for London.

The King's Theatre being now finished, the Drury Lane company were transplanted there, *pro tempore,* until Drury Lane was ready for their reception. On the 22nd of September it opened, under John Kemble's management, with a prelude written by Cobb, for the occasion, called, 'Poor Old Drury', 'The Haunted Tower', and 'The Pannel'; the prices were raised, the boxes to six shillings, and the pit to three and sixpence. The doors were not opened at the hour announced in the bills of the day; the crowd was immense, and when they entered the house, they could not find their way to the different places; all was hurry, bustle, and confusion. The prelude began with Palmer and Parsons, who attempted to address the infuriated audience in vain; they were obliged to retire; the manager was called for, and Kemble came forward; a paper was given to him from the pit, stating that the cause of their disapprobation was the delay in opening the doors, and the great inconvenience of the passages. Kemble stood the fire well, and assured them, those inconveniences should be remedied on the next evening's performances.

The storm then ceased; the handing up the paper (which was done by a friend of the management) was a lucky *ruse*, and did great credit to the projector, General John Kemble himself. The prelude contained some comic points, alluding to the size of the Opera House, compared with Old Drury, and some beautiful scenery, particularly Mount Parnassus, by Marinari.

'The Haunted Tower' followed: I had to sing the first song. I was in good voice, and it filled the theatre well, which was by far the best for sound I ever sang at, not even excepting St. Carlos, at Naples. All the performers were welcomed with applause, and Mrs. Jordan, in the afterpiece of 'The Pannel', came in for a great share of it. Madame Mara was prevailed upon to perform for a few nights, and Artaxerxes was got up for her in great style. Kemble at this time had to fulfil an engagement which he had previously made at Newcastle. Mrs. Siddons and Mrs. Jordan were also going away, and Signora Storace was confined with severe illness;—all this crippled the theatre very much. Mr. Sheridan gave a dinner at the Piazza Coffee House to Mr. Holland, the architect of New Drury, and a number of his friends were present on the occasion; amongst others invited, Mr. Kemble, Storace, and myself. I happened to be placed near Mr. Sheridan, who at that time knew very little of me except my being one of his performers; in the course of the evening, he was lamenting to me, the situation the theatre was placed in by the illness and absence of some of its leading performers, and wished me to suggest what operatic piece could be got up without them. After a little thought, I proposed to him to get up 'Cymon', which could be done without any of the absent performers. Mr. Sheridan replied, 'Cymon, my good Sir, would not bring sixpence to the treasury.'

'Granted, Sir,' said I, 'Cymon as it now stands certainly might not; but my reason for proposing it, is, that I saw at Naples an opera, at the end of which, was a grand procession and tournament, triumphal cars, drawn by horses, giants, dwarfs, leopards, lions, and tigers, which was eminently successful; and it is my opinion, that Cymon might be made a vehicle for the introduction of a similar spectacle. I recollect all the spectacle part as done at Naples; and I think, with the novelty of your present theatre, and the manner in which the piece can be cast, Cymon would bring a mint of money to the house.'

After a moment's reflection, he said he thought it would, that he felt obliged to me for the suggestion, and that he would give directions to have it brought forward with all possible speed. The evening was spent with great good humour; my friend, Jack Bannister, contributed to its hilarity, by giving us excellent imitations of several of the performers of both theatres. At the conclusion, we adjourned to another room to take coffee; as Kemble was walking somewhat majestically towards the door, and Jack Bannister getting up to go after him, I hallooed out, 'Bannister, follow that lord, but see you mock him not,'[1] as Bannister, a moment before, had been mocking the actors; the quotation was thought rather apt, and produced much laughter.

Mr. Sheridan told Storace that night, that he was very much pleased with me, and desired him to bring me the Sunday following to dine with him in Bruton Street; he did so, and surprising to relate, Mr. Sheridan was at home to receive us. I spent a delightful day; and, after that, to the lamented day of that great man's death, I had the happiness to enjoy his confidence and society. Great preparations were made to prepare Cymon;[2] no expense was spared; and the piece was produced with all splendour and magnificence.

There was some new music introduced by Stephen Storace and others; the scenery was beautiful, and the procession magnificent; generally speaking, it was admirably performed.

The car, in which were Sylvia and Cymon, was drawn by two beautiful horses; and at my feet, as Cymon, lay a beautiful cupid. Before the piece was brought out, I had a number of children brought to me, that I might choose a Cupid. One struck me, with a fine pair of black eyes, who seemed by his looks and little gestures to be most anxious to be chosen as the representative of the God of Love; I chose him, and little then did I imagine that my little Cupid would eventually become a great actor; the then little urchin, was neither more nor less than Edmund Kean. He has often told me, that he ever after this period felt a regard for me, from the circumstance of my having preferred him to the other children. I consider my having been the means of introducing this great genius to the stage, one of my most pleasurable recollections.

It was in this year that Mr. and Mrs. Crouch separated[3] by mutual consent, he never appreciating the gem which he possessed.

On the 14th of January, 1792, the Pantheon theatre was burned. Mr. Sheridan was with me on that day; I went with him into Oxford Street, to view the conflagration. While Mr. Sheridan was observing how very high the flames were, he said, 'Is it possible to extinguish the flames?' An Irish fireman was close to us, and who heard him make the observation, said, 'For the love of Heaven, Mr. Sheridan, don't make yourself uneasy, Sir; by the Powers, it will soon be down; sure enough, they won't have another drop of water in five minutes.' Pat said this in the natural warmth of heart, for he imagined that the burning of the Pantheon theatre must have been gratifying to Mr. Sheridan, as the proprietor of Drury Lane.

A part of Mr. Sheridan's conduct, relative to the Opcra company at the Pantheon, I was witness to, and thought it reflected great credit on him. The noble directors of that theatre wished to get a patent for Italian operas at the Pantheon;—they opened it in the year 1791 with a splendid serious comic opera, and grand ballets, but they found the stage so contracted, that it was hardly possible to produce any thing like spectacle.

At the back of the Pantheon stage there was a large piece of ground which went as far back as Marlborough Street, which, with a house adjoining it, belonged to a Mr. Thompson. The noble directors of the Pantheon offered to give a large sum for the purchase of the ground, which would have enabled them to increase their stage.

Mr. Thompson, whose property it was, had been an old and faithful servant in Dublin to Mr. Thomas Sheridan, the father of Mr. Richard Brinsley Sheridan; and when Mr. Sheridan was in office in Mr. Fox's administration, he procured Thompson a place in one of the public offices, and also made him stage property-man of Drury Lane Theatre. The Duke of Bedford wrote a letter, which I have seen, to Mr. Sheridan, to request of him to compel Thompson to sell the piece of ground they wanted, without which, they could not have an efficient stage. Sheridan replied to his Grace, (the letter was sent from my house,) 'that he was sorry he could not grant his request, as the carrying on Italian operas at the Pantheon was most unjust and unfair towards the claimants on the Opera House in the Haymarket, as well as to Mr. Taylor, the chief proprietor, who was making every effort to rebuild it; and that, so far from aiding it, he would do every thing in his power to counteract it.' He immediately saw Thompson, and made a point with him, not to accept of any proposals from the Pantheon, which Thompson conceded, and so ended the business.

In the summer of 1792[1] I went to Paris to see what I could pick up in the way of dramatic novelty for Drury Lane, and a most interesting period it certainly was, and not to be forgotten by those who were there.

I found my old friends and comrades still at the Italian Opera at the Théâtre Feydeau; there also I fell in with my worthy countrymen, Colonel Stark Macarthy, and Captain Fagan; the latter possessed a vast portion of the ready wit of his country. I was walking with him one day in the Place Vendôme, in company with a French officer; and we stopped to admire the fine piece of sculpture which then stood there, representing the figure of Victory, holding a laurel crown of victory over the head of Louis XIV. The French officer was enumerating the splendid achievements of that heroic King, and particularly desired us to observe the attitude of the figure of Victory;—'Pray, Sir,' said Fagan, 'may I take the liberty of asking a question—is Victory putting the laurel on His Majesty's head, or taking it off?' The question puzzled the Frenchman, and made me laugh heartily.

At day-break, one morning, I was awakened by the beating of drums, and an uproar in the street; I found the King and Queen had made their escape from Paris; the tumult was terrific; all the gates of Paris were closed; the national guards called out; in short, all was anarchy and confusion; and although those dreadful scenes have been too accurately described to need an observation, it is impossible for one who has been an eye-witness to the horrors of a revolution, to refer to the period without touching on the subject.

One evening, I was sitting at the Café de Foix, in the Palais Royal, with my two friends, Macarthy and Fagan, and at the same table was seated the notorious republican, Tom Paine, and with him the well-known Governor Wall;[1] these two worthy persons were pouring forth to a group that crowded round the table, the most horrid invectives against the King and Queen; my blood boiled to hear the miscreants vomit forth their infernal doctrines, and revolutionary principles. In the midst of their harangue a courier entered the coffee room with intelligence, that the King, Queen, and family had been taken prisoners at Varennes; never shall I forget the delight of that caitiff Tom Paine; his Bardolph face blazed with delight, and Governor Wall loudly vociferated curses on their heads. I and my friends left the coffee-house with grief and horror, but were obliged to stifle our feelings: the sad news we found too true; it was proclaimed in the Palais Royal, on the Boulevards, and all over Paris; and at night there was a general illumination.

The next day Paris was all in a bustle; couriers gallopping backwards and forwards, dragged off their horses by the mob, and obliged to show their dispatches before they were allowed to proceed. In the evening, the

Richard Cumberland by George Romney

John Bannister, by J Russell, 1799

Madame Catalani in Semiramide *in 1806*

King and Queen were expected to arrive at the Thuilleries, accompanied by their family and suite. I procured a place to see their entry, and, through the interest of a friend, mounted a tree quite close to the palace. The road through which they were to pass was crowded for miles.

About six o'clock they entered the Thuilleries. I shall never forget it; it was a heart-breaking sight to see them brought prisoners into their own palace; their faithful followers and servants were seated on the top of their carriages, covered with dust, accompanied by an immense body of national guards. The conduct of the populace I thought most praiseworthy; not a voice was heard; all was silence; no exultation, no disapprobation; in every countenance around me I saw nothing but depression and sorrow.

I was quite close to the carriage when they dismounted; nothing could be more majestic than the conduct of the Queen, when Dupont (member of the National Assembly,) offered to hand her from the carriage; she waved her hand, and walked with a firm step into the palace, without accepting his aid. She was plainly dressed, and, I remember, wore a black bonnet, covered with dust. What a reverse of fortune! not quite six years previously I had seen both the King and Queen dining in public at Versailles, in health, in happiness, and in greatness, the very idols of their subjects; and now I beheld them brought back by force to their capital like malefactors.

17

I wished to quit such scenes as soon as possible, and the next morning went to Mr. Merry, His Britannic Majesty's minister, to procure a passport, but was more than a week before I could obtain one. I met at Mr. Merry's, Johnstone's friend, Mr. England, who was also waiting to get a passport to take him to Boulogne-sur-mer; he kindly offered me a seat in his carriage, which I thankfully accepted; we both got passports, and at nine o'clock at night left Paris. I had the precaution to put a national cockade in my hat; while my companion, who by the way had been taking so many parting bottles with his friends that he was greatly intoxicated, fell fast asleep.

When we got to the post house, at Ecouen, to change horses, a crowd of men and women surrounded our carriage, armed with pikes, pitchforks, &c. and demanded our passports; a monster of a woman, with a pike clenched in her extensive hand, opened the carriage-door, woke England out of his sleep, and gave him a hearty shake; he could not speak any French, except, unluckily, a few abusive words, which he did not fail to bestow upon all around him. I jumped out of the carriage, and addressed the huge Sycorax, who appeared to be the spokeswoman of the infuriated party; I told her that my companion and myself were English republicans, shewed her the national cockade which I wore in my hat, and added, that the gentleman in the carriage was, unfortunately, very much intoxicated with drinking republican toasts before he left Paris. I shewed her our passports, and, in short, soothed and flattered the huge harridan so much, that she let us proceed without further molestation. Our lives would not have been worth a sous, had I not spoken French, and taken the method which I did; notwithstanding which, I felt very uneasy until I reached Boulogne, for Mr. England was rather of a choleric temper, and could not disguise his dislike to the French.

When I got to Boulogne, I remained with him at his house there for two days, which were all I could spare, as the time was approaching at which I was obliged to be at Oxford, where Mrs. Crouch and I were engaged to sing at the grand musical festival. After this short delay, therefore, I took my leave of Dick England, grateful for the many attentions he paid me. I cannot omit mentioning a circumstance that happened, which I thought reflected great credit on him.

When I was at Dover, previous to my going to France the last time, there was at the same inn with me, a young man, a native of Dublin, and a Quaker, who was going to Dunkirk on some commercial business; but there being no packet at that port, and I, being pleased with his society, prevailed upon him to accompany me to Boulogne, where I knew he would find plenty of land conveyances to Dunkirk.

He was a jolly dog, and recounted many stories of his partiality to the stage, and how he used to disguise himself to go to the theatre, for fear of its coming to the knowledge of the elders: he was a wet Quaker, a fac-simile of O'Keefe's young Sad Boy; and, among other innocent propensities which he appeared to have, had certainly a great passion for gaming. We got to Boulogne early in the morning, and I proposed to stay there for three or four days.

On the pier I met with Mr. B——, with whom I had formed a slight acquaintance when at Boulogne the year before; he invited himself to dine with me and young Sad Boy; we drank a good deal of wine, and the

Spirit moved my young Quaker to excess; he was an open-hearted fellow, and told us that his business at Dunkirk was to receive a large sum of money, at which intelligence, our visitor, honest Mr. B—— seemed specially delighted. Now, this self-invited, dinner-taking friend, I knew to be a great gambler, and leagued with a number of English gamblers in Boulogne and at Paris, to scramble for what they could get. When Sad Boy had returned to rest, my *honourable friend* removed all doubts upon the subject by saying, 'Shall we do the foreigner?' I asked him what he meant,—'to get part of that money which he is going to fetch from Dunkirk,' said he, 'and divide it between us.' I said I would think of it, and confer further on the subject in the morning.

I knew that the fellow who made the vile proposition derived his chief support from the liberality of Dick England, and that the gambling transactions of the precious junto were all known to him. The post was in an hour to set off for Paris; so before I went to bed I wrote a letter to Dick England, at that city, informed him of the proposition made to me, and the intention of Mr. B—— to follow my friend to Dunkirk, and pillage him. I added, that my Quaker friend was an open-hearted, good-natured, unsuspicious Irishman, and entreated him to write to Mr. B——, and lay his injunction on him to avoid following young Sad Boy, and stated that I would wait at Boulogne, at Parker's Hotel, till I received his answer to my letter, which I entreated might be immediate.

I waited accordingly; by return of post I got a letter from Mr. England, stating that he had written to worthy Mr. B—— to caution him against directly or indirectly meddling with the Quaker; on the contrary, to watch him, and take care that he did not fall into the hands of any other decoy.

I shewed England's letter to young Sad Boy, advised him to be more upon his guard before strangers, and less communicative; I saw him safe off for Dunkirk, and got into my calassetto, on my way to Paris; and never, from that day to this, have I seen Mr. B——, who wished me to become a partner in his iniquity.

As soon as I reached Dover, I started for London, where I remained but one day. Mrs. Crouch, an attached friend of hers (Mrs. Williams), and I, set off in a travelling carriage for Oxford, where we had lodgings taken for us, at the moderate rate of twelve guineas for the festival week.[1] When we got to Salt Hill, Mrs. Crouch was attacked by dreadful shiverings and spasms; and when we reached Henley, found herself unable to proceed. I immediately sent for medical assistance, and had the good fortune to meet with Mr. Bayley, a skilful surgeon and apothecary, who found his patient in such a state that her removal would have been undertaken at the hazard of her life. We had to sing at the festival the next morning, but there was no alternative; I was obliged to leave her, and post to Oxford by myself: I got there just as the performance was beginning. I informed Dr. Hayes, the conductor, of Mrs. Crouch's illness, who advised me to go, after church, to Dr. Wall, the principal physician in Oxford, and prevail upon him to visit Mrs. Crouch, at Henley. The Doctor's house was full of company, and he had a large party to dine with him; notwithstanding which, he instantly put post horses to his carriage, and went off to Henley.

Immediately after the evening concert was over I set off for that place myself, and there found the worthy Doctor, who told me his patient was in great danger. He remained with her four days and nights: each morning, at break of day, I was obliged to post for Oxford, and after the business of the day return at night to Henley. The fatigue was wearing to the body, not to speak of the agony of singing in the church in the morning, and at the concerts in the evening, with an aching heart and anxious mind.

On the fifth day the worthy Doctor Wall pronounced his patient out of danger, and took his departure for Oxford, leaving her under the care of Mr. Bayley. We were obliged to remain there nearly four weeks, at the end of which period, I had the gratification to see my valued friend restored to her usual health and beauty. We went to Worcester and Birmingham for a few nights, and returned to London for the opening of the winter season at the King's Theatre, October 18th.

At that theatre was introduced to the public, for the first time, the musical romance, called 'The Prisoner'; written by the Rev. Mr. Rose, one of the masters of the Charter House. It was a piece of much interest; the principal scene (and a most effective one it was,) I saw at Paris, and gave it to the author, who, with a great deal of ingenuity, ingrafted it on his own drama. It was that where the prisoner escapes by the aid of the gaoler's children. Chenard, the French actor's performance of the gaoler, was very fine acting; and it is but justice to say, that Wewitzer's representation of the same character in its English garb, suffered nothing by comparison. The music by Attwood was very pleasing.

On the 20th of November, the opera of 'The Pirates' was produced; the drama by Cobb, the music by Storace. The male performers in it were Kelly, Dignum, Sedgwick, Suett, John Bannister, and Parsons.

The females, Mrs. Crouch, Miss Decamp, Mrs. Bland, and Signora Storace; the scenery was picturesque and beautiful, from designs taken on the spot by Stephen Storace, at Naples. The magic-lantern scene, representing Hero and Leander, and the crossing of the Hellespont, was peculiarly beautiful. Mr. Sheridan directed that no expense should be spared in decorating the opera, and his orders were fulfilled.—The music was a master-piece; but, above all, the finale at the end of the first act, which I thought Storace's chef-d'œuvre, and worthy to be placed by the side of Mozart's first finale to the 'Nozze di Figaro'.

All the performers had characters suited to their respective abilities, and the opera had a most successful run to crowded houses. There was a scene and a quintetto in the third act; the music composed by Guglielmi, a beautiful morceau, from the Italian opera performed at the Pantheon, entitled 'La Bella Pescatrice'. Stephen Storace thought so, and therefore introduced it. Whenever Storace selected, his knowledge of stage-effect was so great, that the selections were always appropriate and never-failing.

Mr. Sheridan had this year entered into an arrangement with Mr. Taylor, the proprietor of the Opera House, to carry on Italian Operas twice a week. On those nights (Tuesday and Saturday), the Drury Lane Company performed at the Little Theatre in the Haymarket; and at the Opera House on Monday, Wednesday, Thursday, and Friday.

On the 24th of January, 1793, there was not any play performed, from respect to the memory of the unfortunate monarch, Louis the Sixteenth, who was murdered in Paris on that day. Mr. Kemble, without consulting Mr. Sheridan, closed the Theatre. Mr. Sheridan, who was out of town, arrived late that evening, and finding there was no play, came to my house in Suffolk Street, accompanied by the present Earl Grey, and was highly incensed at the shutting up of the theatre upon such an occasion; for, he said, it was an invariable maxim with him, that neither politics nor religion should be taken notice of in his playhouse; though, I believe, no man deplored the tragical event more sincerely than he did.

Mr. Sheridan appointed Stephen Storace and myself joint directors of the Italian Opera, with a carte blanche; but he was proprietor, and of course consulted on all important points; and whose advice on theatricals, or any thing else, indeed, was so good, when he chose to give it? Amongst other things, he desired that the boxes should be newly decorated, and the seats in the pit and gallery covered with new cloth.

One day, when I returned from a late rehearsal to a hurried dinner, having to return to the theatre to act in 'Cymon', I saw a man waiting in the passage of my house in Suffolk Street, with patterns of different coloured cloth, that I might select one wherewith to cover the seats of the theatre. In a great hurry, I examined them, and chose one; the sequel will prove, that it would have been better for me had I professed myself no judge of upholstery.

The Italian Opera Company was good, in both the serious and comic departments. Signor Bruni, the first soprano singer, possessed a fine voice and fine person; Madame Mara was the prima donna; and myself the serious tenor. For the comic opera, Morelli was the primo buffo; Rondini, the second buffo; Signora Storace, the prima donna; with several others.

Paesiello's charming comic opera, the 'Zingari in Fiera', was produced that season; its popularity lasted many years. The ballets were of the first class; the great Noverre was the ballet-master, and there was a numerous and well-chosen corps de ballet. Among others, Didelot, L'Abune,[1] Miss Novelon, Gardel, Aumer, D'Egville, &c. Mademoiselle Millau (now Madame Gardel,) and the fascinating Hillisberg. Noverre produced his magnificent ballet of 'L'Iphigénie en Aulide'; the splendour of the spectacle, the scenery, the richness of the decorations and dresses, could not have been surpassed: the dancing was of the first order, and the acting of D'Egville, in Agamemnon, inimitable; the triumphal cars, with horses; the grand marches, processions, and above all, the fine grouping of the corps de ballet, all was *vrai* classicality, and proved Noverre to be the greatest master of his art. But he was a passionate little fellow; he swore and tore behind the scenes, so that, at times, he might really have been taken for a lunatic escaped from his keeper.

I once felt the effects of his irritability:—The horses attached to the car in which D'Egville was placed, were led by two men from Astley's, one of whom was so drunk that he could not go on the stage. I had been acting in the opera, but was so eager for the affray, and so anxious that things should go on right, that I had taken off my opera dress, and put on that of a Grecian supernumerary, and, with a vizor on my face, of course was not known. I held one of the horses, and all went correctly. I was standing behind the scenes, talking to one of the men, in my supernumerary dress, and perhaps rather loudly; Noverre, who was all fire and fury, came behind me and gave me a tremendous kick. 'Taisez-vous, bête!' exclaimed he; but when I took off my vizor, and Noverre found he had been kicking his manager, he made every possible apology, which I of course accepted, and laughed at the incident; at the same time begging him not to give me another such *striking* proof of his personal attention to the concern. By the way, the carpenters seemed, by their looks, to say, that the kicking was better bestowed on *me,* than on one of themselves; however, I can assure the reader it was the manager's *last* kick.

At the Little Theatre, the Drury Lane company performed, on March 7th, a very pretty operatic piece, called 'Osmyn and Daraxa'. The drama was written by Mr. James Boaden, and well received; the music by Attwood was very good. On the 11th of the same month, was acted for the first time, for Storace's benefit, the 'Prize; or, 2. 5. 3. 8.'[1] written by Prince Hoare, the music by Stephen Storace; it was received with great applause, and certainly not more than it merited, for it proved a prize to the theatre.

On the 20th of June, at the same house, with Mr. Colman's summer company, was performed, 'The London Hermit; or, Rambles in Dorsetshire', one of O'Keefe's pleasantest productions; the part of the Irish cicerone was a *chef-d'œuvre,* as performed by Johnstone. O'Keefe and Johnstone dined with me on the day it was produced, and I was highly gratified in having at my table O'Keefe, who had played with me in Dublin, in 'Lionel and Clarissa', before my departure for Italy. But, alas! how changed I found him!—When he acted Jessamy, he was a fine, sprightly, animated young man; now, poor fellow, broken down, and almost blind; but still full of pleasantry and anecdote. I went to see the comedy, which was admirably performed, and perfectly succeeded.

This year Drury Lane lost one of its most efficient members, in Mr. Wrighten, the Prompter, a man most esteemed and respected. I have often heard Mr. Sheridan say, that he thought an intelligent prompter of the greatest importance to a well-regulated theatre: a stage-manager was only required for *state days* and *holidays,* but a steady prompter was the *cornerstone* of the building. Wrighten's funeral was attended by all the School of Garrick, of which I was a member. Jack Bannister was detained on some particular business, and did not arrive until we were just setting out to the burial. Charles Bannister said, 'For shame, Jack—why are you so much after your time?—If Wrighten were alive, he'd forfeit you for being late.'

Speaking of the School of Garrick, and of my belonging to it, I ought perhaps, to explain, that it was a club formed by a few of the contemporaries of the British Roscius, who dined together during the theatrical winter season, once a month. They did me the honour (unsolicited on my part) to admit me among them. I was highly flattered as a young man, and duly appreciated the favour. It was, of all societies I ever have been in, perhaps the most agreeable; nothing could surpass it for wit, pleasantry, good humour, and brotherly love. When I was admitted, I found the following members belonging to it:

King,	James Aickin,
Dodd,	Farren,
Moody,	Wroughton,
Parsons,	John Palmer,
Baddely,	Robert Palmer,
J. and C. Bannister,	and
Frank Aickin,	Burton.

In mentioning their names, I need not say what were the flashes of wit and merriment that set the table in a roar; and yet, with the exception of my worthy friend, Jack Bannister, (whom God long preserve!) they are all gone to that bourne from which no traveller returns.

As they fell off, the following members were elected in their room:—

Holman,	Cherry,
Henry Johnstone,	Dowton,
Pope,	Mathews,
Suett,	Charles Kemble.

My friend Pope gave an excellent dinner, upon the occasion of his election, at his house in Half Moon Street; and the first Mrs. Pope, the ci-devant Miss Young, who had acted many of the principal characters of our Immortal Bard, with distinguished éclat, was requested to become a member of the club, by accepting the silver medal of Garrick, which each member wore at the meetings of the society. She came amongst us, and seemed to appreciate the flattering attention paid to her high professional merits. She was the only female who ever had the compliment paid her; but, alas! she, among the rest, is now no more; and, delightful as the society was, and intellectual as its recreations were, it gradually dwindled, either from deaths or desertions, until at last it has become extinct.

Old Moody, who was delighted with every thing which reminded him of his great master, was almost broken-hearted at the event. I was always partial to Moody's agreeable society; so, to indulge the old gentleman, I proposed that he and I should meet once a month, dine together, and keep up the form of the club, which we did for some time.

I remember upon one of these occasions, I perceived, as we sat over our bottle, that he was more than usually low spirited, and I ventured to ask, what made him so? 'My dear fellow,' said he, 'I feel myself the most miserable of men, though blessed with health and affluence. Such is the detestable vice of avarice, which I feel growing upon me, that parting with a single sixpence, is to me like parting with a drop of my heart's blood, for which reason, unconquerable as the growing passion is, I feel that I ought to be abhorred and detested by mankind.'

I endeavoured to rally him out of so singular a feeling; and as far as I am personally concerned, I can vouch for it, that he had no just reason for indulging it; for when I was desirous of purchasing the lease of my house, in Pall Mall, and happened to say in his presence, that I wanted £.500 to complete the bargain, he called upon me the following day and offered me the loan of that sum, upon no other security than my simple note of hand.

At the *tête-à-tête* meetings of the club he was, at times, very entertaining, and told me many stories of himself. Amongst others, he said that, early in life, he was sent out to Jamaica; and on his return to England, went on the stage, unknown to his friends. I do not recollect the name of the ship in which he told me he came back to England; but he informed me, that he worked his passage home as a sailor before the mast.

One night, some time after he had been on the stage, when he was acting Stephano in the 'Tempest', a sailor, in the front row of the pit of Drury Lane, got up, and standing upon the seat, hallooed out, 'What cheer, Jack Moody, what cheer, messmate?'

This unexpected address from the pit, rather astonished the audience. Moody, however, stepped forward to the lamps, and said, 'Jack Hullett, keep your jawing tacks aboard—don't disturb the crew and passengers; when the show is over, make sail for the stage-door, and we'll finish the evening over a bowl of punch; but till then, Jack, shut your locker.'

After the play was ended, the rough son of Neptune was shewn to Moody's dressing-room, and thence they adjourned to the Black Jack, in Clare Market (a house which Moody frequented,) and spent a jolly night over sundry bowls of arrack. This story, told by himself in his humourous manner, was very amusing.

Previous to the dissolution of the club, one night, when we were full of mirth and glee, and Moody seated, like Jove in his chair, and Mathews, amongst other members, present, a waiter came in to tell Mr. Henry Johnstone, that a gentleman wished to speak to him in the next room. In a few minutes we heard a great noise and bustle, and Henry Johnstone, in a loud tone say, 'Sir, you cannot go into the room where the club is; none but members are on any account admitted; such are our rules.'

'Talk not to me of your rules,' said the stranger; 'I insist upon being admitted.'—And after a long controversy of, 'I will go;' and 'You shan't go;'—the door was burst open, and both contending parties came tumbling in.

The stranger placed himself next to me, and I thought him the ugliest and most impudent fellow I ever met with. He went on with a rhapsody of nonsense, of his admiration of our society, that he could not resist the temptation of joining it,—filled himself a glass of wine, and drank to our better acquaintance.

Moody, with great solemnity, requested him to withdraw, for no one could have a seat at that table who was not a member.

The stranger replied, 'I don't care for your rules;—talk not to me of your regulations—I will not stir an inch!'

'Then,' cried the infuriated Moody, 'old as I am, I will take upon myself to turn you out.'

Moody jumped up, and throttled the stranger, who defended himself manfully;—all was confusion, and poor Moody was getting black in the face; when the stranger threw off his wig, spectacles, and false nose, and before us, stood Mathews himself, *in propriâ personâ*. So well did he counterfeit his assumed character, that except Henry Johnstone, who was his accomplice in the plot, not one amongst us suspected him.

Moody, when undeceived, was delighted, and added his tribute of applause to Mathews; and the evening passed off as usual, with glee and revelry. The part was admirably managed by Mathews, who had taken an opportunity of leaving the room to prepare himself for his disguise, while a song was going on, which engrossed the attention of the company, and so slipped out unnoticed. I have mentioned this circumstance in perhaps a wrong place, for it happened many years after the period of which I was previously treating; but as I was on the subject of the School of Garrick, I thought the anachronism excusable.

In the summer of 1793, Mrs. Crouch and I had engagements at Birmingham, Manchester, Chester, Shrewsbury, Worcester, and Liverpool; and at Dublin, for December, January, and February.[1]

Previous to going there, we played a few nights at Liverpool. My benefit was the last night of our engagement. In the morning of that eventful day, crossing Williamson Square to go to the theatre, a gentleman stopped me, and, accosting me with the most pointed civility, informed me that he had a writ against me for 350*l.*; I, at the time, not owing a sixpence to any living creature.

I said he must be mistaken in his man. He shewed me the writ, which was at the suit of a Mr. Henderson, an upholsterer in Coventry Street, and the debt, he said, had been incurred for furnishing the Opera House with covering for the boxes, pit, &c. &c. So, instead of preparing for the custody of Lockit, on the stage, (for 'The Beggar's Opera' was the piece to be acted,) I was obliged to go to a spunging-house.

I requested the sheriff's officer, who was extremely civil, to accompany me to Mrs. Crouch, to consult what I had best do; she advised me by no means to acknowledge the debt, but to go to the Exchange, and state publicly the cause of my arrest, and to ask any gentleman there to become bail; making over to such bail, as a security, nearly five hundred pounds, which we luckily had paid into Mr. Heywood's Bank, in Liverpool, three days before; but Mr. Frank Aickin, who was then manager, rendered any such arrangement unnecessary, as he very handsomely came forward and bailed me. I was therefore released, and performed Macheath that night to a crowded house.

I sent my servant to London by the mail, with an account of the transaction to Mr. Sheridan, who immediately settled the debt in his own peculiar way. He sent for Henderson the upholsterer, to his house, and after describing the heinous cruelty he had committed, by arresting a man who had nothing to do with the debt, and who was on a professional engagement in the country, expatiated and remonstrated, explained and extenuated, until he worked so much upon the upholsterer, that in less than half an hour, he agreed to exonerate me and my bail; taking, instead of such security, Mr. Sheridan's bond; which, I must say, was extremely correct in the upholsterer. But Mr. Sheridan never did things by halves; and therefore, before the said upholsterer quitted the room, he contrived to borrow 200*l.* of him, in addition to the original claim, and he departed, thinking himself highly honoured by Mr. Sheridan's condescension in accepting the loan.

I have seen many instances of Mr. Sheridan's power of raising money when pushed hard; and one among the rest, I confess even astonished *me*. He was once 3000*l.* in arrear with the performers of the Italian opera: payment was put off from day to day, and they bore the repeated postponements with Christian patience; but, at last, even their docility revolted, and finding all the tales of Hope flattering,[1] they met, and resolved not to perform any longer until they were paid. As manager, I accordingly received on the Saturday morning their written declaration, that not one of them would appear at night. On getting this, I went to Messrs. Morlands' banking house, in Pall Mall, to request some advances, in order to satisfy the performers for the moment; but, alas! my appeal was vain, and the bankers were inexorable,—they, like the singers, were worn out, and assured me, with a solemn oath, that they would not advance another shilling either to Mr. Sheridan or the concern, for that they were already too deep in arrear themselves.

This was a pozer; and with a heart rather sad I went to Hertford Street, Mayfair, to Mr. Sheridan, who at that time had not risen. Having sent him up word of the urgency of my business, after keeping me waiting rather more than two hours in the greatest anxiety, he came out of his bed-room. I told him unless he could raise 3,000*l.* the theatre must be shut up, and he, and all belonging to the establishment, be disgraced.

'Three thousand pounds, Kelly! there is no such sum in nature,' said he, with all the coolness imaginable; nay, more than I could have imagined a man, under such circumstances, capable of. 'Are you an admirer of Shakspeare?'

'To be sure I am,' said I; 'but what has Shakspeare to do with 3,000*l.* or the Italian singers?'

'There is one passage in Shakspeare,' said he, 'which I have always admired particularly; and it is that where Falstaff says, "Master Robert Shallow, I owe you a thousand pounds."—"Yes, Sir John," says Shallow, "which I beg you will let me take home with me."—"That may not so easy be, Master Robert Shallow," replies Falstaff; and so say I unto thee, Master Mick Kelly, to get three thousand pounds may not so easy be.'

'Then, Sir,' said I, 'there is no alternative but closing the Opera House;' and not quite pleased with his apparent carelessness, I was leaving the room, when he bade me stop, ring the bell, and order a hackney-coach. He then sat down, and read the newspaper, perfectly at his ease, while I was in an agony of anxiety. When the coach came, he desired me to get into it, and order the coachman to drive to Morland's, and to Morland's we went; there he got out, and I remained in the carriage in a state of nervous suspense not to be described; but in less than a quarter of an hour, to my joy and surprise, out he came, with 3,000*l.* in bank notes in his hand. By what hocus-pocus he got it, I never knew, nor can I imagine even at this moment; but certes he brought it to me, out of the very house where, an hour or two before, the firm had sworn that they would not advance him another sixpence.

He saw, by my countenance, the emotions of surprise and pleasure his appearance, so provided, had excited; and, laughing, bid me take the money to the treasurer, but to be sure to keep enough out of it to buy a barrel of native oysters, which he would come and roast at night, at my house in Suffolk Street.

After my benefit, at Liverpool, we performed a few nights at Chester, where I met a Major Haliday, who was doatingly fond of the stage, and particularly of acting Hamlet. He did so one night at the Chester theatre to a crowded house. I have seen many worse professional Hamlets; Mrs. Crouch was the Ophelia. I went to spend a couple of days with him at his place, within a few miles of Parkgate, accompanied by Messrs. Banks and Ward, the proprietors of the Chester and Manchester theatres, where we were entertained most hospitably. He had, living with him, a very pleasant and agreeable fellow, a Captain Stanley, who, for many years, was no slouch at the bottle, any more than the Major himself, who studied quantity as well as quality; however, poor Captain Stanley was nearly blind, and one dark night, he was found drowned. It was strange that water should have been the cause of a man's death, who had a natural aversion from it during his life: he was lamented by all who had enjoyed his pleasant society.

After concluding our Chester engagement, we set off for Dublin. Mrs. Siddons was just finishing her performances there;—then King was to play for a fortnight, and then Mrs. Crouch and myself were to take the field.

During the whole of my friend King's stay in Dublin, he used to come every night after acting, and sup with me, and delightful indeed was his society. He had an inexhaustible fund of anecdote, which he told in a way peculiar to himself; and, like Anacreon, blended to the last, the flower of youth with the hoary frost of age.

I was standing behind the scenes, in Crow Street, one night, and I saw him for once rather put out of temper. The play was the School for Scandal; he was at the side wing, waiting to go on the stage, as Sir Peter Teazle. At the stage-door was seated an immensely fat woman, the widow of Ryder, the celebrated Irish actor, who had been the original Sir Peter Teazle, in Dublin, in the summer of 1777.

The lusty dame, looking at King, who was standing close to her, hollowed out, with an implacable brogue, and the lungs of a Stentor,

'Arrah! agra! there was but one Sir Peter Teazle in the world, and he is now in heaven, and more is the pity. Ah! Tom Ryder! Tom Ryder! look down upon Sir Peter Teazle here, your dirty representative:' and after this complimentary harangue, the wretched lady began to howl most piteously, to the great annoyance of all behind the scenes, but most particularly to that of King, who appeared really disconcerted. However, the widow was removed, tranquillity was restored, the cloud dispersed, and King acted with his usual excellence. Two nights after this rencontre, he had to act his favourite part, Lord Ogilby. I was at dinner, with a couple of friends, at my own house, and received the following note from him:—

'My dear Kelly,

'I am just come to the theatre, to dress for Lord Ogilby, and asked my dresser to hand me a wine-cork, to mark the lines of my face; he has seriously sworn to me, that he had been looking every where, all over Dublin, and could not procure a cork. Now, my good friend, if you should have such a thing, by any chance, as a cork, and will send it to me, Lord Ogilby's visage will be much indebted to you for the donation.'

I thought he was hoaxing; but when he came to sup with me after the play, he assured me it was a true bill; and when I found who his dresser was, I was not surprised. He was a merry wag, of the name of Tuke, a fellow of low humour,—a veritable Dicky Gossip;[1] whose former profession had been hair-dressing, and who was then the stage property-man at the Dublin Theatre.

When John Kemble was performing the part of Alexander there, with great éclat, he wore armour and a helmet, which were made by Tuke, of which Tuke was very proud. After Kemble had quitted the theatre, upon some particular occasion, the play was again performed; and Daly, the proprietor and manager, undertook to act the part of Alexander himself, and ordered a new helmet. Tuke took the helmet to him, but Daly found it so very much inferior to the one which he had made for Kemble, that he flung it in his face, and bestowed upon him a torrent of abuse, for attempting to give him so shabby a helmet for Alexander.

Tuke replied, 'Mr. Daly, Sir, I think the helmet is a proper good one; Mr. Kemble, (God Almighty bless him!) would not have found fault with it. Ah! he is a player! and would know how to put it on his head; and if you, Mr. Daly, could act the part of Alexander the Great as well as Mr. Kemble, by my soul, you would believe yourself to be the son of

Jove in right earnest.' The remark, coming from a common man, was rather good. This anecdote I heard from Mr. Daly himself.

18

At this period, the Beggar's Opera was prohibited by the Irish Government from being acted, which of course made the public more eager to see it. It was suggested, that if I could make interest to get permission to have it acted for my benefit, it would draw a great house. I, therefore, waited on my good friend, Mrs. Jefferies, sister to Lord Clare, the Lord Chancellor, to entreat her to use her influence with his Lordship to get me permission to have it acted. She pleaded my cause with great zeal, got a verdict in my favour, and the performance of it brought me an overflowing house.

The managers ought to have been well pleased that I took this measure and carried it; for the piece, ever since that time, has kept its station on the Dublin stage.

I found my sojourn in Dublin very pleasant; all kindness and hospitality. I had the pleasure of associating, a great deal, with my friend Mr. Curran; and at his house, on Stephen's Green, had the honour of meeting the late Messrs. Ponsonby and Egan, Lord Norbury, and several of the stars of the Irish bar. I never spent a pleasanter time; not could I perceive, amongst any of those learned gentlemen, an illustration of Dr. Johnson's remark—'that there must be a kind of solemnity in a professional man.'

After a very profitable and pleasant campaign, we finished our Dublin engagement, and prepared to fulfil those made in Manchester, Shrewsbury, and Birmingham, in our way to open New Drury. We agreed, for the first time in our lives, to go by a Liverpool packet, and sent our trunks, &c. to the Marine Hotel, to be put on board.

On the morning proposed for our departure, Hitchcock, Daly's stage-manager, called upon us to say, that they were going to perform the ensuing evening (for the first time), 'The Mountaineers', and called to ask us, as we had seen it performed in London, what kind of scenery, dresses, and decorations, ought to be got ready for its representation. I laughed heartily at the idea of having only one day to prepare all those materials, and said to Mrs. Crouch, I would give any thing to see in what possible way the play could be done in the time.

'Well,' said she, 'that matter is easily arranged; the term of our lodgings is not up for four days to come; and by our engagement we are not obliged to be at Manchester until this day week; send for our trunks, and let us stop.' The proposition pleased me much, and we remained, and saw 'The Mountaineers' the night following; and it was a discredit to any barn. But blessed are the ways of Providence; had not my apparently idle curiosity induced us to remain, most certain it is that we should have met a watery grave; the Liverpool packet, in which we were to have sailed, foundered on the Welsh coast, and every soul on board perished.

Three days after that melancholy event, we took our passage in a packet for Holyhead, where we arrived safe, after a pleasant passage of seven hours, and set off to fulfil our engagement at Manchester. We went to the Bridgewater Arms Hotel, and in the coffee-room I saw a London newspaper, mentioning the loss of the Liverpool packet; and, among the names of the unfortunate passengers who were lost, were Mrs. Crouch's and my own, with an elegiac eulogium deploring our fate, and making many handsome remarks upon us. Never did I read praise of myself with such unfeigned and lively feelings of pleasure.

On the following day, in another London paper, was a letter addressed to the editor, dated Liverpool, with Mr. Frank Aickin's name forged to it, stating that he had just returned from the funeral of poor Kelly and Mrs. Crouch, who were followed to the grave by a vast concourse of people, all bitterly lamenting their untimely end. I never discovered the fellow who wrote this letter, but, whoever he was, he must have had a heart callous to every right feeling.

There was an odd coincidence at the time.—Mrs. Crouch (who was always kindly attentive to her father), before she left Liverpool to go to Dublin, gave Mr. Packer, of Drury Lane Theatre, with whom she was intimate, a paper for Mr. Phillips, wherein she bequeathed to him, in case any accident happened to her, a certain property; but begged of Mr. Packer not to deliver the paper to Mr. Phillips, unless he heard that any disaster had befallen her. Packer, when he heard of her supposed death, went immediately to Mr. Phillips, who was confined to his bed with the gout, to reveal to him the melancholy catastrophe, and deliver the paper consigned to his charge. Just as he was about to open the business, the postman came to the door, with a letter from Mrs. Crouch herself, to her father, dated at Manchester, informing him of her being in excellent health and spirits. Of course, the letter was satisfactory to all parties, and the contradiction of the report was inserted in all the newspapers.

On our appearance at Manchester, our reception was enthusiastic, as it was every where, both on and off the stage; we were well known on the roads, and at all the inns we went to, on our way to Shrewsbury, Birmingham, and London, we were overwhelmed with congratulations on our safety; and, after all our adventures, arrived, at the beginning of February, in Suffolk Street, where we found my friend, Stephen Storace, waiting for us.

On the 3rd of February, I witnessed an appalling spectacle, at the Little Theatre in the Haymarket:—Their Majesties, on that night, had commanded three pieces,—'My Grandmother', 'No Song, no Supper', and 'The Prize', all written by my friend, Prince Hoare.[1] To have them all performed on the same night, by royal command, was no small compliment to the author, and must have been highly satisfactory to him. The crowd was so great, that at the opening of the doors, in going down the steps which led to the pit, three or four persons slipped and fell, and several others were hurried over them; sixteen persons were trampled to death, and upwards of twenty were taken up with broken limbs. The news of this fatal accident was, very judiciously, kept from their Majesties until after the performance was over, when they evinced the deepest sorrow and regret at the event.

On the first Friday in Lent, March 12th, 1794, was opened the New Drury Lane Theatre, with a sacred oratorio, commencing with Handel's immortal Coronation Anthem; the orchestra represented the interior of a Gothic cathedral, and had a most sublime effect. And on the 21st of March, the theatre opened for the representation of dramas, with 'Macbeth'. A prologue, from the pen of the Right Honourable Major-General Fitzpatrick, was spoken by Mr. Kemble, with great applause.

The day previous to the opening of the theatre, Colonel North, Sir Charles Bampfylde, Messrs. Richardson, Nield, Reed, Sheridan, and John Kemble, were to dine with me in Suffolk Street; an hour and a half before dinner, Kemble and I called at General Fitzpatrick's, to get the prologue, which Kemble was to speak the next night. Kemble came with me to Suffolk Street; and had I not seen it, I could not have thought it possible:—while we were waiting dinner for Mr. Sheridan, Kemble studied the prologue, which consisted of fifty lines, and was perfect in every word of it before dinner was announced; a powerful proof of his retentive memory and quick study, for, to my certain knowledge, he had it not in his possession, altogether, more than an hour and a half.

I have often heard him say, that he would make a bet that in four days he would repeat every line in a newspaper, advertisements and all, *verbatim,* in their regular order, without misplacing or missing a single word.

The epilogue for the opening, was written by George Colman, and spoken in a fascinating manner by Miss Farren, explaining to the audience the utility of an iron curtain and a reservoir of water, in case of accidents by fire, which told remarkably well at the time, although the theatre was subsequently burnt to the ground. It ended with a well-turned compliment to Shakspeare, whose statue was discovered under a mulberry tree at the rising of the iron curtain.

Macbeth[1] was splendidly got up, the costume appropriately preserved; the choruses were finely executed with all the strength of the company. I had the direction and getting up of the delightful music, and suggested a change which has been ever since adopted, and I think with good effect. It has been the custom for one witch only to sing—

He must—he will—he shall
Spill much—more blood.

My alteration was—

FIRST WITCH.—He must!
SECOND WITCH.—He will!
THIRD WITCH.—He SHALL!
Spill much more blood!

laying great stress upon the climax, '*He shall*!' The alteration was much approved of.

There was another novelty in the witchery,—at the words 'Mingle, mingle ye, that mingle may,'—a great number of little boys came on as spirits; I must confess it produced something like laughter; they were, however, persisted in, for several nights, but at last discontinued, for there was no keeping the little boys in order; they made such a terrible noise behind the scenes: one little urchin used to play all kinds of tricks; and that one, odd enough to say, was my ci-devant Cupid, Edmund Kean, and, on his account, Kemble dismissed the whole tribe of phantoms.

The play was powerfully cast: Macbeth, Kemble; Macduff, John Palmer; Banquo, Bensley; Malcolm, Charles Kemble, who, on that night, made his first appearance before a London audience; Charles Bannister was the Hecate, and admirable he was in it; Mrs. Siddons was Lady Macbeth; and Parsons, Moody, and Baddely, the speaking witches.

On the 9th of June, the splendid musical spectacle of 'Lodoiska', translated from the French by John Kemble, was produced; the translation was highly creditable to his talents, and the poetry admirably suited to the music, which Storace, with his never-failing taste and judgment, selected from the rival composers Cherubini and Kreutzer.

I was in Paris[1] at the first representation of 'Lodoiska' at both theatres. Kreutzer's was performed at the Théâtre des Italiens, and Cherubini's at the Feydeau,—both got up with great effect and care; but, partiality apart, the Drury Lane piece surpassed them both. Storace selected the most effective music from either, and enriched the piece with some charming melodies of his own composition;—the scenery was picturesquely grand and beautiful, the dresses in perfect costume. Mr. Kemble took great pains in getting up the piece, all the minutiæ were specially attended to, and it was enthusiastically received by the public.

In the last scene, when Mrs. Crouch was in the burning castle, the wind blew the flames close to her; but still she had sufficient fortitude not to move from her situation;—seeing her in such peril I ran up the bridge, which was at a great height from the ground, towards the tower, in order to rescue her; just as I was quitting the platform, a carpenter, prematurely, took out one of its supporters, down I fell; and at the same moment, the fiery tower, in which was Mrs. Crouch, sank down in a blaze, with a violent crash; she uttered a scream of terror. Providentially I was not hurt by the fall, and catching her in my arms, scarcely knowing what I was doing, I carried her to the front of the stage, a considerable distance from the place where we fell. The applause was loud and continued. In fact, had we rehearsed the scene as it happened, it could not have appeared half so natural, or produced half so great an effect.—I always afterwards carried her to the front of the stage, in a similar manner, and it never failed to produce great applause.—Such are, at times, the effects of accident.

On that night, Mr. Sheridan came to sup with us; and I told him I was lucky in not having broken my neck. He left us earlier than usual, to go to the Duchess of Devonshire's. The Duchess, who had been at the theatre, asked him if I was much hurt; to which (with his usual good nature in making blunders for me) he replied, 'Not in the least; I have just left him very well, and in good spirits; but he has been putting a very puzzling question to me, which was,—"Suppose, Mr. Sheridan, I had been killed by the fall, who would have *maintained me* for the rest of my life?" '

The overture to 'Lodoiska',[1] is one of the most spirited compositions I ever heard, and was admirably played by the Drury Lane band. Storace had the second movement of it struck off in an allegro spirituoso time, which electrified the audience, who called for its repetition with vehement applause; yet, when I went to Paris, I heard the same overture, (which by the way was not the original one, nor that which I had heard when before in Paris) of which the second movement, so brilliantly performed at Drury Lane, was played slow, by which it lost all its effect. I was introduced to Kreutzer, the composer of it, and sat down to the piano-forte, and played it in the time in which it was played in England; he thought himself the effect would be better: and on the 18th of August, 1802, Napoléon's birthday, there was a grand orchestra in the Thuilleries, conducted by Kreutzer, who was the first violin; he led his overture to 'Lodoiska', in the same time as it was played at Drury Lane; the effect was prodigious, and shouts of applause followed.

At this period, Mr. Sheridan was getting largely in my debt; I, myself, was not keeping out of debt, and my wine bills were very large; the purple tide flowed by day and night; and I never stopped it, for then 'I took the DRUNKARD for a GOD.'

One day, I called upon him, and requested he would let me have a little money; he put me off, as usual, with promising he would let me have some to-morrow. To-morrow was always his favourite pay-day; but, like the trust-day at a French inn, that morrow never did I see. In the midst of all this, he told me how much he was pleased with Tom Welsh,[2] (then a boy,) and his singing 'Angels, ever bright and fair', the night before. 'He should be encouraged,' said he: 'go and tell him, that, in addition to his salary, I shall send him a present of 200*l.*; and you shall take it to him.' 'Shall I?' said I, (making the quotation from Lionel and Clarissa), 'I think the borough may be disposed of to a worthier candidate;' but neither Welsh nor I ever got a halfpenny of the money.

On the 2nd of July, a new musical piece was produced, entitled, 'The Glorious First of June!' written by Mr. Cobb, for the benefit of the widows of the brave men who fell on that day. It was well suited to the purpose, and was a sequel to 'No Song, no Supper'; it was all got up in three days. Mr. Joseph Richardson wrote an elegant prologue on the occasion, which was spoken, with great feeling, by John Kemble; the piece concluded with a grand sea-fight,[3] and a sumptuous fête, in honour of our glorious victory. Storace and myself gave it some new songs; but the music was chiefly old. I had to represent the character of Frederick;

and as I was so much employed in writing the music, I begged Mr. Sheridan (who wrote a good many speeches for it), to make as short a part for me, and with as little speaking in it as possible. He assured me he would.

In the scene in which I came on, to sing a song (written by Cobb), 'When in war on the ocean we meet the proud foe!' there was a cottage in the distance, at which (the stage direction said) I was to look earnestly, for a moment or two; and the line which I then had to speak was this:—

> 'There stands my Louisa's cottage; she must be either
> in it or out of it.'

The song began immediately, and not another word was there in the whole part. This sublime and solitary speech produced a loud laugh from the audience.

When the piece was over, Mr. Sheridan came into the green-room, and complimented me on my quickness, and being so perfect in the part which he had taken so much pains to write for me; which, he said, considering the short time I had to study it, was truly astonishing. He certainly had the laugh against me, and he did not spare me.

Mrs. Crouch and I were engaged at the Edinburgh Theatre, during the Leith Races; I had a letter from my Apicius, Tate Wilkinson, asking us to stop and play one night at Leeds, on our way thither, which we did. 'The Siege of Belgrade' drew an excellent house; we spent a very pleasant evening, and picked up a little loose cash to pay turnpikes.

I was delighted with the journey, and very much pleased with Edinburgh; the New Town appeared to me to resemble Florence, with the superlative advantage of a sea-view. The prospect from the Calton Hill, and Arthur's Seat, filled me with admiration. I was also struck with the great resemblance between the Old Town and many parts of Paris, particularly in the height of their houses, and some other points which shall be nameless.

I found Mr. Jackson, of Edinburgh, a pleasing, well-informed man, and rather popular as a manager; and to be *that,* is no easy matter any where. I remember, when a child, to have heard his performance of Alcanor, in the tragedy of 'Mahomet', highly spoken of; and that, in the famous speech of

> 'Curse these vipers,' &c. &c.

he was encored three times a night; during which period, parties ran so high, that, between the pros and cons, they kept the theatre, for many nights, in tumult and riot. Mrs. Jackson was rather a popular tragic actress with the Edinburgh audience, and possessed much merit. There was a Mr. Wood in the company, a very great favourite, who was esteemed an excellent master of elocution, and a very worthy man, but a great oddity. His great ambition was to do every thing that Garrick used to do; he rose at the same hour, shaved, breakfasted, and dined at the same hour; and drank whatever he heard was Garrick's taste; in short, nothing could please him more than to copy Garrick implicitly, and to be thought to do so.

I was walking with him one day; and, knowing his weak point, assured him that King had often told me, that when Garrick was to perform any part to which he wished to give all his strength and energy, he used to prevail upon Mrs. Garrick to accompany him to his dressing-room at the theatre, and, for an hour before the play began, rub his head, as hard as she could, with hot napkins, till she produced copious perspiration; and the harder he was rubbed, and the more he was temporarily annoyed by it, the more animation he felt in acting. This (as I thought it) harmless joke of mine, turned out a matter of serious importance to poor Mrs. Wood; for, a long time afterwards, whenever he had to act, particularly in any new part, he actually made her go to his dressing-room, as I had suggested, and rub away, till *she* was ready to drop with fatigue, and *he,* with the annoyance which her exertions produced. The effect of the process upon his performance, however, did not, by any means, keep pace with the labour.

During our stay in Edinburgh, we brought very good houses, and had two excellent benefits. My late friend Perry, proprietor of the Morning Chronicle, gave me several letters to his literary friends and others; among whom was Mr. Gillies, now Lord Gillies, whose brother is a merchant in London, and who shewed me many attentions. I had the honour also to be particularly noticed by his Grace the Duke of Queensberry, who was at Edinburgh for Leith Races. It was a novel sight to me, to see from the sands, horses at full speed, and ships in full sail, at no great distance from each other; and the shore covered with gay equipages.

I cannot omit mentioning the many pleasant days I spent with Signor Natali Corri,[1] his wife and sister. Signor Corri was the first singing master in Edinburgh; his wife and sister sang at the Subscription Concerts, which he carried on there with great éclat. They were natives of Strasburg and Alsace, and sang duets most pleasingly. Signor Corri had also a large magazine, for the sale of music and musical instruments; he was in partnership with his brother, a very worthy man, married to a beautiful woman, a native of Rome. At these concerts, I heard a Signor Urbani, a good professor, and, like his countryman, David Rizzio, very partial to Scotch melodies, some of which he sang very pleasingly, though in a falsetto voice. There was also a young Italian, of the name of Stabilini, a first-rate violin; and a Signor Cecchi, a good violoncello performer. I used to meet them at the house of the great Scotch physician, Dr. Cullum, who was devoted to music, and gave the professors of it the greatest encouragement. His hospitable mansion was always open to them, and his much-esteemed professional advice always gratuitously at their service.

After enjoying a delightful and profitable excursion, we took leave of our kind Edinburgh friends for Lancaster, and went, in our comfortable travelling-carriage, to visit the Lakes of Cumberland and Westmoreland; and an enchanting tour we had.

We remained two days at Keswick. Lord William Gordon was then at his picturesque cottage on the Lake,[1] and did us the favour to give us an invitation, which we had great pleasure in accepting. In our way through York, we stopped at our hospitable friend, Tate Wilkinson's, and had a pleasant day, with the exception of a slight quarrel between Tate and his wife,—a thing which will occur in the best regulated families. The latter was guilty of the enormous neglect of not having apple-sauce with a huge roasted goose. Tate, all dinner-time, exclaiming, —'Fie! Mrs. Wilkinson,—oh! fie!'—'No apple-sauce, Ma'am!'—'Mrs. W. is a mighty good woman, Ma'am!'—'but goose without apple-sauce!' —'Ugh!'

We got to Lancaster in time for the assize week, during the whole of which we performed at the theatre to crowded houses. Nothing occurred to merit particular notice while we remained there.

We also performed a few nights at Birmingham; and while there, were on a visit at the house of Mr. Cox, a respectable, well-informed man; a great book-collector, and very fond of theatricals. He had made an ample fortune in business, and was then on the point of retiring. The attentions which I received from him and his amiable lady, can never be forgotten by me; nor can I omit mentioning Mr. William Macready, the manager of the Birmingham Theatre, who, in theatrical business, I ever found honest, upright, obliging, clever, and friendly, and in all his dealings, whether Fate smiled or frowned, a man of punctuality and rectitude. I am extremely happy here to pay a just tribute to his worth.

For the opening of the winter season, we arrived at our house in Suffolk-street, in cheering health and spirits.

About this time, we used to pass many pleasant evenings with Mrs. Robinson, the ci-devant beautiful Perdita, at her house in St. James's Place. She and Mrs. Crouch had a sincere esteem for each other; she gave very pleasant petits soupers, where she and her daughter, with their wit and good humour, contrived to make the hours glide away insensibly; I often talked with her of the many pleasant hours I passed with her brother, Mr. Darby, at Leghorn, on my first arrival there.

She produced, in November, at Drury Lane, a petite pièce, entitled 'Nobody'; and I was sorry to see it condemned after the third night, though Bensley, Bannister, Barrymore, Miss Decamp, and Mrs. Jordan, exerted their talents to support it.

On the 20th of November, Drury Lane Theatre lost one of its greatest props in a particular walk of the drama, in poor Baddely. On the evening before his death, he was taken ill as he was dressing for the character of Moses, in the 'School for Scandal', which part was originally written for him. His Canton, in the 'Clandestine Marriage', will ever be remembered with King's Lord Ogilby; and in Jews and Frenchmen, he was very good. He was a worthy man, although he was nick-named 'Old Vinegar,' only from the excellent manner in which he acted a character of that name in O'Keefe's farce of 'The Son-in-Law'. In his younger days, he had been a cook, and an excellent cook, to my knowledge, he was, and moreover extremely proud of his skill in the culinary art. He had been cook to Foote, in whose service he imbibed a taste for the drama. He married a celebrated beauty, Miss Snow.[1] He told me once, that when he was acting at the Haymarket, of which Foote was the proprietor, they had a quarrel, and Baddely challenged him to fight with swords. On receiving the challenge, Foote said,—'Hey! what! fight!—Oh! the dog! —So I have taken the spit from my kitchen-fire, and stuck it by his side; and now the fellow wants to stick *me* with it.'

In his will, he left a twelfth-cake and wine for the performers of Drury Lane Theatre, of which they partake every Twelfth-night, in the Green Room, and drink to the memory of the donor. He had a habit of smacking his lips always when speaking. In allusion to this, Charles Bannister said to him one day at the School of Garrick (when boasting of his culinary qualifications), 'My dear Baddely, every body must know that you have been a cook, for you always seem to be *tasting your words*.'

He bequeathed his house and premises, at Upper Moulsey, in Surrey, to Mrs. Baddely; and after her death, these, and money arising from an annuity, to the Theatrical Fund of Drury Lane Theatre; the house, and premises belonging to it, at Moulsey, to be an asylum for decayed actors. The house stands facing the Temple of Shakspeare, on Mr. Garrick's Lawn, at Hampton. The trustees of the fund, however, thought proper to sell it; and it has been purchased, and is now in the possession of my friend, Mr. Savory, of Bond-street, at whose hospitable table I have many times been a welcome guest. In his parlour is an excellent likeness of Baddely, in the character of Moses, in 'The School for Scandal', painted by Zoffany; and on a part of the premises are the boards of the old Drury Lane stage, on which the immortal Garrick displayed his unrivalled powers. It seems no unnatural coincidence, that the ci-devant cook's property should have found a savoury purchaser.

On the 20th of November, Cobb produced his opera of 'The Cherokee'; the music by Storace. The Cherokee chorus was one of the grandest ever composed; the effect was sublime. Mrs. Crouch acted very finely in it. Tom Welsh had a part which he played very impressively: the scenery and decorations were of the most splendid description. I performed the character of an English officer in it; and had some good situations, and good songs. That delightful warbler, Mrs. Bland, in the character of a Welsh peasant, sang that ballad, afterwards so universally popular, 'A little bird sang on a spray',[1] with great simplicity and truth; indeed, what did she not sing well? As far as her powers went, she was perfect as an English ballad-singer. I remember dining one day with those two great musicians, Haydn and Pleyel, and requesting them to go to Drury Lane, and hear a female singer; saying, that in my opinion no real judge of the art could find a single blemish in her style or taste. They went to hear Mrs. Bland, and told me, that my praise was not at all exaggerated.

I have, at different times, composed a number of songs for her, and may safely say, that she never introduced a grace unseasonably, or one that was not full of taste and meaning.

Mrs. Bland, when Miss Romanzini, first sang at Hughes' Riding School, now the Circus,[2] in St. George's Fields, in the spring of 1773; she then travelled with Breslau; and made her first appearance at Drury Lane, the 24th of October, 1786, in 'Richard Cœur de Lion'. Her sensible manner of singing reminds me of an anecdote which Mozart once told me of the Emperor Joseph the Second, relative to himself:—His Majesty, speaking of a piece of music of Mozart's,[3] said to him,—'Mozart,

I like your music very much, but there are too many notes in Madame Lange's song.'—'Sire,' replied the composer, 'there are just as many notes in it as there ought to be.'

I feel much pleasure in recording here an anecdote, which must prove highly gratifying to a young lady, now engaged at Drury Lane Theatre, as well as to her friends. When Miss Wilson appeared at Drury Lane Theatre, in 'Artaxerxes', Mr. Elliston wished me to hear her, and give him my opinion of her. I was, at the time, too ill with the gout, to be able to attend the theatre. My old and valued friend, Madame Mara, was then in London. I wrote to her to call upon me, and requested her to go and hear Miss Wilson, to give me her true and candid opinion of her abilities, as I could not go myself; and after the performance, to return to me, and make her report; which she did, and a favourable one it was.—'But,' said she, 'I was at Drury Lane, a few nights since, to see the pantomime; there was a little girl, who sang a ballad,—"Up, Jack, and the day is your own"; that girl, depend upon what I tell you, has one of the finest voices I ever heard; and could I be induced to take a pupil, to bring forward on the stage, that girl should be the person of my choice.' The young lady is Miss Povey; and proud may she be of having been so mentioned by such a person as Madame Mara.

Yet, with all her great skill and knowledge of the world, Madame Mara was induced, by the advice of some of her mistaken friends, to give a public concert at the King's Theatre, in her seventy-second year, when, in the course of nature, her powers had failed her. It was truly grievous to see such transcendent talents as she once possessed, so sunk—so fallen. I used every effort in my power to prevent her committing herself, but in vain. Among other arguments to draw her from her purpose, I told her what happened to Mombelli, one of the first tenors of his day, who lost all his well-earned reputation and fame, by rashly performing the part of a lover, at the Pergola theatre, at Florence, in his seventieth year, having totally lost his voice. On the stage, he was hissed; and the following lines, lampooning his attempt, were chalked on his house-door, as well as upon the walls of the city:—

'All' età di settanta
Non si AMA, nè si CANTA.'

i.e.

With the great age of seventy,
Singing and loving don't agree.

Would she had taken the sage counsel of the Spanish poet, Balthazar Garcia,—'Learn to retire from public situations with dignity.'—She was an excellent, kind-hearted woman; but, in this instance, certainly not well advised.

19

On the 24th was produced, at Drury, Cumberland's play of 'The Wheel of Fortune'. About three weeks previous to the bringing out of this play, I went into the prompter's room, and found Kemble, who was going to dine with me, sealing up a parcel. He said, 'My dear Mic, wait a moment, until I send off this to Cumberland; it is a comedy of his, which I write to tell him is accepted; and, if I am not greatly mistaken, there is a character in it that will do something for *me*; at least I feel that I can do something with *it*. Mind, you and Nancy (meaning Mrs. Crouch) must promise to see me act it the first night.' We accordingly did, and were delighted; and, ever after, considered Kemble, Penruddock; and Penruddock, Kemble: indeed, the whole play was finely acted.—Miss Farren's Emily, Mrs. Powell's Woodville; King's Governor Tempest, R. Palmer's Sir David Daw, Palmer and Charles Kemble, and, though last not least, Suett's Lawyer Weazle, were all excellent.

I remember well, after poor Suett's death, Kemble, in lamenting the event, and saying to me,—'My dear Mic, Penruddock has lost a powerful ally in Suett; Sir, I have acted the part with many Weazles, and good ones too, but none of them could work up my passions to the pitch Suett did; he had a comical impertinent way of thrusting his head into my face, which called forth all my irritable sensations; the effect upon me was irresistible.'

About the middle of May, an opera was acted, at Drury Lane, in which I had to perform an Irish character.[1] My friend Johnstone took great pains to instruct me in the brogue, but I did not feel quite up to the mark; and, after all, it seems my vernacular phraseology was not the most perfect; for, when the opera was over, Sheridan came into the green-room, and said,—'Bravo! Kelly; very well, indeed; upon my honour, I never before heard *you speak such good English* in all my life.' This sarcastic compliment produced much laughter from the performers who heard him.*

* A similar criticism was made by the elder Colman, when he went to Ireland,

This season Miss Mellon made her first appearance. Mr. Sheridan had seen her the previous season at Stafford, where she was acting; she was much patronised at that place by the leading families, particularly by Mr. Horton, an intimate electioneering friend of Mr. Sheridan's. She was engaged at Drury Lane, and proved herself a valuable acquisition to our dramatic corps. She was a handsome girl, and much esteemed; and in gratitude, I feel called upon to say, that, both as Miss Mellon and Mrs. Coutts, I have received from her the most marked and friendly attentions; and am happy to have it in my power, thus publicly, to express my acknowledgments.

The same season, the votaries of true comic humour sustained an irreparable loss in the demise of poor Parsons; his health had been rapidly declining, but not his inimitable comic powers. On the evening of the nineteenth of January, he played Sir Fretful Plagiary, and died on the 3rd of February. The following epitaph was written on him by Mr. Dibdin, sen.

'Here Parsons lies;—oft, on Life's busy stage,
With Nature, reader, you have seen him vie;
He friendship knew—knew science—knew the age;—
Respected knew to live—lamented die!'

At Drury Lane Theatre, March 12, 1796, was the first representation of the 'Iron Chest', written by my friend George Colman. The music, composed by Storace, was, I believe, the cause of his premature and lamented death. On the first rehearsal, although labouring under a severe attack of gout and fever, after having been confined to his bed for many days, he insisted upon being wrapped up in blankets, and carried in a sedan-chair to the cold stage of the playhouse. The entreaties and prayers of his family were of no avail,—go he would; he went, and remained there to the end of the rehearsal. The agony I suffered, during the time, is beyond my power of description. He went home to his bed, whence he never rose again. The last twelve bars of music he ever wrote, were the subject of the song (and a beautiful subject it is), 'When the robber his

---

chiefly to see the actors of the Dublin theatre. Among other plays, he saw there his own comedy of 'The Jealous Wife'. On being questioned, by a friend, how he was pleased with the acting of it, he replied,—'Faith, I did not well understand what they were saying; for every man and woman in the play spoke with the most determined brogue, except the gentleman that acted Captain O'Cutter (the only Irish character in the piece) for *he* spoke the most pure and perfect English, throughout the whole of the performance, without a vestige of the brogue.'

victim had noted'; which I sang in the character of Captain Armstrong. I called upon him the night of the day in which he had been at the rehearsal; he sent for me to his bed-side, and pressing my hand, said,—'My dear Mic, I have tried to finish your song, but find myself unable to accomplish it; I must be ill, indeed, when I can't write for you, who have given so much energy to my compositions. I leave you the subject of your song, and beg you will finish it yourself; no one can do it better; and my last request is, that you will let no one else meddle with it.' Saying these words, he turned on his side, and fell into a slumber; and never, never did I see him more!

His memory will for ever live in the hearts of all who have heard his compositions; for the drafts of true genius, though they may not be honoured so soon as they come due, are sure to be paid with compound interest in the end: this is an old maxim, and, I hope, a true one. He died March the 16th, in the thirty-third year of his age. It is a singular coincidence, that three such great musical geniuses as Purcell, Mozart, and Storace, were nearly of the same age when fate ordained them to their early graves.

On the 30th of the same month, was first performed, the opera of 'Mahmoud', written by Prince Hoare; the music chiefly by Storace. Previous to the opera, the following lines were written, at the short notice of a few hours only, by the author of the piece; who, from his earliest days, was the bosom friend of the gifted composer, both in Italy and in England.

'When vain is every anxious hope to save,
And genius sinks to an untimely grave!
The waken'd feelings of a generous mind,
A momentary void consent to find.
How difficult, alas! the task we try,
The blank with equal value to supply.
To-night we mourn a loved, composer lost;
By all lamented, but by us the most.
Deprived, alas! of that inspiring beam,
That touch'd the tuneful lyre with fleeting gleam;
Yet what remains, and long, we trust, shall live,
We aim, with anxious industry, to give.
Imperfect, if you view th'intended plan,
Accept it as we give,—'tis all we can.
Faults will, no doubt, too evidently glare,
And haply teach you our regrets to share.

But shall we humbly for compassion sue,
And lift our hands, for pity, up to you?
No! Shall the gen'rous Briton, taught to bless
His deadliest foe, when prostrate in distress,
Await our voice, his pitying ear to call,
When native genius, native virtues fall?
Oh! be it still the honest Briton's boast,
To shield the flow'rets of his native coast;
Unprompted, to protect their op'ning bloom,
And zealous guard them, scatter'd o'er the tomb.'

The whole of the profits arising from the opera were generously given, by the author, to Storace's widow and orphan.

All the performers took the greatest pains to do justice to the posthumous work of the composer. Kemble's acting, as the hero of the piece, was a masterly performance. The opera had a run of many nights, and was much applauded; it had the powerful support of Mr. Braham, who made his first appearance in it at Drury Lane, and sang a hunting cavatina, in a masterly style; as well as a beautiful ballad,—'From shades of night!' with great truth of expression, and lovely simplicity. Mr. Braham[1] was received with the greatest applause, and deservedly so, for there is no such singer, when he pleases; he is, decidedly, the greatest vocalist of his day; and, from a long professional intercourse with him, I ever found him replete with liberality and kindness; and ever ready to give his meed of applause to real merit.

On the 7th of April, Madame Banti took for her benefit, at the Opera, Gluck's grand serious opera of Alceste. Mr. Taylor, the then proprietor of the Opera House, and Madame Banti, made a request to Mr. Sheridan, to give me permission to act the principal part in the opera, which I had so often performed at Vienna, under the tuition of the great composer. The knowledge of my having successfully performed it at that theatre, induced Madame Banti to ask me to act it at the Haymarket. I got permission, and the opera made so great a hit, that Mr. Taylor, with the consent of Mr. Sheridan, engaged me for twenty nights. Madame Banti's performance of Alceste was a *chef-d'œuvre*; her acting sublime, her singing charming; for twenty nights the opera drew crowded houses. Banti possessed all the power of voice which she had when I heard her first at Venice—her figure was much improved; and, as a serious actress, she was unrivalled. She had wonderful natural powers, but as I have already said, no great knowledge of music.

It was the fashion of the day for the subscribers to the Opera to attend the rehearsals; amongst others, the late Duke of Queensberry was a constant attendant; no weather kept him away—there he was, on the stage, muff and all. I had the pleasure, for many years, to be honoured with his peculiar notice; and have been frequently invited to his hospitable table, both in Piccadilly, and at Richmond. In my intercourse with mankind, I never met superior for worldly knowledge and acuteness; he was a nobleman of polished manners, of the *vieille cour*; he had his foibles, it is true; but then, who has not? On Tuesdays and Saturdays he had generally a large dinner party of the French nobility, who were obliged to seek shelter in this country, from the horrors of the Revolution; he was well aware that a French lady or gentleman is *au désespoir*, unless they can go to some spectacle; and he used the following delicate mode of indulging them in their favourite amusement, knowing that they were too poor to indulge themselves, and too proud to accept of pecuniary assistance.

After coffee had been handed round, he used to ask, 'who is going to the Italian Opera tonight? I long to use my family privilege.' I was present one evening, when the Duchess de Pienne asked him what this privilege meant? He said, it was that of writing admissions for the theatres to any amount he pleased, without entailing any expense. This was apparently a joyful hearing to the theatrical amateurs, and nine of the party went that evening to the Opera with his written admissions. He had previously made an arrangement with my worthy friend, Mr. Jewel, the Opera House treasurer, and also, as I understood, with other theatres, that his orders were always to be admitted, and the next morning sent to his steward, who had directions to pay the amount of the admissions which his Grace had sent in. This delicate manner of conferring a favour needs no comment.

I never saw in any country such comfortable dinners as those of his Grace; at his side-board there was a person to carve every joint, and he never had more than three dishes at a time on his table; but all were hot and comfortable, and the viands the most *recherché*. His chief French cook, whom he denominated his *officier de bouche*, was a great artist, a real *cordon bleu,* who ought to have had, like Cardinal Wolsey's master-cook, a crimson velvet dress, with a collar and a gold chain. His wines too were of the most exquisite kind, for his Grace was a votary of Bacchus as well as Venus.

He was passionately fond of music, and an excellent judge of the art;

but his being very blind and very deaf, was certainly somewhat against him. A favourite propensity of his, was, that of giving instructions in singing: he was kind enough to offer Mrs. Billington and myself, to teach us the songs of Polly and Macheath, in the Beggar's Opera; and, to humour him, we have often let him sing to us. It was extremely amusing to all parties, one person excepted, who always accompanied him on the piano-forte, and who lived in the house with him,—his name was Ireland; but I always called him Job.

His Grace asked me one day to dine with him, *tête-à-tête*; after dinner, he told me, he had formed a resolution never to have more than one guest at a time; the reason he gave was, that he had grown so deaf, that he could scarcely hear. 'Had I', said he, 'at table more than one person now, they would be talking one to the other, and I sitting by, not able to hear what they were talking about, which would be extremely provoking; now if I have but one to dine with me, that one must either talk to *me,* or hold his tongue.'

This season the Opera House was very attractive. I was stage manager; Viotti,[1] the celebrated violin player, was leader of the orchestra, and a masterly leader he was. He asked me one day to dine with him at the Crown and Anchor, in the Strand, to meet three friends of his, who formed an economical little dinner-club, which they held there once a month. I went, and found his friends three of the greatest revolutionists: —Charles Lameth, who had been President of the National Assembly; Dupont, the popular orator of that time, also a Member of the National Assembly, and who was the very person whom I had seen offer to hand the poor Queen of France out of her carriage, when brought prisoner back from Varennes, which she indignantly refused; and the Duke D'Aiguillon, one of the twelve Peers of France, who, in former days, had an immense fortune, was a great patron of the arts, and so theatrical, that he had a box in every theatre in Paris. He was particularly fond of music, and had been a scholar of Viotti. I passed a pleasant day with these émigrés, who were all men of high endowments, and truly polished manners; nor did they seem at all depressed by change of circumstances; all was vivacity and good humour.

The Duke sat next to me at dinner. I asked him if he had seen Drury Lane Theatre; his reply was, I have seen the outside of it, but I am now too poor to go to theatres; for did I indulge in my favourite amusement, I should not be enabled to have the pleasure of meeting you and my worthy friends at dinner to-day—I cannot afford both.

I told him, that as manager of the Opera House, and musical director of Drury Lane Theatre, I should have great pleasure in giving him and his friends admissions nightly, for either of those theatres; and that my box at the Opera House was at their service on the following Saturday, and I requested they would do me the honour to dine with me on that day, and afterwards visit it. They favoured me with their company, and much delighted they were: often and often afterwards did they dine and sup with me. I introduced them to Mr. Sheridan and many of my friends. It was certainly, I thought, to be lamented, that men possessing such amiable manners, should, from strong republican principles, bring themselves into misfortune; but I had nothing to do with their politics: I only saw the bright side of their characters, and felt a sincere pleasure, as far as lay in my power, in administering, in my little way, comfort to those who were labouring under so sad a reverse of fortune; for, in this country, the French noblesse would not associate with them. Even the Duke D'Aiguillon, though one of the highest noblemen of France, was never received by the Duke of Queensberry, nor did he visit any where.

One morning he called on me, and said he had a favour to beg of me. I requested him to command my services: he said, 'My dear Kelly, I am under many obligations for your repeated acts of kindness and hospitality to me and my friends; but still, though under a cloud, and labouring under misfortunes, I cannot forget that I am the Duke D'Aiguillon, and *cannot stoop to borrow or beg from mortal*; but I confess I am nearly reduced to my last shilling, yet still I retain my health and spirits; formerly, when I was a great amateur, I was particularly partial to copying music,—it was then a source of amusement to me. Now, my good friend, the favour I am about to ask, is, that, *sub rosa,* you will get me music to copy for your theatres, upon the same terms as you would give to any common copyist, who was a stranger to you. I am now used to privations, my wants are few; though accustomed to palaces, I can content myself with a single bed-room up two pair of stairs; and if you will grant my request, you will enable me to possess the high gratification of earning my morsel by the work of my hands.'

I was moved almost to tears, by the application, and was at a loss what to answer, but thought of what Lear says,

'Take physic, pomp!'[1]

and 'to what man may be reduced.' I told him I thought I could procure him as much copying as he could do, and he appeared quite delighted;

and the next day I procured plenty for him. He rose by day-light to accomplish his task—was at work all day—and at night, full dressed, in the Opera House in the pit. While there, he felt himself Duke D'Aiguillon; and no one ever suspected him to be a drudge in the morning, copying music for a shilling per sheet; and strange to say, that his spirits never drooped: nine Englishmen out of ten under such circumstances would have destroyed themselves; but the transitory peace of mind he enjoyed was not of long duration; an order came from the Alien Office for him and his friends to leave England in two days; they took an affectionate leave of me: the Duke went to Hamburgh, and there was condemned to be shot. They told me that he died like a hero.

He had a favourite Danish dog, a beautiful animal, which he consigned to my protection, until, as he told me, he had an opportunity to send for him with safety. I pledged myself to take every care of him, and never shall I forget his parting with this faithful animal; it seemed as if the last link which held him to society was breaking; the dog had been the faithful companion of his prosperity—his adversity;—he caressed, and shed a flood of tears on quitting it—the scene was grievous; but I did not then think that I should never see the Duke more. I took every care of his poor dog—who, missing his kind master, after a little, refused *all nourishment,* and actually *pined, and died.* Yet he survived the being who had fed and cherished him.

On May 6th, 1796, Mr. Bensley, whom I am proud to have called my friend, took leave of the stage on his own benefit night, in the character of Endeavour, in the 'Grecian Daughter':—he was a good actor, and a perfect gentleman. In his younger days, he had been in the army, and I was told had been at the Havannah. I have seen him often, with great pleasure, act Prospero in the Tempest, and Iago and Pierre: his Malvolio, in Twelfth Night, was considered a fine performance. He had a manner of rolling his eyes when speaking; and a habit, whenever he entered the green room, of stirring the fire with great ceremony, secundùm artem, in which habit, I was in the habit of imitating him; he caught me once in the very fact, and joined heartily in the laugh against himself.

I remember there was a tragedy brought out at Drury Lane, written by a hatter, which was completely condemned: towards the end of the play, Palmer and Bensley had in their characters to *die* upon the stage; a torrent of hisses accompanied their latter moments, and the curtain fell in the midst of the tumult. When the play was over, Palmer and Bensley came into the green room; and Palmer said to Bensley, 'You see,

Bensley, the audience have settled 'The Hatters.'—'So I perceive,' answered Bensley; 'and they did not spare the *dyers*.'

On Mr. Bensley's quitting the stage, he was appointed barrack-master; and subsequently a near relation of his, Sir William Bensley, Bart. died, and left him a very large fortune; he then retired to Stanmore, where he died, regretted and respected by all who had the pleasure of knowing him.

My friend Elliston, (of whom Mrs. Crouch, it will be remembered, prognosticated at York, that he would one day become a distinguished actor,) made his début at the Haymarket, on the 25th June, 1796, in Octavian, in 'The Mountaineers', and Vapour, in 'My Grandmother'. His admirable voice and excellent acting in both characters, stamped him, at once, a favourite, which he continues to this day; I need hardly say, how very deservedly so.

The same season, Thalia lost one of her most powerful supporters, by the demise of Mr. Dodd. He was an actor of the good old school. On my first appearance at Drury Lane, he performed the part of Jessamy, in 'Lionel and Clarissa'; and although then bordering on his sixtieth year, I never saw it so admirably represented; indeed, all his fops were excellent, particularly Lord Foppington, and Sparkish, in the 'Country Girl'. I have often seen him, with infinite pleasure, in Sir Andrew Ague Cheek, Abel Drugger, and Old Kecksey, in the 'Irish Widow'. He was an entertaining companion, very fond of convivial meetings; he knew a vast number of comic songs, and was *renommé* for recounting good stories, although it must be confessed they were somewhat of the longest. He was a constant attendant of the Anacreontic Society, held at the Crown and Anchor, in the Strand, which was admirably conducted by a set of bankers and merchants. They had a good concert in the early part of the evening, by a most excellent band, led by Cramer; after which, the company retired to the large room, where supper was provided. The principal vocal performers of the day were to be found there. Old Charles Bannister, after supper, uniformly sang, with powerful effect, 'Anacreon in Heaven',[1] which was there originally sung by Webster. There were the best catches and glees, sung by Webbe, Danby, Dignum, Hobbs, Sedgwick, Suett, &c. relieved by some famous songs of Dodd's. I passed many delightful evenings in this society, and was extremely sorry when it was discontinued. I deeply regretted the death of my poor friend Dodd, and with true sorrow followed his remains to the grave. He was one of the original members of the School of Garrick, and always spoke of his great master with the highest veneration and respect.

In the early part of this summer, I went to Dover Castle, on a visit to my worthy and esteemed friend, the Honourable Colonel North, who was then Deputy Governor. I passed three days delightfully in his endearing society. The coast of France is very distinctly seen from the windows in clear weather.

One very fine morning, I was seated at a little distance from the Castle, looking at the opposite shore, and took my pencil and a little music book (which I always carried about me, to put down any musical idea that might strike me,) from my pocket: a subject I thought pretty came across me, and I was writing it in the book, when one of the soldiers belonging to the Castle came behind me, and without the smallest ceremony, laid hold of me, saying, in a tremendous Tipperary brogue, 'Ah, my tight fellow, have I caught you in the fact?—Och, Mr. Mounsier, how got you here, Sir?'

I began to laugh, but the Tipperary man of war said, 'By the powers! I'll teach you to laugh out of t'other side of your mouth, my fine fellow, in a minute of two.'

I asked what my offence was?

'What,' said he, 'have I not caught you taking views of the fortifications?[1] you seem mighty fond of looking at it, but, please the pigs, you don't get out of the black hole in it, in a little time;' and, with all his might, he proceeded to surround me, and drag me to the donjon keep, accompanying each lusty pull with a volley of abuse.

Luckily for me, before we got a great way on the road to durance vile, we met Colonel North, who, much to my delight, released me from the gripe of Old Tipperary, and his military ardour. He laughed heartily at my adventure; but told me that the soldier had done no more than his duty,—'And you ought to have known *that,* Kelly,' said the Colonel.—'Making *notes* is a sure way of getting into a *scrape*; and you should have bargained for the *bars* before you began.'

The next day, we went to his brother's, the Earl of Guilford's seat at Waldershare, where we remained two days, and then returned to London. I then accompanied Mrs. Crouch to Cheltenham, where she had been ordered to drink the waters. Our excellent friend, the Colonel, promised to meet us there; and, punctual to his word, was there before us. We agreed, during our stay at this delightful place, to take a house together, and we were fortunate enough to get a beautiful cottage, in the midst of cornfields, then called Wyatt's Cottage; there, indeed, I enjoyed his delightful society; for in repartee and ready wit, who was his equal?

The Colonel was stinted by his medical adviser, while drinking the Cheltenham waters, not to exceed one pint of wine a day; he promised not to exceed his pint, nor did he; but it was a Scotch pint; six of claret or port, which was his daily portion; white wine, at dinner, he said, went for nothing, though he flirted with the best part of a bottle of old Madeira every day.

Here I had the pleasure of meeting an old friend of my father's, my eccentric countryman, the Earl of Howth, whose skill in coachmanship was so celebrated. The very apex of his ambition—the pride of his heart—was, not only to be thought a coachman-like Lord, but actually a coachman;—his wig—his coat—every part of his dress—was a coachman's; and in his conversation, he imitated the slang of the fraternity: but his actions, and manner of thinking, were those of a perfect gentleman; he was upright, good-natured, and honourable. He rarely visited his beautiful place, near Dublin. He resided, in the winter, chiefly at Bath; and, in the summer, at Cheltenham, with his daughters, the Ladies St. Lawrence, and a particular friend of theirs, a Miss Georges, a lady of polished manners and education, respected by all who had the good fortune to be acquainted with her.

The theatre at Cheltenham was, at that time, under the management of its proprietor, the eccentric Watson, who was a fellow of infinite jest and humour; full of Thespian anecdotes, and perfectly master of the art of driving away loathed melancholy.

Many a hearty laugh have I had with him: he was an Irishman, and had, although I say it who should not say it, all the natural wit of his country about him. He was of a very respectable family (Quakers) in Clonmell. In John Kemble's younger days, he was a near ally of his, and both belonged to a strolling company. They lived, or rather, by Watson's account, *starved together*. At one time, in Gloucestershire, they were left pennyless; and after continued vicissitudes, Watson assured me, such was their distress, that at that time they were glad to get into a turnip-field, and make a meal of its produce uncooked; and, he added, it was while regaling on the raw vegetable, that they hit upon a scheme to recruit their finances; and a lucky turn-up it turned out. It was neither more nor less than that John Kemble should turn methodist preacher, and Watson perform the part of clerk.

Their scheme was organized; and Tewkesbury was their first scene of action. They drew together, in a field, a numerous congregation; and

Kemble preached with such piety, and so much effect, that, positively, a large collection rewarded his labours. This anecdote, Kemble himself told me was perfectly true.

Watson had brought together, at Cheltenham, a respectable dramatic corps; he wished Mrs. Crouch and myself to perform for a limited number of nights, and offered us a clear half of the receipts of the house, every night, and each of us a clear benefit; but as we were there for the benefit of health, I refused his liberal terms. Lord Howth, however, called on me, one day, and said, 'My dear Kelly, every body is wishing you would perform here for a few nights; you will get a good deal of money; and, in the name of fortune, why not pick up your crumbs; sure, it will be only just an amusement to you; the house will always be full, and I will let the boxes for you myself.'

Such a good-natured offer was too tempting to be refused, and we agreed with Watson for six nights. We played to overflowing houses, and the noble box-keeper fulfilled his part of the contract; for on the morning of the first performance, while the company were assembled in the Spa-room, after paying their devoirs to Mrs. Forty, there was his Lordship with the box-book in his hand, saying to one,—'Now, my lady, remember you have got the stage-box; as for the Countess, she can only have a second and third row;'—and so on. Nothing could exceed the warmth of his Lordship's heart, although he was so eccentric; he even left his coach-box, to let boxes for me.

I went one morning into a poulterer's shop, and found the Noble Earl buying some poultry. I ordered the poulterer to send me home a fine goose, wished his Lordship good morning, and was walking homeward at a quick pace, when I heard my name hallooed out; and turning round to see who was calling me, I saw his Lordship in the middle of the High Street; his Lordship shouting out, with a determined Irish accent,—'Kelly! Kelly! I say, Kelly! Corn your goose! corn your goose!—I tell you, now do, Kelly, corn him! keep him in salt four days, and then boil him with a whisp of white cabbage; and, by the Powers, he'll be mighty fine eating.' I took his Lordship's advice, and found it a delicious dish.

One day I was saying to him, that I had a very bad sore throat; he told me he had a never-failing recipe for a sore throat. His directions were, —just before going to bed, to get scalding water, and the finest double-refined sugar, with two juicy lemons, and above all, some good old Jamaica rum; and when in bed, to take a good jorum of it, as hot as bearable.

'Why, my Lord,' said I, 'your prescription seems to me to be nothing more than punch.' 'And what is better for a sore throat than good punch?' said his Lordship; 'good punch at night, and copious gargles of old Port by day, would cure any mortal disease in life.'

I passed some pleasant weeks at Cheltenham; and, among other agreeable recollections, it is not the least to think, that I there formed an acquaintance with my excellent friend, Mr. Savory, now a celebrated chemist, in Bond Street, who, at that time, was under Mr. Cotter, the principal apothecary and chemist at Cheltenham. I also had the advantage of originating a friendship with that great and worthy man, and friend to the human race, Dr. Jenner, who often did me the honour to take his dinner with me: he wrote a very excellent Bacchanalian song, for which I composed the music.

When I was about leaving Cheltenham, I was lamenting to the Doctor the loss of the Spa waters, which had done Mrs. Crouch and myself so much essential service; he told me, under an injunction of secrecy, (which I never violated during his life-time,) that I had no cause to regret the loss of the waters, 'for, depend upon it,' said he, 'the Cheltenham salts, which you can procure of Mr. Patheyrus, chemist, in Bond-street, and of him alone, are to the full as efficacious, and conducive to health, as the water from the well. This,' concluded the excellent man, 'is the candid opinion I give you. I should not wish to promulgate it, as it might prejudice many industrious people, by keeping company from the Spa, which I should be sorry should be the case.'

I repeat this opinion for the information of those who have it not in their power to go to the Cheltenham Spa, either from want of time, or the means of accomplishing the journey there.

I associated with many Irish families who came to drink the waters, and had the pleasure of being introduced, by Colonel North, to Mr. Coutts, as his most particular friend. The introduction was very flattering to me; and I had the pleasure, for many years, to be kindly remembered, and favoured by the notice and attentions of one, who was ever a liberal patron of the arts and sciences, and of those who professed them.

I went to London, to meet Mr. Taylor, of the Opera House; but Mrs. Crouch remained at Cheltenham. Mr. Taylor wished to submit to His Royal Highness the Prince of Wales (who was then at Brighton), for His Royal Highness's approbation, a plan of alterations in the Opera House, for the ensuing season, and wished me to go down to Brighton with it, which I did. The day after I arrived there, I was honoured with an audience at the Pavillion, to which I was introduced by my kind friend and countryman, Colonel M'Mahon.

I found, as I always had the good fortune to do, His Royal Highness every thing gracious, kind, and condescending; a Prince who needs but to be known to be beloved and respected, for the rich variety of his talents, attainments, and knowledge, which seem to belong to every age, and to every country.

After a week's delightful sojourn at Brighton, I returned to London; and the following day took my seat upon the Cheltenham coach, to join Mrs. Crouch, who was waiting at Cheltenham till I returned to accompany her to London. I was full of life and spirits, and found some pleasant companions on the roof of the carriage; and laugh, fun, and hoaxing, were the order of the day; for although the latter word is of more modern origin, still the meaning was the same, and the joke as winning.

About twelve miles from Cheltenham, near Northleach, a man, (a native of the latter place,) on the coach-box, said that the two men walking before us up the hill, were the gaoler of Northleach, and a man in his custody for debt. When we overtook them, the coach was moving at a very slow pace, and I could not resist the allurement of a quotation; a trick I was ever prone to indulge in, when it came in my way. Hallooing out aloud, and imitating, and my face looking like, old Macklin's, in 'The Merchant of Venice', I quoted Shylock's speech to the astonished Northleach prison-keeper:—

'I do wonder,
Thou naughty gaoler, that thou art so fond to come
abroad with him, at his request.'[1]

'And what is that to you?'—quoth the gaoler, (with a face as red as a turkey-cock,)—'What business is it of yours, to ask me what I do? If I had you down here, I'd break every bone in your body.'

I should have been sorry to be within his reach, for the varlet was tall, and had a *striking* appearance; however, the coachman relieved me from his threats, by quickening his pace, laughing, as well as the passengers, while the infuriated gaoler was giving me a volley of abuse: however, to say truth, I deserved it for my impudence.

I passed some very pleasant days at Plymouth, and received many marked attentions from Mr. Hawker, an English gentleman who was Dutch Consul. He took me to see the French prisoners confined in Mill Prison; it was astonishing to witness the apparent gaiety of their minds, and the perfect happiness with which they were enjoying themselves at all kinds of games and gambols; but the ingenuity of some was beyond my conception. They made toys of all descriptions, and sold them to the visitors of the prison. I bought from a French lieutenant the model of a ship, of his own making, completely rigged—the workmanship was admirably good. Amongst other things which I saw there, was a trait of French honesty, which amused me extremely.

A fellow who was locked up, had a large bench in front of the place where he was confined, on which were several articles for sale; an old man, who could speak a little English, stood by the side of them, and kept bawling out, to all the passers by:—

'Come here, Monsieur le Capitaine, look here, my pretty things—Monsieur le Capitaine, come buy de pretty things for Madame.'

I went up to him, and wished to purchase a handsome writing desk, for which the spokesman asked four guineas. I refused to give so much, but offered him one; the owner (who was locked up) in speaking to the salesman in French, told him to insist upon four guineas, adding, 'I am sure you will get it; Monsieur le Capitaine, there, looks very like a simpleton.'

I replied, that I would give no more than the guinea; and also speaking to him in French, which he had no notion I understood, told him that, simpleton as I was, I could purchase just such another writing desk for a louis d'or in Paris, either in the Palais Royal or on the Boulevards.

He made me a low bow, and said, smiling, 'Ma foi, Monsieur, vous avez de l'esprit—et pour çà—for *that,* you shall have the desk for one guinea.' I gave him the money, with a few complimentary observations upon his honesty and good manners.

Having seen all I wished to see, I went to Plymouth Dock, with an intention of going into Cornwall. On alighting from the chaise, I strolled about while dinner was preparing, gaping around me. I found a gate open, and walked into a large yard, and seeing a person there, asked him the name of the place?

'What!' said the man, 'Don't you know?'

I told him that I did not, but having seen a large gate open, *I had walked in.*

'Then, my good fellow,' said the man, 'take my advice, and *walk out* as fast as you can; for if you are found examining the Dock Yard without permission, you will be forthwith lodged in the Mill Prison, whence you will not find it a very easy thing to get away.'

I thanked my honest friend for his kind intelligence, and with a hop, step, and jump, was outside the gates of the Dock Yard in two minutes. I was afterwards informed, that I really had a narrow escape, for, as we were then at war, no stranger was allowed to enter, without a special order from the Commissioner.

I was very often at Mount Edgecumbe, where, at that time, the Somerset Militia were encamped. I had an invitation from the late Lord Cork, to dine with him at the mess, which I accepted, and that indeed, was the place where I first met my kind friend, Sir Charles Bampfylde. From that day, until the period of his lamented death, I was favoured with his friendship. There dined at the mess that day, a young gentleman, a lieutenant in the navy, brother to a noble lord, who drank a great deal of wine, and subsequently accompanied me on my return to Dock, in the public passage boat. In the boat were some workmen of the Dock Yard, all of whom had an inveterate aversion to the officers of the navy, so much so, that desperate quarrels frequently occurred between them. My companion was excessively noisy and troublesome, abusing the people of Dock in the grossest and most unqualified terms. I was doing all in my power to persuade him to 'moderate the rancour of his tongue,' but in vain; when he was half seas over, he became more and more violent in his vituperation of the Dockites.

20

When we got on shore, and were walking up the hill, some half dozen of our hard-fisted nautical companions fell upon us. I was pummelled about like a shuttle-cock, knocked down, and left senseless on the ground; while my companion, who was the sole occasion of my being so cruelly mauled, apprehensive, I conclude, of the anger of some strict disciplinarian in command, made all sail from the scene of action, and left me at the mercy of the cowardly ruffians; for I was fool enough to stand my ground, as long as I was able—the fruits of which vain resistance were, that I was carried to my hotel senseless, and confined to my bed for six weeks, attended by two medical men. Independently of the drubbing with which they favoured me, I was a loser of 500*l.* which, like Father Foigard, in the 'Beaux Stratagem', I *intended* to get; for I had engagements in Liverpool, Manchester, Birmingham, and Dublin, all of which I was obliged to relinquish in consequence; so that I had good reason to remember Dock.

Three years after this mishap, however, I ventured again to visit Plymouth. Mrs. Crouch and myself were then engaged to perform at the theatre. Mr. Foote, the father of the lovely Miss Foote, of Covent Garden Theatre, was then manager of Plymouth Theatre; and Mr. Hughes, one of the proprietors of Sadler's Wells, manager of the theatre at Dock. With him, Mrs. Crouch and myself entered into an engagement, when we had finished at Plymouth, to perform for a fortnight at Dock. The theatre was crowded every night we played. One evening, in 'No Song, no Supper', Mrs. Crouch, who acted Margaretta, introduced a pretty ballad, which Dr. Arnold had composed for Miss Leak, at the Haymarket, entitled, 'The Poor Little Gipsey'. Mrs. Crouch sang it delightfully, and it was every where a great favourite. While she was singing the line, 'Spare a poor little gipsey a half-penny,' a jolly tar hallooed from the pit, 'That I will, my darling!' and threw a shilling on the stage. The liberality of honest Jack, produced a roar of laughter from the audience.

On our way to Plymouth, we passed a few very agreeable days at Bath, with my old friend and master Rauzzini, who was the original adviser of the measure of sending me to Italy. Every thing at Pyramid (the name of his residence) breathed content and happiness; professional people, of all descriptions, were welcome to his hospitable table, which was always supplied with the best viands, and choicest wines.

While we were staying with him, Madame Mara and Signora Storace were also his inmates, and every evening we had music of the best sort; Rauzzini himself presiding at the piano-forte, and singing occasionally. He had lost the soprano part of his voice, but his lower contra alto tones were very fine, and his taste was exquisite; he was also a delightful composer. It had been generally asserted and believed, that when he was engaged at the King's Theatre as first soprano singer, most of the popular songs which he sang in Sacchini's operas[1] were composed by himself, although the credit of them was given to Sacchini; but upon a severe quarrel between them, Rauzzini, in a paper war, actually avowed himself the author of them, and accused Sacchini of the greatest ingratitude.

He retired to Bath, where he undertook to conduct the concerts, and continued to reside for many years, beloved and respected by the inhabitants and visitors of that city. He had a great deal of teaching, which, added to the profits of his performances, enabled him to entertain his friends in the hospitable manner he did. The expenses of those performances were to him comparatively small, as it was almost an article of faith amongst the profession to give their services gratis on such occasions. I have known Mrs. Billington renounce many profitable engagements in London, when Rauzzini has required the aid of her talents, and at her own expense, travel to Bath, and back to London, as fast as four horses could carry her, without accepting the most trifling remuneration. The singers engaged at the King's Theatre were always allowed by the proprietors to give him their gratuitous assistance.

Braham was his favourite scholar, and invariably made a point of attending; no pecuniary advantages derivable from any other source, ever induced him to relinquish the opportunity of serving his old master to the day of his death,—a kindness which Rauzzini always spoke of in terms of the highest gratitude. Happy have I ever been to join in such praises, having always found Braham, from his first appearance at Drury Lane Theatre to the present moment, liberal and kind towards me, personally, and ever ready to give his support and approbation to merit wherever he found it. Aware, as he must be, of his own superior talent, he is above envy, and possesses professionally, and in every other sense of the words, a clear understanding, sound sense, and accurate judgment.

After a week's sojourn at Bath, Mrs. Crouch and I took our departure for Plymouth. At Exeter we spent a pleasant day and night, though it was in the church-yard, where our hotel (one of the best in that city) was situated. I went to the cathedral, and heard a beautiful anthem of Jackson's finely sung; he himself was at the organ. I went up to the organ-loft, and introduced myself to him; he did me the favour to call at my hotel, and spend the evening with me. He was a man of great taste and musical research, but very eccentric. His melodies were pure and natural, and some of his madrigals and anthems will live for ever, to the credit of the English school. He was a great friend of the late Mr. Linley, who largely partook of his style and genius.

We arrived at Plymouth, and put up at the Pope's Head. The theatre was then opened under the management of Mr. Jefferson, a good kind of man, who had formerly acted inferior parts with Mr. Garrick at Drury Lane, and was thought very like him. His eye was very expressive, and he was excessively proud to be considered like the great actor, of whom he spoke with enthusiasm. He was a martyr to gout, but a most entertaining man, and replete with anecdotes, which he told with peculiar humour.

Before he became proprietor of the Plymouth theatre, he was manager of a strolling company of comedians, who acted on shares. When they were at Penzance, in Cornwall, performing in a barn, and miserably off for audiences, a French dancer, of the name of La Croix, who had come from St. Malo's, to seek his fortune in Plymouth, finding the theatre there shut, and hearing of Monsieur Jefferson's company at Penzance, formed a resolution to pack up his very 'little all,' and *chassé* on foot to join them.

When he arrived at Penzance, he waited upon Mr. Jefferson, offered his services, and said, that he had no doubt he should draw crowded houses by the excellence of his performance; for Monsieur La Croix, in his own opinion, was 'Le Dieu de la danse.' He was accordingly enrolled in the company on the usual terms, that is to say, that all should share and share alike. He made his appearance in a fine pas seul; but, unluckily, in one of his most graceful pirouettes, a very important part of his drapery, either from its age or slightness, or from the wonderful exertion of its wearer, became suddenly rent in a most unmendable manner. Shouts of laughter and applause followed, which Monsieur La Croix imagined were given for his jumping; nor was the supposition at all unjustifiable, for the higher he jumped, the more he was applauded. At last some one behind the scenes called him off the stage; and he was so shocked at the mishap which had befallen him, that he could never be induced to appear again. But, in the sequel, when he came to receive the recompence of his exertions and exposure, the salvo for his shame amounted only to a few bits of candle ends, which he would not accept; he said, he was a French artiste, and not a Russian, and therefore could not be expected to live on candles, and that Monsieur *Jeff* (as he called the manager) had imposed upon him with false pretences. The poor fellow made his way to Totness, where, as I heard, he got some scholars; but nothing would induce him to hear *Mr. Jeff,* or his tallow provender, ever spoken of again.

After dinner, Mrs. Crouch and I went to the theatre; it was Mrs. Clendining's benefit; the play, Inkle and Yarico, and the house very full: Mrs. Clendining acted Yarico. She, at that time, belonged to the Covent Garden company, and had a very good voice, and was a favourite with the town, in spite of a most implacable Irish brogue. The opera, on the whole, was well performed: Trueman, afterwards engaged at Drury Lane, was the vocal hero of the company, and the band, for a provincial theatre, was really respectable.

Many years afterwards, I was introduced to the late Mr. John Emery, the truly great comedian of Covent Garden Theatre, who told me that I had once caused him much alarm by having been present at the Plymouth theatre, where he was leader of the band. I found this highly-gifted actor a very fine musician, as well as a delightful artist. I have some marine pieces of his, that are, in my opinion, admirable.

On my return to town, I went to spend a few days with my friend George Colman, at his beautiful cottage, called 'Mountains;' there I again met Colonel North, and Mr. Frederic Walsh, of the Custom House. At that time Mr. Dowton, the comedian, was acting at Tonbridge Wells, with his mother-in-law, the eccentric Mrs. Baker, who was proprietress of that theatre. Mr. Colman wrote to Mr. Cumberland to say, that on the following day we should be at Tonbridge Wells (nine miles from Mountains) for the purpose of seeing Mr. Dowton act; and requested him to choose the character in which he should like us to see him.

Mr. Cumberland selected Sheva, in his own play of 'The Jew'; and a part in the farce called 'Hunt the Slipper'. We were all delighted with Dowton's performance, particularly the Jew, which was a very fine specimen of natural acting. I was so struck with it, that I called out to a gentleman, with whom I was acquainted, who was sitting within three boxes of our party,—'This is fine acting; this, I'll answer for it, will do.' My prognostication, it seems, was so loudly expressed, that, as Dowton afterwards told me, he heard it on the stage.

On my return to town, I told Mr. Sheridan what I thought of Dowton; and my opinion being corroborated by George Colman, Dowton had an immediate offer to join the Drury Lane company, which he accepted, and made his first appearance in the same character of Sheva, on the 10th of October, 1796; his success was perfect, and he has continued, to this day, a brilliant ornament of his profession.

Mr. Sheridan, whose praise in theatrical matters was fame, often told me, that he thought Dowton a sterling actor; and that if he ever wrote a comedy, the two performers for whom he should take most pains, would be Dowton and Jack Johnstone—would that he had kept his promise!

Dowton, whom I have proved to be one of the kindest and best-hearted men in existence, was formerly very passionate; and when he believed himself right, nothing could move him from his point. On one occasion, he thought himself slighted, and in a huff, quitted his situation, and retired to the house of his old friend, Mr. Lee, of Bexley, a worthy, kind man, whose hospitality is proverbial in the county of Kent.

Mr. Sheridan was very sorry to lose so excellent an actor, and wrote to him to return, but all in vain. I went down to Mr. Lee's house, at Mr. Sheridan's request, to see what *I* could do, and stopped there two days; but Dowton was inexorable, although every thing he desired would have been granted.

When I returned to town, and told Mr. Sheridan of the failure of my mission, he said to me, 'I compare Dowton to a spoiled child at school, who first cries for bread and butter—that is given him; when he has got that, he must have brown sugar put upon it—it is sugared for him; after that, he is not contented till he has glass windows cut out upon it.' However, without having the bread, butter, brown sugar, or glass windows, by the interference of his staunch friend, Cumberland, and the advice of his equally staunch friend, Mr. Lee, he returned to his situation; and Sheridan, on the occasion, ordered the revival of two comedies for him, 'The Goodnatured Man', and 'The Choleric Man', but, (as may be anticipated by those who knew Mr. Sheridan) neither of them was ever revived.

At Drury, the next musical piece brought out, was the 'Honey Moon', a comic opera, written and composed by Mr. William Linley, son of that excellent musician and composer, William Linley,[1] patentee of the Theatre Royal, Drury Lane, and father-in-law to Mr. Sheridan. It was produced on the 7th of January, 1797, and reflected great credit on the talents of the author; but owing to an unjust cabal, which was clearly proved to exist on the first night of its performance, it did not meet with that success to which its merits entitled it, and the author (with becoming spirit) withdrew it from the stage. 'The Pavilion', a musical entertainment, written and composed also by Mr. William Linley, in which I performed a principal character, was brought out some time after the 'Honey Moon', but did not meet with much greater success, and was also withdrawn for the same reason, though it had some beautiful music in it. The Linley family were all most highly gifted—nature and art combined, did every thing for them. I remember once having the satisfaction of singing a duet with Mrs. Sheridan (William Linley's sister) at her house in Bruton Street; her voice, taste, and judgment, united to make her the *rara avis* of her day.

The last time I beheld her heavenly countenance, was at Bristol Hot Wells, where she went for the benefit of her health, having been attacked with a severe pulmonary complaint, which baffled every effort of art to overcome it. She was, indeed, what John Wilkes said of her, the most beautiful flower that ever grew in Nature's garden; she breathed her last in the year 1792, in the thirty-eighth year of her age; and was buried by the side of her sister, Mrs. Tickell, in the cathedral church of Wells.

Her mother, a kind friendly woman, and in her youth reckoned beautiful, was a native of Wells. Miss Maria Linley, her sister, a delightful singer, died of a brain fever, in her grandfather's house at Bath. After one of the severest paroxysms of the dreadful complaint, she suddenly rose up in her bed, and began the song of, 'I know that my Redeemer liveth', in as full and clear a tone as when in perfect health. This extraordinary circumstance may be depended upon, as my friend, Mr. William Linley, her brother, stated the fact to me a short time since.

I never beheld more poignant grief than Mr. Sheridan felt for the loss of his beloved wife; and although the world, which knew him only as a public man, will perhaps scarcely credit the fact, I have seen him, night after night, sit and cry like a child, while I sang to him, at his desire, a pathetic little song of my composition, 'They bore her to her grassy grave.'

On the 9th of February, 1797, was produced, for the first time, an interesting musical entertainment, called 'A Friend in Need,' written by Prince Hoare, which met with universal approbation;—it was my first appearance in England as a composer.

On the 8th of April, Miss Farren, who had been for many years the favourite child of Thalia, and the elegant representative of fashionable life, quitted the stage, of which she had been so long one of the brightest ornaments, to become Countess of Derby. The theatre, on the occasion, was crowded to the ceiling; and the applauses she received, were as warm as they were deserved. Her demeanour in the theatre, was all affability and good nature; and in every action she was ever kind and lady-like. Lady Teazle, and other characters of high life, she pourtrayed with all the vivid colouring of truth; indeed, she had the advantage, like her great predecessor, Mrs. Abington, of associating with the first society and the greatest wits of the age.

It was in this year that Mr. Cumberland, the author, promised my friend, Jack Bannister, to write a comedy for his benefit, which was to be interspersed with songs, for Mrs. Jordan, which he wished me to compose. He was good enough to give Bannister and myself an invitation to spend a few days with him, at his house at Tonbridge Wells, in order that he might read his comedy to us; and as we were both interested in its success, we accepted his invitation; but fearing that we might not find our residence with him quite so pleasant as we wished, we agreed, previously to leaving town, that Mrs. Crouch should write me a letter, stating, that Mr. Taylor requested me to return to London immediately, about some Opera concerns; by which measure we could take our departure without giving offence to our host, if we did not like our quarters, or remain with him if we did.

Jack Bannister rode down on horseback, and I mounted the top of the Tonbridge coach. Seated on the roof, were two very pretty girls and two livery servants; this party I soon discovered were on the establishment of the Duchess of Leinster, following her Grace to Tonbridge Wells, whither she had gone the day before. While ascending Morant's Court Hill, we overtook Bannister on horseback, who called out to me, 'What, Michael! who would have expected to see you on the top of the stage? I hope you have brought your curling irons with you; I shall want my hair dressed before dinner; come to me to the Sussex Hotel. Tonbridge Wells is very full, and, I dare say, you will get plenty of custom, both as a shaver and dresser.'

At the conclusion of this harangue, he bade me good day, put spurs to his horse, and rode away.

I resolved to follow up the joke; and when the coach stopped at Seven Oaks, I sat down to dinner (my luncheon) with the servants, in the room allotted to outside passengers. We grew quite familiar; the lady's maid and the two footmen promised me their protection, and declared that they would do every thing in their power to get me custom, although they could not invite me to call and see them at the Duchess's house, because nothing but the most rigid stinginess was practised there. 'I suppose,' said I, 'you can give one a glass of ale now and then?'

'Ale,' said one of the footmen, 'bless your heart, we never have ale, never see such a thing,—nothing but small beer, I assure you.'

Until we arrived at our journey's end, the abigails and knights of the shoulder-knot kept entertaining me with anecdotes of the family, which were not very flattering I confess, but which I believe to have been false, having had for many years the pleasure of knowing her Grace, the Duchess, and Mr. Ogilvie, her husband.

On our parting where the coach set us down, we all vowed eternal friendship, and I got to Mr. Cumberland's in time for dinner. The party consisted of myself, Bannister, Mrs. Cumberland, an agreeable well-informed old lady, and our host, who by-the-bye, during dinner, called his wife, mamma. We passed a pleasant evening enough, but wine was scarce; however, what we had was excellent, and what was wanting in beverage, was amply supplied in converse sweet, and the delights of hearing the reading a five-act comedy.

Five acts of a play, read by its author after *tea,* are at any time opiates of the most determined nature, even if one has risen late and moved little; but with such a predisposition to somnolency as I found the drive, the dust, the sun, the air, the dinner, and a little sensible conversation had induced, what was to be expected? Long before the end of the second act I was fast as a church—a slight tendency to snoring, rendered this misfortune more appalling than it otherwise would have been; and the numberless kicks which I received under the table from Bannister, served only to vary, by fits and starts, the melody with which nature chose to accompany my slumbers.

When it is recollected, that our host and reader had served Sheridan as a model for Sir Fretful, it may be supposed that he was somewhat irritated by my inexcusable surrender of myself: but no; he closed his proceedings and his manuscript at the end of the second act, and we adjourned to a rational supper upon a cold mutton-bone, and dissipated in two tumblers of weak red wine and water.

When the repast ended, the bard conducted us to our bed-rooms; the apartment in which I was to sleep, was his study; he paid me the compliment to say, he had a little tent-bed put up there, which he always appropriated to his favourite guest. 'The bookcase at the side,' he added, 'was filled with his own writings.'

I bowed, and said, 'I dare say, Sir, I shall sleep very soundly.'

'Ah! very good,' said he; 'I understand you,—a hit, Sir, a palpable hit; you mean being so close to my writings, they will act as a soporific. You are a good soul, Mr. Kelly, but a very drowsy one—God bless you—you are a kind creature, to come into the country to listen to my nonsense —*buonas noches*! as we say in Spain—good night! I hope it will be fine weather for you to walk about in the morning; for I think, with Lord Falkland, who said he pitied unlearned gentlemen on a rainy day—umph —good night, God bless you,—you are so kind.'

I could plainly perceive, that the old gentleman was not over-pleased, but I really had no intention of giving him offence. He was allowed, however, to be one of the most sensitive of men, when his own writings were spoken of; and, moreover, reckoned envious in the highest degree.

He had an inveterate dislike to Mr. Sheridan, and would not allow him the praise of a good dramatic writer; which, considering the ridicule Sheridan had heaped upon him in 'The Critic', is not so surprising.—

That piece was wormwood to him: he was also very sore at what Sheridan had said of him, before he drew his portrait in that character.

The anecdote Mr. Sheridan told me. When the 'School for Scandal' came out, Cumberland's children prevailed upon their father to take them to see it;—they had the stage-box—their father was seated behind them; and, as the story was told by a gentleman, a friend of Sheridan's, who was close by, every time the children laughed at what was going on on the stage, he pinched them, and said, 'What are you laughing at, my dear little folks? you should not laugh, my angels; there is nothing to laugh at?'—and then, in an under tone, 'Keep still, you little dunces.'

Sheridan having been told of this, said, 'It was very ungrateful in Cumberland to have been displeased with his poor children, for laughing at *my comedy*; for I went the other night to see *his tragedy*, and laughed at it from beginning to end.'

But with all the irritability which so frequently belongs to dramatists, Mr. Cumberland was a perfect gentleman in his manners, and a good classical scholar. I was walking with him on the pantiles one morning, and took the opportunity of telling him (which was the truth) that his dramatic works were in great request at Vienna; and that his 'West Indian' and 'Brothers', particularly, were first-rate favourites; this pleased the old man so much, that (I flattered myself) it made him forget my drowsy propensities.

He took me up to the top of Mount Ephraim, where we met the Duchess of Leinster and a lady walking;—she had just got out of her carriage, and the two identical footmen who had been on the stage-coach with me, were walking behind her. She stopped to speak to Mr. Cumberland; and never shall I forget the countenance of the servants, when her Grace said, 'Mr. Kelly, I am glad to see you, have you been long here?'

I replied, 'No, Madame, only two days.'

'Did you come down alone?' said the Duchess.

'Not entirely,' said I; 'I came down on the coach, and, I assure you, met with some very pleasant chatty companions, who amused me very much, by a variety of anecdotes about themselves, and their masters and mistresses.' While I was saying this, I kept looking at my two sworn friends, the footmen, who seemed struck with wonder and surprise.

'Well,' said the Duchess, 'I hope this place will agree with you.'

I said, 'I fear not, for I am extremely partial to malt liquor, and I am told, that it is execrable here; and that in the very first houses, one meets with nothing but bad small beer.' I again looked at my friends, and I am sure they wished me at Jericho; for it was evident, by their countenances, that they were afraid I should betray their confidence; and they seemed quite relieved when they saw me make my bow and walk away.

A letter arrived the next morning, as we had planned, which called me to London; we informed our host, that we were obliged to quit his hospitable roof early the following day. 'My children,' said he, 'I regret that you must leave your old bard, but business must be attended to; and as this is the last day I am to have the pleasure of your company, when you return from your evening's rambles on the pantiles, I will give you what I call a treat.'

After dinner, Bannister and myself went to the library. 'What,' said I to Bannister, 'can be the treat Cumberland has promised us tonight? I suppose he took notice of your saying at dinner, that your favourite meal was supper; and he intends, as we are going away to-morrow morning, to give us some little delicacies.' Bannister professed entire ignorance, and some doubt; and on our return from our walk, we found Cumberland in his parlour, waiting for us. As I had anticipated, the cloth was laid for supper, and in the middle of the table was a large dish with a cover on it.

When we were seated, with appetites keen, and eyes fixed upon the mysterious dainty, our host, after some preparation, desired a servant to remove the cover, and on the dish lay another manuscript play. 'There, my boys,' said he, 'there is the treat which I promised you; that, Sirs, is my Tiberius, in five acts; and after we have had our sandwich and wine and water, I will read you every word of it. I am not vain, but I do think it by far the best play I ever wrote, and I think you'll say so.'

The threat itself was horrible; the Reading sauce was ill suited to the light supper, and neither poppy nor Mandragore, nor even the play of the preceding evening, would have been half so bad as his Tiberius; but will the reader believe that it was no joke, but all in earnest, and that he actually fulfilled his horrid promise, and read the three first acts? but seeing violent symptoms of our old complaint coming over us, he proposed that we should go to bed, and in the morning that he should treat us, before we started, by reading the fourth and fifth acts; but we saved him the trouble, for we were off before he was out of his bed. Such are the perils and hair-breadth 'scapes which attend the guests of dramatists who live in the country.

The comedy which he read on the first evening of our visit, and which was called 'The Last of the Family', was brought out at Drury Lane, as he had promised, for Bannister's benefit, on the 8th of May, and was repeated four times with moderate success. It contained much elegant dialogue and correct sentiment, but the plot was too meagre and inartificial for effect. Bannister spoke a prologue in the character of Sheva, in 'The Jew'; and Mrs. Jordan an epilogue with a song, which were much applauded.

At this period, I left Suffolk Street, and took a house in Lisle Street, Leicester Square, which Mrs. Crouch fitted up according to her own excellent taste. Upon this scite, an Italian Opera House was to have been erected by a Mr. O'Ryley,[1] a clever and ingenious man, under the patronage of the Marquis of Salisbury (whose estate it was), but the project fell to the ground, and the theatre never rose from it.

On the 14th June, a benefit was given at Covent Garden Theatre, for the widows and children of the brave men who gloriously fell in action on the 14th February, under the late Lord St. Vincent. The three theatres, on that night, combined their forces for the laudable purposes of charity. Mrs. Jordan played Peggy, in 'The Country Girl'; and we performers in 'No Song, no Supper', gave our aid. The whole corps de ballet from the Opera House, represented the ballet of 'Cupid and Psyche'.[2] Several performers of Covent Garden Theatre came forward, and Mrs. Abington, who had not appeared for many seasons, spoke a favourite epilogue.

For Drury Lane, I composed an afterpiece, called, 'The Chimney Corner', translated from the French, by Mr. Walsh Porter, an excellent, though a very eccentric man; to whom, as I have already said, I was indebted for many attentions when at Worcester, and elsewhere. The scenery was very pretty, but the piece was not successful; and after its third representation, was withdrawn.

On the 14th December, the celebrated dramatic romance, called 'The Castle Spectre', was produced at Drury Lane, written by M. G. Lewis, Esq. It had a prodigious run; John Kemble performed in it, as did Mrs. Jordan, and Mrs. Powell, who made a splendid spectre. The first night of its representation, the sinking of the Ghost in a flame of fire, and the beauty of the whole scene,[3] had a most sublime effect. I composed the music for the piece; but for the situation in which the Ghost first appears in the oratory to her daughter, and in which the acting both of Mrs. Powell and Mrs. Jordan, without speaking, rivetted the audience, I selected the chacoone of Jomelli, as an accompaniment to the action. This chacoone had been danced at Stutgard, by Vestris, and was thought an odd choice of mine for so solemn a scene; but the effect which it produced, warranted the experiment.

21

Mr. M. Lewis, the author of this drama, though eccentric, had a great deal of genius. I knew him well, and have passed many pleasant hours in his society. I composed his operas of 'Adelmorn the Outlaw'; 'The Wood Dæmon'; 'Venoni'; 'Adelgitha'; all for Drury Lane; and a romantic drama, which he never brought forward, called 'Zoroaster'. The last I composed was, 'One o'Clock', produced at the Lyceum. Of all his dramas the 'Castle Spectre' was his favourite, perhaps from its having been the most attractive and popular; and yet, it has been said, it was the indirect cause of his death.

After his father's decease he went to Jamaica, to visit his large estates. When there, for the amusement of his slaves, he caused his favourite drama, 'The Castle Spectre', to be performed; they were delighted, but of all parts which struck them, that which delighted them most was the character of Hassan, the black. He used indiscreetly to mix with these people in the hours of recreation, and seemed, from his mistaken urbanity and ill-judged condescension, to be their very idol. Presuming on indulgence, which they were not prepared to feel or appreciate, they petitioned him to emancipate them. He told them, that during his life-time it could not be done; but gave them a solemn promise, that at his *death*, they should have their freedom. Alas! it was a fatal promise for him, for on the passage homeward he died; it has been said, by poison, administered by three of his favourite black brethren, whom he was bringing to England to make free British subjects of, and who, thinking that by killing their master they should gain their promised liberty, in return for all his liberal treatment, put an end to his existence at the first favourable opportunity.

This anecdote I received from a gentleman who was at Jamaica when Mr. Lewis sailed for England, and I relate it as I heard it, without pledging myself to its entire authenticity.

It is, however, notorious, that he died at sea; and it has often been remarked, that the death of a person so well known in the circles of literature and fashion as he was, never created so slight a sensation. This evidently arose from circumstances which had removed him from the immediate *world* with which he had been accustomed to mix; and having been already absent from it for a length of time, his departure from the *general* world, was neither felt nor commented upon.

I once received a command from his present Majesty, when Prince of Wales, to compose a simple English ballad for him; and I had his gracious permission to publish it, as composed for His Royal Highness, and dedicate it to him. I applied to my friend Lewis to write me one, which he did. The song was very popular, and sung by Incledon, at Covent Garden Theatre. The last verse was so applicable to the fate of its author, that I cannot resist giving the words.

TO-MORROW,

A Ballad, written by M. G. Lewis, Esq. *and composed by* Michael Kelly, *expressly for* His Royal Highness the Prince of Wales.

I.

A bankrupt in trade, fortune frowning on shore,
All lost—save my spirit and honour;
No choice being left, but to take to the oar,
I engaged in the Mars, Captain Connor.
But the winds call me some few words to say,
To Polly these moments I borrow,
For surely she grieves I leave her to day,
And must sail on the salt seas to-morrow.

II.

Nay, weep not, though Fortune her smile now denies,
Time may soften the gipsy's displeasure;
Perhaps she may throw in my way some rich prize,
And send me home loaded with treasure.
If so lucky, Oh! doubt not, without more delay,
Will I hasten to banish your sorrow,
And bring back a heart that adores you to-day,
And will love you as dearly to-morrow.

III.

But, ah! the fond hope may prove fruitless and vain,
Which my bosom now ventures to cherish;
In some perilous fight—I may haply be slain,
Or, o'erwhelmed, in the ocean may perish.

Should such be the fate of poor Tom, deign to pay
To his loss a fit tribute of sorrow,
And sometimes remember our parting to-day,
Should a wave bc his coffin to-morrow.

Mr. Lewis had many advantages as an author; he was a good German, understood Spanish, and was perfect master of French and Italian.

After the success of the 'Castle Spectre', I determined to endeavour to get the French programme of 'Blue Beard' (which I had brought from Paris) dramatized. I accordingly called upon my valued friend, George Colman, and told him that I had brought him the outline of a French romance, which, I believed, if he would undertake to write it, would prove highly successful; I told him moreover, that my object was to endeavour to establish my name as a composer, by furnishing the music for it; that I was perfectly sure a week's work would accomplish the literary part of the two acts, for which I would give him a couple of hundred pounds.

After having discussed the subject, and two bottles of wine, the witty dramatist agreed to my terms, and I promised to accompany him to his country-house, and remain with him for a week; I did so, and before the week was ended, the piece was complete, and those who have seen it,— and who has not? will bear testimony to the admirable manner in which he executed his task.

The drama was immediately accepted at Drury Lane; orders were issued to the machinists, painters, and decorators, to bring it forward with the greatest possible splendour and magnificence; and it must be admitted, that nothing could exceed its brilliancy; the music, which fortunately became extremely popular, I composed, with the exception of two selected pieces, and the success of the whole was beyond expectation and precedent. It may be worth noticing, that the Blue Beard, who rode the elephant in perspective over the mountains, was little Edmund Kean, who, at that time, little thought he should become a first class actor.

The 16th January, 1798, was the first night of its production. From the bungling of the carpenters, and the machinery going all wrong, at one time, as it drew near the conclusion, I gave it up as lost: but never shall I forget the relief I experienced when Miss Decamp sang, 'I see them gallopping! I see them gallopping!' She gave it with such irresistible force of expression, as to call from the audience loud and continued shouts of applause.

At the end of the piece, when Blue Beard is slain by Selim, a most ludicrous scene took place. Where Blue Beard sinks under the stage, a skeleton rises, which, when seen by the audience, was to sink down again; but not one inch would the said skeleton move. I, who had just been killing Blue Beard, totally forgetting where I was, ran up with my drawn sabre, and pummelled the poor skeleton's head with all my might, vociferating until he disappeared, loud enough to be heard by the whole house, 'D—n you! d—n you! why don't you go down?' The audience were in roars of laughter at this ridiculous scene, but good-naturedly appeared to enter into the feelings of an infuriated composer.

The next day, the piece was much curtailed; the scenery and machinery were quite perfect; and, on its next representation, it was received with the most unqualified approbation, by overflowing houses, and has kept its standing for six-and-twenty years. The music had an unparalleled sale, but I could not escape the shafts of envy and malice. The professional, would-be theatrical composers, the music-sellers and their friends, gave out that the music was not mine, and that I had stolen it from other composers. But I laughed them to scorn; conscious that I never even selected a piece from any composer to which, when I printed it, I did not affix his name; always bearing in mind what Colley Cibber tells us of himself,—that when he produced his first comedy, which was successful, of 'Love's Last Shift', his enemies gave out that it was not his own; Cibber said, if they knew the person to whom it really belonged, he had been true to his trust, for he had never yet revealed the secret. The Italian proverb was ever present to my mind, which says,

> Lasciategli dire, pure che
> Lasciamo fare.

In English:—

> Let them go on saying,
> So they let me go on doing.*

* The second Act of Blue Beard opened with a view of the Spahi's horses, at a distance; these horses were admirably made of pasteboard, and answered every purpose for which they were wanted. One morning, Mr. Sheridan, John Kemble, and myself, went to the property-room of Drury Lane Theatre, and there found Johnston, the able and ingenious machinist, at work upon the horses, and on the point of beginning the elephant, which was to carry Blue Beard. Mr. Sheridan said to Johnston, 'Don't you think, Johnston, you had better go to Pidcock's, at Exeter 'Change, and hire an elephant for a number of nights?'—'Not I, Sir,' replied the enthusiastic machinist; 'If I cannot make a better elephant than that at Exeter 'Change, I deserve to be hanged.'

In the grand march, where Blue Beard comes over the mountain, there was to be a military band. I was not sufficiently conversant with wind instruments; and therefore I went to Mr. Eley, a German, and Master of the band of the guards. I took my melody to him, and he put the parts to it most delightfully. A considerable bet was made, that the melody was *his,* and not *mine*; to decide the wager, and put the matter at rest, I was induced, after twenty-two years had elapsed, to write to Mr. Eley, and received his answer, a copy of which I insert:—

July 18th, 1821.
48, Frith Street, Soho.

Dear Sir,

I received your letter concerning the march in Blue Beard, of which you gave to me the melody, to put parts for the orchestra wind instruments, to which I added some part to finish the trio, and to lead into the next chorus. I wrote this score in the music room, at Covent Garden Theatre, during the acts of the play, which several of the orchestra did see, and concluded it was my melody; though I assured them it was not; from whence this error has arose.

I remain, dear Sir,
Most truly yours,
R. T. ELEY.

I was now finally settled in my house in Lisle Street, and about the same period, my esteemed friend, Mr. Thomas Philips, the singer, called on me, and wished me to take him as a pupil, and offered me a most tempting premium, but I was too much occupied to accept it. He went to Dr. Arnold, under whose able instruction he became a sound musician and an accomplished singer; he is still in the profession, and by far the very best acting singer on the English stage: to any profession which he had embraced, he would have been an ornament; his conduct is ever honourable,—his feelings always gentlemanly.

About the same time, a less agreeable incident occurred to me, which, although purely of a domestic nature, may be serviceably mentioned here, in order to put others upon their guard, under similar circumstances. I had advertised, in the newspapers, that I was in want of a man-servant; a middle-aged man came after the place—an Irishman. He said he had lived with a gentleman of fortune, of the name of Pritchard, who resided chiefly at his country house, in Epping Forest, but was often at an hotel in South Molton Street; if I could make it convenient to call there the next day, he would be in town, and I might get his character. I went the next day to the hotel; the waiter informed me that Mr. Pritchard had been there, and waited for me as long as he could, but would call upon me in Lisle Street. When I returned to dinner, Mrs. Crouch told me that an elderly gentleman, in deep mourning, of the name of Pritchard, had called upon me, in a job-carriage. She described him as a particularly interesting old gentleman. He gave the Irishman an excellent character, and said that he should not have parted with him upon any account, but that having recently become a widower, he felt it necessary to reduce his establishment.

Mrs. Crouch gave so favourable a description of the 'elderly gentleman,' and the elderly gentleman had given her such a favourable description of his Irish servant, that we were perfectly satisfied, and the man was directed to come to his place.

After he had been in my service some days (it was in the winter time), Mrs. Crouch's own maid came into my room, about four o'clock in the morning, and said she heard such a noise in the passage, as convinced her that somebody was endeavouring to break into the house.

I rose, and crept softly to the head of the stairs, and listened, when I heard the respectable Hibernian protegé of the highly respectable elderly gentleman from Epping Forest, say, through the keyhole of the street door, 'Be quiet! the maid-servants are not gone to bed; come back in an hour;—the plate is in the back drawing-room.' This was pretty conclusive evidence of the liberal intentions of my new servant, touching the disposition of my property. I immediately got my sword, and proceeded to the passage, where I found the object of my search. I told him that if he stirred one inch, I would run him through the body. In the mean time, one of the maids called a watchman, and the culprit was consigned to the coal cellar for the rest of the night.

In the morning, I consulted Mr. Holloway, my solicitor, as to my future conduct in the business; and he knowing, professionally, the difficulties, doubts, and expense of prosecuting and punishing criminals, advised me to profit by my experience, and turn the fellow away; I followed his counsel, and discharged my servant.

One morning, about six weeks afterwards, while I was at the Opera House, superintending a rehearsal, a Bow Street officer came to me from Mr. Bond, with his compliments, to request my immediate attendance at the Police Office. I obeyed the magistrate's wishes, and, to my great astonishment, found seated on the bench, beside the magistrates, Mrs. Crouch, and her sister, Mrs. Horrebow; my *ci-devant* Hibernian servant at the bar, in custody, in company with his ally, the respectable elderly gentleman, who had so liberally given his friend, that which he had not himself—a character. He was, however, no longer dressed in mourning, but in a light-coloured coat, all in tatters, looking quite miserable.

It appeared that, through the recommendation of Mr. Pritchard, the worthy Irishman got into the service of a clergyman at Clerkenwell, into whose house, one night, the family being all at rest, he admitted two thieves, who stripped it of every thing moveable. Upon closer examination of the circumstances, it turned out, that he belonged to a gang of house-breakers, who kept Mr. Pritchard in pay for the express purpose of giving false characters. Mr. Pritchard was sent to Newgate: and the Irishman, having been found guilty at the Old Bailey, was hanged, after having confessed the commission of innumerable atrocities.

As I before said, I relate this to serve as a caution to my readers against receiving the characters of servants from persons to whom they have not a respectable reference, however respectable their personal appearance, or however amiable or gentlemanly their manner.

This summer I took a cottage at Battersea, and accepted an engagement for part of the season, at Colman's theatre,[1] in order to introduce a pupil of Mrs. Crouch, a Miss Griffiths, who afterwards married a Mr. Stewart, a comic performer on the Dublin Stage. She played Polly, at the Haymarket, to my Macheath, and Clarissa to my Lionel; she was a girl of great promise, and becoming a great favourite. She was the daughter of the stage-door keeper of the Edinburgh theatre, and was employed about the house to sweep the stage, &c. when Mrs. Crouch and myself acted at Edinburgh. She was so delighted with Mrs. Crouch's performance, that some time after we had quitted the theatre, without intimating her intention to her father, or any person belonging to her, she travelled *on foot* all the way from Edinburgh to London, and found out Mrs. Crouch in Lisle Street, who took her under her tuition and patronage, and bestowed the greatest pains in instructing her. She had a sweet voice, a fine ear, and a great share of intellect.

On the 2nd of August, the stage had an irreparable loss, by the death of that excellent actor, John Palmer, who expired on the stage, while acting in 'The Stranger', just as he uttered—

'There is another, and a better world!'

A similar melancholy event happened in the year 1758, when Joseph

Pethren, playing the Duke, in 'Measure for Measure,' dropped down dead, after repeating these words:—

'Reason thus with life—If I do lose thee, I lose a thing that none but fools would keep;—a breath thou art.'[1]

Alas! poor Palmer! his fate was a lamentable one; he had been continually involved in difficulties, brought on him by struggling to support and educate a numerous family; and at the very moment that a hope of extrication from his difficulties gleamed upon him, he sank into the grave: for it is perhaps not generally known, that two days previously to his going to Liverpool, at my house, and I may safely say, through my influence, Mr. Sheridan appointed him stage-manager of Drury Lane Theatre, with a stipend of 400*l.* per annum, exclusive of his salary as an actor; and commissioned me to be the bearer of the pleasing intelligence to him.

The next morning, when I was singing a song at rehearsal, at the Haymarket, Palmer, who had been in the country, came on the stage to speak to one of the actors; when I espied him, without stopping the band, I went on singing the air; but, for the right words of it, substituted the following:—

'My good Jack Palmer, don't go away:
I've got something pleasing to you to say.'

This piece of sublime poetry produced a hearty laugh. I informed him of the appointment, with which, poor fellow, he was truly delighted; it was indeed, the very summit of his hopes and wishes. That evening he set off for Liverpool, whence he never returned. It was supposed, that the death of his youngest boy, on whom he doted, broke his heart.

No actor was ever more generally efficient; in some characters he was excellent, in none indifferent. His acting, in 'Joseph Surface'; 'The Suicide'; Stukely, in 'The Gamester'; Dionysius, in 'The Grecian Daughter'; Young Wilding, in 'The Liar'; Sir Toby Belch, in 'Twelfth Night', was perfection. Mr. Aickin, the Liverpool manager, gave a benefit at his theatre, for the orphan children; Mr. Colman gave his company for the same laudable purpose; the Opera House was lent them, as Mr. Colman's theatre was not sufficiently large. Drury Lane Theatre opened on the 15th of September, with 'The Stranger', and 'The Citizen', for the benefit of his orphan family; the house overflowed in every part; and there were a number of handsome presents made them. The receipts of the night were upwards of 800*l.*; a just tribute to the talents of their unfortunate father.

This benefit has recently been referred to publicly, in consequence of the melancholy occurrence which awakened a fresh interest in the public for one of the surviving sons. An allusion was made by Mr. Palmer, Jun. to the non-payment of the receipts of the house by Mr. Sheridan; but from a correspondence which appeared in the newspapers, it seems that the allegation was founded on a mistake.

The next musical piece I produced at Drury Lane, was in conjunction with Mr. Dusseck, the celebrated piano-forte player; he composed the serious part of it.—I the comic. What he did, was masterly and effective. The piece was entitled, 'The Captive of Spilburg';[1] the story from the French piece, 'Camille; ou, le Souterrain'; it was ably managed by Prince Hoare, and had a run of seventeen nights. My next musical productions were in a play taken from Mr. Lewis's romance of 'The Monk',[2] by Mr. Boaden, and performed at Drury Lane, called 'Aurelio and Miranda'. I thought there was a great deal of merit in the writing; but it was only acted six nights: many thought it indecorous to represent a church on the stage (which, by the way, was a fine specimen of the art,—painted by Capon). But the powerful objection was, the unearthly appearance of Kemble, as the Monk. I never shall forget his attitude immediately after his entrance; his dress—the look—the *tout ensemble*—struck me to be more than human. He was hailed with the most rapturous applause; but he stood motionless, with uplifted eyes, and apparently regardless of the public tribute.

The great sums of money produced to the theatre by 'Blue Beard', induced the Drury Lane proprietors to prevail on Mr. Colman to write a musical afterpiece, to vie with it in splendour. The piece was entitled, 'Feudal Times; or, The Banquet Gallery'. I composed the whole of the music for it. Although the scenery was grand, and the piece well acted, it was not so successful as Blue Beard; although performed, in the course of the season, for many nights. It was brought out in January 1799.

On the 5th of April, 1799, the musical world had to regret the demise of the veteran Cramer, the admirable violin performer, leader of the Opera band, King's concert, and all the music meetings.

On the 24th of May, in the same year, Mr. Sheridan's celebrated play of 'Pizarro', from Kotzebue, was produced; it was admirably acted, and I had the proud distinction of having my name joined with that of Mr.

Sheridan, in its production, having been selected by him to compose the whole of the music.[1]

Expectation was on tip-toe; and strange as it may appear, 'Pizarro' was advertised, and every box in the house taken, before the fourth act of the play was begun; nor had I one single word of the poetry for which I was to compose the music. Day after day was I attending on Mr. Sheridan, representing that time was flying, and that nothing was done for me. His answer uniformly was, 'Depend upon it, my dear Mic, you shall have plenty of matter to go on with to-morrow;' but day after day, that morrow came not, which, as my name was advertised as the composer of the music, drove me half crazy.

One day I was giving a dinner to the Earl of Guilford, the Marquis of Ormond (then Lord Ormond), my valued friend Sir Charles Bampfylde, Sir Francis Burdett, George Colman, J. Richardson, M. Lewis, and John Kemble; and, about ten o'clock, when I was in the full enjoyment of this charming society, Mr. Sheridan appeared before us, and informed my friends, that he must carry me off with him, that moment, to Drury Lane; begged they would excuse my absence for one hour, and he would return with me. I saw it would be useless to contradict him, so I went to the theatre, and found the stage and house lighted up, as it would have been for a public performance; not a human being there, except ourselves, the painters, and carpenters; and all this preparation was merely that he might see two scenes, those of Pizarro's tent, and the Temple of the Sun.

The great author established himself in the centre of the pit, with a large bowl of negus on the bench before him; nor would he move until it was finished, I expostulated with him upon the cruelty of not letting me have the words which I had to compose, not to speak of his having taken me away from my friends, to see scenery and machinery, with which, as I was neither painter, nor carpenter, nor machinist, I could have nothing to do: his answer was, that he wished me to see the Temple of the Sun, in which the choruses and marches were to come over the platform.—'To-morrow,' said he, 'I promise I will come and take a cutlet with you, and tell you all you have to do. My dear Mic, you know you can depend upon *me*; and I know that I can depend upon *you*; but these bunglers of carpenters require looking after.'

After this promise, we returned to my house; I found my party waiting; nor did we separate until five o'clock in the morning.

To my utter surprise, the next day, according to his own appointment,

Mr. Sheridan really came to dinner; after the cloth was removed, he proposed business. I had pen, ink, music-paper, and a small piano-forte (which the Duke of Queensberry had given me, and which he had been accustomed to take with him in his carriage, when he travelled,) put upon the table with our wine. My aim was, to discover the situations of the different choruses and the marches, and Mr. Sheridan's ideas on the subject; and he gave them in the following manner:—'In the Temple of the Sun,' said he, 'I want the virgins of the Sun, and their high priest, to chaunt a solemn invocation to their deity.'—I sang two or three bars of music to him, which I thought corresponded with what he wished, and marked them down. He then made a sort of rumbling noise with his voice (for he had not the slightest idea of turning a tune), resembling a deep gruff bow, wow, wow; but though there was not the slightest resemblance of an air in the noise he made, yet so clear were his ideas of effect, that I perfectly understood his meaning, though conveyed through the medium of a bow, wow, wow. Having done this, and pointed out their several situations, he promised me, faithfully, that I should have the poetry in a couple of days; and, marvellous to say, he actually did send me Cora's song, which Mrs. Jordan sang; and the trio, sung by Mrs. Crouch, Miss Decamp, and Miss Leak, 'Fly away, time,'—which they made very effective. The poetry of the last, however, was written by my good friend, Mr. Richardson; the song really by himself. Having extracted these, I saw that it was perfectly ridiculous to expect the poetry of the choruses from the author of the play; and as I knew a literary gentleman, whose poverty, if not his will, would consent to assist me, I gave him Mr. Sheridan's ideas, as I had caught them from his bow, wow, wows, and got him to write words to them, which he did very well; at least well enough to answer my purpose.

But if this were a puzzling situation for a composer, what will my readers think of that, in which the actors were left, when I state the fact, that, at the time the house was overflowing on the first night's performance, all that was written of the play was actually rehearsing, and that, incredible as it may appear, until the end of the fourth act, neither Mrs. Siddons, nor Charles Kemble, nor Barrymore, had all their speeches for the fifth? Mr. Sheridan was up-stairs in the prompter's room, where he was writing the last part of the play, while the earlier parts were acting; and every ten minutes he brought down as much of the dialogue as he had done, piece-meal, into the green-room, abusing himself and his negligence, and making a thousand winning and soothing apologies, for having kept the performers so long in such painful suspense.

One remarkable trait in Sheridan's character was, his penetrating knowledge of the human mind; for no man was more careful in his carelessness; he was quite aware of his power over his performers, and of the veneration in which they held his great talents: had he not been so, he would not have ventured to keep them (Mrs. Siddons particularly) in the dreadful anxiety which they were suffering through the whole of the evening. Mrs. Siddons told me that she was in an agony of fright; but Sheridan perfectly knew, that Mrs. Siddons, C. Kemble, and Barrymore, were quicker in study than any other performers concerned; and that he could trust them to be perfect in what they had to say, even at half-an-hour's notice. And the event proved that he was right: the play was received with the greatest approbation, and though brought out so late in the season, was played thirty-one nights; and for years afterwards, proved a mine of wealth to the Drury Lane Treasury, and, indeed, to all the theatres in the United Kingdom.

Such, however, were the delays during the first night's performance, that the play did not end, until within five minutes of midnight! The farce of 'My Grandmother', was to follow, but the exhaustion of the audience was so complete, that, when the afterpiece commenced, only seventeen persons remained in the whole dress circle, and twenty-two in the pit.

John Kemble is so perfectly identified with the character of Rolla, that perhaps, as anecdotes of such a person, however trifling, if characteristic, are always interesting, I may be permitted to mention an instance of his coolness in the midst of difficulty, which I had forgotten to relate in its proper place, as far as dates are concerned.

In the summer of 1783, he and his unrivalled sister, Mrs. Siddons, were engaged at Limerick; and Mrs. Crouch, then Miss Phillips, was also there, playing on the alternate nights with the tragedians. She was beyond measure popular, and the theme of universal admiration. One evening, after having performed Rosetta, in 'Love in a Village', some officers of a militia regiment, quartered in Limerick, being very much intoxicated, avowed their intention of escorting her home; and, in order to carry their plan into execution, obtained admission behind the scenes, and proceeded to address her on the subject. She, terrified, ran into her dressing-room and locked the door, which these heroes declared they would forthwith break open.

It so happened, that Mr. Phillips, her father, was laid up with the gout at that juncture, and had commissioned Kemble to see his daughter home after the play; and thus authorised, the moment he heard the disturbance and its cause, he proceeded to the scene of action, and politely requested the military force to withdraw; but they positively refused to stir without Miss Phillips. Upon which, Kemble took his sword, and said, that having been deputed by the lady's father to escort her to her house, he should execute his commission at the hazard of his life, and requested Miss Phillips to open the door of the dressing-room.

With this request she complied; but they had not proceeded many paces, before one of the officers, of the name of Yelverton, came behind Kemble, and made a cut at his head with his sabre.—A woman, of the name of Judy Cameron, one of the stage-dressers, perceived the intention; and catching the man's arm, wrested the sword from him, and, in all probability, saved Kemble's life. Kemble saw the whole transaction; and, without the smallest alteration in look or manner, or being in the slightest degree moved, he turned to his preserver, Judy, and said, 'Well done, Euphrasia!'[1]—He then drew his sword, and conducted his fair charge in safety to her chair.

Lord Muskerry, who was Colonel of the regiment, called upon Kemble in the morning, and told him that every apology he might require should be made by the officers. This anecdote, extremely illustrative of character, I had both from Mrs. Crouch and her father, who always mentioned it with gratitude, and admiration of the high spirit and perfect coolness which Kemble displayed upon this trying occasion.

My next production, at Drury Lane, was an afterpiece, from the German of Kotzebue. I do not recollect the German title of it, but it was literally translated into English by Mr. Papendick, a native of Germany, a very worthy man, and page to her Majesty Queen Charlotte. He shewed it to my friend John Bannister, who told me he approved of the incidents and situations; but in the state in which it then was, he thought it impossible to produce it on the English stage with any effect; but he proposed to me to join with him in purchasing the copyright, and getting it adapted, by some skilful hand, for Drury Lane Theatre.

Having a reliance on his judgment, I agreed to go with him the next day to Windsor, where Mr. Papendick was the page in waiting, to propose terms for the purchase of his translation; we did so, and agreed for a certain sum, and returned the next day to town. Bannister prevailed on our worthy friend, Tom Dibdin, to take the main incident, and write a piece from it; which (sub rosâ) he did admirably. He called it 'Of Age Tomorrow.' I composed the whole of the music, with the exception of the opening piece, which I selected from Paesiello. This farce was, and is, a great favourite; nothing could be more perfect than the acting and singing of Mrs. Charles Kemble, then Miss Decamp; by those who had the pleasure of witnessing it, I think it impossible it can ever be forgotten. Bannister's personification of the Hair Dresser, was excellent; had he served a seven years' apprenticeship to the trade, he could not have been more *au fait* in it, nor have handled the comb, curling irons, and powder puff, more skilfully. Wewitzer, in the Old German Soldier, was excellent, and Suett, as the Country Sportsman, highly amusing.

This piece was very productive to the treasury, at little or no expense. In it there was a ballad, written by Mr. M. G. Lewis, and composed by myself, which was sung by Miss Decamp, entitled, 'No, my love, no'. I believe I may say, it was the most popular song of the day; it was not alone to be found on every piano-forte, but also to be heard in every street, for it was a great favourite with the ballad-singers: but the primitive cause of its gaining such popularity was, its being sung delightfully by a distinguished amateur, and more completely too, with the expression I intended, than by any other person I ever heard;—I allude to Mr. Charles Calvert, the present Member for Southwark. Many and many a time have I heard him sing it charmingly, and often have I enjoyed his kind hospitality and social qualities. To Miss Decamp I had also great obligations for the animation and spirit she infused into it.

Amongst other friends who used to favour me with their company to dinner, was Signor Ferdinando Mazzanti, a native of Rome, who had been formerly a celebrated soprano singer in Italy and Germany. Dr. Burney, in his Musical Tour, speaks highly of his merits. He mentions him as a great musician, and an eminent classical scholar. When he first came to England he was sixty years of age, and when I knew him was turned seventy. He did not speak a word of English on his first arrival in London, yet, strange as it may appear, for a person at a period of life so advanced, in a very few years he made himself master of the English language, and was fully acquainted with most of the works of our poets and dramatic writers. He was very intimate with Mr. Swinburne, who formerly wrote a Tour of Italy, and gave instructions in singing to his daughter, who afterwards married Mr. Paul Benfield,[1] on his return from India. Mazzanti was a most entertaining companion, possessed a fund of wit as well as information, was full of anecdote, and had a memory scarcely equalled.

He received an invitation from his friend Mr. Swinburne, on his arrival in London, to stay with him, which he accepted; and he told me, that the first time he ever went to an opera in England, the performance was 'The Beggar's Opera Travestied',[1] at the Little Theatre in the Haymarket, which he mistook for the Opera House in the same street. The part of Polly upon that occasion was represented by the elder Bannister, who gave her tender airs with all the power of his deep and sonorous bass voice; and he told me that his astonishment and horror were unspeakable, when he saw the part of a young woman acted by an old man; for he had not been informed, nor did he even guess at the time, that the part of Polly was burlesqued; on the contrary, he thought it had been so intended by the author, and always so acted. A few nights afterwards, he was asked to go and see the tragedy of 'Isabella',[2] at Drury Lane. 'No, no,' said he, 'I will not go to your theatres to see heroines acted by old bass singers with beards;' nor could he be prevailed upon, for a long time, to attend any of our theatrical exhibitions, in consequence of his early disgust.

Mr. Taylor, of the Opera House, wished me (if I could have got permission from Mr. Sheridan) to go abroad and engage a first woman singer for his theatre. I was one morning talking to Viganoni, and mentioned Mr. Taylor's desire. 'Indeed,' said Viganoni, 'you need not go so far as Italy; you have only to go over the way to Badioli's shop, and in his first floor you will find a most beautiful woman, an excellent singer and admirable actress, who only arrived in London from the Continent late last night.' I communicated this intelligence to Mr. Taylor, who requested me, as stage manager, to wait upon her; and, if I could hear her sing, and approved of her, to offer her an engagement for the season.

The next day I waited on Madame Bolla, introduced myself to her, and found her an accomplished beautiful woman, without the slightest affectation. I stated my business to her,—she said she was very willing to engage. On her piano-forte, there was, amongst other music, a duet, which I asked her if she would favour me so far as to sing with me. She replied, 'Most willingly; I perceive you wish to hear me, before you engage me: and I think you are perfectly right.'

She sang the duet, and I was highly pleased. She asked 800*l.* for the season. I acquainted Mr. Taylor with her terms, and he ordered articles to be drawn out, which I took to her the next day, and which she immediately signed, and made her début in Paesiello's opera of 'Il Zingari in Fiera', and met with the most decided success. She was perfect mistress of the English language, and spoke it fluently. She had been brought to

England from Milan when a child, and placed at school at Hampstead, where she remained six years, returned to Italy, and performed in all the principal theatres on the Continent. She acted Lilla in 'The Siege of Belgrade', at Drury Lane, for the benefit of Mrs. Crouch, and gave all the points of the dialogue as if she had been for years on the English stage, and was received with just and merited applause.

On the 15th of May, 1800, (a memorable day, as it afterwards proved,) I went to see His Majesty, King George the Third, review the grenadier battalion in Hyde Park. In firing one of the vollies, a ball struck Mr. Ongley, a clerk in the Navy Office, who was standing only a few paces from the King. It was said, that had the wound been two inches higher it must have been mortal. On the same evening, an event took place at Drury Lane Theatre, which, combined with what had occurred in the morning, gave the most serious alarm. When the arrival of the King was announced, the band, as usual, played 'God save the King'. I was standing at the stage-door, opposite the royal box, to see His Majesty. The moment he entered the box, a man in the pit, next the orchestra, on the right hand, stood up on the bench, and discharged a pistol at our august Monarch, as he came to the front of the box. Never shall I forget His Majesty's coolness,—the whole audience was in uproar. The King, on hearing the report of the pistol, retired a pace or two, stopped, and stood firmly for an instant; then came forward to the very front of the box, put his opera-glass to his eye, and looked round the house, without the smallest appearance of alarm or discomposure.

The late Marquis of Salisbury, then Lord Chamberlain, was behind His Majesty, in attendance in the box; and, on hearing the report of the pistol, fearing some further attack might follow, respectfully requested His Majesty would retire from the box into the adjoining room. His Majesty's reply to him was, 'Sir, you discompose me as well as yourself, —I shall not stir one step.' The Queen and Princesses then entered the box. On ascending the staircase, the Queen asked Mr. Sheridan what all the noise and uproar was about? He replied, it arose from some boys, who had been firing off squibs. Hatfield, the ruffian who committed the crime, was seized by the performers in the orchestra, and dragged over its spikes into the music-room, which was under the stage: the audience from all parts vociferating, 'Bring forward the assassin, bring him on the stage—shew him, shew him.'

I was at that moment on the stage. The Queen called me to her, and asked me if the man was in custody; I told Her Majesty that he was secured. I then came forward and addressed the audience, assuring them, that the culprit was in safe custody, undergoing an examination by His Royal Highness the Duke of York, Mr. Sheridan, and Sir William Addington; but with the immense crowds about the doors, and under the stage, in the confusion, he might possibly escape, should they insist on his being brought forward. This appeal produced tranquillity. 'God save the King' was then called for, and received with shouts of applause, waving of hats, &c. During the whole of the play, the Queen and Princesses were absorbed in tears;—it was a sight never to be forgotten by those present. At the end of the play, 'God save the King' was again demanded by the whole house; and while we were singing it, a paper was sent to me by Mr. Sheridan, with a verse which he had written on the spur of the moment. It was handed to me by Mrs. Jordan, and I sang it, although with an agitated voice. It was as follows—:

From every latent foe,
From the assassin's blow,
  God save the King.
O'er him thine arm extend,
For Britain's sake defend
Our father, prince, and friend,
  God save the King.

This stanza was three times repeated, with the most rapturous approbation. His Royal Highness the Prince of Wales was assisting in the music-room at the examination, and evinced the most anxious solicitude and joy for the safety of his royal and august father. The play was Cibber's comedy, 'She would, and she would not'. Never was a piece so hurried over, for the performers were all in the greatest agitation and confusion. When it concluded, His Majesty left the theatre, amidst the shouts of the audience within, and the enthusiastic cheers of the populace without.

I remember perfectly well, I had dined that day with Mr. Frederick Walsh, in Fludyer Street, with Lord Guilford, Sir Charles Bampfylde, and Mr. Taylor of the Opera House. I was obliged to leave the table almost as soon as we sat down, being under the necessity of going to the theatre to sing in 'God save the King'. Mr. Taylor (who was a great joker) said, 'Mark me, when that fellow returns from the theatre, he will come to us with some marvellous story in his mouth.' When the performance was over, I returned to Mr. Walsh's, and found the party over their wine. I went into the parlour and exclaimed, that the King had been shot at, in the theatre. Mr. Taylor burst into a roar of laughter, saying,

'Did not I tell you that he would come back with some quiz in his mouth?' Nor could I for a long time convince them what I had said was truth; so naturally improbable did it appear, that so good and gracious a monarch should have been exposed to the perils of assassination.

On the 29th of April, 1800, Miss Baillie's play of 'De Montfort' was produced at Drury Lane Theatre. I composed the music:—the scenery was magnificent; the cathedral scene, painted by Capon, was a *chef-d'œuvre*; it had also the support of excellent acting. Mr. Kemble took every pains in the getting it up, but it would not suit the public taste, and was withdrawn after a few nights.

On the 22nd of May, 1800, was produced, for Banti's benefit at the Opera House, an opera, entitled, 'Zenobia and Arminia', the music composed by the Earl of Mount Edgcumbe; some of it was extremely pretty, and did infinite credit to the noble amateur, who is an excellent musician, and a good counterpointist.

At Drury Lane, 11th of December, 1800, was revived, under the classical superintendence of John Kemble, with great splendour of dresses and decorations, Shakspeare's 'King John'. Kemble acted King John with great force and discrimination. In my humble opinion, it was one of his very best characters; his scene with Hubert was great indeed: but what words can describe the magnificent performance of Mrs. Siddons, in Lady Constance! By those who have had the good fortune to witness it, I am convinced it can never be forgotten. Charles Kemble's Faulconbridge was, and is to this day, a masterpiece. Miss Kelly was the representative of Prince Arthur; and, although so very young at the time, evinced a promise of future excellence which she has most amply realised.

Mr. Sheridan called upon me one day, and said, 'Last night I was at Brookes's; Charles Fox came there with Lord Robert Spencer,—they had both been at Drury Lane to see "King John". I asked him if he was pleased with the performance. He replied, that he was, particularly with Mrs. Siddons. But, he added, there was a little girl who acted Prince Arthur, with whom I was greatly struck; her speaking was so perfectly natural; take my word for it, Sheridan, that girl in time will be at the head of her profession.' Mr. Sheridan at that period did not know that Miss Kelly was a relation of mine; but upon this favourable report, went to see her, and told me that he perfectly agreed with Mr. Fox; and further said, 'that he should like to read the character of Monimia in the "Orphan", to her; for, at some future day, he was convinced she would act it admirably.' Praise from two such men, and such judges of the drama, as Fox and Sheridan, must have been highly flattering to any performer.

When Miss Kelly left Drury Lane, and went for some time to act at Glasgow (where she was a great favourite), Mrs. Siddons one day inquired after her, as the promising girl who had performed with her in 'King John'. I told Mrs. Siddons she was gone to act in Scotland. 'Well,' said that incomparable actress, 'I shall be glad to see her return to Drury Lane, where she ought to be; for, if she continue to improve, I am much mistaken if she do not become at some time a very conspicuous ornament to her profession.'

In February 1801, the popular play of 'Deaf and Dumb', was brought out at Drury Lane. Miss Decamp's, John Kemble's, and Wroughton's acting in this piece were, in my opinion, beyond all praise. Mrs. Mountain sang a song, of my composing, in it, charmingly—the poetry by Mr. M. G. Lewis; it was very popular, and always encored. This piece was originally translated by Holcroft, and afterwards altered and adapted to the English stage by Kemble.

Mr. M. G. Lewis brought out, on the 4th of May, 1801, at Drury Lane Theatre, his drama of 'Adelmorn the Outlaw', to which I composed the music. On the whole, it was successful.

I had the pleasure this year to meet Mr. Thomas Moore, the poet, at Mrs. Crouch's cottage in the King's Road; my brother, Joseph, introduced him there. I was much entertained with his conversation, and cultivated his pleasing society; and, in the course of our acquaintance, persuaded him to write a musical afterpiece, for the Haymarket Theatre. I engaged with Mr. Colman to compose the music, and to perform in it. It was called 'The Gipsey Prince', and was performed for the first time on the 24th of July, 1801; part of the poetry was very pretty; but the piece did not succeed, and was withdrawn.

As a sample of the poetry, I subjoin a song, sung by me, in the character of the Gipsey Prince:—

'I have roam'd through many a weary round,
  I have wander'd East and West;
Pleasure, in every clime, I found,
  But sought, in vain, for rest.

'When Glory sighs for other climes,
  I feel that one's too wide;
And think a home which Love endears,
  Is worth a world beside.

'The needle, thus, too rudely moved,
Wandered unconscious where;
Yet, having found the place it loved,
It, trembling, settled there.'

The same year I entered into a new sort of speculation, of which I will detail the particulars:—It will be remembered, that at the corner of Market Lane, in Pall Mall, there was an old house, almost falling, the lease of which (it had sixteen years to run) was to be sold. The owner was Mr. Rice, boxkeeper to the Little Theatre in the Haymarket. Mr. Taylor, the proprictor of the Opera House, suggested a plan to me, which, he said, he was convinced would make my fortune; namely, to buy the lease of that house, put it into thorough repair, and make a large shop in it, to sell my own compositions. As a further temptation, he told me that I should have a door opening to the stage of the Opera House, and that all the subscribers to the Opera, for the great convenience of having a private passage, and easy access to their carriages and sedan-chairs, would, most willingly, subscribe two guineas a year each, which would amply reimburse me for the expense attending it. And also, that by paying a portion of the salaries of the opera composers from abroad, I should have the music of the operas and ballets to publish, exclusively, for my own emolument. And moreover, that being manager of the Opera House, living, as it might be said, under its roof, would be a great advantage to me, in attending rehearsals and performances; and, in being always on the spot where my services were required. All these advantages were very alluring; no situation could be better for a music-shop; in short, through Fancy's aid, I hoped, in sixteen years, to be as rich as Crœsus; but,—

'Hope told a flattering tale.'[1]

Five hundred guineas were required for the lease; and, on a moderate calculation, a thousand more to make the requisite alterations.

At this time, I had the distinguished honour of attending His Royal Highness the Prince of Wales, when he had music at Carlton House. I humbly took the liberty to mention to His Royal Highness the plan I had formed to open a shop for the sale of my own music, and to entreat his royal opinion. He condescendingly gave his opinion, that I was perfectly right: 'for,' graciously added His Royal Highness, 'in a commercial country like ours, nothing can be more creditable than for a man to sell the produce of his own abilities, or, indeed, of any other person's.'

Sanctioned by such an opinion, I made up my mind; and with the assistance of my good friend Moody (to which I have before alluded), I purchased the lease of the house, and almost rebuilt it. The expenditure was far beyond what I was led to anticipate. However, I spared no cost, stocked it well with other music, besides my own; engaged shopmen, porters, &c. and opened it to the public on the 1st January, 1802. The crowds of people who came to purchase music, by way of bringing me (as they said) good luck, were immense. The subscription was opened, for the opera visitors to get an easy access to their carriages. The ladies subscribers said, it was delightful to have such an accommodation. Most of them immediately put down their *names,* but very few of them ever put down their *money,* although there was a considerable current expense attending it, for fires, lighting, and extra servants.

I began to think I was not fitted for what I had undertaken, and reflected on the proverb, 'the eye of the master fattens the horse.' Indeed, my occupations at Drury Lane, Covent Garden, and Haymarket, both as performer and composer, besides being manager of the Italian Opera, and musical director at Drury Lane and the Little Theatre in the Haymarket, were quite enough to engage any one man's mind, without entering into a business which required every attention paid to it, from morning till night. Too late, alas! was I convinced of my error; but I was in for it, too deep to retract.

On the 22nd January, 1802, at Drury Lane Theatre, the Honourable William Spencer produced a musical afterpiece, entitled, 'Urania'. The music of it was the joint production of his brother, the Honourable John Spencer, and myself. I felt much honoured and flattered by the association. Mr. Spencer, who was a scientific writer and a sound musician, composed some very good music for it. I had the pleasure of being known to him at Vienna, when on his travels. It is by his tasteful selection, I understand, that the chacoone of Jomelli (which I selected for the appearance of the Ghost in 'The Castle Spectre') was first introduced by him into our churches, and known in all of them by the title of 'The Sanctus of Jomelli'.

The dialogue in 'Urania', was classically beautiful, as well as the poetry. There was one song in it sung by Mrs. Bland, (which was a great favourite,) entitled, 'Nature with swiftness armed the horse'; a liberal translation from Anacreon, written with true poetic taste, to which I composed the music. The scene of Urania's descent was entirely new to the English stage, and produced an extraordinary effect. The piece was received with uncommon applause.

I formerly had the pleasure of being often in the society of Mr. William Spencer, at his own house, and of meeting him at that of my friend Mr. William Maddocks. Both these gentlemen were lovers of the stage, encouragers and judges of the drama, and of the chosen few who know the value of it, under judicious regulations. Mr. William Maddocks possessed a large fund of wit and humour, and wrote a farce for a private theatre to which he belonged, which possessed much merit.

I often regretted, that Mr. William Spencer did not continue to write for the stage. His knowledge of various languages, particularly German, would have furnished him with many good subjects. He is also perfect master of Italian, and well versed in all the poets of that enchanting language.

Mrs. Billington returned to England this season, after an absence of several years, and was engaged at Drury Lane and Covent Garden, to perform a certain number of nights at each theatre. At both she appeared in Mandane, in 'Artaxerxes'; she went through all her operatical characters, in all of which I performed with her. She was received with rapturous applause, and on each night drew crowded houses.

On the 11th March, 1802, Drury Lane Theatre was closed for the night. Francis, Duke of Bedford, was buried on that day; and, having been ground-landlord of the theatre, this mark of respect was paid to his memory.

22

On the 28th March, Mrs. Billington performed 'Merope', at the Opera House, for Banti's benefit, who, on this occasion, appeared for the first time in male attire. Curiosity was on tip-toe to hear these two great singers, in the same opera, and the performance drew an overflowing house. The worthy Signor Zacharia Banti, to be sure of laying hold of the money, had the pit-door barricadoed, and posted himself there, with some of his friends. An immense crowd had collected at the doors, before the usual time of admission; and on their being opened, the rush was so great, that smash went the barricado, which, together with the cautious Signor Banti, was carried forward, money-boxes and all, in the van of the crowd to the very extremity of the pit.

Recovering himself, and getting on his legs, he gazed around him, and in disappointed anguish, exclaimed, 'O Santa Maria! de pit full! de gallery full! all full—and no money in de box!—what will Brigida—my angel wife say, when I shall have nothing in my box for her?'

A similar circumstance happened at one of my benefits at the Opera House, when Madame Catalani did me the favour to sing for me; the rush was so great, that the doors were broken down, and the pit crammed to excess: the return in money was only 25*l.* Of course great numbers got in to the pit without paying; and though an appeal was made, and a request that those who had not paid, would send the price of their admission to the box-office the following day, not a single person sent; they seemed all to be of Falstaff's way of thinking,—'They did not like that paying back.'

The same year my old friend, King, quitted the Drury Lane stage, which he had trodden fifty-five years—an ornament to his profession.

Mrs. Billington had her benefit at Drury Lane, 30th April. On this occasion the opera of 'Algonah'[1] was brought forward; the drama by Cobb, the music by myself. The opera was successful, though, on the first representation of it, poor Mrs. Billington had a terrible fright; and no wonder, poor thing, for at the end of the first act, who did she find sitting in her dressing-room, but her beloved husband, Monsieur de Felican, whom she thought safe and snug at Venice, whence she had escaped from him; but he, good soul, was deeply in love with her English guineas, and all at once vowed he could no longer bear to be separated from his *beloved Bettina*, as he called her.

Monsieur Felican had been in the Commissariat department, in Buonoparte's service; and having laid strong siege to Mrs. Billington's affections, succeeded. He was a remarkably handsome man, and (as Mrs. Billington told me) before marriage, a most insinuating monster of meekness: but the very first week after their union, the dove assumed the fierceness of the hawk. It was said, that he used to treat her unmercifully; and if she dared to complain, plates, dishes, or any other moveable, were thrown at her.—Such was *her* story. I never would have any communication with him. How it was managed, I know not, but his stay in this country was very short; I have reason to believe, that he had many *weighty* arguments put to him, to hasten his departure. I never saw any woman so much in awe of man, as poor Mrs. Billington of him, whom she had married for love.

At this period, Drury Lane was in a very bad way,—the actors' salaries were greatly in arrear. Mr. Grubb, one of the proprietors, and

Messrs. Hammersley, applied to the Lord Chancellor, praying, that their demands on the theatre, with those of the old and new renters, might be taken out of the receipts before the performers were paid. Sheridan resisted this; and the actors, one and all, threatened to strike, if such an order were granted. The cause came on before the Chancellor. Sheridan pleaded his own cause against the whole Chancery bar, which was retained on the other side. In a most elaborate and eloquent speech, he stated the embarrassments of the theatre, the necessity of paying the performers, as no work could go on without workmen: if they withdrew their services, the doors must be closed, the property fall to pieces, and general ruin ensue. From his eloquent tongue persuasion flowed, and won the high debate. The consequence was, that the performers gained the day; and an order was granted, that they should be the first persons paid.

The Lord Chancellor, after passing a high eulogium on Sheridan, quoted, in addressing him, (as I was told, for I was not near enough to hear it,) Doctor Johnson's last lines in the 'Life of Savage'.—'Negligence and irregularity, long continued, make knowledge useless, wit ridiculous, and genius contemptible.'

I thought at the time, that the quotation might have been spared, and that it was perhaps harsh to speak truth at all times. However, he left the Court amidst the loud congratulations and admiration of his friends, and the envy and discomfiture of his enemies. He walked with me to my house in Pall Mall, where he dined, and told me that he should have spoken better, if I had not kept him up so late the night before. I was so happy and delighted, that I could not help reminding him of Mr. Pitt's eulogium on him, during Warren Hastings's trial. That illustrious statesman designated Mr. Sheridan's speech, on that occasion, as 'an astonishing effort of eloquence, wit, and argument united; surpassing all the eloquence of ancient and modern times, and possessing every thing that genius and art could furnish to agitate and controul the human mind.' For although Mr. Sheridan was a follower of Mr. Fox in politics, Mr. Pitt had the liberality to pay the above tribute to his talent and genius.

In the month of July 1802, Viganoni and I set off in a post-chaise for Dover, and got on board a packet for Calais; we were four-and-thirty hours at sea; among the passengers, were Lady Carhampton and Mr. Lewis Goldsmith, whom I had the pleasure of knowing. We got to Nampont at night, where I sat upon the very bench which Sterne mentions in his 'Sentimental Journey'; and, all the time, I could think of nothing but the 'poor old man and his dead ass.' When we got to Paris, we went to an excellent hotel, in the Rue Neuve St. Marc. On going past the Thuilleries, on our way to dinner, over the gate, in the Place Carousel, the first objects which caught my eye, and grieved my heart, were my old friends the horses, which I used so much to admire in the Piazza St. Marc, at Venice. Then they were of bronze, the pride of the Venetians; and to have had them gilt, seemed to me like sacrilege.

There were (at this short period, we were at peace with France) a vast number of English in Paris, amongst whom, I had the pleasure to be known and noticed by Lord Erskine, Mrs. Damer, Mr. and Mrs. Fox, Lord and Lady Holland, whose condescension I always experienced, whenever I had the honor of meeting them. There were also in Paris my very kind friend, the Earl of Guilford, the Honourable Mrs. and Miss St. Leger, with Doctor Mousley, on their way to Barège, to drink the waters. Viganoni took me with him to a friend of his, in the Place Carousel, to see the First Consul, Buonaparte, review the troops. It was a magnificent sight. He was mounted on his charger, in a plain blue coat, white pantaloons, and a plain cocked hat; and close to him, mounted on a fine Arabian horse, his favourite Mameluke, who seemed an admirable horseman. All the general officers on the ground wore rich and splendid uniforms. The contrast was great between their gorgeous attirements and the simple costume of the *little great man,* who seemed perfectly conscious of his adventitious superiority.

On my return from the review, I met my worthy friends, John Kemble and Mr. Robert Heathcote, in the Rue Richelieu—we agreed to dine together, and go in the evening to the Théâtre François, to see Talma act Orestes, in 'The Distressed Mother'.[1] I was much pleased with the performance of that great actor; but there was a scene performed in the front of the house more curious to an Englishman. Charles Fox, accompanied by his lady, and some male friends, occupied a box in the first tier. After the first act of the play, there was a buzz through the parterre, that Charles Fox was in the house; the moment it was known, there was a general call from the parterre, for him to come forward and shew himself. The cry from all parts of the house was, 'Monsieur Fox! Monsieur Fox! come forward, we want to see you.' For several minutes he was deaf to the call, but the audience seemed determined not to let the performance go on, until he did, for Mr. Fox was as naturally a favourite with the revolutionary French, as Mr. Pitt was the contrary. At length, his friends pushed him forward. The moment he appeared, there was very general applause, which continued for some time, he bowing most respectfully to the audience.

Just as the applause ceased, Buonaparte, accompanied by some of his officers, entered his box, which was *vis-à-vis* to the one Fox occupied. On his entré he was received with the clapping of a few hands. He seemed somewhat dissatisfied with his reception; at all events, he did not remain above a quarter of an hour in the box, and left it without taking the slightest notice of the audience.

The next day the First Consul held a grand levee at the Thuilleries, and all the English were presented to him, myself excepted; but though I was not there in *propriâ personâ,* my opera hat was; for my Lord Guilford, not having his own with him, borrowed mine, which many a time and oft I had worn on the stage when acting Captain Macheath. On the day of the levee I dined with Lord Guilford, who gave me an account of his reception.

He was introduced by the Préfet du Palais as Lord Guilford, son of Lord North, at one time prime minister of His Britannic Majesty.

Buonaparte, darting one of his spiteful looks at him, said, 'My Lord, your father was a very great man;' and turning to the Marshal, said, sneeringly, 'Was it not he who lost America for England?—yes, he was a very great man, indeed;' then turning upon his heel, he walked on.

The vulgar rudeness and uncalled for impertinence of the remark, were received by the noble Earl with contemptuous silence.

I saw Buonaparte one evening at the Italian Opera: the performance was Paesiello's 'Nina', in which Rovedino and Viganoni both sang, particularly a duet, with which Buonaparte seemed much pleased. Josephine was in the box, and appeared a charming woman. He was very attentive to her throughout the performance, although he afterwards divorced her for his personal convenience. He was very partial to Paesiello's music, and sent to Naples for him, gave him an appointment of two thousand louis a year, excellent apartments in the Thuilleries, and a carriage, with servants who had permission to wear the Buonaparte livery. Acts like these pass for liberality and magnanimity in a Corsican tyrant. What would the English nation say, if an English monarch ventured to do such a thing?

The composer and eminent teacher, Signor Ferrari, who resided many years in London, was in Paris at this period, and visited his old master Paesiello daily. I requested him to introduce me into Paesiello's apartments without mentioning my name, and accordingly was ushered up stairs; and when I came to the drawing-room door, where Paesiello and Signora Luigia his wife were, I sang on the outside, the favourite song which he had composed for me at Vienna; and although fifteen years had elapsed since he wrote it, he recollected the tone of my voice, opened the door, and embraced me, saying, 'Bene venuto, mio caro O'Kelly.' I stopped with him and dined, and passed a charming day.

Twice or thrice a week during my stay, I dined with Madame Montansier in the Palais Royal. This lady was the proprietress of two theatres, the Italian Opera and the Comic Theatre, named after her, the Théâtre Montansier, in the Palais Royal. I frequented all the theatres, but chiefly the Feydeau, to hear those excellent singers, and actors, Ellivien and Martin. At this period they were acting 'La Maison à vendre'. The once beautiful Madame Dugazzon played the Old Lady in it, nor did she think herself degraded by it. Another piece, which was a great favourite of the Parisians, was 'La Folie'. I procured both these operas, and brought them to London. 'La Maison à vendre' I gave to Mr. Cobb, who brought it out at Drury Lane, under the title of 'A House to be Sold'; and 'La Folie' to George Colman, who produced it at the Haymarket Theatre, under the title of 'Love laughs at Locksmiths', and an excellent morceau it was rendered by his masterly genius; indeed, far superior to the French drama. The original music of both pieces was very good, but not calculated for an English audience; I therefore recomposed the whole of the music for them. Both pieces met with prodigious success on our stage, but particularly 'Love laughs at Locksmiths', which is, to the present time (1824), a great favourite.

I was invited by Monsieur Ellivien, to dine with him at his hotel in the Rue Mirabeau. Viganoni was asked to meet me. I was unknown to our host as a performer, and was introduced to him by Rovedino, as his friend, who was also of the party. After dinner, I was saying to my host, that I thought if he had seen 'Richard Cœur de Lion', and 'Lodoiska', as performed in London, he would have been pleased; he laughed, and said, it was out of the nature of things, that such music as 'Richard Cœur de Lion', and 'Lodoiska', could be sung by English singers, who, to his ears, were detestable; that he had been in London the last summer, for two days,—that he went to the theatre, and was quite disgusted with the vulgarity of the performers. In the course of conversation, I found that he had obtained leave from the Paris theatre to come to England for a week or ten days, to liberate a great friend of his, who was confined in the King's Bench for debt; that he was taken to an hotel, near Westminster Bridge, and that the only theatre he went to, was Astley's;[1] and from the performances he heard there, he had formed his opinion of all English music, and English singers. Ellivien has since married a rich widow, and retired from the stage.

Paris, to me, always appeared a delightful place. I had many friends,—was free of the principal theatres, and found it, by one half, less expensive than Brighton or Margate. I found the people, generally speaking, courteous, attentive, and obliging.

After breakfast, one morning, on the Boulevards, I was reading the bills of the different theatres, stuck against the walls; in order to fix upon the one I should visit in the evening; when near me, I observed, similarly occupied, a tall elderly man, seemingly without a shirt, with a pipe in his mouth, a greasy red woollen night-cap on his head, a coat in tatters, and, to judge from appearances below, a *true sans culotte*. After having made me a low bow, he said, in very good French, 'Apparently, Sir, you are a stranger in Paris, and are examining the play bills, to choose the best performance to go to, to-night.—Amongst those announced, for my own part, I should prefer the "Athalie" of Racine; the choruses are superb, and the music by Rameau,[2] though of the old style, is magnificent. The last time I heard it was on the night the Grand Opera House on the Boulevards was burned down. If you are a lover of music, I would advise you to go and hear it; I shall go there myself, this evening.'

Saying which, he made me a low bow, and walked away, wishing me much pleasure from hearing Racine's 'Athalie'.

Some people might call the poor ragged admirer of Racine and Rameau, intrusive; for my part I took his remarks for disinterested politeness, for he neither knew me, nor wanted any thing of me; and as a proof of the generality of taste and information amongst the French, I think the anecdote worthy of notice.

Mr. Biggin, who was once called in London the handsome Biggin, and who ascended in a balloon from Sloane Street, with the pretty Mrs. Sage, was at that time in Paris: he was a literary man, and had a great taste for the fine arts. He was appointed, by Mr. Taylor, his trustee for the Opera House, during the period that Lord Kinnaird and Mr. Sheldon managed that concern. In conjunction with Mr. Biggin, I engaged the celebrated Winter, to compose three Italian operas, and three grand ballets, for our Opera. I agreed to pay half his salary for the exclusive right of publishing his music for my own emolument; and had I not been pillaged, that engagement alone would have been a fortune to me, so popular were his works, and so very extensive the sale of them.

I left Viganoni in Paris to finish his engagement, and returned to England with Mr. Small, a young Irish singing master settled in London, who had been a scholar of the celebrated Millico at Naples, and was a very pleasant fellow.

On the 25th October, 1802, the burletta of 'Midas' was revived at Drury Lane Theatre, with unqualified approbation. It had a run, the first season, of twenty-seven nights. From my earliest days, I was fond of the music of 'Midas', which, in my humble opinion, is delightful. It was entirely selected by Kane O'Hara, who was a distinguished musical amateur; his adaptations were not alone elegant and tasteful, but evinced a thorough knowledge of stage effect. I have heard him, when a boy, sing at his own house in Dublin, with exquisite humour, the songs of Midas, Pan, and Apollo's drunken song of, 'Be by your friends advised, too harsh, too hasty Dad'. When I acted the part of Apollo at Drury Lane, I formed my style of singing and acting that song from the recollection of his manner of singing it.*

The simple and pretty melody of, 'Pray Goody, please to moderate the rancour of your tongue', (before I sang it at Drury Lane,) was always sung in a quick jig time;—it struck me, that the air would be better slower, and I therefore resolved to sing it in the 'andantino grazioso' style, and added a repetition of the last bars of the air, which I thought would give it more stage effect. When I rehearsed it the first time, as I had arranged it, Mr. Kemble was on the stage, who, with all the performers in the piece, as well as the whole band in the orchestra, *unâ voce,* declared, that the song ought to be sung in quick time, as it ever had been; but I was determined to try it my own way, and I did so: and during

* O'Hara was so remarkably tall, that, among his intimate friends in Ireland, he was nick-named St. Patrick's Steeple. At one time, Giardini's Italian glee was extremely popular, and sung every where, in public, and in private. The words in Italian are,—

'Viva tutte le vezzose
Donne, amabile, amorose,
Che non hanno crudeltà.'

It was parodied, and for the last line—

'Che non hanno crudeltà,'

they substituted this,—

'Kane O'Hara's cruel tall:'

a combination of sounds which, from early association, I am unable entirely to overcome whenever I hear the glee.

the run of the piece, it never missed getting a loud and unanimous encore. When 'Midas' was revived at Covent Garden Theatre, it was sung by Mr. Sinclair in the exact time in which I sang it, and with deserved and additional success. It is not, I believe, generally understood, that Rousseau was the composer of it.[1]

23

On the 17th November, 'A House to be Sold,' was brought out at Drury Lane, and received with much applause. Bannister and Miss Decamp were excellent in their parts, so were Suett and Wewitzer, and I acted in it the Manager of an Italian Opera;—the piece had a run of several nights. There was a supper scene, in which I was obliged to eat part of a fowl. Bannister told me, at rehearsal, what then I could hardly believe, that it was very difficult to eat and swallow food on the stage. But, strange as it may appear, I found it a fact, for I could not get down a morsel; my embarrassment was a great source of fun to Bannister and Suett, who were both gifted with the accommodating talent of stage feeding; whoever saw poor Suett in the Lawyer, in 'No Song, no Supper', tucking in his boiled leg of lamb; or in the 'Siege of Belgrade', will be little disposed to question my testimony to the fact.

The next novelty at Drury Lane, was an historical musical drama, called the 'Hero of the North', produced on the 19th February, 1803. I composed the music, and also performed in it. It was received with distinguished applause.

On the 16th of May, I went to see the first appearance of my friend Mathews, at the Haymarket, in the characters of Jabel, in Cumberland's comedy of the 'Jew', and Lingo, in the 'Agreeable Surprise': he was received by a crowded house with unanimous applause. He came from the York theatre, where he had been a distinguished favourite of the eccentric Tate Wilkinson (who knew well how to value his talents), as well as of the York audience, and the other theatres of the circuit he belonged to.

He married a favourite pupil of Mrs. Crouch's, a Miss Jackson, who is half-sister of Miss Fanny Kelly; she had a sweet voice, was extremely pretty, with a beautiful figure; possessing amiable manners, and good sense. Mrs. Crouch recommended her strenuously to Tate Wilkinson, as his first singer, and she was very successful. Her exemplary conduct, and unassuming deportment, induced the principal people in Yorkshire to take great notice of her, and introduce her into the best society. She there became the second wife of Mathews; and, having accompanied him to London, made her first appearance at the Haymarket, in 1803, as Emma, in 'Peeping Tom'; her *début* was very successful, and she continued for several years to fill many of the principal vocal characters at that theatre and Drury Lane. She has now retired from the stage, and plays her part in private life, in a manner which secures her the esteem and affection of all who know her.

On the 25th July, Colman produced his translation from 'La Folie', of 'Love laughs at Locksmiths', for which I composed the music. It was very strongly cast, and well represented in all its parts. Elliston's Captain Beldair was full of buoyant gaiety. Mathews's Risk was an inimitable piece of acting; he had two songs, 'The Farm Yard', and 'Miss Bailey', both of which were always encored; 'Miss Bailey' was a universal favourite, and the piece ran the whole of the season.

Mrs. Billington, and I were engaged this year by Mr. Francis Aickin, for Edinburgh and Liverpool. Accompanied by her brother, Charles Weichsell, we left London in a post coach and four for Liverpool. Her fame drew crowded houses every night during a fortnight. 'Artaxerxes' was performed several nights; she was the Mandane, I, the Artabanes, and Miss Duncan (now Mrs. Davison) the Arbaces; and it was really surprising how well that lady sang and acted the part, considering that she had never been accustomed to recitative. I took a great deal of pains to instruct her, and was highly repaid, by her assiduity and truly amiable manners.

In my intercourse with theatrical ladies, I never met with more equanimity of temper and good nature than in Mrs. Davison. Her mother was then with her, and played the old ladies in comedy and opera extremely well, and bore the character of an excellent parent, and kind-hearted woman.

Mrs. Billington and I took our benefits, and both had crowded houses. After finishing our engagements at Liverpool, we went to Edinburgh. On our way thither we passed through Dunbar, where we dined; but, when we offered to pay the innkeeper his bill, he refused English Bank notes, and informed us, that they would be of no use to us on the road, as they would not be taken at any of the inns between Dunbar and Edinburgh. The reason he gave was, that a few days previous, a gentleman and lady, who came in their carriage, had paid their bill with a forged ten pound note; and at all the inns, till they got to Edinburgh, defrayed their expenses by changing forged five and ten pound notes. So that with a *quantum sufficit* of bank notes in our pocket, we were absolutely in pawn at a little Scotch inn. Weichsell and I went to a banker's in the place, (who, by the way, kept a whiskey shop), and told him our situation; he turned out to be a good kind of fellow, and agreed to advance us 25*l.* in *Scotch* Bank notes, on our depositing 100*l.* English until we returned them. This bargain, singular as it may sound, we were forced to make, and accordingly restored his provincial paper, when we got to Edinburgh. When we arrived in the Scotch metropolis it was the time of Leith races, and the place was crowded, as was the theatre nightly.

We were most hospitably entertained at that beautiful sea-bathing place, Musselburgh, by Mrs. Esten, (the present Mrs. Scott Waring,) who had then quitted the stage, of which she had been a distinguished ornament; she had a lovely, amiable, and highly-accomplished daughter, since married, to whom I had the pleasure of giving lessons in singing.

Mrs. Powell, of Drury Lane Theatre, was at Edinburgh; I accompanied her in a carriage to the races. Amongst the throng of fashionables, on the Sands, was the present King of France, on horseback, who was then residing at Holyrood House. He came up to the carriage in which we were, and discoursed nearly an hour with us, with the most condescending affability.

After reaping a golden harvest, in the fields of Thespis, we took leave of Scotland, and agreed, on our way to London, to play two nights at Newcastle. Stephen Kemble was the manager, who received us kindly, and we had two overflowing audiences. It was at Newcastle, I first had the pleasure of meeting that genuine child of Momus, Liston; and, on my return to London, strongly recommended Messrs. Sheridan and Richardson to engage him for Drury Lane: but procrastination was their motto; and it is to George Colman's discernment, that the public are indebted for the invaluable acquisition of Liston's unrivalled talents to the London stage: he made his first appearance in Zekiel Homespun, in the 'Heir at Law', at the Haymarket Theatre (14th June, 1805.)

I this year had the pleasure of spending some weeks in Wales, with my friend Mr. William Maddocks, M.P. at his beautiful seat at Tre Maddock, where there was a large party of ladies and gentlemen assembled. All was hospitality, frolic, and fun, which the brilliant wit of our host contributed in a great degree to promote. We had horse-racing, balls, concerts, plays, and every kind of amusement.

Mrs. Billington was engaged this year as prima donna at the Opera House. She made her first appearance in the serious opera of 'Ferdinand in Mexico', by Nassolini,[1] a charming composer; and in the month of May, Winter composed, expressly for her, the opera of 'Calypso', the music of which she sang delightfully, and looked the character divinely.

My next musical production at Drury Lane, was 'Cinderella;[2] or, the Glass Slipper'. The piece was written by a Mr. James; the story was well told in action, and the poetry of the songs appropriate. I was rather fortunate in composing the music. The scenery, machinery, and decorations, were profusely splendid; and nothing could surpass the fine acting of Miss Decamp, as Cinderella. It was produced in January 1804, and performed, during its first season, fifty-one nights.

In the midst of all the *éclat* and success of this season I had returned my income to the Commissioners of Income Tax, at 500*l*. per annum, which, it appeared, they did not think a sufficient return, and sent me a summons to appear before them on their next day of meeting. In consequence of receiving this, I consulted a kind friend, who was my counsellor on all occasions, who advised me, if I felt myself justified by the truth, to adhere firmly to the amount which I had at first fixed. He promised to accompany me, which he did, and was witness to the following conversation between the Commissioners and myself.

'So, Mr. Kelly,' said one of the men of authority, 'you have returned your income to us, at 500*l*. per annum:—you must have a very mean opinion of our understandings, Sir, to think that you could induce us to receive such a return, when we are aware that your income, from your various professional engagements, must amount to twice or three times that sum.'

'Sir,' said I, 'I am free to confess I have erred in my return; but vanity was the cause, and vanity is the badge of all my tribe. I have returned myself as having 500*l*. per annum, when, in fact, I have not five hundred pence of certain income.'

'Pray, Sir,' said the Commissioner, 'are you not stage-manager of the Opera House?'

'Yes, Sir,' said I; 'but there is not even a nominal salary attached to that office; I perform its duties to gratify my love of music.'

'Well, but Mr. Kelly,' continued my examiner, 'you teach?'

'I do Sir,' answered I; 'but I have no pupils.'

'I think,' observed another gentleman, who had not spoken before, 'that you are an oratorio and concert singer?'

'You are quite right,' said I to my new antagonist; 'but I have no engagement.'

'Well, but at all events,' observed my first inquisitor, 'you have a very good salary at Drury Lane.'

'A very good one, indeed, Sir,' answered I; 'but then it is never paid.'

'But you have always a fine benefit, Sir,' said the other, who seemed to know something of theatricals.

'Always, Sir,' was my reply, 'but the expenses attending it are very great, and whatever profit remains after defraying them, is mortgaged to liquidate debts incurred by building my saloon. The fact is, Sir, I am at present very like St. George's Hospital, supported by voluntary contributions, and have even less certain income, than I felt sufficiently vain to return.'

This unaffected exposé made the Commissioners laugh, and the affair ended by their receiving my return. The story is not very dissimilar to one told of the celebrated Horne Tooke, who, having returned to some Commissioners under the same Act, his income at two hundred pounds per annum, was questioned much in the same manner as myself; till at last one of the inquisitors said,

'Mr. Horne Tooke, you are trifling with us sadly; we are aware of the manner in which you live, the servants you keep, the style you maintain; this cannot be done for five times the amount you have returned.—What other resources have you?'

'Sir,' said Horne Tooke, 'I have, as I have said, only two hundred pounds a year; whatever else I get, I beg, borrow, or steal; and it is a perfect matter of indifference to me to which of those three sources you attribute my surplus income.' And thus ended the examination.

On the 5th December of this year, Mr. Reynolds, the prolific dramatist, produced a musical afterpiece at Drury Lane, entitled 'The Caravan; or, the Driver and his Dog.' There was some pretty music in it, composed by Reeve, and it had a very great run, and brought much money to the treasury. The chief attraction of the piece was a dog called Carlo; and when he leaped into some real water and saved a child, the most unbounded tumults of applause followed. It was truly astonishing how the animal could have been so well trained to act his important character.

One day Mr. Sheridan having dined with me, we went to see the performance of this wonderful dog: as we entered the green-room, Dignum (who played in the piece) said to Mr. Sheridan, with a woeful countenance, 'Sir, there is no guarding against illness, it is truly lamentable to stop the run of a successful piece like this; but really'—'Really what?' cried Sheridan, interrupting him.

'I am so unwell,' continued Dignum, 'that I cannot go on longer than to-night.'

'You!' exclaimed Sheridan, 'my good fellow, you terrified me; I thought you were going to say that the dog was taken ill.'

Poor Dignum did not relish this reply half so much as the rest of the company in the green-room did.

In the year 1804 the Opera House was opened by Mr. Francis Goold, who had been a schoolfellow of mine at the Rev. Dr. Burke's academy in Dublin; he had passed the greatest part of his life on the Continent, and was extremely well acquainted with the arts, and theatrical matters in particular. He was well suited for the management of an extensive theatre, and knew music scientifically; and was, moreover, a truly honest, friendly man. From the day of his entering on the management, until the day of his death, I was his stage-manager, his confidential friend and adviser.

He had the merit of engaging, for his prima donna, the celebrated Grassini, who made her first appearance in the serious opera of 'La Virgine del Sole': she possessed a fine counter-tenor voice, the lower tones of which were sublimely pathetic. In the sweet duet composed by Meyer, 'Parto, ti lascio', with Viganoni, she was delightful. The melody of the effective grand chorus, 'Qual orror', in the opera, was extolled by the amateurs for its peculiar beauty and originality. The production of this melody by Meyer is rather curious, as it was recounted to me by Madame Grassini herself. Meyer, while composing the opera of 'La Virgine del Sole',[1] at Venice, was at a supper party, where a young Englishman was present; after supper there was some singing, and the young Englishman was asked to sing in his turn; he sang the Scotch ballad to O'Keefe's words, in the musical entertainment of 'Peeping Tom',—'Pretty Maud, pretty Maud'. Meyer was so pleased with the melody that he got pen and ink, and having requested to hear it again, wrote it down; and from that simple melody, produced the effective chorus in question.

Grassini was an admirable actress, and a beautiful woman; her merits obtained for her the society and countenance of people of the highest rank in this country. Mrs. Siddons, amongst others, had often been heard to express her admiration of her acting, and has repeatedly visited the Opera expressly to see her action; and she once told Grassini so.

When she was a performer at the theatre of St. Carlos at Naples, and a great favourite there, in the year 1796, she was honoured by the patronage of His Royal Highness the Duke of Sussex, whose name, in the various countries through which he has travelled, will be remembered with gratitude by those artists whom he liberally supported and protected. His Royal Highness is a perfect linguist, an excellent judge of music, and sings with taste. I have often had the honour of being admitted into his society, and always found him full of condescending good nature and affability.

The grand triumph of the Opera House however was, when Mrs. Billington and Grassini sang together in 'Il Ratto di Proserpina',[1] composed expressly by Winter, for those two beautiful women, and exquisite performers. The charming duet, sung by them, 'Vagi colli', was always loudly encored; the beautiful trio, also sung by them accompanied by Viganoni,—the cavatina, 'Che farò senza la madre?' in which Grassini's fine pathos shone so conspicuous, and Mrs. Billington's brilliantly executed air, 'Apri la madre il core', will ever be remembered by the musical world; indeed, the whole of the opera was admirable, and Winter's *chef-d'œuvre*; he had only three weeks to write it, and, to keep his time, had the able assistance of his countryman, Mr. Cramer,[2] the excellent master of His Majesty's private band, as well as composer. He instrumented a great part of the opera; and in what he did, proved himself perfectly competent to the task.

The attraction of the beautiful Proserpine (Grassini), and her mother, the lovely Ceres (Billington), drew great houses. 'Il Ratto di Proserpina' was the only opera in which these theatrical divinities appeared together; for Mr. Goold, contrary to all advice, engaged them on condition that (with the exception of the one opera,) they should appear singly, on alternate Tuesdays and Saturdays; and it was a *sine qua non* with these goddesses, that their Saturdays should be held sacred; for, strange as it may appear, (such is the power of fashion) with the same performers and the same opera in the same week, I have known five hundred pounds taken at the doors on the Saturday, and the Tuesday's receipts under sixty. If any thing were wanting to prove the influence of fashion, and how very secondary, after all, the attraction of talent at that theatre is, this fact perhaps would be decisive.

This silly engagement had, one Tuesday night, nearly shut up the house. It was Mrs. Billington's turn to perform, but she was taken with so severe a hoarseness that she could not sing a note, nor, indeed, leave her bed. Grassini was entreated by Mr. Goold to sing in her stead, but she declared that no power on earth should induce her to do so, as Saturday was her night, and not Tuesday. I did all in my power, by every argument, to prevail upon her, but the inexorable Syren was deaf to my entreaties. I found there was no method to gain my point but by a *ruse de guerre,* and to fib through thick and thin.

Fibbing, as I delicately call it, is a necessary accomplishment for the stage-manager of an Italian Opera House; without it, one of the most difficult and necessary objects could never be attained, (I mean, keeping the ladies quiet). The art is only to be acquired by practice, aided by a certain proportion of impudence; in neither of which I was altogether deficient. For instance, I said, upon this occasion, 'My dear Grassini, as manager, I ought to prevail upon you to perform, but as a performer myself, I enter certainly into your feelings, and think you perfectly right not to sing out of your turn—the Saturday is yours—but what I say to you, I trust you will not repeat to Mr. Goold, as it might be of serious injury to me.'

'Depend upon it, my dear Kelly,' said Grassini, 'I will not; I look upon you, by what you have just said, to be my sincere friend.'

As I was leaving the room, I said, 'To be sure, it is rather unlucky you do not sing tonight, for this morning a message came from the Lord Chamberlain's Office, to announce the Queen's intention to come *incog.*, accompanied by the Princesses, purposely to see you perform; and a *loge grillé* is actually ordered to be prepared for them, where they can perfectly see and hear without being seen by the audience; but, of course, I'll step, myself, to the Lord Chamberlain's Office, and state that you are confined to your bed, and express your mortification at disappointing the Royal Party.'

'Stop, Kelly,' said she; 'what you now say alters the case; if Her Majesty Queen Charlotte wishes to see "La Virgine del Sole", and to hear me, I am bound to obey Her Majesty's commands:—go, then, to Goold, and tell him I *will* sing.'

She accordingly did perform on the Tuesday. When I went into her dressing-room after the first act, Her Majesty not having arrived, Grassini suspecting that I had made up a story to cajole her, taxed me with the trick, and when I confessed it, she took it very good naturedly, and joined in the laugh at her own credulity. The feeling of respect to the wishes of our excellent Queen Charlotte which she evinced, did her infinite credit.

On the 3rd July, 1804, I produced a musical piece, called 'The Hunter of the Alps'. It was a very pleasing drama, and was received with the greatest applause, having run thirty nights the first season; it is occasionally acted even now at different theatres. Independent of its merit, the admirable acting of Elliston must have ensured its success. I must here observe, that Harry Horrebow, when in his fifth year, played the Boy; and his bye-play with Elliston was excellent, and always received with laughter and applause. He is the son of Captain Horrebow, of the Danish naval East India Service. His mother is a sister of Mrs Crouch. She married while very young, and very handsome, and went to India with her husband; and his ship having been wrecked on the Indian coast, she appeared professionally at the Calcutta theatre, then under the management of Mr. Rundell, a favourite actor, and near relation of Mrs. Bannister. Mrs. Horrebow subsequently returned to England with a small independence.

Harry Horrebow performed also in a Grand Ballet at the Opera House, and in a Ballet of Action at Covent Garden Theatre, entitled 'Aggression!' The piece was chiefly indebted, for its reception, to the fine acting of Mrs. St. Leger. Little Harry was her son in the piece; she held him aloft in one hand, while she fought her assailant with a tomahawk. The whole of the Action was picturesque and beautiful, and always ardently applauded. Harry's performance in one scene, in which he was preparing his bow and arrow for action, was as beautiful as any thing ever seen on the stage.

One of those whimsical errors, which in *my* countrymen are called blunders, occurred on the first representation of 'The Hunter of the Alps', which is sufficiently whimsical to be recorded here.

It was rumoured (why, it would be difficult to say) that a party had been made to oppose the piece at its production; and I told the circumstance to an intimate friend, an Irish gentleman, who took fire at the bare mention of such under-handed treachery.—'Just give me,' said he, 'half a dozen orders, and I'll send in a few regular Geary Owen boys, who shall take their shilelahs under their arms; and we'll see who'll be after trying to hiss your music.'

I accordingly furnished him with the necessary passports; and, being quite aware of the presence of my adherents, sat in perfect security during the performance, although it must be confessed I occasionally heard the discordant whizzings of hisses; however, the applause predominated, and the piece was entirely successful.

After quitting the theatre, I had some friends to sup with me in Pall Mall, and amongst them, the author of the piece.[1] We were enjoying ourselves with all sorts of merriment, when in bolted my Hibernian supporter, who, as he entered the room, vociferated exultingly,

'Here we are, Mic, here we are! We are the boys! We did it, Mic! Oh, Sir, the music is movingly beautiful; and when the fellow in green howled about the Hill of Howth (a hunting chorus, 'Hilloa ho!') we made no small noise. Beautiful indeed was the tune: but as for the play—may I never stir if ever I saw such stuff and botheration; by my honour and soul I think nobody hissed the speaking part half so much as we did.'

It never entered the head of my exclusive friend, that the success of the piece and of the music were identified; on the contrary, he thought the effect of contrast would heighten the personal compliment to me. The author, whom he had never seen, and who was present, bore the explanation of his discernment with very good humour; and we washed down the subject in copious draughts of that universal panacea, whiskey punch.

On the 22nd of August Colman wrote a piece for his own theatre, called 'Gay Deceivers', for which I composed the music. It had many comic incidents, smart dialogue, and some sweet songs. One called 'The Spartan Boy', was truly poetical; the piece was performed a number of nights, and was much liked. Colman grounded it upon a French comic opera, entitled 'Les Evénemens Imprévus', one of the pieces I had brought with me from Paris. The author of the French drama, strange to say, was an Irishman of the name of Hale,[2] an officer in the French military service; all his songs were versified for him, as he could not compose French poetry, though he furnished all the subjects.

He wrote a very pretty comic opera, entitled 'L'Amant Jaloux', and 'Midas', which was in high favour with the Parisians. I saw it twice played at the Théâtre Rue Favart: the subject is differently treated from ours; and, in my opinion, Kane O'Hara's burletta is worth a million of it. In Paris, it in a great degree gained its popularity by the acting of the inimitable Monsieur Trial, who represented the Singing Shepherd; his imitation of the old school of French singing (which he caricatured with irresistible humour) was admirable. 'L'Amant Jaloux', 'Les Evénemens Imprévus', and 'Midas', were all composed by Grétry, and beautiful music he gave them, although not sufficiently effective for the English taste; which, in the musical way, requires more Cayenne than that of any other nation in the world.

At this period of my life, although eminently successful in my professional career, my mind was deeply embarrassed by perceiving the gradual decline of the health of my dearest friend, Mrs. Crouch. I prevailed upon her to accompany me to Brighton, but grieved to find that she derived no benefit from change of air.

24

On the 31st January, 1805, Tobin's popular and successful play of the 'Honey Moon' was produced at Drury Lane Theatre. It had lain for several seasons on the shelf, and would have remained there, had not Wroughton, who was then stage manager of Drury Lane (having nothing in the shape of a new comedy to produce), rummaged the prompter's room, where many other plays lay neglected,—it may be, never looked at. Luckily, one of the first that came to hand was 'The Honey Moon', which Wroughton took home to read, and on his own judgment and at his own risk, had it copied, cast, and put into rehearsal. Thus did chance bring to light one of the most popular comedies that had been produced for many years.

It was finely performed in all its parts, particularly the Duke by Elliston, Juliana by Miss Duncan, and Jaques by young Collins, who was a true disciple of Nature, and, in my opinion, had not death cut short his career, would have been an ornament to the stage. There was a country dance at the close of the fourth act, in which Elliston and Miss Duncan displayed such grace and agility, that it was always encored. There were also two songs, one sung by Miss Duncan, and the other by Miss Decamp, both composed by me.

Poor Tobin had not the satisfaction to see his play performed. Before it was produced he took a voyage to the Mediterranean, in hopes that change of climate and sea air would restore his health, which was very delicate, but death struck him in the flower of his youth.

I had the pleasure of being well acquainted with him, and was introduced to him by one of his dearest friends, the late Miss Pope, the admirable actress of Drury Lane, who wished very much that we should write an opera together, which we had agreed to do. Many and many a time have I accompanied him to Mr. Joseph Richardson's house in Argyll Street, to get back his comedy of 'The Honey Moon' from Drury Lane; but he never succeeded even in obtaining a glimpse of it: excuse upon excuse was made for not restoring it; and no wonder, for, in fact, they were ignorant that it was in their possession; and after repeated calls, waiting jobs, and denials, the unfortunate and disappointed author gave up the piece as lost.

Mr. Richardson was a good man, and one of my most intimate friends, but, like his great prototype and bosom friend, Sheridan, was indolence personified; and *to-morrow* was, as with Sheridan, his day of business. He even seemed ambitious of imitating the foibles of Sheridan, which was bad taste, considering the disparity of their talents; for, as the Spanish poet Garcia observes, 'the eagle may gaze stedfastly at the sun, while the butterfly is dazzled by the light of a taper;' not but that Richardson possessed considerable literary talent. He was one of the chief writers in the 'Rolliad',[1] and author of that elegant comedy, 'The Fugitive'. He lived in intimate friendship with Lord John Townsend, the Earl of Thanet, and Mr. Tickell, Mr. Sheridan's brother-in-law, who was the author of a comic opera called 'The Carnival of Venice', and the adapter of Allan Ramsay's 'Gentle Shepherd'.[2]

Sheridan had assigned to Richardson a quarter share of Drury Lane Theatre, said to be worth twenty-five thousand pounds. The Dukes of Northumberland and Bedford, Earls Fitzwilliam and Thanet, raised fourteen thousand pounds to enable him to complete his purchase. He was in high favour with the late Duke of Northumberland, who brought him into Parliament for the borough of Newport in Cornwall.

When last in Paris, I had been to the Théâtre Français to see a petite comedy performed, entitled 'Les Deux Postes', and delighted I was with the manner in which it was acted. Baptiste, the elder, played the Blind Old Man to admiration. Indeed, the whole dramatis personæ were perfect. I procured a copy of the piece, and gave it to my friend George Colman, who, being pleased with the subject, resolved to write a musical afterpiece from it; and his adaptation was far superior to the original, as indeed was every thing he did in the same way.

It was brought out on the 28th January, under the title of 'We Fly by Night; or, Long Stories', at Covent Garden Theatre. I composed the whole of the music. Munden's personification of the Old Story-teller was perfect; indeed, all the performers in the piece gave it their best support: it was strongly cast. Liston and Fawcett were exquisitely comic; the part of the Englishman (in the French original so well performed by Baptiste the younger) was transposed into a Frenchman, and very well acted by Farley; Miss Tyrer, now Mrs. Liston, was truly comic in the Landlady, and sang with her usual sweetness; Miss Davies was the Heroine. The piece was eminently successful, and had a great run. Both Miss Tyrer and Miss Davies were pupils of Mrs. Crouch and myself. Mrs. Liston was always attentive to her profession, and scrupulously honourable in fulfilling all her engagements.

A musical entertainment, written by Mr. Dimond for my benefit, was produced on the 23rd May, 1805, entitled, 'Youth, Love, and Folly'. I composed the whole of the music. It combined the talents of Elliston, Dowton, Mrs. Bland, and Mrs. Mountain; and I had an excellent part in it. Miss Decamp acted a Jockey with such vivacity, dressed it, and looked it, so completely, that she might have passed as having been brought up at Newmarket. The versatility of this lady's talent was very great; as was, to my knowledge, her zeal for her employers, and affability of manners to every person in the theatre. When she quitted her home, Drury Lane, her departure was regretted by all.

My management at the Opera this season was going on triumphantly. Winter produced a new serious opera, entitled 'L'Amore Fraterno'. The music was very fine. Mrs. Billington was the Heroine, and sang with all her usual fascination, ably supported by the two tenor singers, Viganoni and Braham. Winter also composed the music of the grand ballet of 'Achilles', which was excellent; as well as the ballet itself, composed by D'Egville, who in this, as well as many other pieces of a similar nature, has proved himself a great master of his art. His powerful acting, and that of the graceful and handsome Deshayes, will long be remembered.

The 'Orazj', or, 'Gli Orazj ed i Curiazj', was got up for Grassini with all care and attention: the music (the finest serious opera Cimarosa ever produced) was delightful, and drew crowded houses to the King's Theatre, as it did at Venice, where it had been originally produced. In my opinion, the acting of Grassini in this opera was almost as fine as Mrs. Siddons': higher praise she could not wish for; the passage, where she exclaimed 'O, Orazio, mio bene,' leaning over her dead husband, was positively heart-rending.

On account of the length of the operas and ballets, and never being able to get the lady-singers ready to begin in time, the operas seldom finished till after twelve o'clock on Saturdays. The Bishop of London sent to inform me, that if the curtain did not drop before the twelfth hour, the licence should be taken away, and the house shut up. Against his fiat there was no appeal, and many nights have I been obliged to order the dropping of the curtain in the midst of an interesting scene in the ballet. This, for a few nights, passed on without any notice being taken of it by the subscribers and the public; but on Saturday, the 15th of June (Oh! fatal night!), the demon of discord appeared with all his terrors in this hitherto undisturbed region of harmony. The curtain fell before twelve o'clock, just as Deshayes and Parisot were dancing a popular pas de deux. This was the signal for the sports to begin; a universal outcry of 'Raise the curtain!—Finish the ballet!' resounded from all parts of the house; hissing, hooting, yelling, (in which most of the ladies of quality joined) commenced.

The ballet master, D'Egville, was called for, and asked, 'Why he allowed the curtain to drop before the conclusion of the ballet?' He affirmed, that he had directions from me to do so. I was then called upon the stage, and received a volley of hisses, yellings, &c. I stood it all, like brick and mortar; but at last, thinking to appease them, I said the truth was that an order had been received from the Bishop of London, to conclude the performance before midnight. Some person from the third tier of boxes, who appeared to be a principal spokesman, called out, 'You know, Kelly, that you are telling a lie.' I turned round very coolly, and, looking up at the box from whence the lie came, I said, 'You are at a very convenient distance; come down on the stage, and use that language again, if you dare!'

This appeal was received by the audience with a loud burst of applause, and a universal cry of 'Bravo, bravo, Kelly; well replied!—Turn him out! Turn the fellow out of the boxes!' The gentleman left the box, but did not think proper to make his appearance on the stage. This was a lucky turn as it regarded myself, but did not appease the rioters; for, finding their mandate for drawing up the curtain and finishing the ballet not obeyed, they threw all the chairs out of the boxes into the pit, tore up the benches, broke the chandeliers, jumped into the orchestra, smashed the piano-forte, and continued their valorous exploits, by breaking all the instruments of the poor unoffending performers. Having achieved deeds so worthy of a polished nation, and imagining no more mischief could be done, they quitted the scene of their despoliation with shouts of victory; but there was a finale to the drama, which they did not expect. Mr. Goold identified some of the ring-leaders, and commenced actions against them for damages, which cost them many hundreds of pounds. Mr. Goold gave up the actions (for, as Gay says, 'Goold from law could take out the sting;'[1]) on condition of their acknowledging

Frances Kelly,
by T Uwin, 1822

John Philip Kemble

Richard Brinsley Sheridan in old age

their ill-behaviour, and amply satisfying those who had been injured.

At the close of the season I went to Brighton, and took a house on the West Cliff, for Mrs. Crouch; but she gradually grew worse. She was attended first by Sir Charles Blicke, and afterwards by Dr. Bankhead and by my worthy friend and countryman, Sir Matthew Tierney, whose assiduous attentions on that trying occasion, must ever call for my warmest gratitude. But alas! the decree had gone forth.

When her immediate danger was known, friends flocked in from all quarters. Her sister, Mrs. Horrebow, arrived from London, and our faithful and attached friend, Mr. Rose, the merchant, with whose family we had been for many years on the most affectionate and confidential terms. With him she at all times communicated unreservedly, and to him confided her cares and anxieties for my future prosperity; for, to the last, she was utterly incapable of a selfish feeling. She arranged every thing relative to her affairs and her funeral as if she had been going a journey, and was to return and reap the benefit of her care.

At length the dreadful hour arrived, over the occurrences of which, feelings of affection, still unsubdued, prompt me to draw a veil.

The grief, however deep and sincere, of affectionate relatives and friends, can afford no interest to a common reader; but I hope that I, who knew her best, may be permitted to say, that had she been so fortunate as to meet with a husband capable of appreciating and cherishing her estimable qualities and superior talents, she would have lived and died without a blemish on her fame.

The following year, I caused a monument to be erected to her memory, bearing the inscription which follows:—

THE REMAINS OF
ANNA MARIA CROUCH,
During many Years a Performer at Drury Lane Theatre.
She combined with the purest Taste, as a Singer, the most
elegant Simplicity as an Actress: beautiful almost beyond
parallel in her Person; she was equally distinguished
by the Powers of her Mind.

They enabled her,
when she quitted the Stage,
to gladden Life by the Charms of her Conversation, and
refine it by her Manners.
She was born April 20th, 1763, and
died October 2nd, 1805.

THIS STONE
is Inscribed to her beloved Memory, by him whom she esteemed the most faithful of her Friends.

25

At a period so painfully distressing as this, I received the greatest kindness and attention from my friends Major and the first Mrs. Scott Waring. I left Brighton with an aching heart, and went to my friend Rose, at Richmond, where I received a letter from Lord Guilford, inviting me to Wroxton Abbey;[1] to such an invitation, so warmly pressed, there was but one reply; and I set off for that delightful spot, where I knew consolation and kindness awaited me. I wrote thence to Mr. Graham, then at the head of the Board of Management of Drury Lane, to say, that I could not return to the theatre for some time; and received a very kind letter in reply, conveying permission to absent myself as long as I thought fit. I remained at Wroxton Abbey for two months.

On leaving the Earl of Guilford's, I went to pass a week with the Marquis of Ormonde, at Ditchley, in Oxfordshire, which his Lordship rented of Lord Dillon. The Marquis was a great lover of the drama, and well versed in all our dramatic poets. The Marchioness was a most accomplished woman. Every kindness and hospitality were shewn me by my noble host and hostess, who were too suddenly and shortly after snatched from this world themselves.

My two months having passed, I took my departure for London, and played Henry, in 'The Deserter'. On my first appearance, I was received, as I thought, with kind and sympathetic applause, by my friends and the audience; but I took a thorough dislike to the stage, and resolved to quit the profession, so soon as I had made some necessary arrangements to enable me to do so. In the interim, I composed the music to the splendid spectacle of 'The Forty Thieves',[2] produced at Drury Lane, in April 1806, which had a very great run. Miss Decamp acted, sang, and danced, in the character of Morgiana, with wonderful effect.

The same season, in conjunction with Attwood, I composed for Covent Garden, an operatic play, called 'Adrian and Orrila'. Cooke played the part of the Prince in it, and the very deuce he had liked to have played with it: for, on the morning of the day on which the piece was to be performed, he came to rehearsal so intoxicated, that he could scarcely stand. Both the author and myself were on the stage, alarmed, as may well be imagined, for the fate of a play, the principal serious character of which, was to be performed by a man dead drunk.

We were determined not to let our play be acted. Mr. Kemble, on the contrary, (who then was stage manager, as well as co-proprietor with Mr. Harris,) insisted, that the play should be done, at all risks. Mr. Harris was sent for, to decide. In the interim, Cooke was pouring out a volley of abuse against Kemble, calling him, 'Black Jack', &c. all which Kemble bore with Christian patience, and without any reply. At length Mr. Harris, with his faithful ally on all emergencies, the late James Brandon, the box book-keeper, on seeing Cooke's situation, decided that the play should not be performed on that night; but that Kemble should make an apology to the audience, on the plea of Cooke's sudden indisposition; which Kemble refused to do.—'When Greek meets Greek, then comes the tug of war.'

Harris declared he would have the play changed. Kemble, on the contrary, was as peremptory to have it performed; and vowed, that if it were changed, under the pretence of Cooke's indisposition, he would go forward to the audience, and inform them of the true cause of their disappointment.

Harris said, 'Mr. Kemble, don't talk to me in this manner. I am chief proprietor here, and will have whatever orders I give, obeyed.'

I shall always remember Kemble's countenance, when, with the greatest calmness, he replied:

'Sir, you are a proprietor—so am I. I borrowed a sum of money to come into this property. How am I to repay those who lent me that money, if you, from ill-placed lenity towards an individual, who is repeatedly from intoxication disappointing the public, choose to risk the dilapidation of the Theatre, and thereby cause my ruin? By Heavens, I swear the play shall be acted.'

Words were getting to a very high pitch, when Brandon coaxed Cooke into his house, put him to bed, and applied napkins, steeped in cold water, to his head, in the hopes of sobering him. He slept from twelve till five o'clock, when he took some very strong coffee, which brought him to his senses, and he consented to play the part; and considering all circumstances, I was struck with astonishment to see how finely he acted it. To be sure, he had nearly made one trifling omission, namely, cutting out the whole plot of the piece. And had it not been for the promptness and presence of mind of the then Miss Smith (the present Mrs. Bartley) who played the character (and finely she did play it,) of Madame Clermont, he would have succeeded in doing so. 'Oh! that men should put an enemy into their mouths to steal away their brains!'

No man, when sober, was better conducted, or possessed more affability of manners, blended with sound sense and good nature, than Cooke; he had a fine memory, and was extremely well informed. I asked him, when he was acting at Brighton one day, to dine with me and Mrs. Crouch; and we were delighted with his conversation and gentleman-like deportment. He took his wine cheerfully; and as he was going away, I urged him to have another bottle; his reply was, 'Not one drop more. I have taken as much as I ought to take; I have passed a delightful evening, and should I drink any more wine, I might prove a disagreeable companion, therefore, good night;' and away he went. Nor could I then prevail upon him to stop.

In the memorable time of the O. P. riot,[1] some of the actors belonging to Covent Garden seemed to enjoy the disagreeable situation in which Kemble, as manager, stood. I was one night in Covent Garden Theatre, when one of them absolutely and roundly asserted, that Kemble was but an indifferent actor. Cooke was in the green-room at the time, and I said, 'What do you think of the assertions of those gentlemen, Mr. Cooke; do you think Kemble an indifferent actor?'

'No, Sir,' he replied; 'I think him a very great one; and those who say the contrary are envious men, and not worthy, as actors, to wipe his shoes.' It gave me unspeakable pleasure, to hear him give so liberal an opinion of my esteemed friend, even though the expression of it was somewhat of the coarsest.

In the same season, the Italian Opera acquired a powerful acquisition in Naldi, the celebrated buffo singer, who made his *début* in a comic opera, entitled 'Le Due Nozze ed un sol Marito', and was received with great and deserved applause;—he was a fine comic actor. His performance in 'Il Fanatico per la Musica', was unique; he was, besides, an excellent musician, and a good performer on the violoncello. I always had a strong partiality for Naldi,—he was a fine generous fellow. When he was engaged at the Opera House, Morelli, the *once* fine bass singer, was discharged; and from an inordinate passion which he had for insuring in the lottery, was steeped in poverty. Naldi, until the day of his death, furnished him with every necessary of life, and allowed him a weekly stipend of two guineas for his pocket, which was regularly transmitted to him every Saturday night.

Naldi, previous to the Revolution, was a lawyer of considerable eminence at Bologna; he was an excellent scholar, and his manners were those of an extremely well-bred man. Like many others of his ill-fated countrymen, he was obliged to quit his native city, and make a profession of that, which he had only studied as an accomplishment. Whilst performing at Venice, the beauteous eyes of Madame Vigano, a celebrated dancer, enslaved his heart. They went to Lisbon, both having an engagement at the Italian Opera-house there. He remained many seasons in London, a justly deserved favourite. His ill stars took him to Paris, where, one day, just before dinner, at his friend Garcia's house, in the year 1821, he was shewing the method of cooking by steam, with a portable apparatus for that purpose; unfortunately, in consequence of some derangement of the machinery, an explosion took place, by which he was instantaneously killed. The awful and untimely fate of this worthy man was lamented by all, but by none more than myself, for I had always lived with him on terms of the most cordial and sincere friendship.

I have often heard him describe the great hatred he felt for the French nation, and every thing belonging to it; indeed, he carried his dislike so far, that although often offered most tempting engagements at Paris, as first buffo at the Italian Opera, nothing could prevail upon, or induce him to go thither, until urgent business took him there to meet his death. His principal inducement for visiting Paris, was to see Madame Naldi's daughter (whom he loved as his own child) make her *début*, which she did previous to his untimely end, and was much liked. She is still at the theatre, and a favourite of the Parisians.

On the 13th December, 1806, Madame Catalani, and Signor Siboni, made their *début* in the serious opera of 'La Semiramide'. Madame Catalani's personification of Semiramide, was a powerful effort of the scenic art—she looked beautiful, and a queen;—her songs were given in a manner which electrified her audience;—she possesses, in truth, what the Italians call the *novanta nove,* i.e. the ninety-nine. When a singer possesses a superior fine voice, the Italians say, he, or she, has got the ninety-nine points out of the hundred, to make a fine singer. Her reception, by a crowded audience, was enthusiastic. Siboni, in addition to a fine tenor voice, and a commanding figure, was a tasteful singer, and a good musician; his reception was also very flattering. At the close of the season, Mademoiselle Parisot, who had been a popular dancer for some years, took leave of the stage, and married a Mr. Hughes, a man of property.

In April 1807, Mr. M. G. Lewis brought out, at Drury Lane Theatre, his romantic drama, called the 'Wood Dæmon'. It was, unquestionably, a work of genius;—I composed the music to it. It was brought forward with magnificent scenery, and was a favourite.

On the 12th May, Mr. Dimond's operatic piece, in two acts, called the 'Young Hussar', was produced at Drury Lane Theatre. I also composed the music to that, and it was, on the whole, successful.

Musical pieces were often performed at Drury Lane: among others, Mr. Sheridan's opera of 'The Duenna', in which I performed the part of Ferdinand. It was customary with me, when I played at night, to read my part over in the morning, in order to refresh my memory. One morning, after reading the part of Ferdinand, I left the printed play of 'The Duenna', as then acted, on the table. On my return home, after having taken my ride, I found Mr. Sheridan reading it, and with pen and ink before him, correcting it. He said to me, 'Do you act the part of Ferdinand from this printed copy?'

I replied in the affirmative, and added, 'that I had done so for twenty years.'

'Then,' said he, 'you have been acting great nonsense.' He examined every sentence, and corrected it all through before he left me; the corrections I have now, in his own hand-writing. What could prove his negligence more, than correcting an opera which he had written in 1775, in the year 1807; and then, for the first time, examining it, and abusing the manner in which it was printed?

I know, however, of many instances of his negligence, equally strong, two of which I will adduce as tolerable good specimens of character. I can vouch for their authenticity.

Mr. Gotobed, the Duke of Bedford's attorney, put a distress into Drury Lane Theatre, for non-payment of the ground rent; and the chandeliers, wardrobe, scenery, &c. were to be sold to satisfy his Grace's claim. Sheridan, aroused and alarmed at the threat, wrote a letter to the Duke, requesting him to let his claim be put in a state of liquidation, by Mr. Gotobed's receiving, out of the pit door money, 10*l.* per night, until the debt should be paid; this was agreed upon by his Grace. More than a twelvemonth passed, and Sheridan was astonished at receiving no reply to his letter. In an angry mood he went to Mr. Gotobed's house, in Norfolk Street (I was with him at the time), complaining of the transaction; when Mr. Gotobed assured him, on his honour, that the Duke had sent an answer to his letter, above a year before. On hearing this, Sheridan went home, examined the table on which all his letters were thrown, and amongst them found the Duke's letter, unopened, dated more than twelve months back. To me, this did not appear very surprising; for, when numbers of letters have been brought to him, at my house, I have seen him consign the greatest part of them to the fire, unopened.

No man was ever more sore and frightened at criticism than he was, from his first outset in life. He dreaded the newspapers, and always courted their friendship. I have many times heard him say, 'Let me but have the periodical press on my side, and there should be nothing in this country which I would not accomplish.'

This sensitiveness of his, as regarded newspapers, renders the following anecdote rather curious:—after he had fought his famous duel, at Bath, with Colonel Matthews, on Mrs. Sheridan's (Miss Linley's) account, an article of the most venomous kind was sent from Bath, to Mr. William Woodfall, the editor of the Public Advertiser, in London, to insert in that paper. The article was so terribly bitter against Sheridan, that Woodfall took it to him. After reading it, he said to Woodfall, 'My good friend, the writer of this article has done his best to vilify me in all ways, but he has done it badly and clumsily. I will write a character of myself, as coming from an anonymous writer, which you will insert in your paper. In a day or two after, I will send you another article, as coming from another anonymous correspondent, vindicating me, and refuting most satisfactorily, point by point, every particle of what has been written in the previous one.'

Woodfall promised that he would attend to his wishes; and Sheridan accordingly wrote one of the most vituperative articles against himself, that mortal ever penned, which he sent to Woodfall, who immediately inserted it in his newspaper, as agreed upon.

Day after day passed; the calumnies which Sheridan had invented against himself, got circulation, and were in every body's mouth; and day after day did Mr. Woodfall wait for the refutation which was to set all to rights, and expose the fallacy of the accusations; but, strange to say, Sheridan never could prevail upon himself to take the trouble to write one line in his own vindication; and the libels which he invented against himself, remain to this hour wholly uncontradicted.

I was well acquainted with Mr. Woodfall, who declared to me that this was the fact.

Another instance of his neglect for his own interest, came (amongst many others) to my knowledge. He had a particular desire to have an audience of his late Majesty, who was then at Windsor; it was on some point which he wished to carry, for the good of the theatre.—He mentioned it to his present Majesty, who, with the kindness which on every occasion he shewed him, did him the honour to say, that he would take him to Windsor himself; and appointed him to be at Carlton House, to set off with His Royal Highness precisely at eleven o'clock. He called upon me, and said, 'My dear Mic, I am going to Windsor with the Prince the day after tomorrow; I must be with him at eleven o'clock in the morning, to a moment, and to be in readiness at that early hour, you must give me a bed at your house; I shall then only have to cross the way to Carlton House, and be punctual to the appointment of His Royal Highness.'

I had no bed to offer him but my own, which I ordered to be got in readiness for him; and he, with his brother-in-law, Charles Ward, came to dinner with me. Amongst other things at table, there was a roast neck of mutton, which was sent away untouched. As the servant was taking it out of the room, I observed, 'There goes a dinner fit for a king;' alluding to his late Majesty's known partiality for that particular dish.

The next morning I went out of town, to dine and sleep, purposely to accommodate Mr. Sheridan with my bed; and got home again about four o'clock in the afternoon, when I was told by my servant, that Mr. Sheridan was up-stairs still, fast asleep—that he had been sent for, several times, from Carlton House, but nothing could prevail upon him to get up.

It appears that, in about an hour after I had quitted town, he called at the saloon, and told my servant-maid, that 'he knew she had a dinner fit for a king, in the house, a cold roast neck of mutton,' and asked her if she had any wine. She told him there were, in a closet, five bottles of port, two of madeira, and one of brandy; the whole of which, I found that he, Richardson, and Charles Ward, after eating the neck of mutton for dinner, had consumed:—on hearing this, it was easy to account for his drowsiness in the morning. He was not able to raise his head from his pillow, nor did he get out of bed until seven o'clock, when he had some dinner.

Kemble came to him in the evening, and they again drank very deep, and I never saw Mr. Sheridan in better spirits. Kemble was complaining of want of novelty at Drury Lane Theatre; and that, as manager, he felt uneasy at the lack of it. 'My dear Kemble,' said Mr. Sheridan, 'don't talk of grievances now.' But Kemble still kept on saying, 'Indeed we must seek for novelty, or the theatre will sink—novelty, and novelty alone, can prop it.'

'Then,' replied Sheridan with a smile, 'if you want novelty, act Hamlet, and have music played between your pauses.'

Kemble, however he might have felt the sarcasm, did not appear to take it in bad part. What made the joke tell at the time, was this: a few nights previous, while Kemble was acting Hamlet, a gentleman came to the pit-door, and tendered half-price. The money-taker told him, that the third act was only then begun.

The gentleman, looking at his watch, said, It must be impossible, for that it was half past nine o'clock.

'That is very true, Sir,' replied the money-taker; 'but recollect, Mr. Kemble plays Hamlet to-night.'

Mr. Sheridan, although a delightful companion, was by no means disposed to loquacity—indeed, quite the contrary; but when he spoke, he commanded universal attention; and what he said, deserved it. His conversation was easy and good natured, and so strongly characterised by shrewdness, and a wit peculiarly his own, that it would be hard, indeed, to find his equal as a companion. That he had his failings, who will deny? but then, who amongst us has not? one thing I may safely affirm, that he was as great an enemy to himself as to any body else.

One evening that their late Majesties honoured Drury Lane Theatre with their presence, the play, by royal command, was the 'School for Scandal'. When Mr. Sheridan was in attendance to light their Majesties to their carriage, the King said to him, 'I am much pleased with your comedy of the "School for Scandal"; but I am still more so, with your play of the "Rivals";—that is my favourite, and I will never give it up.'

Her Majesty, at the same time, said, 'When, Mr. Sheridan, shall we have another play from your masterly pen?' He replied, that 'he was writing a comedy, which he expected very shortly to finish.'

I was told of this; and the next day, walking with him along Piccadilly, I asked him if he had told the Queen, that he was writing a play? He said he had, and that he actually was about one.

'Not you,' said I to him; 'you will never write again; you are afraid to write.'

He fixed his penetrating eye on me, and said, 'Of whom am I afraid?'

I said, 'You are afraid of the author of the "School for Scandal".'

I believe, at the time I made the remark, he thought my conjecture was right.

One evening, after we had dined together, I was telling him, that I was placed in a dilemma by a wine-merchant from Hockheim, who had been in London to receive orders for the sale of hock. I had commissioned him (as he offered me the wine at a cheap rate) to send me six dozen. Instead of six dozen, he had sent me *sixteen*. I was observing, that it was a greater quantity than I could afford to keep, and expressed a wish to sell part of it.

'My dear Kelly,' said Mr. Sheridan, 'I would take it off your hands with all my heart, but I have not the money to pay for it; I will, however, give you an inscription to place over the door of your saloon:—Write over it, "Michael Kelly, composer of wines, and importer of music".'

I thanked him, and said, 'I will take the hint, Sir, and be a composer of all wines, except old Sherry; for that is so notorious for its intoxicating and pernicious qualities, that I should be afraid of poisoning my customers with it.'

The above story has been told in many ways; but as I have written it here, is the fact. He owned I had given him a Roland for his Oliver, and very often used to speak of it in company.

About this time, my good friend Major Waring bought Peterborough House, at Parson's Green, which before had been the property of Mr. Meyrick; and certainly there never was a more hospitable one. The society consisted chiefly of persons of genius. There have I met, month after month, Lady Hamilton, Mrs. Billington, the Abbé Campbell; the Irish Master of the Rolls, Mr. Curran; and a worthy countryman of mine, Mr. John Glynn, of the Commissariat Department; and many a time and oft have we heard the chimes of midnight, for that was the hour at which Curran's lamp burned brightest; and round the social board, till morning peeped, all was revelry and mirth.

While I am on the subject of revelry and mirth, it may not be amiss to give the reader an idea of the extraordinary mixtures of serious splendour and comical distress, which occasionally take place in the world.

Every body knows, that during the short administration of Mr. Fox's party, Mr. Sheridan held the office of Treasurer of the Navy, to which office, as every body also knows, a handsome residence is attached. It was during his brief authority in this situation, that he gave a splendid fête, to which, not only the ministers, and a long list of nobility were invited, but which, it was understood, His Royal Highness the Prince of Wales, His present Most Gracious Majesty, would honour with his presence:—a ball and supper followed the dinner. Morelli, Rovedino, and the Opera company, appeared in masks, and sang complimentary verses to the Prince, which Pananti wrote, and I composed. The music in 'Macbeth'[1] was then performed; and, in short, nothing could surpass the gaiety and splendour of the entertainment, which went off as well as was anticipated.

But, previous to the great consummation of all the hopes and wishes of the donor, I happened to call at Somerset House, about half past five; and there I found the brilliant, highly-gifted Sheridan, the star of his party, and Treasurer of the Navy, in an agony of despair. What was the cause?—had any accident occurred?—bad news from the Continent?—was the Ministry tottering?—In short, what was it that agitated so deeply a man of Sheridan's nerve and intellect, and temporary official importance? He had just discovered that there was not a bit of cheese in the house—not even a paring.—What was to be done? Sunday, all the shops shut—without cheese, his dinner would be incomplete.

I told him I thought some of the Italians would be prevailed upon to open their doors and supply him; and off we went together in a hackney-coach, cheese-hunting, at six o'clock on a Sunday afternoon—the dinner-hour being seven, and His Royal Highness the Prince expected.

After a severe run of more than an hour, we prevailed upon a sinner, in Jermyn Street, to sell us some of the indispensable article, and got back just in time for mine host to dress to receive his company. I forget now who paid for the cheese, but the rest of the story I well remember, and have thought worth recording.

It was during this season, that Mr. Frederick Jones, the proprietor of the Dublin Theatre, induced by the extraordinary popularity of Madame Catalani, came to London, for the purpose of engaging her. He also came to me, to engage me to perform with her, and conduct the operas and concerts, and make up an Italian Company for the Rotunda, and the Dublin Theatre, which I did. The company consisted of Madame Catalani, Signors Morelli, Rovedino, Deville, and myself. There were two operas to be performed; 'Semiramide', and 'Il Fanatico per la Musica'. I was to have for my engagement, a free benefit. Madame Catalani was to have a clear half of the receipts of each night's performance; and Mr. Jones the other half, for paying all the performers, orchestra, &c. The agreement was signed and sealed in my saloon in Pall Mall. M. Valabrique, Madame Catalani's husband, was kind enough to offer me a seat in their travelling-carriage to Dublin, which I accepted.

I was their guest throughout the whole journey, which was really delightful: indeed, their attention on this and every other occasion to me, can never be forgotten by me. I always found Monsieur Valabrique, a very good-natured man; aware, certainly, that he possessed an inestimable gem in the splendid talents of his wife. He was a strict guardian of those talents, and very properly turned them to the best advantage for their lovely possessor.

Of Madame Catalani herself, I could relate numberless traits of goodness; no woman was ever more charitable or kind-hearted; and as for the quality of her mind, I never knew a more perfect child of nature. She was delighted with the beauties of Wales, and I remember was particularly struck by the vale of Langollen.

At Bangor, she heard the Welsh harp for the first time. The old blind harper of the house was in the kitchen; thither she went, and seemed delighted with the wild and plaintive music which he played. But when he struck up a Welsh jig, she started up before all the servants in the kitchen, and danced as if she were wild. I thought she never would have ceased. At length, however, she finished; and, on quitting the kitchen, gave the harper two guineas.

When we arrived in Dublin, she was received and caressed in every society. The concerts at the Rotunda, which I conducted, and in which I sang, were nightly crowded. The orchestra was ably led by my friend Tom Cooke, whose versatility and genius, in my opinion, cannot be too highly appreciated.

One morning, at a rehearsal at the Rotunda, Madame Catalani was so ill with a sick headache, that she could not rehearse her song; and as it was extremely difficult for the orchestra, she begged of me to have it rehearsed by the band. Cooke asked me for the part from which Madame Catalani sang; I gave it him. He placed it on one side of his music desk, and on the other, his first violin part, from which he was to play; and, to my great astonishment, Madame Catalani's, and that of all present, he sang every note of the song, at the same time playing his own part on the violin, as leader; thus killing, as it were, two birds with one stone, with the greatest ease.

The song was one of Portogallo's, in manuscript, and had never been out of Madame Catalani's hands; therefore, it was impossible that he could have seen it previously; it was full of difficult divisions, of which he did not miss one. Had I not been an eye-witness of this extraordinary exhibition, I could not, as a musical man, have believed it.

The prices at the theatre, on the nights Catalani performed, were raised to half a guinea for the pit and boxes, and five shillings for the gallery. At the piano-forte sat my old, revered, and first teacher, Dr. Cogan. Madame Catalani was received, and hailed by the Irish audience, with rapturous applause. She sang divinely, both in the serious and comic operas. I always acted with her, and had a hearty reception from my generous countrymen. I had the honour of dining with her and her husband, at the Earl of Harrington's, Commander-in-Chief; amongst others, whom I had the pleasure of meeting at his Lordship's, were Mr. W. Browne, of Castle Browne, whom I first met at Venice; and Major Kelly, who was then Lord Harrington's Aid du-Camp, and whose gallantry at the battle of Waterloo, will long be remembered, and duly appreciated, by his country.

I was also particularly honoured by the notice of his Grace the Duke of Richmond, then Lord Lieutenant. When, accompanied by the Duchess and family, his Grace honoured the opera with his presence, it was my duty, as director, to light the vice-regal party to their box, as they came in state. His Grace was particularly kind in his conversation and remarks; and, at the conclusion of the opera, when I again lighted them to their carriages, her Grace the Duchess would not permit me to attend them beyond the box. I had the honour of being invited to the Lodge, at the Phœnix Park, and there found the Viceroy the same accomplished gentleman I knew him at Vienna, when he was the gay and lively Colonel Lennox.

From Mr. Jones, the patentee of the theatre, his amiable wife, and charming family, I experienced the greatest hospitality and kindness; their house was my home, and every thing was done for my comfort. Indeed, it would be invidious in me, to particularise the many acts of kindness I received from my friends in Ireland.

I went one day to dine with my witty countryman, Curran, the Master of the Rolls, at his pretty place at Rathfarnham. Among his guests was Counsellor Mac Nally, the author of the opera of 'Robin Hood'. I passed a delightful day there. Many pleasant stories were told after dinner; among others, one of Mac Nally's, to prove the predilection which some of our countrymen formerly had, for getting into scrapes when they first arrived in London.

The night his opera of 'Robin Hood', was brought out at Covent Garden Theatre, a young Irish friend of his, on his first visit to London, was seated on the second seat in the front boxes; on the front row were two gentlemen, who, at the close of the first act, were saying how much they liked the opera, and that it did great credit to Mrs. Cowley, who wrote it. On hearing this, my Irish friend got up, and tapping one of them on the shoulder, said to him,

'Sir, *you* say that this opera was written by Mrs. Cowley; now, *I* say it was not: this opera was written by Leonard Mac Nally, Esq. Barrister at Law, of No. 5 Pump Court, in the Temple.—Do you take my word for it, Sir?'

'Most certainly, Sir,' replied the astonished gentleman; 'and I feel very much obliged for the information you have so politely given me.'

'Umph! very well, Sir,' said he, and sat down.

At the end of the second act, he got up, and again accosted the same gentleman, saying, 'Sir, upon your honour, as a gentleman, are you in your own mind perfectly satisfied that Leonard Mac Nally, Esq. Barrister at Law, of No. 5, Pump Court, in the Temple, has actually written this opera, and not Mrs. Cowley?'

'Most perfectly persuaded of it, Sir,' said the gentleman, bowing.

'Then, Sir,' said the young Irishman, 'I wish you a good night;' but just as he was leaving the box, he turned to the gentleman whom he had been addressing, and said,

'Pray, Sir, permit me to ask, is your friend there convinced, that this opera was written by Mr. Mac Nally, Barrister at Law, of No. 5, Pump Court, in the Temple?'

'Decidedly, Sir,' was the reply; 'we are both fully convinced of the correctness of your statement.'

'Oh, then, if that is the case, I have nothing more to say,' said the Hibernian, 'except that if you had not both assured me you were so, neither of you should be sitting quite so easy on your seats as you do now.'

After this parting observation, he withdrew, and did not return to the box.

I have often heard it said, that Irishmen are generally prone to be troublesome and quarrelsome. Having, in the different countries I have visited, had the pleasure of mixing much with them, I can aver, from experience, that the contrary is the case, and that, generally speaking, they are far from being either the one or the other; and if they find that an affront is not intended, no nation in the universe will join more freely in the laugh, if even against themselves. I will take leave to quote an example,—Curran versus Mac Nally:

Mac Nally was very lame; and when walking, had an unfortunate limp, which he could not bear to be told of. At the time of the Rebellion, he was seized with a military ardour; and when the different volunteer corps were forming in Dublin, that of the lawyers was organized. Meeting with Curran, Mac Nally said, 'My dear friend, these are not times for a man to be idle; I am determined to enter the Lawyers' Corps, and follow the camp.'

'You follow the camp, my little limb of the law?' said the wit; 'tut, tut, renounce the idea; you never can be a disciplinarian.'

'And why not, Mr. Curran?' said Mac Nally.

'For this reason,' said Curran; 'the moment you were ordered to march, you would *halt*.'

But I fear I am digressing somewhat too wildly. To resume:—

After spending a delightful summer, which was productive both of pleasure and profit, I returned to London about the end of September 1807. On the 3rd May, 1808, Mr. Cumberland produced, at Drury Lane Theatre, a piece entitled 'The Jew of Mogadore', to which I composed the music. It was with great reluctance that the Board of Management at Drury Lane accepted it: therefore, when I had finished the music of the first act, I rested on my oars until I knew their final determination. I met Mr. Sheridan one day in Essex Street in the Strand, and told him of it. He desired me to go on with it by all means; 'for,' said he, 'if the opera should fail, you will fall with a fine classical scholar, and elegant writer, as well as a sound dramatist,' (such was his expressed opinion of Cumberland's abilities). 'Go, instantly,' continued he, 'to those discerning critics, who call themselves the "Board of Management", and tell them, from me, if you please, that they are all asses, to presume to sit in judgment on the writing of such a man as Cumberland; and say, further, that *I order* the opera to be accepted, and put into rehearsal.'

'And pray, Sir,' said I, 'in what light am I to view this "Board of Management?"—What are they?'

'Pegs to hang hats upon,' said Sheridan.

I went to the *pegs*, communicated Mr. Sheridan's command, and the opera was performed accordingly. Braham sang in it charmingly.

On the 26th May, 1808, my friend, Miss Pope, quitted Drury Lane stage, as Deborah Dowlas, in the 'Heir at Law', and spoke a farewell address in the character of Audrey. I went there to witness it. No lady, on or off the stage, bore a higher character than Miss Pope. She was an actress of the old school, and had the honour of being patronised by his late Majesty George the Third. She made her first *entrée* at Drury Lane Theatre in the year 1759, in the part of Corinna, in the comedy of 'The

Confederacy'. She had been the favourite pupil of the celebrated Kate Clive, and was brought forward under the auspices of that great comic actress.

On the 30th May, 1808, I witnessed the retirement of my friend, Madame Storace, from the stage, in her favourite part of Margaretta, in 'No Song, no Supper'. Colman wrote a farewell address for her, which she sang in character; and quitted public life, esteemed and regretted by all those who were acquainted with her. I continued in intimate friendship with her to the day of her death.

One Thursday[1] she dined with me in Russell Street. Signor Ambrogetti, the comic singer, and my friend, Mr. Savory of Bond Street, met her at dinner; in the course of the evening, she was all at once taken with a shivering fit, and appeared very ill. When her carriage came to take her home, Mr. Savory requested her to be bled, and to send for Dr. Hooper. On the following day Dr. Hooper went to her country-house at Herne Hill, and advised her by all means to be bled, but she would not consent because it was Friday; thus, in fact, she sacrificed herself to superstition. It was confidently asserted, that had she lost blood, her life might have been saved.

26

Superstition often takes possession of the strongest minds. A more powerful instance of the truth of this cannot be cited than that of Mr. Sheridan. No mortal ever was more superstitious than he, as I can aver from my own knowledge. No power could prevail upon him to commence any business, or set out upon a journey, on a Friday; nor would he allow, if he possibly could avoid it, a piece to be produced at his theatre on a Friday night. It is a well-known fact (which he never denied), that when Tom Sheridan was under the tuition of Doctor Parr, in Warwickshire, his father dreamt that he fell from a tree in an orchard, and broke his neck. He took alarm, and sent for his boy to London, instanter. The Doctor obeyed the mandate, and brought his pupil to town; and I had the pleasure to meet him at Mr. Sheridan's, at dinner. I thought him (though an oddity) very clever and communicative; he was a determined smoker, and, on that day, not a little of a soaker; he drank a great deal of wine, to say nothing of a copious exhibition of hollands and water afterwards.

The music room at Brighton Pavilion in 1824 from Illustrations of His Majesty's Palace at Brighton, *by John Nash*

Michael Kelly c. 1825

I remember, when he was asked whom he considered the first Greek scholar in Europe, he answered, 'The first Grecian scholar living is Porson, the third is Dr. Burney,—I leave you to guess who is the second.'

On the 13th June, 1808, Madame Catalani performed a scena from 'Semiramide', at Drury Lane Theatre, for my benefit, in which I also performed. On the 17th June, 1808, I played in 'No Song, no Supper', which was my last appearance on the Drury Lane stage, where I had been chiefly the principal male singer for twenty years, but I did not think myself of sufficient consequence to take a formal leave of the public.

I then made an arrangement with Mr. Sheridan, to be Musical Director of Drury Lane Theatre, and to continue Stage Manager of the Opera House. While on the stage, I did every thing in my power, by persevering industry in my profession, to merit the patronage and liberality which I experienced from an indulgent public. From the first moment I trod the boards of Drury Lane, to the moment I quitted it, as far as my feeble efforts went, I endeavoured to support it, through all its perplexities. I had a veneration for the theatre where Garrick and Sheridan had presided, and its best interests were nearest my heart. I felt a proud distinction at having been so fortunate, as for five and twenty years to have enjoyed the most friendly intimacy and unreserved confidence of its highly-gifted proprietor; whom I look upon, take him for all in all, to have been one of the most extraordinary men of the age in which he lived. Mr. Sheridan did me the honour (as his friend,) to introduce me to the best society, and the first literary men in the kingdom, who all sought his company. They were sure to find him almost every night at my house, where he was the great magnet of attraction.

One day, I had the pleasure of having at my table to dinner, the Marquis of Ormonde, the Earl of Guilford, Sir Charles Bampfylde, Messrs. Sheridan, Richardson, Colman, my countryman Curran, John Kemble, and Tom Sheridan. A greater power of talent seldom or ever was congregated; but, alas! every one of those highly-distinguished individuals (my valued friend George Colman excepted) have been taken from us.

Some time previous to my retirement from Drury Lane stage, I had made Madame Catalani a promise to accompany her, for the second time, to Dublin. I set off with them on the first of August, 1808; she was engaged by Mr. Jones, on similar terms to those she received on her first engagement there; mine, too, were the same. Signor Siboni and Signor Spagnoletti were also engaged. We had to perform two grand serious operas, 'La Mitridate', and 'La Didone Abbandonata', in both of which Madame Catalani exerted herself beyond her former efforts; but 'La Didone' was her *triomphe,* both as an actress and a singer. Siboni performed the haughty Iarbas, the Moorish king; and I, the pious Eneas. After performing six nights in Dublin, we proceeded to give six performances at Cork. The Cork audience are passionately fond of music, and Catalani's reception was enthusiastic; and I experienced the most hospitable reception from numerous friends.

Walking on the Parade, on the second morning of my arrival, with Mr. Townsend, proprietor of the Correspondent newspaper, he pointed out a very fine-looking elderly gentleman, standing at the club-house door, and told me that he was one of the most eccentric men in the world—his name was O'Reilly; he had served many years in the Irish Brigade, in Germany and Prussia, where he had been distinguished as an excellent officer. Mr. Townsend added, 'We reckon him here a great epicure, and he piques himself on being a great judge of the culinary art as well as of wines. His good nature and pleasantry have introduced him to the best society, particularly among the Roman Catholics, where he is always a welcome guest. He speaks German, French, and Italian, fluently; and constantly, while speaking English, with a determined Irish brogue, mixes all those languages in every sentence. It is immaterial to him, whether the person he is talking to understand him or not—on he goes, stop him who can. He is a great friend of Frederick Jones; and it is an absolute fact, that Jones took such a liking to him the first day he came to dine with him, that he made him stay at his house all night, and he has lived with him ever since—that is to say, for seven years. Jones now never comes to Cork, but sends the Captain down when the Dublin company perform here. He is extremely useful, keeps a strict look-out for every thing that concerns his friend's interests, and is a perfect Cerberus among his door-keepers at the theatre; but let us cross over, and I will introduce you,—I am sure you will be pleased with him.'

I was accordingly presented to him. No sooner had the noble Captain shaken me heartily by the hand, than he exclaimed,

'*Bon jour, mon cher Mic, je suis bien aise de vous voir,* as we say in France. *J'étois fâché* that I missed meeting you when you was last in Dublin; but I was obliged to go to the County Galway to see a brother officer, who formerly served with me in Germany; as *herlick à carle,* as we say in German, as ever smelt gunpowder. By the God of war, *il est brave, comme son épée—c'est-à-dire,* as brave as his sword. Now tell me, how go on your brother Joe, and your brother Mark;—your brother Pat, poor fellow, lost his life I know in the East Indies—but *c'est la fortune de la guerre,* and he died *avec honneur.* Your sister, Mary, too, how is she? By my soul, she is as good a hearted, kind creature, as ever lived; but *entre nous, soit dit,* she is rather plain, *ma non è bella, quel ch' è bella, è bella quel che piace,* as we say in Italian.'

'Now, Captain,' said I, 'after the flattering encomiums you have bestowed on my sister's beauty, may I ask how you became so well acquainted with my family concerns?'

'*Parbleu*! my dear Mic,' said the Captain, 'well I may be, for sure *your* mother and *my* mother were sisters.'

On comparing notes, I found that such was the fact. When I was a boy, and before I left Dublin for Italy, I remember my mother often mentioning a nephew of hers, of the name of O'Reilly, who had been sent to Germany when quite a lad (many years before) to a relation of his father, who was in the Irish Brigade at Prague. Young O'Reilly entered the regiment as a cadet; he afterwards went into the Prussian service, but my mother heard no more of him.

The Captain told me, furthermore, that he had been cheated some years before out of a small property which his father left him in the County Meath, by a man whom he thought his best friend. 'However,' said the Captain, 'I had my satisfaction by calling him out and putting a bullet through his hat; but, nevertheless, all the little property that was left me is gone. But, *grace au ciel,* I have never sullied my reputation, nor injured mortal, and for that, "the gods will take care of Cato". In all my misfortunes, cousin, I have never parted with the family sword, which was never drawn in a dirty cause; and there it hangs now in a little cabin which I have got in the County Meath. Should ever Freddy Jones discard me, I will end my days in *riposo e pace* with the whole universal world.'

I have often thought, if Mr. Sheridan or Colman had been acquainted with this worthy, yet eccentric man, he would have served them as a model for an Irish character; and how Jack Johnstone would have acted it.

One of the captain's eccentricities I had nearly forgotten to mention:—he was never without lemons, shalots, and Cayenne pepper, in a case in his pocket, which he always produced at table. The lemons, he said, were to squeeze over his oysters, *à la Française.* The shalots for a beefsteak, *à l'Anglaise*; and the Cayenne for every dish, foreign and domestic; nor should I, in justice to my relation, omit a joke of his which is almost as piquant as his sauce.

One day he was in the streets of Clonmel, when the Tipperary militia were marching out of that town; their Colonel's father had formerly been a miller, and amassed a large fortune, which he had bequeathed to the colonel himself. O'Reilly, seeing the gallant officer at the head of the corps, exclaimed, 'By the God of war, here comes Marshal *Sacks*, with the *flour* of Tipperary at his back.'

I quitted Cork for Limerick, with gratitude for the many favours bestowed upon me by its warm-hearted inhabitants. I was delighted to see how the place had improved since I last saw it. The new town is beautiful. We had only time to perform four nights there—the prices of the theatre were doubled,—the houses overflowed every night,—all the nobility of the county of Clare poured into the city, and the hotels and inns were crowded to excess. I passed a delightful week there; and my cousin, the Captain, seemed as much at home in Limerick as he had been at Cork.

Mr. Logier, the inventor of a method of teaching music, to which he has given his name, was living in the barracks at Limerick at that time. He belonged to the Marquis of Ormonde's regiment of militia, which was quartered there. The finest trumpet player I ever heard in any country played in our orchestra; his execution on the instrument almost baffled belief;—his name was Willman, and he is the brother of Mr. Willman, the principal clarionet, and an equally talented performer on that instrument, at the King's Theatre.

On our last night in Limerick, just in the middle of a most impressive and beautiful duet, which Catalani and I were singing in 'Didone', and at a moment when the whole house was wrapt in attention, a man vociferated from the gallery, 'Mr. Kelly, will you be good enough to favour us with—"O thou wert born to please me"?' This unexpected request produced a loud laugh from the audience. Catalani asked me what the meaning of it was; I answered, that it was nothing but a peculiar manner of applauding. My gallery friend, I suppose, recollected poor Mrs. Crouch and myself, singing, 'Oh, thou wert born to please me',[1] at the same theatre many years previous, and wished to hear it again.

After concluding my engagement at Limerick, we returned to Dublin, where we were to perform six nights, previous to our quitting Ireland. Having no occasion for rehearsals, I used to visit the environs every day.

One morning, riding with an old friend of mine, we saw, near the Black Rock, two strapping, shirtless fellows, real *sans culottes,* on the back of a poor half-starved horse, which seemed to be sinking under the weight, hardly able to crawl along the road. On my friend saying, what a pity it was to load the poor beast with two outside passengers, one of the riders who overheard him, cried out, 'Please your honour and glory, Sir, will you be pleased to tell us, are the hounds far before us?'

At the close of my engagements in Ireland, I set off for London, and in Wales, met my friend, Mr. William Maddocks, who joined me, and a delightful journey we had. I arrived in Pall-Mall on the 21st of September, and heard with real concern of the destruction of Covent Garden Theatre, the night previous, by fire. However, the managers opened the Opera House in six days (so that the performers suffered little or nothing), with the tragedy of 'Douglas', and the musical entertainment of 'Rosina'.

My first production at Drury Lane this year was the music to 'Venoni', a play by M. G. Lewis, Esq. It was produced on the 1st December, but was withdrawn after five nights, not meeting with success at first. The last act of this piece, as originally constructed, proved offensive to the feelings of the audience; and although the previous acts excited the deepest interest, and received sufficient applause, nevertheless the unlucky catastrophe was as constantly hissed. The author finding the public determined on this point, conceived the whimsical (and I believe unexampled) idea of withdrawing the play for a time, and reproducing it with an entirely new last act, constructed out of the most opposite materials from those of the original one. Strange as this scheme may appear, it succeeded. 'Venoni' re-appeared with a bran-new catastrophe, and proved a favourite with the town through the remainder of the season.

Though the destruction of Covent Garden Theatre fell lightly on the performers, it was severely felt by the proprietors, particularly by Kemble, who had staked his all, in the purchase of his share; however, the sympathy his loss excited was powerful, and the liberality he met with, noble; it was said that his present Majesty presented him with a thousand pounds, and that the Duke of Northumberland offered him ten thousand, which he refused as a gift, but accepted as a loan, for a term of years, and gave his bond to his Grace for the repayment.

There is a little history connected with this subject, which from being highly creditable to all parties concerned, the public may feel pleased to know:—

Mr. Richard Wilson, of Lincoln's Inn Fields, (whom I am proud to call a friend of mine, having received many marks of kindness and hospitality from him, as well as from his lady and amiable daughter, now

Mrs. Randolph,) was the solicitor and confidential man of business of his Grace, the late Duke of Northumberland, who, knowing that he was on terms of intimacy with Kemble, wished him to prevail upon that great actor to give Earl Percy, the present Duke, some lessons in elocution.

Kemble, when the request was made, instantly acceded to it, making only one in return, which was that no remuneration should be offered him, as he felt amply repaid by having it in his power to gratify the Duke.

The origin of this feeling in Kemble is curious, and from its trivial nature not generally known. He told me himself, that in the year 1779 he was acting at York, where a play was in preparation, in the success of which he was deeply interested: the Duke of Northumberland commanded two troops of the King's own Dragoons, then quartered in the city. Kemble applied to one of the officers to permit some of the men off duty to attend the theatre to walk in the processions, to which application he received a somewhat ungracious reply, accompanied by an observation that the soldiers had other duties to attend to. He then wrote to the Duke, to ask *his* permission, as commanding officer, and immediately received a favourable answer.

'The handsome manner,' said Kemble to me, 'in which his Grace conferred the favour, enhanced the obligation, and never has been forgotten by me; to be able to evince the feeling I entertain by shewing his Grace's son every attention in my power, is my highest gratification and sufficient inducement to me to become, as you facetiously call me, "a master of scholars," which no sum of money could induce me to do.'

On the 31st of December, 1808, the first stone of the new theatre was laid by his present Majesty, then Prince of Wales, as Grand Master of Freemasons; and a brilliant sight it was. On that day Kemble, it is reported, received a letter from the Duke of Northumberland, enclosing the bond for ten thousand pounds, which I have just mentioned, in which his Grace said, 'That as it was a day of rejoicing, he concluded there would be a bonfire, and he requested that the enclosed obligation might be thrown in to heighten the flames.' This magnificent donation was worthy of the house of Percy; and the delicate and handsome manner in which it was conferred, richly deserves to be recorded.

On the 24th February, 1809, Mr. Richard Wilson gave a dinner to the principal actors and officers of Drury Lane Theatre, at his house in Lincoln's Inn Fields. All was mirth and glee: it was about eleven o'clock, when Mr. Wilson rose and drank 'Prosperity and Success to Drury Lane Theatre;' we filled a bumper to the toast; and at the very moment we were raising the glasses to our lips, repeating 'Success to Drury Lane Theatre,' in rushed the younger Miss Wilson, now Mrs. Montague Oxenden, and screamed out, that 'Drury Lane Theatre was in flames!' We ran into the square, and saw the dreadful sight; the fire raged with such fury, that it perfectly illuminated Lincoln's Inn Fields with the brightness of day. We proceeded to the scene of destruction; Messrs. Peake and Dunn, the treasurers, dashed up stairs, at the hazard of their lives, to the iron chest, in which papers of the greatest consequence were deposited. With the aid of two intrepid firemen they succeeded in getting the chest into the street;—little else was saved.

I had not only the poignant grief of beholding the magnificent structure burning with merciless fury, but of knowing that all the scores of the operas which I had composed for the theatre, the labour of years, were then consuming:[1] it was an appalling sight; and, with a heavy heart, I walked home to Pall-Mall.

At the door, I found my servant waiting for me, who told me that two gentlemen had just called, and, finding I was not at home, had said, 'Tell your master, when he comes home, that Drury Lane is now in flames, and that the Opera House shall go next.' I made every effort to trace these obliging personages, but never heard any thing more of them.

Mr. Sheridan was in the House of Commons when the dreadful event was made known, and the debate was one in which he was taking a prominent part; in compliment to his feelings, it was moved that the House should adjourn.

Mr. Sheridan said, that he gratefully appreciated such a mark of attention, but he would not allow an adjournment, for that 'Public duty ought to precede all private interest;' and with Roman fortitude he remained at his post while his playhouse was burning.

The next morning, several of the principal performers called in Pall-Mall to consider what could be done in the dreadful position of affairs; and while we were debating, a message came from Mr. Sheridan, to know where he could meet us? Wroughton, who was at that time our stage-manager, asked John Bannister, Dowton, myself, and a few more of the principal actors to dine with him in Gower Street; and wrote to Mr. Sheridan to request he would meet us there, which he punctually did.

After dinner, lamenting the dreadful situation in which we, as well as himself, were placed by the conflagration, he said, that the first consideration was, to find a place where we could perform, under his 'Drury

Lane Patent;' for, though the theatre was destroyed, the patent was not, and that he would make every effort in his power to forward the interests and wishes of the company, without any private consideration of his own, until arrangements might be made to rebuild Drury Lane Theatre. The only request he would make, which was with him a *sine qua non,* was, that the whole of the company, with heart and hand, should stand by one another, and that there should be no separation; 'For,' said he, 'I am aware that many of the principal performers may get profitable engagements at the different provincial theatres, but what then would become of the inferior ones, some of whom have large families? Heaven forbid that they should be deserted!—No: I most earnestly recommend and entreat, that every individual belonging to the concern should be taken care of. Let us make a long pull, a strong pull, and a pull altogether; and above all, make the general good our sole consideration. Elect yourselves into a committee; but keep in your remembrance even the poor sweepers of the stage, who, with their children, must starve, if not protected by your fostering care.'

Such were the sentiments delivered in my presence, by Mr. Sheridan, who, on every occasion which called for the expression of his feeling towards our profession, shewed himself the warmest advocate and supporter of its reputation and prosperity; in confirmation of which, I cannot refrain from quoting the following passage from a letter which he wrote to me some years since, upon my consulting him as to some matters of importance to my professional interests:—

'In my way,' he observes, 'of viewing the profession, and treating its professors, I never considered it fit that the proprietors should, every year, weigh and gauge the decrease of theatrical power which time or accident may have occasioned; and, overlooking past services, hunt after every change and substitute which may, for the moment, be advantageous.'

This feeling was highly honourable to Mr. Sheridan, not only in his character of manager of a theatre, but as indicative of a filial feeling of respect for the profession of which his father had been a member, and by the exercise of which, he had been enabled to give the splendid abilities of his gifted son the advantages of the best cultivation.

On the 25th March, 1809, the Drury Lane company performed at the Opera House; Mr. Taylor, the proprietor, having granted the use of his theatre gratuitously for three nights to the performers.

About this period, Mr. Sheridan took me to dine with his Grace the

Duke of Norfolk, who had a happy knack of telling a story. One, I remember, he told us with great *naiveté*.

Amongst his Grace's owls, at Arundel Castle, was one which was named by its keeper Lord Thurlow, from an imaginary likeness between the bird and his Lordship. One morning, when the Duke was closeted with his solicitor, with whom he was in deep consultation upon some electioneering business, the old owl-keeper knocked at the library door, and said, 'My Lord, I have great news to give your Grace.'

'Well,' said the Duke, 'what is it?'

'Why, my Lord,' said the man, 'Lord Thurlow has laid an egg this morning.'

Not recollecting, at the moment, that the owl had been nick-named 'Lord Thurlow,' the Duke was not a little astonished; and, until the keeper explained, the solicitor was dreadfully scandalized by such an audacious calumny upon a noble Lord, who had been so long sitting upon the woolsack.

The Drury Lane company, under a licence from the Lord Chamberlain, commenced, on the 11th of April, 1809, the regular drama, at the Lyceum, in the Strand. The opening play was 'John Bull'; they closed their season there on the 12th of June, and re-opened on the 25th of September.

On the 18th of September, 1809, the new Covent Garden Theatre opened with 'Macbeth', and the 'Quaker'.

On the 25th of October, Mr. Arnold brought out at the Lyceum, a musical piece of his own writing, entitled 'The Jubilee'. I composed the music, and it ran a number of nights.

The Drury Lane company were performing at the Lyceum, under the firm of Tom Sheridan, the late Colonel Greville, and Mr. Arnold, and were very successful; and every person belonging to the establishment were regularly paid their full salaries. Tom Sheridan, for some part of the time, was manager, and evinced great talent and industry. I had the pleasure of living on terms of intimacy with him; and many a time, when he used to come to town from Cambridge, with his friend, the Honourable Berkeley Craven, have they favoured me with their company.

Tom Sheridan did not 'ape his sire' in all things; for whenever he made an appointment, he was punctuality personified. In every transaction I had with him, I always found him uniformly correct; nor did he unfrequently lament his father's indolence and want of regularity, although he had (indeed naturally) a high veneration for his talents.

Tom Sheridan had a good voice, and true taste for music, which, added to his intellectual qualities and superior accomplishments, caused his society to be sought with the greatest avidity.

The two Sheridans were supping with me one night after the opera, at a period when Tom expected to get into Parliament.

'I think, father,' said he, 'that many men, who are called great patriots in the House of Commons, are great humbugs. For my own part, if I get into Parliament, I will pledge myself to no party, but write upon my forehead, in legible characters, "To be let".'

'And under that, Tom,' said his father, 'write—"Unfurnished".'

Tom took the joke, but was even with him on another occasion.

Mr. Sheridan had a cottage about half a mile from Hounslow Heath,—Tom being very short of cash, asked his father to let him have some.

'Money I have none,' was the reply.

'Be the consequence what it may, money I must have,' said Tom.

'If that is the case, my dear Tom,' said the affectionate parent, 'you will find a case of loaded pistols up-stairs, and a horse ready saddled in the stable,—the night is dark, and you are within half a mile of Hounslow Heath.'

'I understand what you mean,' said Tom, 'but I tried that last night. I unluckily stopped Peake, your treasurer, who told me, that you had been beforehand with him, and had robbed him of every sixpence he had in the world.'

It is curious, after knowing such stories, and remembering the general habits and pursuits of Mr. Sheridan, to look at the effusions of his muse, in which he privately vented his feelings.

One day, waiting at his house, I saw under the table, half a sheet of apparently waste paper; on examining it, I found it was a ballad, in Mr. Sheridan's hand-writing; I brought it away with me, and have it now in my possession. On my return home, the words seemed to me beautiful, and I set them to music. It is, of all my songs, my greatest favourite, as the poetry always brings to my mind the mournful recollection of past happy days. It was also a great favourite with Mr. Sheridan, and often has he made me sing it to him. I here insert it:—

I.

No more shall the spring my lost pleasure restore,
  Uncheer'd, I still wander alone,
And, sunk in dejection, for ever deplore
  The sweets of the days that are gone.

While the sun as it rises, to others shines bright,
 I think how it formerly shone;
While others cull blossoms, I find but a blight,
 And sigh for the days that are gone.

II.

I stray where the dew falls, through moon-lighted groves,
 And list to the nightingale's song,
Her plaints still remind me of long banish'd joys,
 And the sweets of the days that are gone.
Each dew-drop that steals from the dark eye of night,
 Is a tear for the bliss that is flown;
While others cull blossoms, I find but a blight,
 And sigh for the days that are gone.

My kind friends, Major and Mrs. Waring, in the month of August 1810, were going to spend some time at Southampton, and make the tour of the Isle of Wight; they offered me a seat in their carriage, which I accepted. We spent a most agreeable fortnight at Southampton; the theatre was then open under the management of Messrs. Kelly and Maxwell, also managers of the Portsmouth theatre. Mrs. Siddons, who was in the neighbourhood, on a visit to Mrs. Fitzhugh, was performing, as were also my friends, Jack Bannister and Pope.

I there saw Mrs. Brereton, an actress belonging to the company, perform Mrs. Haller in the 'Stranger', and thought so highly of it, that I recommended my friend, George Colman, to engage her at the Haymarket, which he did; and afterwards I recommended her to Drury Lane.

I was delighted with the tour of the Isle of Wight, where we staid till the beginning of October.

At this time I had frequent invitations from the late Lord Eardley, to visit his beautiful mansion, Belvidere, in Kent. I often experienced great hospitality from his Lordship there, as well as in London, and at Brighton; and had the pleasure of meeting Lord and Lady Say and Sele, and their amiable and accomplished daughter, the Honourable Miss Twiselton, who is a proficient in music, and speaks Italian in all its native purity. I did myself the pleasure, on the 21st of October, 1810, to commemorate the natal day of Lord Eardley, by composing the music of an ode, for three voices, written on the occasion. It was sung by my brother, Captain Kelly, Mr. Bellamy, and myself, at Belvidere, before a large company invited on the occasion, amongst whom were all the artillery officers from Woolwich:—their band was also in attendance. The day was passed with great hilarity, our noble host was in high spirits; and as the jovial glass went round, told a number of anecdotes; among others, one that seemed to amuse his visitors very much.

He told us that, a few days previous, he was walking in the Strand, going to his bankers, Messrs. Child, near Temple Bar, in company with a friend, an officer, who had served under the Duke of York, in Flanders. Walking along, they were followed by a middle-aged man, rather shabbily dressed, who, by his brogue, they found to be an Irishman. He kept close on the heels of the military gentleman, crying 'God preserve your honour, may all blessings from above be showered down upon you; there is not a day that my wife, my children, and myself, do not offer up our prayers, that you may never lose the use of your legs.'

'And pray, my good friend,' said the man of war, 'what good have I ever done you, to merit such unbounded gratitude?'

'Please your honour,' said the man, 'you saved my life, that's all.'

'In what way, my good fellow?' asked the officer.

'Please your honour,' said the Irishman, 'when *you* served with the Duke of York, in Flanders, *I* was a private in your regiment; and one hot morning, you were so deucedly frightened, that you took to your heels like a lamplighter and ran away; and I, because you were my own particular officer, ran after you, and thereby saved my life; for which, as I said before, the blessings of me and mine ever attend you.'

His Lordship gave the above anecdote with genuine humour; and I joined with others in laughing at the story, but thought of the Italian proverb, 'Se non è vero, è ben trovato.'

In the month of February, 1811, 'Blue Beard' was produced at Covent Garden Theatre; and Mr. Harris requested me to superintend the getting up of my music, which I did. On the first morning of my going to the theatre, at the back of the stage, I perceived a number of horses, and, on inquiry, found they were to prance about in 'Blue Beard'. I was making my way to the green-room, when, in the middle of the stage, I came in contact with John Kemble, and pointing to the place where the horses stood, I thus accosted him,—

'Now are we in Arden!'[1]

His reply was, 'More fools we!' We bowed to each other, *à-la-mode de* Noodle and Doodle, in 'Tom Thumb', and passed on without further remark.

This season, a musical drama, called 'Gustavus Vasa', for which I composed the whole of the music, was produced. Mr. Young was the hero of the piece, and acted very finely. Mrs. Dickons was the heroine, and sang all the songs allotted to her, with great effect. Few singers possessed so much science as Mrs. Dickons;—she, at different periods, held the situation of first singer at Drury Lane, Covent Garden, the Lyceum, and Italian Opera House; and wherever she was placed, was esteemed for her many valuable qualities. 'Gustavus Vasa' met with approbation, and was performed a number of nights.

I went to pass the summer at Wroxton Abbey, with my kind friend, Lord Guilford. Mr. and Mrs. Kemble were there on a visit, as was his Lordship's sister, Lady Charlotte Lindsay; indeed, the house was full of visitors, amongst whom was Sir William Gell. At that time, Lord Guilford was preparing for his annual theatricals. Foote's 'Mayor of Garratt', and the 'Old Maid', were to be represented;—the part of the 'Old Maid' was admirably acted by Lady Charlotte; but the favourite piece was the 'Mayor of Garratt', which was thus cast:—

Major Sturgeon	The EARL OF GUILFORD.
Sir Jacob Jollup	Mr. KEMBLE.
Jerry Sneak	The Hon. BARRY ST. LEGER.
Mr. Bruin	The Hon. RICHARD ST. LEGER.
Crispin Heel-tap	SIR WILLIAM GELL.
Roger	Mr. MICHAEL KELLY.
Mrs. Bruin	Mrs. KEMBLE.
Mrs. Sneak	LADY CHARLOTTE LINDSAY.

The noble Earl was an inimitable Major Sturgeon; Lady Charlotte, an excellent Mrs. Sneak; the Honourable Barry St. Leger was extremely comical and effective; and the rest of the *dramatis personæ* were ably filled. But the *bonne bouche* of the whole, was the Sir Jacob Jollup of John Kemble, which he acted with the greatest gravity in a full bottomed wig. And never did he take more pains, with Coriolanus at Covent Garden, than he did at Wroxton Abbey with Sir Jacob Jollup.

An old gentleman from Banbury, who had never seen Kemble act before, sat next him at supper; thinking to say something civil, he complimented him very much on his performance of Sir Jacob. 'Sir!' said he 'it was a fine piece of acting; but I always understood, that your powers lay more in the tragic than the comic line.'

The sapient observation of this Banbury cake, having been overheard, caused more laughter than even Kemble's performance.

There were two nights' performances at Wroxton; on the first, the theatre was open to his Lordship's tenantry, and the farmers and their daughters. After the performance there was a ball, where the servants exhibited high life below stairs,[1] and tripped merrily away with their masters and mistresses; the Lord had, perhaps, a kitchen maid for his partner—the Countess, a footman, or a groom,—a mélange which, it must be confessed, appeared highly agreeable to all parties;—then followed a plentiful supper, at which they enjoyed themselves the remainder of the night.

The second day's performance was for the nobility and gentry of the neighbourhood;—but the first audience was always the best pleased, and the loudest in applauding. The whole, however, was a scene of joy and hilarity; and his Lordship was delighted to witness the happiness which he diffused, and which was pourtrayed in every countenance.

Lord Guilford did not confine his theatricals solely to Wroxton Abbey. He treated his numerous tenants in Kent, and the nobility and gentry within many miles of his magnificent seat at Waldershare,[2] with similar entertainments.

One time I was there, when O'Keefe's 'Son-in-Law' was acted, in a manner to reflect credit on any regular theatre. Major Dawkins played the part of 'Bowkit' admirably; indeed, he possesses a great deal of theatrical talent. My friend, Mr. Joseph Maddocks, was an excellent representative of 'Arionelli', and 'Orator Mum'. I never on any stage witnessed a better representative in many of the scenes of 'Falstaff'. Had he made the stage his profession, in many characters he would have stood unrivalled. I have heard Mr. Sheridan say, that his performance of Sir Anthony Absolute was unique. I have seen him at the Marquis of Abercorn's, at the Priory, and thought Mr. Sheridan's opinion very just. Lord Guilford's 'Old Cranky', in 'The Son-in-Law', was excellent; he gave the song with stentorian lungs, and true humour. The whole fortnight I remained there, was nothing but festivity. Poor Mr. William Maddocks, who was to have played the character of 'Old Vinegar', was all the time laid up with the gout. But he wrote the following stanzas, which I set to music, and which were often sung in full chorus.

SONG,

Written by W. A. Maddocks, Esq. M.P. and composed by Michael Kelly.

I.

I wish I had, I wish I had
Some Muse as Clio fair,
My voice to raise, in lasting praise,
Of festive Waldershare;
Here Comus and his jovial train
Collect from day to day,
Reluctant all to part again,—
Time only flies away.
Chorus, I wish, &c.

II.

Here all the laughing Hours give birth
To something ever new,
And Wisdom, in the mask of Mirth,
Bids nonsense join the crew.
The Muses here the buskin fit,
The Graces dance the hay,
Here gives the host to all, but wit,
Eternal holiday.
Chorus, I wish, &c.

III.

Then sound the lay—then sound the lay,
Aloud full chorus bear,
Commemorate this holiday,
At festive Waldershare.
Long may the host and hostess know
The same delight they give,
And may they, free from every woe,
Long live, this life to live.
Chorus, Then sound the lay, &c.

On the 31st of January, 1811, a musical drama, called 'The Peasant Boy', was brought out at the Lyceum Theatre, for which I composed the whole of the music. The piece had very good success.

In the middle of March, I composed the music to a ballet[1] of Deshayes's composition, at the Opera House. It was a pretty pastoral, and pleased much.

On the 10th of June, 1811, an historical play, called 'The Royal Oak', was produced at the Haymarket. To this drama, also, I composed the music. Elliston was the representative of the merry monarch, and it was an excellent piece of acting.

Connected with my recollections of this play, is an anecdote relative to my deceased friend, Lady Hamilton, so characteristic of that talented, but unfortunate woman, and at the same time so demonstrative of her warmth of feeling, that I cannot suffer it to pass unrecorded.

I had composed a plaintive ballad in the second act, for a Miss Wheatley (formerly a pupil of Attwood's), who possessed a fine deep contre alto voice—the poetry was descriptive of a warrior, who had fallen in recent battle. Upon the fifth representation of the new play, Lady Hamilton, with a party of friends, occupied one of the stage-boxes, appearing all gaiety and animation. Scarcely, however, had this ballad commenced, when she became tremulous and agitated; and at its conclusion, upon the *encore* being loudly demanded, she exclaimed, 'For God's sake, remove me—I cannot bear it.' Her terrified friends withdrew her from the box, whence she was immediately conveyed home in a fainting condition.

The following morning, Miss Wheatley received a note from her Ladyship, (to whom she had previously been unknown,) inviting her to her house, where, after complimenting her upon the force and feeling with which she had given the melody, she added, 'The description brought our glorious Nelson with such terrible truth before my mind's eye, that you overwhelmed me at the moment, but now I feel as if I could listen to you in that air for ever.' She prevailed upon her visitor to repeat the ballad no less than four times at the piano-forte, 'as if increase of appetite grew by what it fed upon.'

Eventually, so powerful became this sentiment, that she induced Miss Wheatley to retire from the stage altogether, and accept, under her roof, the post of musical governess to the young Horatia Nelson, who had been confided to her Ladyship's guardianship. Not a day afterwards elapsed, but the favourite song was put in requisition. I published it under the title of 'Rest, warrior, rest'. It was generally esteemed one of my happiest efforts; and at the present day is perpetually performed at concerts and music-meetings, by that delightful singer, the charming Miss M. Tree, who has given it a renewed fashion and zest.

On the 1st of August, Mr. M. G. Lewis re-wrote his 'Wood Dæmon';—he only made use of the subject—several new characters were introduced;—nothing could be more effective. The piece was then called, 'One o'Clock'. In conjunction with M. P. King, I composed the music.

It was got up with great splendour, and had a considerable run.

August 1811, Signora Bertinotti, Naldi, Signor Cavini, a very sweet tenor singer, and his wife, a very pretty singer, and beautiful woman, Madame Naldi, Miss Naldi, and myself, were engaged by Mr. Jones to perform two Italian operas at the Dublin Theatre. One of them was 'Il Furbo contro il Furbo', the other, Mozart's 'Così fan tutte'. Signora Bertinotti, who was one of the most popular prima donnas on the Italian stage, pleased very much; but the houses not answering the expectations either of ourselves or Mr. Jones, we performed very few nights, and the party set off, *viâ* Belfast, for Scotland, to appear under the management of Corri, at Edinburgh; afterwards to go back to Liverpool for a few nights, and then return to London. It was proposed to me to accompany them, but I declined.

On the 5th of September, 1811, I made my last appearance on any stage, on the stage where I had made my first appearance, when a boy, in 1779. Mr. Bartlett Cooke accompanied me on the flute and hautboy, when I acted first in 1779, and when I last performed in 1811, both in my native city.

When I got to Shrewsbury, on my way from Holyhead to London, while supper was getting ready, I took up a London newspaper, and the first thing I saw, struck me with astonishment; I read in the gazette, these portentous words—'Bankrupt, Michael Kelly, of Pall-Mall, music-seller,' —an announcement so unexpected, confounded me. I instantly wrote to my principal man of business, who had the management of all my money transactions (his name I shall not mention, for the sake of his family, part of which I know to be very respectable,) to know by whom the docket was struck. Unfortunately for me, I had reposed the greatest confidence in him, and would have trusted my life, as well as my property, in his hands. He was recommended to me by a particular friend, and came into my employ a poor man, but he left it amply stocked with every thing; and, *sans cérémonie*, took himself abroad.

I heard nothing more of him, until I was told that, from the badness of the climate to which he went, he was seized with illness, and there died.

When I got to town, I found the docket had been struck against me by a particular friend of his, on account of a dishonoured bill. It was certainly a planned thing: my solicitor, looking into my affairs (which I unluckily did not), found I was plunged, by my *fidus Achates*, deeper in the mire than I could possibly have imagined; and therefore advised me, though my property might have paid all demands three times over, and though I might have superseded the commission, to let the bankruptcy take its course,—and so I did,—and all the property in my saloon was disposed of, for one tenth of its value.

To be a professional man, and a trader at the same time, is, I believe, impossible; but this I found out too late; for if a man be fond of his profession, it must, and ought to engross all his time and thoughts; and, therefore, he is constantly liable to be cheated by his subordinates. To a man occupied in the service of the public, his mind fully occupied with the honourable ambition of standing well in their opinion, it is perfectly immaterial at the time, whether meat be four-pence, or a shilling a pound, and so on in all other things; and from want of looking into his affairs, which prudence, not nearly allied to genius, requires him to do, he gets involved, and sinks deeper and deeper until he is gone past recovery, while those about him are revelling and fattening upon his credulity and inattention.

Locke says, in his 'Conduct of the Human Understanding', that 'let a man be much engaged in the contemplation of any one sort of knowledge, and that alone becomes every thing to him;' and from experience, in my own humble way, I found the philosopher's remark too true. It was, however, rather an odd coincidence, that the docket of my unconscious insolvency should have been struck against me in London on the 5th of September, 1811, the very day upon which I made my last appearance upon any stage in Dublin.

The Drury Lane company ceased performing at the Lyceum the 18th June, 1812, with the play of 'John Bull', for the benefit of the British prisoners in France. On the 29th of the same month, that luminary of the British stage, Mrs. Siddons, took leave of the public at Covent Garden Theatre. I was determined to see her, and got into the orchestra. The play was 'Macbeth'; she acted Lady Macbeth divinely, and looked as beautiful as ever: the house was crowded to excess. After her sleeping scene was concluded, the audience unanimously called for the curtain to drop, and would not allow the play to finish; a marked and just compliment to the most splendid actress the British stage ever possessed; and whose private character has little less contributed to the exaltation of the profession which she adorned, than the unrivalled greatness of her public talents.

On the 10th of October, 1812, New Drury Lane Theatre, built by Mr. Wyatt, one of the sons of the late well-known architect, opened with 'Hamlet', under the immediate direction of the Honourable Thomas

Brande, M.P. (now Lord Dacre,) Mr. Cavendish Bradshaw, the Honourable Douglas Kinnaird, Samuel Whitbread, Esq. William Adam, Esq. M.P. Alderman Coombe, M.P. Mr. Peter Moore, Richard Sharpe, Esq. M.P. Richard Wilson, Esq. Lord Holland, Captain Bennett, Launcelot Holland, Esq. Sir Robert Barclay, Bart. George Templar, Esq. Thomas Hope, Esq. John Dent, Esq. M.P. the Right Honourable John Mac Mahon, M.P. Mr. Richard Ironmonger, Mr. Ward, Mr. Crawford, and George William Leeds, Esq. The novelty of the house drew full audiences during the season, under the management of Mr. Arnold.

On the 25th November, 1813, was produced at Drury Lane, a musical piece, written by Mr. Arnold, called 'Illusion'. The subject was taken from the popular tale of 'Nourjahad', written by Mr. Sheridan's mother, the authoress of 'Sidney Biddulph', &c.; I composed the music; it was received with great applause.

On Wednesday, 1st December, 1813, an Ode was performed at Freemasons' Hall, for the Installation of His Royal Highness the Duke of Kent and Strathern, as Grand Master of Masons in England, according to the old institution. The Ode recited by brother Pope; the music composed by brother Kelly. The military band of His Royal Highness the Duke of Kent, who were Masons, attended; together with several eminent professional singers; and the whole formed a grand *coup-d'œil*. Brother Bellamy sang the following song with great animation, and it was received with unanimous applause:—

SONG.

'Mountains may fall, and rocks decay,
And isle on isle be swept away,—
But Masonry's primeval truth,
Unbroke by force, unchanged by time,
Shall bloom in renovated youth,
And energy sublime.'

The following duet met with the same meed of approbation:—

'For see! from Heaven the peaceful dove,
With olive branch descend;
Augustus shall with Edward join,
All rivalry to end;
And taught by their fraternal love,
Our arms, our hearts shall intertwine,
The union to approve.'

'Then Edward and Augustus hail!
For now beneath the Brunswick line,
One system shall prevail;
O'er all the earth, with truths divine,
Shall Masonry extend its sway,
Till time itself shall pass away
In unity to shine.'

FULL CHORUS.

'Then, brothers, hail the kind decree
That gave them both to—Masonry.'

The 23rd January, 1813, Mr. Coleridge produced, at Drury Lane, his tragedy, entitled 'Remorse'.[1] There were some musical situations in the play which I had to compose. The poetry of the incantation was highly animating; it was sung by Mrs. Bland, with all the refreshing purity of her unsophisticated style, and with that chaste expression and tenderness of feeling which speak at once as it were to the heart. The chorus of boatmen chaunting on the water under the convent walls, and the distant peal of the organ, accompanying the monks while singing within the convent chapel, seemed to overcome and soothe the audience; a thrilling sensation appeared to pervade the great mass of congregated humanity, and, during its performance, it was listened to, with undivided attention, as if the minds and hearts of all were rivetted and enthralled by the combination presented to their notice; and at the conclusion the applause was loud and protracted.

I was fortunate enough to hear, from the highly-talented author of the play, that my music was every thing he could have wished. I felt this as a high compliment from Mr. Coleridge; for I understood, when he was in Sicily, and other parts of Italy, he had this '*Miserere, Domine*' set to music by different Italian composers, none of whom satisfied him by giving his poetry the musical expression which he desired.

On the 16th June, 1813, I took my annual benefit at Drury Lane, and brought out the sequel to the 'Beggars' Opera' (Gay's 'Polly',) altered by Mr. Horace Smith, one of the authors of 'The Rejected Addresses';[2] but the subject was a bad one. I composed new music to it, but it did not succeed, and was withdrawn.

There was, about this time, a law-suit to come on, in Dublin, in which I was subpœnaed, against a Mr. Hime, a music-seller in Dublin, who had pirated and published a number of my compositions. I was labouring under severe illness at the time, and was attended daily by my worthy friend, Dr. Hooper; however, I had promised to go, let the consequence be what it might. On the 13th July, I left Tavistock Row for Dublin, in a travelling-carriage, in company with Mrs. Horrebow, Mr. Addison, and Henry Horrebow.

I travelled slowly, and by short stages, (still being very ill,) and on the seventh day, reached Holyhead, and put up at the Stanley Arms, kept by Mr. Spenser, from whom, and his family, I received the greatest possible attention. I remained nine weeks in his house, as I was unable to cross the sea, I was told, without the risk of my life.

While I was there, a little fellow, a great ally of mine, called upon me every morning. In his person he verified the old adage, that every eye forms its own beauty. This said droll little fellow, surnamed, by the inhabitants of Holyhead, 'Billy-in-the-bowl', though a dwarf, having lost both his legs, or rather, never having had any, went crawling about, literally seated in a bowl-dish; yet, in spite of his deformities, he captivated the heart of a beautiful Welch girl, who would have him for better for worse. Her father, a wealthy farmer, offered to give her a good fortune, and a young and handsome man for her husband; but no! she would have Billy-in-the-bowl. She bore him two fine boys, and is, I am told, even now, very jealous of him.

On the 25th of August, being somewhat restored to health, though still afflicted with the gout, and unable to venture on a sea voyage, I quitted Holyhead for the Earl of Guilford's seat, Wroxton Abbey.

We crossed Bangor Ferry, and I sent Henry Horrebow on to Jackson's, to get horses; those which brought us from Gwyndee we left on the other side of the ferry. I was yet on the beach alone, in the carriage, unable to move, owing to my gout. The tide was coming in rapidly; no appearance of a human being to extricate me from what, I thought, a perilous situation; for every moment I expected the carriage would be afloat, and carried down the stream. At length, by the arrival of horses, I was relieved from my apprehensions, and proceeded on my way to Auber,[1] about eight miles from Bangor, where I dined and slept at the Bull, a charming Welch inn—the accommodation excellent,—and the situation tranquil and picturesque.

The road from Auber to Conway Ferry is beautiful. The view of the sea, on one side, and a highly-cultivated country on the other, with the lofty mountain of Penman Maur, towering to the skies, form indeed a splendid prospect; and to add to the earthly beauties round me, the morning was serene, with a true Neapolitan sky.

I crossed the ferry in the carriage; and when passing Conway Castle, the place where (in the 'Castle Spectre',) it was supposed, 'Megin ho, Megin he', was sung, it gave me great delight to recal the melody, nor could I resist singing it all through; while the boatmen and passengers, who of course did not participate in the feelings by which I was actuated, seemed much astonished, and, by their silence, not ill pleased at the animated manner in which I was singing.

In getting near the shore, I observed a picturesque castle, about half a mile from the place at which we were to land; I inquired of one of the boatmen, to whom it belonged; and at that moment, a pleasure boat being alongside of the ferry boat, a gentleman who was in it, dressed like a sailor, jumped up, and addressing me, said, 'That castle belongs to Lord Kirkwall, who is expected there to-morrow; and I am sure his Lordship will be most happy to see Mr. Kelly, as long as he can make it convenient to remain with him. In the mean time, Mr. Kelly, if you will do me the favour to come into my boat, and join our fishing-party, I shall be happy to give you a bed at my house, and a hearty welcome, and in the morning will accompany you to Lord Kirkwall's.'

I returned the gentleman my acknowledgments for his politeness, but excused myself, as I was in a great hurry to continue my journey on pressing business.

On inquiring of the boatmen who the gentleman was, they told me it was Colonel Lloyd, who had a beautiful house near the ferry.

On the 28th of August, I got to Warwick, dined and slept at the Warwick Arms, and the next day reached Wroxton Abbey to dinner, where I was received by the noble host and hostess with their usual kindness and attention. On the 3rd of September, I went with Lord Guilford to Banbury, where, as Lord High Steward, he gave a dinner to the mayor and aldermen, with whom he was wonderfully popular. I remained at Wroxton till the end of September.

The day before I took my departure, my ever-kind patron said to me, 'My dear Mic, do not be in such a hurry to leave us; stay here a fortnight longer; stay a month; or (at the same time shaking me by the hand), stay here for ever. When we were riding the other day near the entrance of the park, you were admiring a spot of ground there, and saying how happy you should be to spend the remainder of your days there, and so you shall, if you keep in the same mind. You have no family; I will build you a cottage on that very spot, where you shall not have the trouble of going up and down stairs; you shall have a garden, and a paddock for a poney and a cow attached to it; remember this is a serious promise; and, whenever you quit public life, I will fulfil it: we will be neighbours, Mic; my wife shall sing with you, my chaplain shall drink with you, and I will talk with you.'

This liberal offer, and the kind-hearted manner in which it was made, deeply affected me. But death deprived me of my patron and friend. He went to Italy, where he died on the 28th of January, 1817, in the fifty-fifth year of his age, esteemed and regretted by all who had the happiness of being acquainted with the qualities of his head and heart. His amiable Countess did not long survive his lamented loss.

On the 26th of January, 1814, I had the pleasure to witness the first appearance of Mr. Kean, as Shylock, in 'The Merchant of Venice', and was delighted with the performance of my original Cupid in 'Cymon'. There was not a good house, but the audience gave him that applause, on his *entrée*, which they are always liberal enough to bestow on a first appearance; but during the principal part of his scenes in the play, and at his exit, the applause lasted for some moments.

It is pretty generally known, that Mr. Whitbread received a letter from the Rev. Dr. Drury, recommending Mr. Kean in such strong terms to Drury Lane Theatre, that Mr. Whitbread requested Mr. Arnold to go to Dorchester (I think) to see, and engage him for Drury Lane: Mr. Arnold dined with me on the very day he set off on his mission. He saw Mr. Kean in a principal part in a play, and after it, as Harlequin, in a pantomime:—in the latter character, he is universally allowed to have no competitor. Mr. Arnold, with a discerning eye, saw his merit, and offered him terms for Drury Lane, which he could not accept; as a few days previous to Mr. Arnold's seeing him, he had engaged himself to the manager of the Olympic Theatre,[1] in Wych Street, as principal Harlequin, and to superintend the getting up of the pantomimes, for which he was to receive two or three pounds per week. Mr. Arnold and the Drury Lane Committee made interest with the proprietor of the Olympic, to let Kean off his engagement, which he liberally consented to do.

I was present at his first appearance in 'Richard the Third'; there was a crowded house, and I believe that his acting that part drew more money to the treasury than any other actor's ever did. I wrote to him, to know if he had ever been in Ireland; in his reply he informed me he had been to Waterford, but never to Dublin. I wrote to my friend Jones, recommending him strongly to make him the best offer his theatre could afford, as I was sure he would draw him full houses every night. Mr. Jones wrote to me immediately, saying, he would give him similar terms to those which Mrs. Siddons and Mr. Kemble had. Kean accepted them, and set off for Dublin, accompanied by my friend, Pope, who was also very instrumental in procuring him the engagement. He drew a crowded audience every time he acted: Pope performed with him in all his plays, and for his reward had a good house at his benefit.

In my humble opinion, Kean's acting in the third act of 'Othello', is his best performance. The first night he acted it at Drury Lane, I sat in my seat in the orchestra, which was appropriated to me, as Director of the Music, and next to me was Lord Byron, who said, 'Mr. Kelly, depend upon it, this is a man of genius.'

Mr. Sheridan, though very curious to see him, would not go to the theatre; having made a vow, in consequence of some offence he had received from the Committee of Management, never to enter its walls. Mrs. Sheridan, who at this time was very ill, and confined for many weeks, had also a great curiosity to see Mr. Kean perform the part of 'Othello'; but as she could not venture to the theatre, Mr. Sheridan requested Kean to come to his house, and read the play; which he did.

The following day I saw Sheridan, and asked his opinion of Kean: he told me he was very much pleased with him, that he had once studied the part of Othello himself, to act at Sir Watkin William Wynn's private theatre, in Wales; and that Kean's conception of Othello was the precise counterpart of his own. This, which, as it was intended, no doubt, for a compliment, would have sounded like vanity in any body else, in a man of Mr. Sheridan's acknowledged ability, must have been highly flattering to Mr. Kean. I have always considered Mr. Kean an actor of great genius; but I feel much pleasure in mentioning a trait in his private character, which came under my own cognizance. There was a Mr. Conyngham, a native of Ireland, who, in former days, I remember a favourite with the Irish audience, and for many years a member of the Bath company. He was acting at Brighton—his circumstances were not the most flourishing, and a good benefit would, he said, release him from all his embarrassments. A brother actor advised him to write to Mr. Kean; for if he would come and act for his benefit, he might be assured of an overflowing house.

'My good fellow,' replied Conyngham, 'I should be afraid to make so bold a request. It is true, at one time, when we were acting together, we were very intimate, and he was a good-natured fellow; but Ned Kean, then the strolling player, and Mr. Kean, the prop of Drury Lane Theatre, are not one and the same person.'

Conyngham, however, was persuaded to write to Kean, and received the following letter in reply, which I have read.

Dear Tom,

'I am sorry that you are not as comfortable in life as I wish you; put me up for any of my plays next Thursday, and I shall be most happy to act for your benefit. In the mean time, accept the enclosed trifle to make the pot boil.'

The enclosure was a ten-pound note.

On the Thursday he arrived at Brighton, and his performance drew poor Conyngham an overflowing audience. But nothing could induce him to accept one sixpence for his travelling or other incidental expenses: —to descant on the kindness of such an action is useless—it speaks for itself.

On the 16th of June, Drury Lane was honoured with the presence of the Emperor of Russia and King of Prussia; and, on the 17th, they conferred the same honour on Covent Garden Theatre. Their reception by the audience was enthusiastic.

This season, my worthy friends, John Bannister, Mr. Heath, the eminent engraver, and Mr. Nield, the solicitor, made a party to go to Paris.—I agreed to accompany them; and took Henry Horrebow, then quite a boy, with us. None of the party, with the exception of myself, could speak French. However, we had a delightful journey. We stopped a day and a half at Calais, where I hired an excellent roomy post-coach with three horses; and made an agreement, that we should be set down on the fourth day at Paris, or be on the road eight days—at our option;—the latter seemed most agreeable to my party, as they wished to see every thing worth looking at on the road, and none of us were pressed for time.

Our coachman, with whom I made the agreement, was very communicative. One part of the road, between Calais and Boulogne, was rather bad. Our coachman was walking by the side of the coach, and I was singing the romance, in 'Richard Cœur de Lion'.—'Bravo! bravo!' exclaimed coachee; '*sur mon honneur, vous chantez très-bien*—and sing as if you knew music too.' '*Allons, donc—ventre bleu*—let you and I sing a duet.'

'With all my soul,' said I.

He asked me if I knew the duet in the Opera of 'Nina'. I told him I did. '*Allons, donc, commencez*,' said he; and to it we went, pell-mell—he had a strong bass voice, and sang perfectly in tune. After the duet, he sang the songs of 'O, Richard! O! mon Roi', and the chanson, 'Je suis Lindor',[1] with excellent expression, and much to our astonishment.

We arrived at Boulogne-sur-mer, and alighted at Mrs. Parker's Hotel, where we had an excellent dinner, and good beds; and set off early the next morning for Montreuil. We here lost our chaunting guide, which I at first regretted; his successor was quite a young man, very good-natured, and of engaging manners; so much so, that we christened him Le Fevre.[2] While we were at breakfast, I expressed my surprise to Le Fevre, at hearing the coachman, who drove us from Calais to Boulogne, sing so well. 'Sir,' said he, 'that *gentleman* is considered, amongst us, a perfectly good musician. A few years back, he was a captain in the army, but very dissipated and wild—in short, there was no end to his extravagance. His father left him a pretty patrimony, which he soon got rid of; and for reasons, with which I am not acquainted, he was obliged to give up his commission, and leave the army, and now gains his living by driving a coach between Calais and Boulogne; but let him only have his music, his brandy, and his pipe, he will sing, drink, and smoke day and night, and seems the happiest man in all France.'

At that time, recent as is the date of the occurrence, reverses like these were not so common in England as they are now; at present, extravagance in time of war, and half-pay in time of peace, have driven men to drive coaches, who had every just expectation at one time of keeping them; but, 'all the world's a stage,' and it is not at all anomalous, to find some obliged to take up with the commonest fare; nor is any employment, for the support of a family, to be considered dishonourable, which is not dishonest.

At Montreuil, we went to the hotel, kept by the two Brothers with enormous Cocked Hats;—the eldest, near ninety years of age, in full possession of all his faculties, was as garrulous as need be. He seemed very proud of having known Sterne, with whom, he told us, he had conversed, and whom he remembered perfectly.

I would advise those who are fond of good living, and particularly of woodcock-pies, to dine at Montreuil,—the younger Cocked Hat is esteemed a perfect *cordon bleu* in cookery.

We slept at Abbeville, at the Hôtel de l'Europe, an excellent house. We took luncheon at Beauvais, where it was market-day; and the street, in which our inn was situated, was crowded with market-people, listening to a French ballad-singer, roaring away on the steps of the coffee-house, opposite to our inn. I was in high spirits, and determined to rival the said Stentorian ballad-singer; so I mounted the steps, and sang a strophe of a French song. The crowd gave me great applause, and loud cheering; so much indeed, that the mistress of the coffee-house declared, that if I would remain at Beauvais, and sing to the frequenters of her coffee-room, she would board and lodge me, free of expense.

27

After loitering on the road for six days, on the seventh (Sunday) we arrived at Paris, where lodgings had been taken for us by the elder Vestris, close to the Boulevard du Temple, which were very comfortable. We passed a delightful time while we remained in Paris.

We went one evening to the Théâtre Vaudeville, and saw the first representation of 'La Route à Paris'. Joly, the favourite actor, played several characters in different disguises. His personification of an English gouty Lord, was perfect. Bannister thought him excellent. Madame Belmont, the original Fanchon, belonged to this theatre; and is an excellent actress, and a fine woman. We also witnessed the first representation of the 'Two Boxers', at the Théâtre des Variétés, performed by those two excellent comic actors, Brunet and Potier. In the line of simple characters, there are no actors like them,—they are real comedians, without buffoonery or grimace.

We accompanied Mr. Heath on a visit to the late Monsieur Denon, the once favourite of Buonaparte. He resided in a fine house upon the Quai Voltaire, furnished in a style of the greatest magnificence. His pictures, prints, cameos, intaglios, statues, &c. were of the first description. Indeed, when accompanying Buonaparte in Egypt, Italy, &c. he had the picking and choosing of the best; and, to do him justice, he did not appear to have forgotten number one.

He received us with the greatest politeness, inquired most affectionately after Mr. Heath's son, with whom he was very well acquainted; and spoke with the most unqualified praise of his talents as an artist, and the amiability of his character as a private individual.

Denon's countenance was replete with intelligence and genius. I introduced Bannister to him, as one of our first-rate actors:—he said, of that he had no doubt, as Mr. Bannister had a fine stage face, and the eye of a good comedian. He gave us recommendations, for the purpose of viewing all the public institutes, colleges, mint, &c. in Paris, which were of great service to us, as they gave us an *entrée* to all those places. We were daily visitors at the Louvre, and were, of course, highly delighted with the works there. Mr. Glover, the English artist, had permission to copy some pictures, and was every day to be seen at work in the gallery. I met there, one morning, my countryman, of whom I have before spoken, Mr. Curran. I asked his opinion of Paris; he replied, that he thought it a mixture of dirt and magnificence—that some of their buildings were very superb, but when once seen, that was sufficient for him; for his own part, he had not the smallest wish to *encore* a building.

My friend, Madame Grassini, was living in the Rue d'Anjou. I dined with her, in company with the celebrated composer Paër, an excellent and jolly fellow. I have seen him take his bottle of champagne, and two of burgundy; after coffee, two or three glasses of brandy, by way of *chasse*, quit the table as sober as a judge, and sit down to the piano-forte, on which instrument he excelled; he also sang with infinite grace and expression.

In the evening, Madame Grassini had a musical party, at which I was introduced to Mr. and Mrs. Crawford, who, extraordinary to say, had, during the whole period of the Revolution, remained at their house in the *Rue d'Anjou*, unmolested by any of the different ruling powers. Grassini, at this period, renewed her engagement for the ensuing season, at the Opera House, with Mr. Waters.

My party were very much struck with the water-works of Marly, the magnificence of Versailles, the Petite Trianon, Malmaison, and St. Cloud; the latter was my favourite. We were shewn every thing worth seeing, and, amongst other curiosities, the chair in which Buonaparte used to sit when he held a council. The person who explained every thing to us, made us examine the number of notches made in it by Buonaparte, who, while giving audience, or transacting business, had a habit of holding a penknife in his hand, and was continually making cuts in the chair, more or less, as he felt pleased, or otherwise. It was said, that when in the council chamber, he would never sit in any other chair. Our cicerone informed us, that he was seated in it when he gave an audience to the Russian ambassador; and on giving him a paper, said 'Read, sign, and be off.' That was said to be the only conversation which passed between them; and from the tyrant's genuine character, it seems very probable to have been so.—The ambassador made no reply, and retired.

The day after our return from St. Cloud, we went to the fair of Vincennes, which was crowded with booths, mountebanks, puppet-shows, &c. From this merry scene, we turned to the mournful task of viewing the castle of Vincennes; and the spot where the ill-fated Duke d'Enghien was, by the sanguinary orders of Buonaparte, barbarously murdered.

Bannister and Heath were obliged to return to England,—the former to fulfil his engagements, and the latter upon business. The last day they remained in Paris, we devoted to see Montmartre; the view of Paris, from the summit of which, is very magnificent.

I was one evening in company, at Madame Grassini's, with a Parisian lady, who had just returned from London, where she had been passing the winter. I asked her how she liked that city?—'To say the truth,' she replied, 'I like two things in London passing well; *par exemple*,—the pavement of your streets, and the mock turtle of your kitchens; in every thing else, Paris is far preferable. I stopped some days longer in England than I at first intended, out of curiosity to see the sun; but the whole time I was there, he never was complaisant enough to make his appearance.' And yet I was informed this lady was a person of some consideration in Paris, and reckoned mighty clever.

My friends took their departure for Rouen, in their way to Dieppe. I had some business to detain me in Paris a week longer, and then purposed following them; but on the eve of my leaving Paris, I was seized with the gout, and kept my bed for ten days. When I was able to move, I hired a cabriolet, and with Henry Horrebow, set off post for Rouen. The first day I was in such pain I could not get further than Pontoise, a town famous for the excellence of its veal. The next day I reached Rouen, and put up at the Hôtel de France, an excellent house. The peasants of Normandy seemed to enjoy themselves; for, in every village through which I passed, they were either dancing or playing at various games. I got to a late dinner at Dieppe, and truly glad I was, as my gout was increasing. My hotel on the quay was lively enough; I saw every thing passing, and remained there five days, waiting for a fair wind for Brighton; and, what was rather strange to meet with in France, I got some of the finest old port wine I ever tasted.

There were three professors of music from London, of the name of Harris, waiting at Dieppe, as well as myself, for a fair wind, who did me the favour every evening to come and sit with me, and were very agreeable company. On the fifth evening, the wind being fair, the Neptune packet was to sail for Brighton. Though unable to move hand or foot, I was determined to go in it; and was carried, in great torture, by four seamen, on board, and packed into my birth. If to have a seventeen hours' rough passage, a violent sea sickness, with a twinging fit of the gout at the same time, be not enough to put a poor fellow's patience to the proof, I know not what is. I sent Henry with the passengers on shore in the first boat to procure a carriage, as I could not walk; and remained on board the packet until he returned with a sedan-chair for me on the beach. I was lifted from the packet into the boat; and luckily Mr. Addison, who was walking on the beach at the time, ran to the Old Ship, and secured me accommodations there. I got better every hour; and the kind attention paid me by Mr. Shugard, the landlord, Mrs. Shugard, and all their family, I shall always be happy to acknowledge.

I found, at Brighton, my friends Philips, Mrs. Philips, Miss Johnstone (now Mrs. Wallack), Messrs. Maddocks, Charles Mathews, Mrs. Mathews, Mr. and Mrs. Poole, and some Irish friends, all forming a party at a boarding house on the Grand Parade. They were like one family; the mistress of the house, a Mrs. White, kept an excellent and plentiful table. Mathews was in excellent spirits, and kept every one alive: there was only one damper, in the shape of an old East Indian officer, just returned from Calcutta, who was most unbending, and did not in the least relish their innocent mirth, for the slightest noise brought on a fit of bile; so that for fear of being disturbed at night, he never went to his bed until every inmate, servants and all, were in theirs.

His bed-chamber adjoined the dining parlour; my friends were kind enough to wish me to join their social party, but that was not feasible, as there was no bed-room in the house unoccupied; however, they determined among themselves to have me *in*, and the Nabob *out*; for which purpose, at the solemn hour of midnight, when all the house were thought to be at rest, Mathews left his room, and on the staircase began howling and barking in different tones, in imitation of a kennel of hounds, and squalling and mewing with all his might, like a dozen of wild cats. The Nabob was terrified, and declared the next morning at breakfast, that he would not pass such another miserable night to be made Commander-in-Chief. The second night, he had another dose, if possible, more potent than the first. The scheme succeeded; for the following morning the restless Nabob requested Mrs. White to let him give up his bed-room in the house, and remain with her as a boarder only. He took a lodging in the next street, and I became possessed of his bed-chamber.

He soon found out the cause of the noises, which, he said, at first he implicitly believed came from a legion of demons. I thought myself extremely fortunate in becoming his *locum tenens*, a situation which I could not have attained but for the excellent imitations of my friend Mathews, combined with the good wishes of my other friends, who were inmates of the house.

At the theatre at Brighton, Mr. Harley (then a provincial performer in Mr. Trotter's company) was acting. I went to see him in 'Bombastes Furioso', in which he introduced a song of his own writing to Braham's air, 'Said a smile to a tear', from the opera of 'False Alarms'. His acting and singing pleased me so much, that I wrote the next day to Mr. Arnold, recommending him as a most promising subject, more particularly for his own theatre, the English Opera House;[1] and strenuously advised him to engage Harley without delay. By return of post, I received Mr. Arnold's reply, enclosing his proposals for an engagement, which Mr. Harley accepted. The rapid strides he has made, and is still making, in the good opinion of the public, and his employers, prove that my early opinion of his merits was not without foundation; and I am happy to have been, in some degree, instrumental in introducing so useful an actor, and worthy a young man, to the London stage. He made his first appearance in London, at the English Opera House, on the 15th of July, 1815, in the part of Marcelli, in the opera of 'The Devil's Bridge'.

I remained at Brighton, until summoned by Mr. Arnold to Drury Lane, to get up and superintend the music in Macbeth, which was to be produced with uncommon splendour for Mr. Kean. I had all the principal vocal performers in the choruses; who all, as well as a numerous list of choral singers, both male and female, took infinite pains to execute the charming productions in a style unequalled in my remembrance; and the enthusiastic applause which the audience gave them, was commensurate with their merits. It was a rare and novel sight, to see so great a body of English chorus singers on the stage, full of appropriate and animated action. Yet in the instance I speak of, such things were; I cannot say such things are,—they find it, perhaps, too troublesome.

I went to see the first appearance of my countrywoman, Miss O'Neil, who made her *entrée* at Covent Garden Theatre, on the 6th of October, 1814; and had the satisfaction of finding her received by the audience with the admiration and applause which she ever afterwards deservedly enjoyed until her retirement from the stage, on her marriage.

Though I had not the pleasure of being personally acquainted with

Miss O'Neil, I felt a great interest for her success. The following anecdote, I believe very little known in the theatrical world, I had from Mr. Jones, the patentee of Crow Street Theatre. Miss Walstein, who was the heroine of the Dublin stage, and a great and deserved favourite, was to open the theatre, in the character of Juliet. Mr. Jones received an intimation from Miss Walstein, that without a certain increase of salary, and other privileges, she would not come to the house. Mr. Jones had arrived at the determination to shut up his theatre, sooner than submit to what he thought an unwarrantable demand; when Mac Nally, the box-keeper, who had been the bearer of Miss Walstein's message, told Mr. Jones, 'that it would be a pity to close the house, and that there was a remedy, if Mr. Jones chose to avail himself of it.'

'The girl, Sir,' said he, 'who has been so often strongly recommended to you as a promising actress, is now at an hotel in Dublin, with her father and brother, where they have just arrived, and is proceeding to Drogheda, to act at her father's theatre there. I have heard it said, by persons who have seen her that she plays Juliet extremely well, and is very young and very pretty. I am sure she would be delighted to have the opportunity of appearing before a Dublin audience; and, if you please, I will make her the proposal.'

The proposal was made, and accepted; and on the following Saturday, *the girl*, who was Miss O'Neil, made her *début* on the Dublin stage as Juliet. The audience were delighted; she acted the part several nights, and Mr. Jones offered her father and brother engagements on very liberal terms, which were thankfully accepted.

In Dublin, she was not only a great favourite in tragedy, but also in many parts of genteel comedy. I have there seen her play 'Letitia Hardy'; she danced very gracefully, and introduced my song, 'In the rough blast heaves the billows', originally sung by Mrs. Jordan, at Drury Lane, which she sang so well, as to produce a general call for its repetition from the audience. She was, in private life, highly esteemed for her many amiable qualities. Her engagement in Dublin wafted Miss Walstein from Dublin (where she had been for many years the heroine of Crow Street) to Drury Lane, where she made her appearance as Calista, in 'The Fair Penitent', on the 13th of November, 1814, but only remained one season.

On the 7th of February, 1815, Miss Mellon quitted the stage,—she made her last appearance at Drury Lane, in the character of Aubrey,[1] in 'As you like it'.

On the 29th of March, Mr. Arnold produced the opera, entitled 'The Unknown Guest'; the subject was taken from a French drama, and managed by Mr. Arnold, with great adroitness. There were some excellent dramatic situations, and some good poetry—he rendered the piece attractive for a few nights—the music I composed.

On the 4th of May, Mrs. Mountain had a benefit at the Opera House, and retired from the stage.

On the 1st of June, 1815, the drama sustained an irreparable loss, in the retirement of the worthy, honest, Jack Bannister, esteemed, beloved, and respected: his career on the stage was long and successful. He made his *entrée* before the public, at the Little Theatre in the Haymarket, in the character of Dick, in Murphy's farce of 'The Apprentice', on the 27th of August, 1778. I lived in habits of intimacy with him for many years; and he has often mentioned to me, Mr. Garrick's partiality for him,[1] who thought his talents much more calculated for tragedy than comedy. He played Zaphne, in 'Mahomet', 'Hamlet', and many other tragic characters. But at last, his comic powers were called into action. In 'Dabble, the Dentist', in my good and kind friend, Mr. Cobb's farce of 'The Humourist', and Tim Tartlet, in 'The First Floor', he burst on the town as a low comedian. On the demise of Edwin, the wide range of comic characters, so ably performed by that truly eccentric actor, at the Little Theatre in the Haymarket, devolved upon Bannister. In Bowkit, in 'The Son-in-Law', 'Peeping Tom', &c. he was eminently successful. In 'The Prize', in 'Of Age To-morrow'; and in a number of characters, in the *outré* line of acting, he had no competitor; but, his great part of all, was Walter, in 'The Children of the Wood'. I saw him in that character, the first night it came out, at the Haymarket, and witnessed also his last appearance in it for his benefit, at Drury Lane; and he then acted the part as finely as on the first night of its representation. With extreme emotion, but with a firm tone of voice, at the close of the afterpiece, he advanced to the audience, whom he addressed, in a speech, the latter part of which I fully recollect:—his words were, 'Consideration of health warns me to retire;—your patronage has given me the means of doing so with comfort. This moment of quitting you, nearly overcomes me. At a period when gratitude and respect call upon me, to express my feelings, with more eloquence than I could ever boast, those feelings deprive me of half the humble powers I may possess on ordinary occasions. Farewell, my kind,—my dear benefactors.'

At the conclusion of his speech, he bowed respectfully to the audience, and was led off by all the performers of the Theatre, who attended to witness his farewell. No performer ever quitted the stage more deservedly respected or regretted. He had been seven and thirty years on Drury Lane stage; and, I am happy to say, that independent of a few attacks of the gout, which all virtuous persons are more or less subject to, he enjoys the comfort of his well-earned fortune, surrounded by his amiable wife and family: that he may long continue to do so, is my most ardent prayer.

This season was also the last of Mr. Wroughton's appearance on the stage. He was a most intimate friend of Bannister—they were scarcely ever to be seen asunder. I used to nick-name them, 'Orestes and Pylades.' Wroughton was for many years stage-manager of Drury Lane Theatre, and had also been, for a number of years, proprietor of Sadler's Wells, and was supposed to have made a great deal of money by that place of amusement. Wroughton was a sterling, sound, sensible performer—he never gave offence as an actor; and in many parts was truly good. His Sir John Restless, in 'All in the Wrong',—Ford, in 'The Merry Wives of Windsor', were among them. But, in my opinion, his performance of the part of Darlemont, in the play of 'Deaf and Dumb', was a master-piece of the art, and ranked with Cooke's Sir Pertinax Macsycophant, Kemble's Penruddock, or Dowton's Doctor Cantwell.

The stage, this season, nearly sustained a loss in Miss Kelly;[1] for, while acting in O'Keefe's farce of 'The Merry Mourners', a pistol-shot was fired at her from the pit, on the 17th of February, 1816, at Drury Lane Theatre, by a Mr. Barnet, who, when taken into custody, proved to be a complete maniac. I was at the theatre at the time.

Mrs. Siddons re-appeared at Covent Garden Theatre (by the express desire of Her Royal Highness the late Princess Charlotte of Wales, who expressed a wish to see her perform Lady Macbeth), on the 16th of June, 1816; but the sudden indisposition of the Princess Charlotte, prevented Her Royal Highness attending the theatre that evening.

I had now to experience the loss of a true and sincere friend, in the death of that great man, Richard Brinsley Sheridan, who expired at his house in Saville Row, on the 7th July, 1816, aged sixty-five. The body was removed to the house of Mr. Peter Moore, Member for Coventry, and thence the Saturday following to Westminster Abbey, near those of Addison, Garrick, and Cumberland, followed by the Dukes of York and Sussex. The pall was borne by the Duke of Bedford, Lord Holland, Earl of Mulgrave, Earl of Lauderdale, the Bishop of London, and Lord Robert Spencer. His son, Mr. Charles Brinsley Sheridan, was chief mourner, supported by Mr. Henry Ogle, The Honourable Edward Bouverie, Mr. William Linley, Sir Charles Asgill, Bart. Mr. Charles Ward; followed by a numerous train of admirers of his splendid talents. Where the body lies, there is a plain flat stone, with this inscription:—

RICHARD BRINSLEY SHERIDAN,
Born 1751; Died 7th July, 1816.
This Marble is the Tribute of an attached Friend,
PETER MOORE.

There were reports industriously circulated through the kingdom, that Mr. Sheridan, in his latter moments, was left in want of the common necessaries of life; and the malignant propagators of the report, went so far to gratify their own malice, as to assert that he called for a lemon, when exhausted with thirst, and that neither he, nor those about him, had the means of procuring him one. I, amongst a thousand others, heard this foolish tale asserted; but I can solemnly aver, from my own knowledge, and from the evidence of those who were nearest and dearest to him, and who remained with him in his last moments, that all such reports were groundless, and fabricated for the most atrocious purposes of scandal.

28

These dealers in malignity stated, that the sum of two hundred pounds was conveyed to Mr. Sheridan in a way that wounded his feelings, and returned by his direction, with the resentment of wounded pride. It is true the money was sent, but in a totally different manner to that described, and returned in a totally different manner to what the world was taught to believe. The real fact is, that Mr. Sheridan's physician, then attending him, and also one of his most intimate friends, undertook to deliver it back to the illustrious donor, and, with all respect, to assure him that Mr. Sheridan was in want of no pecuniary assistance.

I sent, a few days before he died, for his own man, who was in attendance on him during the whole of his illness, and whom I knew to be faithfully attached to his master. He can testify that I entreated him to inform me if his master was in want of any comforts, for with any thing my means would afford I would furnish him; but not to let him or the family know it came from me. John assured me that his master was in want of nothing, and that those who had reported to the contrary, and made up libellous and injurious tales upon the subject, spoke falsely, and were base calumniators.

The loss I sustained by Mr. Sheridan's death, I can but faintly depict: he was, as a companion and friend, to me beyond measure invaluable; his readiness and taste were conspicuous; his wit, though luxuriant and unbounded, never intrusive; and during the five and twenty years through which I enjoyed his friendship and society, I never heard him say a single word that could wound the feelings of a human being.

His quickness in writing may be judged by the circumstances I have already mentioned, relative to the state in which his 'Pizarro' was produced, and he made a similar exertion at the time he brought out 'The Critic'. Two days previous to the performance, the last scene was not written: Dr. Ford, and Mr. Linley, the joint proprietors, began to get nervous and fidgetty, and the actors were absolutely *au désespoir*, especially King, who was not only stage-manager, but had to play Puff; to him was assigned the duty of hunting down and worrying Sheridan about the last scene; day after day passed, until, as I have just said, the last day but two arrived, and it made not its appearance.

At last, Mr. Linley, who, being his father-in-law, was pretty well aware of his habits, hit upon a stratagem. A night rehearsal of 'The Critic' was ordered, and Sheridan, having dined with Linley, was prevailed upon to go; while they were on the stage, King whispered Sheridan that he had something particular to communicate, and begged he would step into the second green-room. Accordingly, Sheridan went, and there found a table, with pens, ink, and paper, a good fire, an armed chair at the table, and two bottles of claret, with a dish of anchovy sandwiches. The moment he got into the room, King stepped out, and locked the door; immediately after which, Linley and Ford came up and told the author that, until he had written the scene, he would be kept where he was.

Sheridan took this decided measure in good part; he ate the anchovies, finished the claret, wrote the scene, and laughed heartily at the ingenuity of the contrivance.

This anecdote I had from King himself. Another instance of his readiness and rapidity, when he chose to exert himself, occurred at the time when his pantomime of 'Robinson Crusoe' was in rehearsal. He happened to call in at the theatre one day, and found them in the greatest confusion, not knowing what to introduce to give time for the setting of a scene; it was suggested to Mr. Sheridan that a song would afford sufficient opportunity to the carpenters for their preparation; accordingly, he sat down at the prompter's table, on the stage, and wrote on the back of a play-bill the beautiful ballad of 'The Midnight Watch', which was set to music by his father-in-law, Mr. Linley, in a style which has established it as one of the most beautiful specimens of pure English melody.

An observation Mr. Sheridan once made to me about Congreve's plays I venture to repeat, it has so much genuine wit about it: he complained to me that 'Love for Love' had been so much altered and modified for the more delicate ears of modern audiences, that it was quite spoiled. 'His plays,' said the wit, 'are, I own, somewhat licentious, but it is barbarous to mangle them; they are like horses, when you deprive them of their vice, they lose their vigour.'

It is of course known, that Mr. Burke, in the early part of his life, enlisted under the banners of Opposition, and was a constant frequenter of the house of a baker of the name of Tarcome, where the aspirants for fame, on that side of the question, used to meet, and debate certain proposed questions; the baker himself was eventually constituted perpetual president of the well-known Robin Hood society; such was the estimation in which he was held by the disciples of Whiggery.

Upon a memorable occasion, Mr. Burke, in the House of Commons, exclaimed, 'I quit the camp,' and suddenly crossed the House; and having seated himself on the ministerial benches, shortly after rose, and made a most brilliant speech in opposition to his *ci-devant* friends and adherents.

Sheridan was a good deal nettled at what he considered a needless defection, and replied with something like asperity to Mr. Burke's attack, and concluded his speech with nearly these words:—'The Honourable Gentleman, to quote his own expression, has "quitted the camp;" he will recollect that he quitted it as a deserter, and I sincerely hope he will never attempt to return as a spy: but I, for one, cannot sympathise in the astonishment with which an act of apostacy so flagrant has electrified the House; for neither I, nor the Honourable Gentleman, have forgotten whence he obtained the weapons which he now uses against us: so far from being at all astonished at the Honourable Gentleman's tergiversation, I consider it not only characteristic but consistent, that he who in the outset of life made so extraordinary a blunder as to go to a baker's for eloquence, should finish such a career by coming to the House of Commons to get bread.'

One of Mr. Sheridan's favourite amusements, in his hours of recreation, was that of making blunders for me, and relating them to my friends, vouching for the truth of them with the most perfect gravity. One I remember was, that one night, when Drury Lane Theatre was crowded to excess in every part, I was peeping through the hole in the stage curtain, and John Kemble, who was standing on the stage near me, asked me how the house looked, and that I replied, 'By J—s, you can't stick a pin's head in any part of it—it is literally *chuck* full; but how much fuller will it be to-morrow night, when the King comes!'

Another of Mr. Sheridan's jests against me was, that one day, having walked with him to Kemble's house, in Great Russell Street, Bloomsbury, when the streets were very dirty, and having gone up the steps while Mr. Sheridan was scraping the dirt off his shoes, I asked him to scrape for me while I was knocking at the door.

Of all our poets, Dryden was Mr. Sheridan's favourite; many a time and oft, when sitting over our wine, have I heard him quote at great length from him. It was truly a treat to hear him recite poetry; he had a powerful voice, and nothing, when animated, could surpass the brilliancy of his countenance, and the fire of his eye.

On the 15th July, 1797, at the Haymarket Theatre, George Colman's excellent comedy of the 'Heir at Law' was produced. Mr. Sheridan, the same year, was passing the autumn in the Isle of Wight, enjoying, as he used to say, one of his greatest delights, sailing backwards and forwards from Cowes to Southampton; and when he returned to town, he told me that he had seen the 'Heir at Law' acted there. He said the play was not well performed, but he was greatly amused with it, and thought it an excellent comedy, and wished Colman could be prevailed upon to write just such another for Drury Lane. Many years after, I went with him, one evening, to Covent Garden (after having dined together at the Piazza Coffee-house), and saw Kenny's admirable farce of 'Raising the Wind' performed. No schoolboy at home for the holidays could have laughed more heartily than he did; he was quite delighted with the character of Jeremy Diddler, and with the acting of Lewis and Emery.

At one time, when hard pressed to pay the Opera Orchestra, who were greatly in arrear, and had resolved not to perform unless their debt was liquidated, threatening to make an application to the Lord Chamberlain; Mr. Sheridan was roused, to make an effort to raise five hundred pounds, which was the immediate sum required. He found a person ready to make an advance for three months, with a proviso, that Stephen

Storace and myself, who then managed the Opera, should give our joint security for the repayment. Being both of us eager that the concern should not stop, we did so, and he promised faithfully to provide for it. The very day the bill became due, Storace was with me, in the morning; we were both in *modo penseroso*, wondering how we could contrive to get it renewed; when, to our great surprise, Mr. Sheridan entered, laughing, with our acceptance dangling between his fingers, the sight of which changed our *modo penseroso* to an *allegro vivace*; he put our security into my hands, at which my heart did verily rejoice, and with all sincerity I made use of the quotation,

'For this relief, much thanks.'

I mention this to shew, however general the impression of Mr. Sheridan's want of punctuality in money matters may be, that there is no rule without an exception.

The last time I saw Mr. Sheridan, was in the room in Drury Lane, formerly the treasury of the old theatre, where a man of the name of Farebrother, an old servant of his, was allowed, by the Drury Lane Committee, to reside. He was sitting alone, reading, with a muffin and a cup of coffee before him. On my entering the room, he told me that he had been reading Davies' 'Life of Garrick', which, said he, 'if you have not read, do read, and advise every actor, from me, to do the same, for it is well worth their attention.'

I remained with him till four o'clock in the morning, *tête-â-tête*. I never saw him more pleasant or communicative. He dwelt particularly on his father's acting the part of King John, and 'without partiality,' he said, 'his scene with Hubert was a master-piece of the art; and no actor could ever reach its excellence.' I had been told by Jefferson, the proprietor of the Plymouth theatre, who had often seen old Mr. Sheridan act King John, in Dublin, that nothing could surpass it.

Mr. Sheridan also spoke of his father's Cato, as a masterly performance, as well as his Brutus, in 'Julius Cæsar'. The Cato of the elder Sheridan was always very popular with the Dublin audience. Mr. Hitchcock, who wrote the history of the 'Irish Stage', remembered him perfectly in the character. I have often heard him say that his declamation was fine and impressive; he pronounced 'Cato' with a broad *a*, as, indeed, all the Irish do. John Kemble always pronounced it 'Cato', and when he acted the part in Dublin, the play was announced from the stage by an old actor of the Sheridan school, who, despising the innovation of Kemble, gave it out thus:—'Ladies and Gentlemen, to-morrow evening will be performed the tragedy of "C*a*to", the part of Cato by Mr. Kemble.' The manner in which he pronounced the same name in two different ways, produced great laughter in the audience, who quite understood the sarcasm. When I related this anecdote to Mr. Sheridan, he seemed to enjoy the pertinacity of the Irish actor.

One day, Mr. Sheridan laughingly said to me, 'It must be allowed, Kelly, that our countrymen always shew more or less of the *potatoe* in their brain. Yesterday, at about four o'clock in the morning, I came out of Brookes's, where I had staid the very last; and, as I was stepping into the carriage, I saw some half-dozen Irish chairmen, loitering at the door, shivering with cold, waiting for a fare. It was a bitter morning, and I said to one of the poor devils, "Why do you remain here, my good fellow?"

' "Please your honour," replied one of them, "we are waiting to take somebody home."

' "You may save yourselves the trouble then," said I, "for I have just come out of the house, and there is nobody left in it."

' "Please your honour, we know there is nobody in it, but who knows how many may come out."

'It was too cold,' said Sheridan, 'to argue with them, so I got into my coach, and left them.'

It would be the height of arrogance and indiscretion in me to descant on, or eulogise the public character of Mr. Sheridan; but I trust that his political life will be handed down to posterity, by some able pen, uninfluenced by favour or enmity; for, take him as a statesman, an orator, a dramatist, and a poet united, I fear we shall scarcely ever see his like again. His good qualities were many; and, after all, the great bane of his life was procrastination; had it not been for that, what could he not have achieved! To me, his memory will be ever dear, and ought to be so to all who admire great and splendid talents. Yet he had many enemies;—some of whom, to my knowledge, his former bounty fed. But, alas! to use the language of our great bard,

> 'The *evil* that men do, lives *after them*;
> The *good*, is often interred with their bones.'[1]

Much *good* remains upon authentic record, relative to Mr. Sheridan, which even his greatest enemies could never deny. Some of the stories which exist against him, however, have a vast deal of humour in them;

and one which has often been told, I think worth inserting, because, having been an eye-witness of the circumstance, I am enabled to show the very 'head and front of his offending.'

We were one day in earnest conversation close to the gate of the path, which was then open to the public, leading across the church-yard of St. Paul's, Covent Garden, from King Street to Henrietta Street, when Mr. Holloway, who was a creditor of Sheridan's to a considerable amount, came up to us on horseback, and accosted Sheridan in a tone of something more like anger than sorrow, and complained that he never could get admittance when he called, vowing vengeance against the infernal Swiss Monsieur François, if he did not let him in the next time he went to Hertford Street.

Holloway was really in a passion. Sheridan knew that he was vain of his judgment in horse-flesh; and without taking any notice of the violence of his manner, burst into an exclamation upon the beauty of the horse which he rode;—he struck the right chord.

'Why,' said Holloway, 'I think I may say, there never was a prettier creature than this. You were speaking to me, when I last saw you, about a horse for Mrs. Sheridan; now this would be a treasure for a lady.'

'Does he canter well?' said Sheridan.

'Beautifully,' replied Holloway.

'If that's the case, Holloway,' said Sheridan, 'I really should not mind stretching a point for him. Will you have the kindness to let me see his paces?'

'To be sure,' said the lawyer; and putting himself into a graceful attitude, he threw his nag into a canter along the market.

The moment his back was turned, Sheridan wished me good morning, and went off through the church-yard, where no horse could follow, into Bedford Street, laughing immoderately, as indeed did several standers-by. The only person not entertained by this practical joke was Mr. Holloway himself.

Another story of him I shall give, because it is very little known, if known at all. Mr. Harris, the late proprietor of Covent Garden, who had a great regard for Sheridan, had at different times frequent occasions to meet him on business, and made appointment after appointment with him, not one of which Sheridan ever kept. At length Mr. Harris, wearied out, begged his friend Mr. Palmer, of Bath, to see Mr. Sheridan, and tell him that unless he kept the next appointment made for their meeting, all acquaintance between them must end for ever.

Sheridan expressed great sorrow for what had been in fact inevitable, and fixed one o'clock the next day to call upon Mr. Harris at the theatre. At about three he actually made his appearance in Hart Street, where he met Mr. Tregent, the celebrated French watchmaker, who was extremely theatrical, and had been the intimate friend of Garrick.

Sheridan told him, that he was on his way to call upon Harris.

'I have just left him,' said Tregent, 'in a violent passion, having waited for you ever since one o'clock.'

'What have *you* been doing at the theatre?' said Sheridan.

'Why,' replied Tregent, 'Harris is going to make Bate Dudley a present of a gold watch, and I have taken him half a dozen, in order that he may choose one for that purpose.'

'Indeed,' said Sheridan.

They wished each other good day, and parted.

Mr. Sheridan proceeded to Mr. Harris's room, and when he addressed him, it was pretty evident that his want of punctuality had produced the effect which Mr. Tregent described.

'Well, Sir,' said Mr. Harris; 'I have waited at least two hours for you again; I had almost given you up, and if——'

'Stop, my dear Harris,' said Sheridan, interrupting him; 'I assure you these things occur more from my misfortunes than my faults; I declare I thought it was but one o'clock, for it so happens that I have no watch, and to tell you the truth, am too poor to buy one; but when the day comes that I can, you will see I shall be as punctual as any other man.'

'Well, then,' said the unsuspecting Harris; 'if that be all, you shall not long want a watch; for here—(opening his drawer)—are half a dozen of Tregent's best—choose any one you like, and do me the favour of accepting it.'

Sheridan affected the greatest surprise at the appearance of the watches; but did as he was bid, and selected certainly not the worst for the *cadeau*.

A punster, in return for Sheridan's hatred of puns, would certainly have made a joke of his affection for watches because they go *tick*; for myself, I have too much respect for Mr. Sherida 's memory, to give way to such a propensity.

Mr. Sheridan was extremely attached to Mr. Richardson; and when Mrs. Sheridan was at Bognor, he used to take Richardson down with him on visits to her. One of these visits Sheridan once described to me with infinite humour, and although I fear it is impossible to impart *literally,* the spirit which he *practically* infused into it, when relating it, I give it as I remember it.

Richardson had set his mind upon going down to Bognor with Mr. Sheridan on one particular occasion, because it happened that Lord Thurlow, with whom he was on terms of intimacy, was staying there. 'So,' said Richardson, 'nothing can be more delightful, what with my favourite diversion of sailing—my enjoyment of walking on the sands—the pleasure of arguing with Lord Thurlow, and taking my snuff by the sea-side, I shall be in my glory.'

'Well,' said Mr. Sheridan; 'down he went, full of anticipated joys. The first day, in stepping into the boat to go sailing, he tumbled down, and sprained his ancle, and was obliged to be carried into his lodgings, which had no view of the sea: the following morning he sent for a barber to shave him, but there being no professional shaver nearer than Chichester, he was forced to put up with a fisherman, who volunteered to officiate, and cut him severely just under his nose, which entirely prevented his taking snuff; and the same day at breakfast, eating prawns too hastily, he swallowed the head of one, horns and all, which stuck in his throat, and produced such pain and inflammation, that his medical advisers would not allow him to speak for three days. So, thus,' said Mr. Sheridan, 'ended in four and twenty hours his walking—his sailing—his snuff-taking—and his arguments.'

Mr. Sheridan was the author of the following dramatic pieces:—

'The Rivals', at Covent Garden, 1775.

'Saint Patrick's Day', a farce, 1775; this was written in two days, for the benefit of the facetious Larry Clinch, a brother actor, and intimate friend of his father, and the original Sir Lucius O'Trigger.

'The Duenna', at Covent Garden, which ran seventy nights without intermission.

The 'Trip to Scarborough', altered from Sir John Vanbrugh; Drury Lane, 1777.

The 'School for Scandal', Drury Lane, 1777.

'The Camp',[1] musical entertainment, in two acts, Drury Lane, 1778.

'The Critic', of which he told me, that he valued the first act more than any thing he ever wrote.

'Pizarro', is his only other production, except the pantomime of 'Robinson Crusoe'. He began an opera, called the 'Foresters', and had written an act or two of a comedy, which he never finished.

It was one of Doctor Johnson's sayings, that if a man do not make new acquaintances as he advances in life, he will soon find himself alone in the world. The truth of the observation I can vouch for by experience. I have found all the friends of my early life drop round me; and honourable and valued as have been many of them, the loss of no one certainly was more deplored by me, than that of Mr. Sheridan. If I have said much of him, it was because I loved and respected him; and the reader, to whom any illustrations of such a man's character must I flatter myself be acceptable, will excuse me.

In the year 1818, I composed the music to a piece called 'The Bride of Abydos'; and in 1820, to another called 'Abudah'; and my last production was a musical entertainment, called the 'Lady and the Devil', for Drury Lane. Between the years 1797 and 1821, I produced, at different theatres, sixty-two pieces, by far the greatest number produced by any one English composer, Bishop excepted. Most of them, I have the satisfaction to say, have been received by the public with favour; and I have thought it might not be disagreeable to my friends to see a list[1] of them, for which reason I have subjoined the titles, dates, the names of their authors, and the theatres where they were performed.

False Appearances (General Conway)	DL	[20 April] 1789	
Fashionable Friends [Horace Walpole?]	DL	1789	
*A Friend in Need (Prince Hoare)	DL	9 Feb. 1797	[238]
Last of the Family (Cumberland)	DL	8 May 1797	[243]
Chimney Corner (Walsh Porter)	DL	7 Oct. 1797	[243]
*Castle Spectre (M. G. Lewis)	DL	14 Dec. 1797	[243–4, 324, 349
*Blue Beard (G. Colman)	DL	16 Jan. 1798	[178, 246–8, 314
Outlaws (Franklin)	DL	16 Oct. 1798	
*Captive of Spilburg (Prince Hoare)	DL	[14 Nov.] 1798	[252]
Aurelio and Miranda (Boaden)	DL	29 Dec. 1798	[252]
*Feudal Times (G. Colman)	DL	19 Jan. 1799	[252]
*Pizarro (Sheridan)	DL	24 May 1799	[252–5]
*Of Age To-morrow (Dibdin)	DL	1 Feb. 1800	[256–7, 335]
De Montfort (Miss Baillie)	DL	29 April 1800	[261]
The Indian (Fenwick)	DL	6 Oct. 1800	
Deaf and Dumb (Translated from the French by Holcroft, and adapted by Mr. Kemble)	DL	24 Feb. 1801	[262]
*Adelmorn (M. G. Lewis)	DL	4 May 1801	[244, 262]
*Gipsey Prince (T. Moore)	LT	24 July 1801	[262]
Urania (Hon. W. Spencer)	DL	22 Jan. 1802	[264]
Algonah (Cobb)	DL	30 April 1802	[266]

House to be Sold (Cobb)	DL	17 Nov. 1802	[270, 273]
Hero of the North (Dimond)	DL	19 Feb. 1803	[273]
Marriage Promise (Allingham)	DL	26 April 1803	
Love laughs at Locksmiths (G. Colman)	LT	25 July 1803	[270, 274]
Cinderella (Mr. James)	DL	8 Jan. 1804	[276]
Counterfeit (Franklin)	DL	13 Mar. 1804	
Hunter of the Alps (Dimond)	LT	3 July 1804	[281–2]
Gay Deceivers (G. Colman)	LT	22 Aug. 1804	[282]
Blind Bargain (Reynolds)	CG	24 Oct. 1804	
The Land we live in (Holt)	DL	29 Dec. 1804	
Honcy Moon (Tobin)	DL	31 Jan. 1805	[283]
Prior Claim (Pye and Arnold)	DL	29 Oct. 1805	
Youth, Love, & Folly (Dimond)	DL	23 May 1805	[285]
We fly by Night (G. Colman)	CG	28 Jan. 1806	[284–5]
Forty Thieves (Ward)	DL	8 April 1806	[288]
Adrian and Orrila (Dimond)	CG	15 Nov. 1806	[288]
Young Hussar (Dimond)	DL	12 Mar. 1807	[292]
Town and Country (Morton)	CG	10 Mar. 1807	
Wood Dæmon (M. G. Lewis)	DL	1 April 1807	[244, 292, 318]
House of Morville (Lake)	DL	23 April 1807	
Adelgitha (M. G. Lewis)	DL	30 April 1807	[244]
Time's a Tell Tale (H. Siddons)	DL	27 Oct. 1807	
Jew of Mogadore (Cumberland)	DL	3 May 1808	[301]
Africans (G. Colman)	LT	29 July 1808	
Venoni (M. G. Lewis)	DL	1 Dec. 1808	[244, 307]
Foundling of the Forest (Dimond)	LT	9 July 1809	
[Britain's] Jubilee (Arnold)	Ly	25 Oct. 1809	[311]
Gustavus Vasa (Dimond)	CG	26 Nov. 1810	[315]
Ballet [Asiatic Divertissement?] (Des Hayes)	KT	1810	[317]
Peasant Boy (Dimond)	Ly	31 Jan. 1811	[317]
Royal Oak (Dimond)	LT	10 June 1811	[317–8]
One o'Clock (M. G. Lewis)	[Ly]	1 Aug. 1811	[244, 318]
Absent Apothecary (Horace Smith)	DL	10 Feb. 1813	
Russians (T. Sheridan)	DL	13 May 1813	
Polly; or, the Sequel to Beggars' Opera [John Gay]	DL	16 June 1813	[322]
Illusion (Arnold)	DL	25 Nov. 1813	[321]
Pantomime [Harlequin Harper] (C. Dibdin)	DL	26 Dec. 1813	
Remorse (Coleridge)	DL	23 Jan. 1814	[322]
Unknown Guest (Arnold)	DL	29 Mar. 1815	[335]
Conquest of Taranto (Dimond)	CG	[15 April] 1817	
Bride of Abydos (Dimond) [from Byron]	DL	5 Feb. 1818	[346]

Abudah (Planché)	DL	13 April 1819	[346]
Lady and the Devil (Dimond)	DL	3 May 1820	[346]

With a numerous list of Italian, English, and French single Songs, Ducts, and Trios.

I have been, with little intermission, stage-manager of the King's Theatre, in the Haymarket, nearly thirty years at which establishment also, I have performed as principal tenor singer, both in the serious and comic operas. The regular emolument for my labours, (and be it known to all, that to manage an Italian Opera is a most laborious task) has been, the use of the house, and the performers belonging to it, for my annual benefit; defraying myself, however, every other expense belonging to the performance of the night. Through all the changes of different proprietorships and lessees, this privilege has been invariably granted me, as a reward for long service.

When I withdrew from Drury Lane Theatre, as a performer, I commuted a very large claim upon the property, for a small annuity.—This agreement has been sanctioned, and punctually fulfilled, by all the noblemen and gentlemen who have subsequently formed the various committees of management; and, since the termination of their authority, has been discharged with equal honour and scrupulousness of attention, by Mr. Elliston, the present lessee; from whom I have uniformly experienced the most friendly,—nay, even brotherly kindness.

There was also a privilege granted me, that upon my benefit at the Opera House, any performers attached to the Drury Lane establishment, and not employed there upon the same night, should be available assistants in whatever English drama I might select for representation. It is a proud gratification to me, to add, that in my brothers and sisters of the sock and buskin, I have always found the most cheerful alacrity upon this occasion. Neither must I omit to observe, that upon many emergencies, the proprietors of the Theatre Royal Covent Garden, (although upon that establishment I have no claim whatever,) have, in the most liberal manner, spontaneously obliged me with any assistance within their power to furnish.

The gout has, of late years, almost deprived me of loco-motion. Both my parents were sufferers from the same disorder,—in me, therefore, it is constitutional, and not my age's penance for my youth's excess;—for in that season, I may say, with Old Adam, in 'As you Like it',—'I never did apply hot and rebellious liquors to my blood.'—'Tis an ancient adage, that the gout grants to its possessor a long lease of life—if it be so, I am sure the lease is held at a *rack-rent*. Upon the whole, however, although *non sum qualis eram,* I may yet say, that my general health is good, and my spirits never better—shall I then complain of my lot? Forbid it, Heaven! —In spite of all the inflictions of my hereditary scourge, I bow my head submissively, and acknowledge, with an humble, yet cheerful thankfulness, that the hand of Providence hath touched me tenderly.

One superior solace, under my worst visitations, I have indeed possessed, which yet remains untold. With some, perhaps, an avowal of it may draw upon me an imputation of pride or vanity; but, if I know myself, gratitude is paramount with me to either of those passions; and all liberal spirits, I trust, will excuse the apparent boast. Let me therefore declare, without equivocation or disguise, that the chief and dearest comfort remaining to me in this life, is the proud consciousness, that I am honoured by the patronage of my beloved Monarch. Even from my earliest arrival in these realms, where George the Fourth now reigns in peace and glory, it was my enviable fortune to be distinguished by the Royal Favour; and the humble individual, who, in 1787, was noticed by the Prince of Wales, is still remembered in 1825 by THE KING!

I cannot here refrain from mentioning a circumstance which occurred to me on the 1st of January, 1822; and I sincerely trust there will not appear any impropriety in my doing so, since it records a trait of gracious goodness and consideration in His Majesty, which, although but one of hundreds, is but little known, and richly deserves to be universally so.

On that evening, the King gave a splendid party at the Pavilion; and His Majesty was graciously pleased to command my attendance to hear a concert performed by his own fine band. His Majesty did me the honour to seat himself beside me, and ask me how I liked the music which I had that day heard in the chapel, amongst which, to my surprise, had been introduced the Chacoone of Jomelli, performed in the 'Castle Spectre', but which since has been called the Sanctus of Jomelli, and is now used in all the cathedrals and churches in England and the Continent, under that title. His Majesty was all kindness and condescension in his manner towards me; but his kindness and condescension did not stop there.

I had taken with me to Brighton that year a god-daughter of mine, Julia Walters, whom I have adopted, and whose mother has been, for years, my housekeeper and watchful attendant during my many severe illnesses. This little girl, at five years old, performed the part of the Child, in the opera of 'L'Agnese', under the name of Signora Julia.

Ambrogetti was so struck with my little *protégée,* that he begged I would let her play the character, which she did with grace and intelligence far beyond her years. This child asked me to procure her a sight of the King, and fixed upon the evening in question to press her request, when she might behold him in the midst of his Court, surrounded by all that was brilliant in the land, and in a palace whose splendour, when illuminated, rivalled the magnificence described in the 'Arabian Nights.'

I told my worthy friend Cramer, the excellent master and leader of His Majesty's private band, the earnest desire of little Julia, and prevailed upon him to admit her behind the organ, with a strict injunction not to let herself be seen; but female curiosity, even in one so young, prevailed; and after the first act of the concert, when the performers retired to take some refreshment, *Signora* Julia crept from her hiding place behind the organ, and seated herself between the kettle drums. The King was sitting on a sofa, between the Princess Esterhazy and the Countess Lieven, and though the orchestra was at a distance, His Majesty's quick eye in a moment caught a glimpse of the little intruder.

'Who is that beautiful little child?' said the King; 'Who brought her here?' and immediately walked to poor Julia, and asked her who she was.

'I belong to *K*,' said Julia.

'And who the deuce is *K*?' said His Majesty.

I was seated quite at the farther end of the room, conversing with Sir William Keppell; and the moment I saw what was going on, I requested Sir William to go to the King, and say that the child belonged to me, which he with great good-nature did.

His Majesty kissed poor little Julia; and taking her into his arms, threw her over his shoulder, and carried her across the room to me, and placed her in a chair by my side, saying, with the greatest condescension, 'Why did you leave the child in the cold? Why not bring her into the room? If she be fond of music, bring her here whenever you like.'

This act of kindness, consideration, and goodness, was duly appreciated by all who witnessed it, and by me will be ever remembered with the most respectful gratitude. On the following evening, when I again had the honour of a command to the palace, His Majesty was pleased to inquire after my pretty little girl.

My friend, Prince Hoare, who was at Brighton at the time, wrote the following lines on the incident:—

ON JULIA, PEEPING

In the music room of the Pavilion, at Brighton, on the 1st January, 1822, and discovered in the fact by His Most Gracious Majesty George the Fourth; who, with his never-failing kindness of heart, and condescension, seized the little culprit in his arms, kissed and caressed her, and bore her in triumph, before the brilliant assembly, to her nearest and dearest friend, Michael Kelly, then present.

Behind the lofty organ's screen,
One gala eve, sly Julia lay,
Intent to peep, at whiles, unseen,
And all the glorious pomp survey.

O, little didst thou dream *that* eye
Which wakes to guard Britania's crown,
Would there thy tiny form espy,
And give thee, Julia, to renown.

For many seasons past, upon my annual night, I have been regularly honoured with a munificent donation from my Sovereign; but, valuable to me as is that bounty in itself, the gift has scarcely been so gratifying to the feelings of his dutiful servant, as the manner of *presenting it*.

A delicacy, which anticipated wishes—
A generosity, which exceeded hopes.

Were I to indulge my feelings, I should be diffuse upon this subject; but I check myself, lest I should offend in a quarter where displeasure would afflict me most.

I therefore shall merely venture to add, that whenever my malady casts me upon a bed of suffering, I do not forget, that the most august hand in the Empire has condescended to place round it additional comforts; and that no sooner does my relenting star restore me to society, than my benefactor's name blesses the first glass I carry to my lips; and I say and sing, with heart and voice, devoutly and gratefully,

'God save the King!'

Explanatory Notes

Page 2. *Galupi:* Dibdin's *Lionel and Clarissa* (Covent Garden 1768) includes music borrowed from other composers, but the only item by Galuppi that Lionel sings is the final love duet—which in the 1770 revision for Drury Lane (often called *The School for Fathers*) Dibdin replaced with a duet by himself.

3. *'Shepherds, I have lost my love':* a 'Scotch Song' by George Ogle, also known as 'The Banks of Banna'. It is in George Thomson's first *Select Collection* of national songs (1793) arranged by Pleyel. Cf. *Poems and Songs of Robert Burns*, ed. J. Kinsley, 1968, iii. 1347.

4. *Fischer's minuet:* the finale theme from one of his oboe concertos; Mozart wrote piano variations on it. Fischer married Gainsborough's daughter.

5. *'The Soldier tired':* Mandane's very difficult aria at the end of Arne's *Artaxerxes*; for many years it was a popular display piece at concerts. Joan Sutherland has recorded it.

6. *'Fuggiam da questo'*, etc.: *recte* 'Fuggiam dove secura in dolce liberta', from Rauzzini's *Piramo e Tisbe* (1775). *The Duenna* was a very popular pastiche opera with a splendid libretto by Sheridan and new music (about a third of the whole) mainly by the younger Thomas Linley, who also arranged the five Scotch Songs. His father wrote some items.

7. (1) *falsetto:* Until Kelly's arrival, all playhouse tenors and baritones sang their high notes falsetto. 'The Charge is prepared' (Air 57 in *The Beggar's Opera*) has several high As; all the second half must have been sung falsetto.

(2) *opera: The Artifice* (1780), an unsuccessful afterpiece.

8. (1) *buffo:* a mistake for buffa.

(2) *La Buona Figliuola:* in fact this opera was first given in Dublin on 17 May 1777, seven months before *La Frascatana*; according to *Faulkner's Dublin Journal*, Kelly played Armedoro in it, 'being his first appearance on any stage'. Signor Savoi was not in Dublin this season; perhaps his illness kept him in London.

10. (1) *not fifteen:* Kelly was almost certainly nearly sixteen and a half.

(2) *The opera was cast thus:* In this footnote Kelly gives a cast that more or less accords with the production first seen on 7 June 1777, in which he is known to have sung Lionel, and it was in this season too that he sang in Michael Arne's *Cymon*. But there were no such productions in 1779 shortly before Kelly sailed

for Italy, and no evidence that he sang in anything at this time. His statement that his voice had not yet broken itself makes 1777 a much more probable date.

Page 14. *'Water parted from the sea':* a deservedly popular song from Arne's *Artaxerxes*. Tenducci had sung it in the original production of 1762.

16. *calashes:* see Kelly's note on p. 21.

17. *poison:* Pergolesi died of consumption, aged twenty-six.

18. *Posilipo:* the volcanic mountain promontory a mile west of Naples. (In 1839 W. S. Gilbert, aged two, was kidnapped there by brigands and ransomed for £25.) At Agnano Terme, on the west side of the promontory, is the Grotta del Cane, the floor of which is covered by carbon dioxide to a depth of two feet; guides no longer demonstrate the effect on dogs.

19. *Mas[s]aniello:* assassinated in 1647 when only twenty-four; Auber was among those who wrote an opera about him.

20. *Gregory:* modern texts show this as said by Samson (*Romeo and Juliet*, I. i), with minor differences. Kelly hardly ever quotes Shakespeare correctly; in the next paragraph but one, 'horses' should be 'horse'. The quotation from Dekker via Malone has several unimportant mistakes; according to Malone it comes from *The Dead Term* (1608).

22. *swore . . . never to become an inmate of it:* In his *Music, Men and Manners in France and Italy* Burney describes how he was astonished by a similar Babel of sound at the S. Onofrio conservatoire on 31 October 1770. Twelve days earlier he had been unimpressed by 'the scholars' of the conservatoire to which Kelly is objecting, 'Santa Maria di Loreto'; he reveals that the obligatory costume (see next paragraph) consisted of 'a white uniform with a black kind of sash'.

26. (1) *'By him we love offended':* hardly an English song (see p. 6). 'Ho sparso tante lagrime' is a canzonetta by Millico (see p. 14).

(2) *Caserta:* a magnificent palace twenty miles inland from Naples; it had been completed in 1774.

27. *Pallone:* Italian version of pelota. The players strike a large ball with a wooden guard worn over hand and wrist.

32. *Piazza di Spagna:* The British consul still has his office there; Keats died there.

33. *piano-forte:* Kelly must mean harpsichord; the change-over can hardly have been earlier than the 1790s anywhere. But information on this subject is surprisingly hard to come by.

35. *the first Italian opera I had ever seen in Dublin:* But long before *La*

Frascatana (December 1777) Kelly must have seen *L'isola d'Alcina* (see p. 8); also he had himself sung in *La buona figliuola*.

Page 38. *four days' journey:* Yet on p. 32 Kelly claims that in a single day he got as far as Terracina, twenty miles further up the coast than Gaeta.

39. (1) *Mr Haydon:* father of the artist, Benjamin Robert Haydon, who gives some interesting information about the Cobley family at the beginning of his autobiography.

(2) *polacre:* a three-masted Mediterranean vessel.

41. *Sarti:* I cannot trace that he ever set this Metastasio libretto. Perhaps Kelly was confused by his *Alessandro e Timateo,* which was not yet written, and meant Piccinni's *Alessandro nell' Indie* (Naples 1774). There were earlier settings by Paisiello, Sacchini, Traetta etc.

42. *Prince B——:* presumably Prince Palagonia, whose extraordinary villa at Bagheria is now a tourist attraction.

43. *Dionysius' Ear:* a cavern near Syracuse with remarkable acoustic properties; the name was invented by Caravaggio and has no historical significance. Acis was transformed into a stream on the slopes of Mount Etna.

46. *the French play: Nicomède* by Corneille: the quotation comes from II. iii. It is surprising that Kelly should have known the play, less so that he should have mis-spelt the title-role. As elsewhere he prints poetry as though it were prose.

48. (1) *capote:* a long cloak with a hood.

(2) *their real name wanted the* t: Yet their father was calling himself Stephen Storace in Dublin at least as early as 1748; there is no evidence that he was ever Sorace, or indeed that there is such a name. Nancy was sixteen, not fifteen, when Kelly met her.

49. *voletta: recte* volata, a rapid 'flying' run. As might be expected, 'bomba' means bomb.

51. *The Battle of the Bridge:* Il Giuoco del Ponte, held on 28 June; this helps to date Kelly's movements.

53. *Della Cruscan:* one of a group of English writers in Florence who took their name from the Accademia nella Crusca; Robert Merry was their leader. They wrote rather insipid verses and supported the French Revolution.

54. *Thomas Linley:* the eldest son of the Thomas Linley who later engaged Kelly for Drury Lane. He was a composer of outstanding promise, but in 1778 he was drowned when only twenty-two in a boating accident on a Lincolnshire lake.

56. *wife:* this word was a last-minute correction in the second

edition which, like the first, had described the Princess as the Pretender's natural daughter.

Page 59. (1) '*Varca il fiume*', etc.: 'Cross the river, go past the hill, and you'll have Siena in front of you.'

(2) *vetturino:* coachman.

64. *Pietà:* Vivaldi had taught for many years at the Ospedale della Pietà; he wrote most of his concertos for the girls there.

66. *La Giudica: recte* La Giudecca, the island immediately south of the fashionable part of Venice.

69. '*Non v'è nessun maggiore dolore*', etc.: more correctly—

Nessun maggior dolore
che ricordarsi del tempo felice
ne la miseria . . . (*Inferno*, v. 121–3)

Francesca is talking to Dante: 'No greater grief than to remember days / Of joy, when Mis'ry is at hand!' (Carey's translation).

70. '*Teco resti, anima mia*': from Sarti's *Demofoonte*. In Domenico Corri's *Select Collection*, vol. i (Edinburgh *c.* 1779) it is given as 'Sung by Sigr. Aprile', who no doubt had taught it to Kelly.

71. '*Could Nature's beauties*', etc.: misquoting *The Traveller*, 111–12.

73. *Gil Blas:* a novel (1715) by Le Sage; Gil Blas is the archetypal hero of the picaresque novel.

75. (1) *As Prior says:* I have not traced this couplet. The following complete poem by Prior is similar in meaning but would have seemed unprintable in Kelly's day:

What trifling coil do we poor mortals keep:
Wake, eat, and drink, evacuate, and sleep.

(2) '*What signify me hear . . .*': *The Padlock* (1768), an operatic afterpiece that merits revival, had words by Bickerstaffe and music by Dibdin. Mungo, the coloured servant, was intended for Moody (just back from the West Indies—see p. 199), but Dibdin wanted the part for himself and got it by making the songs too hard for Moody; he was a big success in it. Mungo's 'coon' English was a novelty at the time.

76. *handsomest man of his kind:* i.e. the handsomest castrato.

82. '*Didone abbandonata*': This Metastasio libretto was set by many composers; Kelly probably saw the version by Traetta.

88. (1) *The tomb of Juliet:* still shown to gullible tourists today.

(2) *chasse:* liqueur.

90. *The most miserable of her existence:* because she was being cruelly treated by her second husband; see p. 266.

95. *Madame Storace:* If the chronology on p. xvii is correct, this was

Kelly's second winter in Venice (1783–4) by which time Nancy Storace was in Vienna. The next six paragraphs should have come between pp. 76 and 80 because they must be about the previous winter.

Page 97. *French company:* Vienna had had French companies at least since the 1750s; French 'dialogue' operas had been popular, especially those written for Vienna by Gluck. The hiatus in Italian opera seasons that Kelly mentions had made possible the production in 1782 of Mozart's German 'dialogue' opera, *Die Entführung aus dem Serail*, usually known as *Il Seraglio*.

98. *Madame Storace was also engaged:* She, Benucci and Mandini were all engaged in the summer of 1783, Kelly (I suggest) not until the summer of 1784. The reasons for so thinking are:

(a) The *General Magazine* (1788) says he spent five years in Italy.
(b) His own account seems to support this (see Chronology).
(c) I can find no evidence of his singing in Vienna's 1783–4 operas.
(d) The *General Magazine* says that 'in a very little time after his arrival he performed the part of Cassario' in *Il re Teodoro*—which was first given in August 1784 (see p. 122–3).

100. *Faubourgs:* suburbs.

104. *Princess Lichtenstein*, etc.: Beethoven, who spelt their names better than Kelly, later dedicated early works to all these families—his Piano Sonata Op.27/1 to Princess Josepha von Liechtenstein, the Piano and Wind Quintet Op.16 to Princess Schwarzenberg's husband, the Op.18 String Quartets to Princess Lobkowitz's son, and the Op.11 Clarinet Trio to the Countess Thun.

108. *Langé:* Joseph Lange married the singer Aloysia Weber, whose sister married Mozart (who had earlier wanted to marry Aloysia).

109. (1) *Stephani:* The younger brother, Gottlieb Stephanie, had written the libretto of Mozart's *Die Entführung aus dem Serail*.

(2) '*Widow of Malabar*': Lemierre's tragedy *La Veuve de Malabar* was staged in London in the 1790s under the title Kelly gives.

(3) *Monologue:* compositions for speaker and orchestra were more usually called melodramas.

110. (1) *Madame Ademberger:* Her husband, Valentin Ademberger, had been Belmonte in *Die Entführung aus dem Serail.* Mrs Jordan made her London début (Drury Lane, 18 October 1785) in a long-popular bowdlerized version of Wycherley's *The Country Wife*.

(2) *Fantoccini:* marionettes.

Page 111. (1) *Italian poet:* he wrote librettos for the resident Italian composer to set as operas.

(2) *'Tally ho!':* a song by Thomas Carter.

113. *'Grazie agl'inganni tuoi':* see Introduction, pp. x–xi.

116. (1) *I compare a good melodist to a fine racer:* Kelly had personal reasons for immortalizing a remark Mozart cannot have meant literally, as had Sir Walter Scott for fastening so gleefully on it in his review of Kelly. See p. 95 where the same rather improbable opinion is attributed to Haydn.

(2) *Mozart's favourite scholar:* Attwood's exercises are in the British Museum, with Mozart's comments and improvements scribbled on them.

(3) *Sprone: recte* Sperone (spur).

118. *for better for worse:* Nancy's marriage must have been in the autumn of 1783, very soon after her arrival in Vienna, for Mozart, working in December on his never-finished opera *Lo sposo deluso*, described the heroine's role as for 'Signora Fischer'.

119. *first visit to the theatre:* Storace's new opera, *Gli sposi malcontenti*, was not produced until 1 June 1785; the date in the preceding paragraph must be one year out.

120. *Both the songs sung by me in the Pirates:* Kelly's memory is at fault; his songs came from *Gli sposi malcontenti*, not *Gli equivoci.* Covent Garden's *Comedy of Errors* (1819) was a 'dialogue' opera with very simple music mainly by Bishop.

122. (1) *'Il Re Teodoro':* Paisiello's opera was first performed on 23 August 1784; Kelly probably made his Viennese début in it. This paragraph should have come much earlier; throughout this Viennese section the order of events is far from chronological.

(2) *Haydn, Dittersdorf, Vanhall, Mozart:* all four players had published string quartets of their own. Dittersdorf's comic opera, *Doktor und Apotheker* (Vienna, July 1786) was in its day as successful as *Figaro;* the Storaces took a copy of it back to London.

125. (1) *palace at Luxemburgh: recte* Laxenburg, just south of Vienna near Mödling.

(2) *Airone:* heron.

127. *Walking Stewart:* an eccentric Scot who had on principle refused all lessons at his schools (which included Harrow and Charterhouse). After melodramatic adventures in India—he had been Prime Minister to the Nabob of Arcot—he had, before meeting Kelly, walked across Arabia and in Ethiopia.

Page 128. (1) *Monsieur Martini: recte* Martinez. Metastasio had come to Vienna as Court Poet in 1730, and he lived with the Martinez family until his death in 1782, fifty-two years in all. Martinez had a daughter, Marianne, who composed oratorios and concertos; Mozart is more likely to have played duets with her than with her aunt.

(2) *high notes:* Aloysia Lange was the first Constanze, and Mozart took her up to high D, which was no higher than Storace took Kelly's friend, Mrs Crouch.

129. *a full-length picture of Handel:* No doubt Gluck acquired this in 1745–6 when he was working in London at the King's Theatre in the Haymarket.

132. *the first act:* Kelly remembered *Figaro* as being in two acts, but it is in four. Thus he means the Act 2 finale and the Act 3 sextet (and see p. 195). It is strange that Kelly should make so much of the tiny part of the 'Stuttering Judge' (in fact only a lawyer) and never mention Don Basilio, a much meatier part which he also sang. Though Kelly writes about *Figaro* after he has discussed *Gli equivoci*, it was in fact produced seven months before Storace's opera; Storace was much influenced by *Figaro*.

133. *the spring of 1787:* Kelly was not in Vienna this spring; he left early in February (see p. 140).

134. *from England:* to compose and supervise the production of *Gli equivoci*.

135. *Milesian:* Irish; from Milesius, a Spanish king alleged to have conquered Ireland about 1300 BC.

140. '*Non anderà . . . cuccitta*': 'It will not always be like this, as the little dog said, turning the roast [on the spit]; the joint will be cooked in the end'.

141. *I . . . delivered his son's letter:* Not so. On 4 April Mozart wrote to his father: 'I am very much annoyed that owing to the stupidity of Madame Storace my letter never reached you.' His father had reported that they passed through Salzburg with unprecedented quantities of luggage.

142. '*Non so d'onde viene*': a superb and very long aria by J. C. Bach, written in Italy before he came to London. Mozart was so entranced by it that he composed decorations for the vocal line. 'Voce de petto': chest notes.

144. *Caferelli*, etc.: Kelly is recalling the past. None of these notables was still in Stuttgart when he passed through it; Jomelli and Hasse were no longer alive.

145. '*Mon bon André*': from Grétry's *L'Épreuve villageoise* (1784).

Storace introduced this song, reharmonized, into *No Song, No Supper;* he had probably seen only the melody line, bought in Strasbourg.

Page 146. *the first representation:* Kelly cannot have seen the first performance, which was on 1 February 1787. The opera *Phèdre*, based on Racine, was by Le Moyne.

147. (1) '*L'univers que j'ai perdu': recte* 'Si l'univers entier m'oublie'.

(2) '*The Fair American':* It was because of this opera that Pilon was abroad. Composers usually got their share of the proceeds from the librettist, but when *The Fair American* failed (1782), Pilon never paid Thomas Carter, and fled to France when Carter sued him.

149. *the Venus of Apelles:* Apelles was a Greek painter employed by Alexander the Great. Nothing of his survives, but in Kelly's day a nude Venus in marble, cut off at the knees, was thought to be based on one of his paintings. It is now in Philadelphia.

151. *facetious:* amusing, without any derogatory undertones.

153. '*Sing ye to the Lord':* from the end of Handel's *Israel in Egypt.*

154. (1) '*Let there be light':* Kelly was probably thinking of a much later occasion, the first London performance of Haydn's *The Creation* (1801), though the words there are slightly different: 'Let there be light, and there was light'.

(2) *12th of June:* there are several small mistakes in what follows. According to Dublin newspapers, Kelly and Mrs Crouch arrived in Dublin on 10 June, and first sang in *Lionel and Clarissa* on 16 June; they seem to have been engaged for six performances, not twelve, and the *Comus* production belongs to their Dublin trip of 1789, not 1787.

155. (1) '*Pace, cara mia sposa':* from *Una cosa rara* by the Spanish composer Martin y Soler, known in Central Europe and London as Martini. Kelly and Nancy Storace had sung in the first performance (Vienna, 17 November 1786).

(2) *Clontarf*, etc.: All these places are on Dublin Bay except for the Dargle and Bray which are a little further south. The Dargle is the river that flows through the Powerscourt estate; the grounds, spectacularly beautiful and open to the public, still look Sicilian.

157. '*Selima and Azor':* Perrault's story is known in Britain as 'Beauty and the Beast'; all the music of the English version was by Thomas Linley senior.

160. '*The Doctor and the Apothecary':* an afterpiece version of Dittersdorf's very long comic opera. Very little of the original

music was kept; about half the score was by Storace. The song Kelly names was borrowed from a Paisiello opera. It had no orchestral introduction; hence the difficulty of starting it when the preceding dialogue was spoken instead of sung in recitative.

Page 161. (1) '*Che sarà, sarà*': What will be, will be.

(2) *The oratorios:* On Fridays in Lent plays were forbidden at the two playhouses, and oratorios were performed instead.

162. '*The Mariners*', '*The Adopted Child*', '*The Smugglers*': All these afterpiece operas had music by Attwood, who included in each score a song from an opera by his master Mozart. The music of 'The Mulberry Tree' had been composed by Dibdin for Garrick's Shakespeare Jubilee at Stratford in 1769.

163. (1) *In the summer of 1788 . . . Birmingham:* Kelly is inadvertently repeating information given on p. 160.

(2) *Purcell:* The music for *The Tempest*, performed for over two centuries as Purcell's, is now thought to be by John Weldon and to date from 1712.

(3) *the 'Haunted Tower':* Kelly has got on to this much too soon; he has yet to describe his activities in the summer of 1789.

164. (1) '*Jephtha's rash vow*': these words do not occur in Handel's oratorio. Kelly may mean the Act 2 recitative and aria 'Open thy marble jaws, o tomb', which Jephtha sings when he realizes the appalling result of his vow. Handel's *L'Allegro* is a secular oratorio based on Milton. Later in 'Haste thee, Nymph', Handel set the words 'Laughter holding both his sides' as though inviting the sort of interpretation that Kelly says he introduced as a novelty.

(2) '*Oft on a plat of rising ground*', etc.: These three songs come respectively from Handel's *L'Allegro*, his opera *Sosarme* (with religious words substituted for the original ones), and his Chandos Anthem No. 9.

165. '*The Haunted Tower*', *in Dublin:* Kelly must mean Storace's adaptation of Dittersdorf's *Doktor und Apotheker;* he has already shown that the first performance anywhere of *The Haunted Tower* was not until the following November.

166. *Joseph Surface:* Palmer had been the original Joseph Surface in Sheridan's *The School for Scandal.*

168. *Macheath, for the first time:* In fact he had played it in Dublin on 23 June 1787—a performance he perhaps preferred to forget, for he had been ridiculed by the critics for his pronunciation.

169. (1) '*No Song, no Supper*': the first performance was on 16 April 1790;

this paragraph should have come later, as should the one below about Edwin's death, which was also in 1790.

(2) *burletta:* an all-sung burlesque of the masque about classical deities; much the most popular example was Kane O'Hara's *Midas*.

Page 170. (1) *'Lord, what is man':* a Sacred Song by Purcell.

(2) *'Total Eclipse':* Sung by Samson when blind in Handel's oratorio of that name.

(3) *'I travelled India's barren sands': recte* 'I travers'd Judah's barren sand', sung by Angelina (not Angelica) in Shield's *Robin Hood.* 'How sweet in the woodlands' was a popular part-song by Henry Harrington, a Bath doctor, which Shield borrowed for *Robin Hood*, where it has different words.

171. *St Peter's:* a village as well as a church, not in Margate but at the back of Broadstairs.

174. *Creole:* a European brought up in the West Indies; in Kelly's day the word carried no implications as regards colour.

178. (1) *Royalty Theatre:* In 1787 Palmer built this theatre near the Tower of London thinking it would not there infringe the playhouses' monopoly, but they went to law and he found himself restricted to short all-sung operas, ballets, and songs. Being no singer, he was pushed into miming such characters as Don Juan, and thus he inadvertently helped to develop *ballet d'action* in London. By 1790 he was back at Drury Lane.

(2) *La Caravane:* For some reason *The Caravan* was never produced at Drury Lane.

(3) *not successful:* Covent Garden's pantomime, *Blue Beard*, was not performed until 21 December 1791; the music, some of it presumably Grétry's, was arranged and added to by Baumgarten, who led the theatre orchestra, but none of it was published.

179. *Pantheon:* see note on p. 243.

180. *Salieri:* None of the music was by Salieri. Most of it was by Storace, as is shown by the attributions in the Song Words published in time for the first night. The music does not survive.

181. *On the first night, I went behind the scenes:* He cannot have done; on 25 June Kelly was in Paris (see p. 189).

182. *'He gave them hailstones for rain':* from Handel's *Israel in Egypt*.

183. *'The Soldier tired of War's alarms':* see note to p. 5.

188. (1) *'See [look] you mock him not':* Hamlet to the First Player about Polonius.

(2) *Cymon:* a Garrick 'spectacular' about knights in armour. Much of the original music by Michael Arne was kept. Storace

composed seven new items and harmonized a tune by Kelly. Thomas Shaw, the leader of the orchestra, composed the overture and one aria, and of the new music only his was published.

(3) *Mr and Mrs Crouch separated:* in the autumn of 1791, according to M. J. Young.

Page 189. *In the summer of 1792:* a mistake for 1791; in June of that year the King and Queen of France escaped and were recaptured at Varennes, and on 6–8 July of that year the Oxford Festival took place. From here to p. 194 should have come earlier.

190. *Governor Wall:* a hot-tempered Irishman who, to escape his embarrassments, accepted the post of Governor of Senegal (1779). Because he flogged a man to death, he was brought to England and court-martialled. He escaped to France but was eventually caught and executed.

193. *the festival week:* This was the Oxford Festival during which Haydn was made a Doctor of Music and his 'Oxford' Symphony (No. 92) performed for the first time in England.

196. *L'Abune*, etc.: Kelly's spelling conceals the following dancers: the two Labories (husband and wife); Nivelon; Hilligsberg; and Millard (who played Iphigénia and Clytemnestra). The latter's father, often known in London as Miller, assembled the music of this ballet. James d'Egville was among the few successful English ballet dancers of the time; he later started a dancing academy.

197. *'The Prize; or, 2, 5, 3, 8':* an afterpiece opera about a lottery ticket; hence the subtitle.

200. *February:* If Kelly was in London by 3 February (see p. 207) he must have left Dublin in January.

201. *the tales of Hope flattering:* a reference to the Paisiello duet popular in Britain as 'Hope told a flattering tale' (see p. 263).

204. *Dicky Gossip:* the garrulous barber-dentist-undertaker in Prince Hoare's afterpiece *My Grandmother* (the music by Storace). It was 'Dicky' Suett's most popular role, and there is a good portrait of him in it at the Ashmolean Museum, Oxford.

207. *Prince Hoare:* and all composed by Storace; three afterpieces in one programme was very unusual.

208. *Macbeth:* Until the 1870s *Macbeth* was always staged with spurious masques for the witches. The music was not published until 1780; and it then occasioned a century of discussion as to whether it was by Locke or Purcell. Once it was found to be by neither, it ceased to be admired or performed. In fact it was

composed by Leveridge in 1702. The earlier *Macbeth* music by Locke survives only in fragments.

Page 209. *I was in Paris:* If so he must have returned immediately after the Oxford Festival (see p. 193) for Cherubini's *Lodoiska* was first performed on 18 July 1791 and Kreutzer's a fortnight later. But two trips in one summer seem out of the question. Perhaps Kelly saw these operas in the summer of 1792. He claims a visit that year (p. 189), and it is a more likely year for his cloak-and-dagger escape (pp. 191–2). Also it was surely Kelly who brought back the libretto of *Lodoiska* for Kemble to translate, and the two scores from each of which Storace borrowed a few pieces.

210. (1) *The overture to 'Lodoiska':* the one played in London was by Kreutzer, later the recipient of a famous Beethoven dedication. Its solemn D minor introduction led to a spate of similar introductions in English opera overtures.

(2) *Tom Welsh:* often called Walsh. He was discovered by Linley in the Wells Cathedral choir, and became the most remarkable boy soprano of the century. He was the hero of Attwood's afterpiece *The Adopted Child,* and virtually the hero of Storace's full-length *Cherokee* (see p. 215). 'Angels ever bright and fair' comes from Handel's *Theodora.*

(3) *a grand sea-fight:* The stage hands told Sheridan that they could not possibly make model ships capable of firing at each other in three days; he said that they could, and they did. Yet he had ridiculed such sea-fights in *The Critic.*

212. *Natali Corri:* his brother Domenico had started publishing music in Edinburgh about 1777. Natale was nearly twenty years younger. About 1794 he took over the business in Edinburgh, which had not been doing well, and Domenico moved to London where he went into partnership with Dussek who married his daughter, Sophia. A useful soprano, she was perhaps the 'sister' Kelly mentions. Natale Corri and Schetky (Kelly's 'Cecchi') set some of the lyrics in Scott's *Lady of the Lake* in the year of its publication, 1810.

213. *Lake:* He owned nearly all the west bank of Derwentwater and had just built his substantial 'cottage', Water End (now Derwent Bay). Kelly and Mrs Crouch cannot really have travelled from Keswick to Lancaster via York.

214. *Miss Snow:* the daughter of Handel's trumpeter, Valentine Snow. As Mrs Baddeley she sang with acclaim in several Dibdin operas.

215. (1) *'A little bird sang on a spray':* Because Mrs Bland, representing a

Welsh girl, sang this charming song with the appropriate accent, it was mistaken for a Welsh folk-song. It was twice arranged by Beethoven (who, however, called it Scottish in his Op.105/1). In fact it must be by Storace.

(2) *the Circus:* Charles Hughes started his riding school in opposition to Astley's in the early 1770s. In 1782 the Royal Circus was built south of the Thames; it offered riding displays organized by Hughes in alternation with short operas and ballets organized by Dibdin and performed mainly by children. Miss Romanzini can hardly have sung for Hughes in 1773 when she was only four. The Royal Circus was later known as the Surrey Theatre; it was pulled down in 1934.

(3) *a piece of music of Mozart's:* the opera, *Die Entführung aus dem Serail.*

Page 217. *Irish character:* Sir Murdock O'Connel in James Hook's *Jack of Newbury*. It is extraordinary that Hook's son allowed (or asked for?) the suppression of his name as the composer of this opera. James Hook is nowhere mentioned in Kelly's *Reminiscences*.

220. *Mr Braham:* A year later he and Nancy Storace left Drury Lane to tour the continent. Nancy became Braham's mistress and in 1801 she had a son by him; they could not marry because Nancy's husband was still alive. The liaison broke up in 1816. Braham then married and became a respectable family man. Subsequently a desire to keep in with the leading tenor of the day led several writers to under-praise Nancy or even to ignore her. Kelly was so anxious not to appear to support Nancy overmuch in their notorious dispute (though she was much wronged) that he repeats his fulsome praise of Braham on p. 234, and never mentions the dispute at all.

222. *Viotti:* the outstanding violinist and violin-teacher of the day. He had come to London from Paris in 1792, his revolutionary leanings too mild for the extremists who were beginning to take over. At the Salomon concerts when Haydn's 'London' symphonies were first performed Viotti often played one of his own violin concertos, and Dussek one of his own piano concertos.

223. *'Take physic, pomp!': King Lear*, III. iv. 33.

225. '[*To*] *Anacreon in Heaven*'*:* published *c.* 1780 'as sung at the Crown and Anchor Tavern', and probably composed by John Stafford Smith (who also wrote that more famous Anacreontic song, 'The Star-spangled Banner'). The Anacreontic Society was dissolved about 1787.

Page 226. *views of the fortifications:* In 1831 Berlioz was similarly interrogated by the police, who had caught him writing suspicious-looking music out-of-doors near Nice (the *King Lear* overture).

230. *'I do wonder'*, etc.: *The Merchant of Venice*, III. iii. 8.

233. *Sacchini's operas:* Between 1773 and 1781 Sacchini composed as many as seventeen operas for the King's Theatre in the Haymarket; he also taught singing to Nancy Storace and had his portrait painted by Reynolds. Burney thought his operas the very peak of modern musical achievement.

237. *William Linley: recte* Thomas Linley, as Kelly well knew, but the slip passed unnoticed in both editions.

243. (1) *Mr. O'Ryley:* As earlier (pp. 179 and 189) Kelly expects the reader to know something of the complex arrangements made for Italian opera after the King's Theatre was burnt down in 1789. There was little support for Gallini's season at the unglamorous Little Theatre, but people flocked to hear Pacchierotti at the Pantheon, Wyatt's beautiful rotunda in Oxford Street. Encouraged by this, the manager, O'Reilly, attempted full-blown Italian opera there in 1791 though there was no proper stage. He even got Paisiello over to compose. With the support of the King he then disputed Gallini's right to open the rebuilt King's Theatre for Italian opera—and thus prevented Haydn's last opera from being staged. However in 1792 the Pantheon was also burnt down, and there was then no sensible reason for opposing Italian opera at the King's Theatre. O'Reilly's plans for building a rival opera house came to nought.

(2) *Cupid and Psyche: L'Amour et Psiche*, with music by Mazzinghi and choreography by Noverre.

(3) *the beauty of the whole scene:* for another description, see Peacock's *Gryll Grange* (1861) ch. 34. The 'chacoone' consisted of 16 bars hacked out of a sonata-form movement by Jomelli.

250. *Colman's theatre:* the Little Theatre in the Haymarket.

251. *'Reason thus with life'*, etc.: *Measure for Measure*, III. i. 6–8.

252. (1) *'Captive of Spilburg':* Dussek's only opera. His fame rested more on the concertos and sonatas he himself played with such brilliance. Kelly published the vocal score which attributes all the music to Dussek; the plot does not suggest the need for any 'comic' music, and Kelly's contribution may have existed only in his imagination.

(2) *'The Monk':* It was from this famous 'Gothic' novel that 'Monk' Lewis got his nickname. 'Novels are all so full of nonsense and

stuff', Catherine Morland remarks in *Northanger Abbey;* 'there has not been a tolerably decent one come out since Tom Jones, except the Monk.'

Page 253. *the whole of the music:* in fact the overture and entr'actes were by Dussek. They were published in piano arrangement.

256. *Euphrasia:* the courageous heroine in Murphy's *Grecian Daughter;* a Mrs Siddons role.

257. *Mr Swinburne . . . Mr Benfield:* Henry Swinburne's *Travels in the two Sicilies* had been published in 1783–5. Paul Benfield had been attacked in a famous speech by Burke for making excessive profits from his estates in India. He died destitute in 1810.

258. (1) *'The Beggar's Opera Travestied':* There had been a performance or two in the 1730s with the male parts taken by actresses and the female by actors, but this version had no success until the elder Colman staged it at the Little Theatre (8 August 1781). Though he looked absurd, Charles Bannister always sang Polly's songs seriously, in his best style, and such Macheaths as Miss Decamp avoided burlesque entirely, but most of the cast behaved outrageously, notably Edwin as Lucy.

(2) *the tragedy of 'Isabella':* Isabella, one of Mrs Siddons's most admired roles, was the heroine of Southerne's *The Fatal Marriage*, which Garrick had freely revised in 1758.

263. *'Hope told a flattering tale':* a very popular duet taken from 'Nel cor più' in Paisiello's *La molinara.* Beethoven wrote variations on the tune for piano.

266. *'Algonah':* a free revision of Storace's full-length opera, *The Cherokee*—revised because the original boy-hero could not now be cast. Any new music by Kelly can have amounted to only a tiny proportion of the whole.

268. *'The Distressed Mother':* Racine's *Andromaque;* Kelly prefers the title of the translation by Ambrose Philips, first given in London in 1712.

271. (1) *Astley's:* In imitation of the Royal Circus, Astley was by now lacing his riding displays with short all-sung operas, but he was never able to employ composers or singers of the slightest distinction.

(2) *Rameau:* this composer never wrote music for *Athalie;* Kelly probably mis-heard the similar-sounding name Moreau, the man who set the choruses and wrote other music for Racine's play in 1691.

273. *Rousseau was the composer of it:* Though possible, this is very unlikely. O'Hara wrote his words to fit a Comic Tune (i.e. one for

miming) in the popular pantomime, *Queen Mab* (1750). The music of *Queen Mab* was published as by 'the Society of the Temple of Apollo', and it is now known that this was a youthful pseudonym of Burney's. It is not likely that any of Rousseau's music reached England until after he had composed his one real musical success, the opera *Le Devin du village* (1752).

Page 276. (1) *'Ferdinand in Mexico', by Nassolini:* In fact the season opened (December 1802) with Mrs Billington in Nasolini's *Merope e Polifonte*. *Ferdinando in Messico* (March 1803) was by Portogallo.

(2) *'Cinderella':* for the first time in Britain.

278. *'La Virgine del Sole':* Andreozzi composed most of this opera. Mayer contributed the duet Kelly praises and presumably the chorus, 'Quel orror'—words that seem quite unsuited to the charming folk-song, 'Pretty Maud'. This looks more English than Scottish; Arnold, who composed *Peeping Tom of Coventry*, often introduced English folk songs into his operas; his source is not known. Scott, reviewing Kelly in the *Quarterly Review*, describes 'Pretty Maud' as 'an English ballad of the reign of George I on the catastrophe of the celebrated pirate, beginning My Name is Captain Kidd'.

279. (1) *'Il Ratto di Proserpina':* Da Ponte, who wrote the libretto for this opera and *Il trionfo dell'amor fraterno* among others (see p. 285), was the official poet at the King's Theatre in as many as seven seasons between 1794 and 1805, and yet Kelly, who boasts of his friendship in Vienna in the 1780s, never once mentions his activities in London. Perhaps for some reason a coolness had developed between them.

(2) *Cramer:* the first edition had Kramer, which is to be preferred. Christian Kramer, unrelated to the London Cramers, was often in Brighton organizing concerts for the King during Kelly's last years, and from 1829 to his death in 1834 he was Master of the King's Musick.

282. (1) *the author of the piece:* William Dimond.

(2) *Hale: Grove's Dictionary of Music and Musicians* calls him Thomas d'Hèle, and attributes to him the plots of *Le Jugement de Midas* (1778), *Les fausses Apparances, ou L'Amant jaloux* (1778), and *Les Evènemens imprévus* (1779).

284. (1) *the 'Rolliad':* a series of political satires aimed ostensibly at Baron Rolle, an M.P. who supported Pitt. Richard Tickell, Sheridan's brother-in-law, was another prominent contributor.

(2) *'Gentle Shepherd':* a poetic eclogue, semi-dramatic, by Allan Ramsay, the artist's father; in 1729 he revised it for the

Edinburgh stage with the addition of a number of 'Scotch Songs'; he was influenced in this by Gay's *Beggar's Opera.* Thomas Linley wrote more elaborate accompaniments for the songs in 1781, and contrived an overture from music by his recently-dead son.

Page 286. '*Goold from law*', etc.: an outrageous pun on the words of Air 67 in *The Beggar's Opera.*

288. (1) *Wroxton Abbey:* near Banbury, and now open to the public.

(2) '*The Forty Thieves*'*:* the first appearance of Ali Baba on the London stage. Other stories from *The Arabian Nights* had been used in London pantomimes since the 1750s.

290. *The O.P. riot:* Covent Garden was burnt down in 1808. The new theatre cost so much to build that Kemble put up the prices, but for two months in the autumn of 1809 there was constant rioting for a return of the Old Prices (O.P.), and eventually Kemble gave way.

297. *The music in* '*Macbeth*'*:* see note to p. 208.

302. *One Thursday:* Kelly has jumped to the year 1817. Nancy Storace was survived by her old mother who lived on in their Herne Hill villa for a few more years.

306. '*O thou wert born to please me*'*:* see p. 155.

309. *were then consuming:* as also, more regrettably, the scores of all Storace's English operas and a good many by Arne and Dibdin.

314. '*Now are we in Arden*'*: As You Like It,* II. iv. Noodle and Doodle come from Fielding's *Tragedy of Tragedies, or The History of Tom Thumb the Great* (1730), which by Kelly's day was more often performed with music as *The Opera of Operas.*

316. (1) *high life below stairs:* the title of a popular comedy of 1759 by James Townley.

(2) *Waldershare:* four miles from Dover.

317. *a ballet:* presumably *Asiatic Divertissement* (23 March) of which the composer is not known. It was popular, with as many as thirty performances. Kelly prefers not to mention his other King's Theatre ballet, *Myrtil et Amaryllis* (21 March 1807), which had only one performance. It is strange that he also does not mention a ballet by Des Hayes of this same season (1810–11) on the plot of *Figaro,* or the first London productions of Mozart's *Così fan tutte* (May) and *Die Zauberflöte* (June).

322. (1) '*Remorse*'*:* This interesting tragedy enjoyed moderate success for which, in the published preface, Coleridge praised most of the cast by name—though not Kelly or Mrs Bland. (He told his friends that he thought both production and acting execrable).

According to the published text all the music came in III. i, in which Alvar, supposed dead by his father and malevolent brother, pretends to conjure up his own spectre in their presence while disguised as a sorcerer. At the start of this scene Coleridge asks for 'Soft music from an instrument of Glass or Steel', meaning perhaps a glass harmonica such as Mozart had written for; but from the vocal score it looks as though Drury Lane allowed him nothing more imaginative than a behind-the-scenes organ. This background music continues off and on up to the only song ('accompanied by the same instrument as before') which has 'Miserere Domine' as its refrain. After a brief chorus (sung 'off'?) Alvar is seized by the Spanish Inquisition. III. ii. shows 'The Interior of a Chapel', and this must be Kelly's 'convent'. Nowhere is there any mention of boatmen or monks singing 'off', or of an organ. Perhaps with these effects in mind, Coleridge complained bitterly of additions made without his consent. His trip to Malta and Sicily took place before *Remorse* was produced, but there was an earlier version, *Osorio*, rejected by Sheridan in 1797. Can 'different Italian composers' really have written music for this earlier version, as Kelly states? His own is infantile beyond belief.

(2) '*The Rejected Addresses*': Helped by his brother James, Horatio ('Horace') Smith wrote a set of amusing parodies on Byron, Crabbe, Scott, Southey, Wordsworth, etc., which he alleged had been submitted for the celebrations when, after the disastrous fire, Drury Lane was reopened in 1812. He also alleged that they had all been rejected, as in truth had his own genuine submission.

Page 323. *Auber: recte* Aber.

325. *Olympic Theatre:* a rough-and-ready building in the Aldwych area put up by Astley in 1805.

328. (1) '*Je suis Lindor*': one of the two songs in Beaumarchais' comedy, *Le Barbier de Séville*. The tune has been attributed both to Monsigny and to Beaumarchais himself. Piano variations on it were written by many composers, notably Mozart (K354) and Clementi (Sonata Op.12/1).

(2) *Le Fevre: recte* Le Fever, my uncle Toby's soldier-servant in Sterne's *Tristram Shandy*.

333. *the English Opera House:* the name given to the Lyceum in 1812 after the Drury Lane company had been able to return to their own theatre.

334. *Aubrey: recte* Audrey; the error escaped notice in both editions.

Page 335. *Mr. Garrick's partiality for him:* In the biography of Bannister by John Adolphus (1838) there is a vivid and amusing account of his audition with Garrick.

336. *Miss Kelly:* Three years later, on 20 July 1819, Kelly's niece received from Charles Lamb a letter which in a charming and round-about way proposed marriage. Miss Kelly's affections were otherwise engaged, but she managed to decline the proposal without wounding the proposer.

342. '*The evil that men do . . .*': *Julius Caesar*, III. ii. 79–80.

345. '*The Camp*': It is now thought that Sheridan wrote no more than a few speeches for this operatic afterpiece, most of which was by his son-in-law, Richard Tickell. The music was by Thomas Linley the elder.

346. Kelly's list has been used as an Index of his Works, with page references added in square brackets. To make room for these, theatre names have been abbreviated as follows:

DL: Drury Lane; LT: Little Theatre ('Haymarket');
CG: Covent Garden; Ly: Lyceum; KT: King's Theatre.

Various spaces have been filled with editorial additions in square brackets. The spelling of five titles has been corrected without comment, and I have changed Kelly's *Fall of Taranto* to Dimond's *Conquest of Taranto*. Asterisks denote published vocal scores, few of which give the music complete. No full scores or orchestral parts seem to survive for any opera by Kelly. Kelly's date for the second item can hardly be right. *The Fashionable Friends*, a comedy and not an opera, was found among Horace Walpole's papers when he died in 1797; he may or may not have been the author. Private theatricals at his home, Strawberry Hill, were not unknown, but if Kelly had been called on for a song or two by Walpole he would certainly have mentioned the fact. The first known performance was at Drury Lane on 22 April 1802, and the second was also the last; the comedy was not liked.

Index

I list all musicians and theatre people about whom I have information; Kelly's society friends are given only selectively. Operas are listed under their composers, plays under their authors, but titles are also indexed individually (with a cross reference) whenever Kelly fails to name the composer or author. Similarly characters are indexed (with a cross reference) whenever Kelly does not say from which opera or play they come. The more important cities and theatres where he worked are included.

Names are often spelt wrongly in the text. I have tried to spell them correctly in the Index, but decisions can be hard to make when people were themselves inconsistent as to how their own names should be spelt; for instance the Aickin/Aicken brothers, and John O'Keeffe/O'Keefe.